RESEARCH METHODS IN CRIMINOLOGY AND CRIMINAL JUSTICE

RESEARCH METHODS IN CRIMINOLOGY AND CRIMINAL JUSTICE

Edwin S. Johnson

PRENTICE-HALL, INC., ENGLEWOOD CLIFFS, N.J. 07632

Library of Congress Cataloging in Publication Data

Johnson, Edwin S. (date)
Research methods in criminology and criminal justice.

Includes bibliographies and index.
1. Crime and criminals–Research. 2. Criminal justice, Administration of–Research.

3. Crime and criminals–Statistical methods. I. Title.
HV6024.5.J64 364'.07'2 80-73
ISBN 0-13-774349-1

Editorial production supervision and
interior design by *Lori E. Wieseneck*
Cover Design by *Frederick Charles Ltd*
Manufacturing Buyer: *Gordon Osbourne*

Prentice-Hall Series in Criminal Justice
James D. Stinchcomb, Editor

Printed in the Unites States of America

10 9 8 7 6 5 4 3 2 1

PRENTICE-HALL INTERNATIONAL, INC., *London*
PRENTICE-HALL OF AUSTRALIA PTY. LIMITED, *Sydney*
PRENTICE-HALL OF CANADA, LTD., *Toronto*
PRENTICE-HALL OF INDIA PRIVATE LIMITED, *New Delhi*
PRENTICE-HALL OF JAPAN, INC., *Tokyo*
PRENTICE-HALL OF SOUTHEAST ASIA PTE. LTD., *Singapore*
WHITEHALL BOOKS LIMITED, *Wellington, New Zealand*

Contents

11 CHI-SQUARE, ASSOCIATION, AND THE CAUSAL CHAIN 264

12 USING TWO OR MORE SAMPLES IN THEORY AND PRACTICE 290

13 USING MORE THAN TWO VARIABLES FOR ANALYSIS 315

14 FALLACY, ETHICS, AND ERROR 343

Preface

This text is designed for both future professionals and students in criminology and criminal justice. It is intended to meet the needs of those professionals who require a working knowledge of research and statistics. Many professionals require a day-to-day interpretation and analysis of masses of material that cross their desks. They read endless reports and are asked to prepare more. They are confronted by technicians whom they must direct or to whom they must reluctantly relinquish control. As a solution to these problems this book is provided as an aid in understanding research methodology, analyzing and preparing reports, and in gaining control by effective decision making.

It is also designed for the student who suddenly finds that he or she must complete research methodology for the degree requirement. In most universities and colleges this comes at the end of the third year or during the senior year. It also means that if the student wishes to go on for graduate work, he or she will continue the research program the following year. Often the student graduates with a bachelor's degree, only to discover that the research methodology already taken is barely sufficient for continuing. I have written this book with that in mind, namely that this text may be used sequentially from the appropriate years of the undergraduate to the continuing years of graduate school.

Although statistics is a requirement for research methods, an understanding of what statistics can do is more important. I have included in the text sufficient statistics to enable the student to progress to analysis and then, with this basic understanding, push on to more difficult work.

Many students will never become research methodologists, but they will all use research in some form or another. The plan of this book is to enable the bewildered student to comfortably find his or her way through the maze of research methodology. Some algebra and some math are necessary, but the course isn't complex; it is more a course in using your mind for analysis—in thinking things out. I also had in mind that research methods should be taught much earlier in the student's career.

The text is designed to ease the student into a "research frame of mind." We begin by discussing science and research, and criminology/criminal justice in particular. Then we discuss current topics and how to select topic material. From the informal topic, we develop propositions and hypotheses, and we begin to define variables. It is at this point that we make the testable research statement and discuss hypotheses in depth. This leads to examination of validity, triangulation, and the use of testing methods other than survey research.

Survey research is looked at in terms of design, data, and research objectives. Here we look at survey work that has been done in the criminal justice field and its value. If we are to examine new problems, verify old solutions, or challenge existing solutions, we must design a research project that will involve sampling, construction of an instrument, and procedure for gathering data. This leads to questionnaire design, interviewing techniques, and sampling techniques. Collection of data now proceeds to scoring, coding, and getting ready to analyze the data statistically. Chapters 9 through 14 cover writing SPSS programs, using statistics and bivariate analysis. Sampling theory and use of multiple samples and multiple variables are also discussed.

Analyzing the results calls for a particularly alert mind that is aware of the pitfalls ahead. Learning analysis is a matter of experience more than of reading. Once you have learned the basics, you can proceed to other methods of technology, such as terminals, programmable calculators, and minicomputers.

Finally, no matter what hardware or software you have used, you must present your findings in the proper form. Examples are given of the work of actual students to help you and to encourage you. These students had never had a course in research before, and they were with me for only one semester. You can do it too if you relax. Getting frustrated and excited only adds to problems that are already there. Follow the text sequentially; if you don't quite grasp some parts, go on to others. It will come to you if you keep at it.

The computer will do all the heavy math for you; you only do the program. However, you *must* be absolutely precise. I am sure that your first printout will give you tremendous satisfaction. Completing your first major project will give you even more.

Research is an exciting and challenging field. Now that you are beginning the research adventure, travel carefully. Challenge findings, especially your own, and do not rush to judgment or jump to conclusions. Research is an exercise in precision. We are not out to prove anything; we are out to discover everything.

Acknowledgments

The writer of a textbook looks back, after the pain of rewriting, correcting, and re-writing, and wonders how he was ever persuaded to embark upon such an arduous endeavor. My primary debt is to those who intimidated me with their research methods classes and made me swear that I would never inflict such agony on my own students. Let them remain unknown. On the other hand, my own affection for research, especially in criminology, was encouraged by Dr. Vernon Fox and Dr. Alex Bassin of Florida State University. Alex Greene and Stephen Cline of Prentice-Hall persuaded me to keep going in the face of adversity. I wish to thank them both. I also owe John Duhring, editor, and Lori Wieseneck, production editor at Prentice-Hall, a further debt of gratitude for their patience and guidance.

The manuscript was reviewed in whole or in part, and improved by the comments of its reviewers: David A. Baxter, Manchester, Missouri; Vernon Fox, Tallahassee, Florida; Ronald J. Niksich, Huntsville, Texas; James D. Stinchcomb, Richmond, Virginia; and Vincent J. Webb, Chicago, Illinois.

I gratefully acknowledge the permission of my wonderful students, Nadine Young (project on escape), and David LiBassi (Casino Gambling Survey), and others in my classes who, advertently or inadvertently, contributed to this text.

I wish to express my appreciation to SPSS, Inc., for permission to include examples of their programs and program sequences for use in research methodology, to International Business Machines Corporation for permission to show illustrations of IBM cards and techniques, and to Appleton-Century-Crofts, Basic Books, Chas. C Thomas, Consumers Union, Dorsey Press, McGraw-Hill, Prentice-Hall, Rand McNally, and Wadsworth, for permission to quote from their various publications as cited in the text.

Finally, I owe a great deal to Dr. Judith J. Johnson, my wife, who assisted with the index and numerous technical problems.

Edwin S. Johnson

1

Introduction

SCIENCE AND RESEARCH

We have often heard the expression, "I've got it down to a science." We accept this without any philosophical analysis and instinctively know that the person is referring to success, progress, and satisfaction. Whether he is talking about business, sports, cooking, or driving, it means that whatever he is doing, he can repeat it again and again with a reasonable certainty of the result. To get to this point, he has practiced, often by trial and error, until most of the uncertainty has been eliminated from the outcome. The person has thought about the activity, carefully considered each move, reduced the problem to points of specific inquiry, and gained mastery.

Science is a systematic mastery of facts, principles, and laws. And even though the person who has "got something down to a science" has done it in a most unorthodox manner, his methods have followed the *principles of basic research* upon which all science depends. He has developed precision of measurement, sophistication of control (removal of error), and probability of prediction of outcomes.

Research as we know it is barely 300 years old. When we consider the 2 million years of man's existence, and the 6,000 years of known records, we can see research is only a mark on the line of time. The indefinable spirit of inquiry that has taken man out of the caves and the jungle has moved him into a world of contemporary science. The last century alone has seen man leap from a pedestrian–equestrian–agricultural age to a jet-powered nuclear space age. Because of research we are surrounded by the marvels of plastics, lasers, modern medicine, satellite TV, supersonic speed, computers, and microprocessors.

It would appear that the social sciences have lagged behind the physical sciences. Ogburn called this "cultural lag."[1] The pressure of survival and an emphasis on time must lead us to intensify our research efforts in the social sciences, in order to improve the quality of life, and to ensure the peaceful direction of social change.

The Traditional View

The scientific method means defining the problem, gathering data, testing the hypotheses, and presenting our findings. Research is the foundation of the scientific method—indeed, the rock upon which science is built. Research is a useful tool; it can do many things. It helps us:

- Explain natural phenomena
- Investigate cause and effect
- Inquire into differences observed
- Question beliefs, superstitions, and myths
- Examine unacceptable "accidents"
- Interpret the unknown
- Predict possible future trends and outcomes

Research requires that the researcher:

- Challenge accepted findings and "absolutes"
- Develop innovative procedures
- Attempt conclusions based upon facts
- Explore new frontiers
- Confirm prior research by replication
- Solve problems
- Ensure the continuation of scientific thought

Research touches every part of our lives, from vital statistics to school records, Society Security, tax returns, medical records, credit cards, bank deposits, passports, and every type of information that is fed into a computer. It is an integral and essential part of modern civilization. In our technological society, research depends upon:

- Collection of data
- Flow of information (communication)
- Verification of facts
- Methods used in the research process
- The sophistication of electronic equipment
- The level of statistical analysis
- Logical and conceptual analysis and findings

The researcher in the behavioral sciences will observe, discover, and formalize. He will use findings to generalize, to make inferences and predictions, and occasion-

[1] William F. Ogburn, "Cultural Lag Theory," *Sociological and Social Research*, 41 (January 1957).

ally to construct theory or solve problems. He is dealing with human beings, few known laws, ambiguous definitions, and variation caused by time and personal subjectivity.

A Contemporary View

The purpose of modern research in the social sciences appears to be:

- The examination and investigation of contemporary everyday phenomena
- The evaluation of historical data
- Evaluation of the growth and change caused by characteristics of the phenomena
- The search for logical explanations of causality
- The development of experimental or controlled situations to anticipate trends or outcomes
- The development of theory and law
- Improvement of the quality of life

Although research is generally categorized as *pure* (seeking information and knowledge for its own sake) or *applied* (using knowledge to solve problems), it can also be *historical* (analyzing past records), *experimental* (manipulating outcomes), and *descriptive* (examining current phenomena). Research may also be *speculative* (simulation).

Research is an aid in constructing theory, which is really an extension and continuation of research. Theory integrates research findings into an organized set of related postulates to explain phenomena. Theory is based upon qualitative (abstract) and empirical (measured) reasoning. It should be simple, clear, parsimonious, logical, and applicable. Theory should contain the built-in quality to generate new research and, ipso facto, new theory.

Research can be a restriction on theory, and vice versa. Most research is based upon theory and usually has a strong underpinning of theoretical structure. When this is the case, the research is designed to discover only what is permitted within the theoretical parameters.

LIMITS AND HORIZONS FOR RESEARCH IN CRIMINOLOGY

When research is not theoretically directed and is merely investigative, the findings (especially if a multifactor approach is used) may be so varied that the researcher is unable to find a particular direction from any of them. Too many factors may be as limiting as single-factor research. For example, if we were researching robbery profiles in the inner city, we would miss entirely (1) why robbery was used as a form of social adjustment, and (2) socioeconomic opportunities for vertical racial mobility; whereas if we were investigating these, we would easily miss the robbery profile we were originally seeking. Research would appear to discover only what it is intended to discover. It is not that the researcher intentionally blinds himself to all the possible issues, but that theoretical immersion, or too broad a base, can lead to ignorance of the issues.

Good research, while considering the extremes, opts for a central position. The researcher:

- Considers extreme theoretical considerations and is conservative
- Considers extreme empirical positions and limits the research to manageable size
- Does not attempt to seek "world reform," "cures for terminal diseases," or "final solutions"
- Considers the end relation of findings to theory
- Considers the possibility of replication/verification
- Evaluates the consequences of the research
- Considers the ethical and philosophical questions involved concerning people, progress, and the quality of life

Great care must be taken in beginning the research adventure, in that preparation should include thinking out what you really want to do, rather than being persuaded to pursue a particular direction.[2]

Research is performed by people—people who have feelings and are motivated and stimulated by emotions as well as intellectual curiosity. We should be aware, as researchers, that the very source of our own personal interests can also be a limitation because of personal opinion, bias, prejudice, and value judgment. Our own humanity contains both the strengths to build research and the weaknesses to destroy it. In researching crime and deviance, we need to be fully alert to our own propensities and deviant human traits. Our inquiries into every uncensored part of human existence should not exclude ourselves, nor should we determine the parameters of our research in our own favor.

Good research will examine the whole spectrum of criminology, from religion to politics, from perversion to morality, from social reality to social pathology,[3] and from ethics to evil. It will examine the causes, the spread, the meaning, and the impact of crime, and the changes in society caused by crime. It will observe and question treatment, modification, rehabilitation, reparation, and medical programs. It will investigate police, legal, probation, and parole administration. Research will inquire into:

- The etiology of crime (the causes of criminal pathology)
- The epidemiology of crime (the control of the spread of criminal social dysfunction)
- The administration of the criminal justice system, including the courts, the police, and corrections

[2] Robert S. Clark, *Fundamentals of Criminal Justice Research* (Lexington, Mass.: Heath, 1977), p. 30. Clark states, "Research design is the tactical plan of the research."

[3] Criminal pathology as used here means the study of suffering from the social dysfunction caused by crime; also, the study of the effects of crime.

- Therapy, behavior-modification, and reparation programs
- Political and governmental systems
- The social and cultural environment
- Social change, trends, and progress in all these areas

PRINCIPLES GUIDING THE RESEARCHER

A researcher is guided by three objectives: He seeks (1) order in the universe, (2) an explanation for natural events, and (3) truth that is independent of himself. Four more objectives should be present in the actual research:

1. *Succinctness*. The research should be clear, concise, lacking in irrelevancies, brief and to the point, nonspurious, consistent, showing related concepts.
2. *Specificity*. The research must demonstrate precision in measurement, methods, and conclusions.
3. *Logical sequentiality*. Rationality and common sense should be the central theme of major research. In the social sciences, problem solving should dominate other considerations.
4. *Verifiability*. The research should be truthful, utilitarian, provable, and accurate. Facts can be checked.

Although not all research is verifiable, no research should be closed to verification. Every scientist, as Blalock has said, should bend over backward to prove himself wrong.[4] The research imagination is backed by an attitude of inquiry, not one of confusion, or aggressiveness and hostility, or of consensus agreement. The research attitude is to find out why things happen, to try things out, to experiment, to explore, to observe, to diligently seek out, and to discover. The researcher aims to advance human knowledge and thereby improve the quality of life. Advancing human knowledge, by inference, means sharing one's findings and avoiding absolutism, which implies that the last word has been said and thus inhibits further research on the subject. All research findings should be treated as tentative, and all should be open to modification.

CRIMINOLOGY AS PART OF THE SOCIAL SCIENCES

Definitions

Before beginning research, it is essential to define the discipline itself. Social science is a systematic explanation of social phenomena. Criminology as a discipline is one part of the social-science spectrum. This becomes more apparent in the definitions of criminology. The following definitions give some idea of its scope.

Sutherland and Cressey have defined criminology:

[4] Hubert M. Blalock, *Social Statistics* (New York: McGraw-Hill, 1972).

> Criminology is the body of knowledge regarding delinquency and crime as social phenomena. It includes within its scope the process of making laws, of breaking laws, and the reacting toward the breaking of laws. These processes are three aspects of a somewhat unified sequence of interactions. Certain acts which are regarded as undesirable are defined by the political society as crimes. In spite of the definition, some people persist in the behavior and thus commit crimes; the political society reacts by punishment, treatment, or prevention. This sequence of interactions is the subject matter of criminology.
>
> Criminology consists of three principal divisions, as follows:
>
> (a) the sociology of law
> (b) criminal etiology
> (c) penology (including methods of social control)[5]

Note that the definition above outlines three "principal divisions," which may be broadly interpreted as law, crime, and corrections. Donald Taft and Ralph England write:

> The term "criminology" is used in both a general and a special sense. In its broadest sense, criminology is the study (not yet a complete science) which includes all the subject matter necessary to the understanding and prevention of crimes and to the development of law, together with the punishment or treatment of delinquents and criminals. In its narrower sense, criminology is simply the study which attempts to explain crime, to find out "how they get that way." If this latter, narrower definition is adopted, one must recognize related fields, including penology, concerned with the treatment of adult criminals, crime detection, the treatment of juveniles and the prevention of crime.[6]

Taft and England have added the idea of criminal behavior, "how they get that way," to the definition.

Hermann Mannheim gives a much lengthier definition, which I have abbreviated:

> Criminology, in the narrower sense in which it is used in this book, means the study of crime. In its wider sense it also includes penology, the study of punishment and of similar methods of dealing with crime, and the problem of preventing crime by nonpunitive measures . . . .
>
> The study of such [criminal] behavior can assume three basic forms:
>
> 1. The descriptive approach . . . the observation and collection of facts about crime and criminals.
> 2. The causal approach . . . the interpretation of the observed facts can be used to search for causes of crime either in general or individual cases. . . . This aspect is called the etiology of crime.

[5] Edwin H. Sutherland and Donald R. Cressey, *Criminology*, 9th ed. (Philadelphia: Lippincott, 1974), p. 1.

[6] Donald R. Taft and Ralph W. England, Jr., *Criminology*, 4th ed. (New York: Macmillan, 1964), p. 11.

3. The normative approach . . . aimed at the discovery of universally valid scientific laws and conformities or trends.[7]

Mannheim has introduced two major ideas, one of nonpunitive methods or modification of behavior, and the other of studying trends.

Walter Reckless writes in his introduction:

> [Criminology is] the understanding of involvement of individuals in delinquent and criminal behavior and understanding the operation of the criminal justice system. The first mentioned concern, namely the study of involvement, has two aspects: (1) the study of the "doer," and (2) the study of the doer's behavior, including the human victim. The second mentioned concern deals with (1) the input of persons into the criminal justice system at all points from complaint to arrest, to court action, to probation, to institutionalization, and to parole; and (2) the output or products of the criminal justice system at its several points of exodus.
>
> Criminology also includes . . . the relation of crime and deviance to law and social values . . . patterns of criminal careers, organized crime and white collar crime; . . . the history and trends in punishment.[8]

Reckless has expanded the notion of criminology by adding victimology and criminal justice proceedings.

Elmer Hubert Johnson, in his definition, raises criminology to the level of an art/science, somewhat like medicine:

> Criminology is the scientific study and practical application of findings in the areas of: (a) crime causation and criminal behavior and etiology, (b) the nature of societal reaction as a symptom of the characteristics of the society, and (c) the prevention of crime.[9]

Johnson's definition infers a diagnosis/treatment approach to criminology—a distinct clinical approach.

Haskell and Yablonsky emphasize the research content:

> Criminology, more specifically, is the scientific study of crime and criminals. It includes the analyses of:
>
> 1. The nature and extent of crime
> 2. The causes of crime and criminality
> 3. The development of the criminal law and the administration of criminal justice

[7] Hermann Mannheim, *Comparative Criminology* (Boston: Houghton Mifflin, 1965), p. 3.

[8] Walter C. Reckless, *American Criminology* (New York: Appleton-Century-Crofts, 1973), p. v.

[9] Elmer Hubert Johnson, *Crime, Corrections, and Society*, rev. ed. (Homewood, Ill.: Dorsey, 1968), p. 13.

4. Characteristics of the criminal
5. The treatment of the criminal
6. Patterns of criminality
7. The impact of crime on social change[10]

David Dressler gets to the idea of basic comparative research:

> A major understanding of criminology is the accretion of data on the etiology of delinquency and crime. What turns men to murder and robbery? Why does one man commit a crime while his brother remains law-abiding? . . . The student of criminology wants to know, "What causes delinquency and crime?"[11]

Gibbons also emphasizes "objective analysis":

> Scientific study of lawbreaking and serious attempts to uncover the causes of criminality have usually taken place within an area of study called criminology, which is concerned with the objective analysis of crime as a social phenomenon. Criminology includes within its scope inquiry into the process of making laws, breaking laws, and reacting to the breaking of laws.[12]

Richard Quinney introduces us to a new criminology with a wider range of inquiry:

> [The new criminology is] an understanding of crime by a presentation that moves back and forth between conventional wisdom about crime and the new conceptions that negate traditional ideas . . . [We will] cover the diverse facets of crime: from the legal system in theory to the law in action, from the theories of criminologists to the public's social reality, from the "criminal's" world to that of legal authority, from the traditional approaches of crime control to the radical notions of social existence.[13]

Quinney also introduces the idea of phenomenology into his research of criminology. His approach is quite different and emphasizes the economic class conflict.

A good idea of the widening scope of criminology may be obtained by examining Daniel Glaser's book, which includes chapters on various aspects of criminology—crime, delinquency, law enforcement, the courts, adjudication, corrections, behavior modification, probation, parole, juveniles, institutions, corrections, and prevention.[14] This very large "handbook" covers a great variety of viewpoints.

[10] Martin R. Haskell and Lewis Yablonsky, *Criminology: Crime and Criminality* (Chicago: Rand McNally, 1974), p. 3.

[11] David Dressler, ed., *Readings in Criminology and Penology*, 2nd ed. (New York: Columbia University Press, 1972), pp. 245–46.

[12] Donald C. Gibbons, *Society, Crime, and Criminal Careers: An Introduction to Criminology*, 3rd ed. (Englewood Cliffs, N.J.: Prentice-Hall, 1977), p. 3.

[13] Richard Quinney, *Criminology—Analysis and Critique of Crime in America* (Boston: Little, Brown, 1975), p. 13.

[14] Daniel Glaser, ed., *Handbook of Criminology* (Chicago: Rand McNally, 1974).

Vernon Fox gives a most comprehensive definition:

> Criminology is the study of criminal behavior and the justice system. It is the study of law, broken law, and the lawbreaker. The understanding of these phenomena requires an understanding of all the social behavioral sciences, the natural sciences, and the ethical systems and controls embodied in law and religion. Criminology is the meeting place of all the disciplines that focus on the emotional and mental health of the individual and the smooth functioning of society.
>
> Criminal behavior can be explained through sociological, psychological, medical and biological, psychiatric and psycho-analytic, economic, political, cultural and other social and behavioral approaches.
>
> Politics define the criminal justice system through the promulgation and implementation of public policy in the law and its enforcement.
>
> Therefore, criminal behavior and the justice system become central to the many disciplines and approaches focusing on the problems of crime in society.[15]

Fox sees criminology as the "meeting place" for interdisciplinary studies on crime and society. He also emphasizes the importance of research in his book.

The definition adopted for this book is as follows: Criminology is the study of the etiology and epidemiology of the pathology and near pathology of crime, criminals, and criminal behavior. It is also the study of:

1. Civil and criminal jurisprudence and lawbreakers
2. Offender sanctions, both punitive and nonpunitive
3. The rights of the offender, the victim, and society
4. Arrest, reparation and corrections, probation and parole
5. Therapy, treatment, manipulation, and rehabilitation of offenders
6. The total criminal justice system (police, courts, etc.)
7. Political definition and enforcement of the law
8. Operational efficiency and effectiveness of the system
9. Effects of social and cultural environment
10. The change in society caused by crime and the changes in crime caused by society

The scope of criminology and criminal justice studies requires a concerted effort in the field of research, for several reasons. First of all, it is a comparatively new discipline and needs to establish lines of research precedents. In former times—indeed, to a great extent in present times—applied criminology has been accustomed to deal with situations on a day-to-day, crisis-survival basis. Situations are so varied that often they are handled in an ad hoc manner, by intuition, or on the basis of limited personal experience. But the enormous input of funds and technology into applied criminology has created the necessity for research for explanation, evaluation,

[15] Vernon B. Fox, *Introduction to Criminology* (Englewood Cliffs, N.J.: Prentice-Hall, 1976), p. 388. See also Chap. 2, "The Emergence of Criminology."

and decision making. Professionals in the field, even those with degrees in criminology or criminal justice, find themselves unable to comprehend the masses of data without the aid of research techniques. In the decision-making process, therefore, they become subordinate to the suppliers of information. Then, too, research understanding will make all the difference in evaluation of data and performance. It will permit the improvement of the quality of society by coping with problems on a scientific basis.

Because research is so vital,[16] the researcher needs a firm understanding of basic principles. The building blocks for research are the same for all sciences, but in handling research problems, there are slight conceptual and quantitative differences, as shown in Table 1.1.

Table 1.1.

Social Sciences	Physical Sciences
Deals with human beings or human problems; research subjects are like the researcher, and have feelings.	Deals with inert, mindless objects, totally unlike the researcher. Research is with "things" that have no feeling.
Researcher may influence or be influenced by subjects (subjectivity).	Researcher is not influenced by research objects (objectivity).
Conclusions are tentative and may be affected by bias, prejudice, incomplete information.	Findings are usually consistent with high degree of objectivity.
Research is subject to few known laws and is based on grand, mid-range, and micro theory.	Findings are subject to known laws. Laws change only in the face of overwhelming evidence.
Research is based on probability, inference, ambiguous variables, unlimited combinations, difficult definitions, language problems, limited sophistication, dubious models.	In physical science, one deals with balanced equations, balanced constructs, precision of measurement, highly specialized technology, planned research programs.
Research is hard to replicate. People, life styles, location, fashions, situations all change very rapidly.	Experiments are easy to duplicate and replication is limited only by time and money.
Quantification and measurement are based upon scales that vary with time and varying statistical procedures.	Quantification is based upon rigid, non-varying scales. Procedures are set.

Uses of Criminological Research

Research is used to test propositions, examine standards and beliefs, investigate statements concerning phenomena, weight the validity of new concepts, replicate the possibility of old concepts, experiment with ideas, manipulate and control

[16] Fox, *Introduction to Criminology*, Chap. 16.

alternate solutions, and demolish prejudice and superstition. Most research begins with an attempt to unravel the relationship expressed in a proposition, which is a statement of a relationship between two or more variables. Such a statement is testable—that is, subject to investigation, scrutiny, and quantitative or statistical test.

A proposition, then, is something put forward or proposed. In the statistical sense, it is a statement of a relationship (either positive or negative) that may be demonstrated or tested. It can be a problem or a theorem, a simple or complex presentation. For research purposes in the social sciences, the proposition is usually tangible, able to be handled or dealt with in some manner, and able to be quantified. Not all propositions are subject to quantification or measurement. Let us look at some propositions in criminology. Remember that the statements need to contain (1) a relationship, (2) testability, and (3) research value.

Take as an example this statement: People who own handguns commit murder; murder rates would decline if civilians were deprived of handguns. Without reflecting on the issues involved, we can see from this statement that certain facts, if ascertainable, would clarify the relationships. For instance, the statement can be read, "Ownership of handguns causes murders to occur"; that is, "A causes B," or "B is the effect of A." Both A and B are identified as variables. Their position in the cause-and-effect chain determines their status. The causal variable (in this case, A, or gun ownership) is known as the *independent* variable; the effect variable (B, murders) is the *dependent* variable. We can now test the relationship between A and B, between murders committed and murderers who own handguns. Chapter 3 deals with variables more explicitly.

Research statements, properly made, permit us to build models for testing and analysis. Research is an exercise in accountability in examining the validity of the research proposition.

Research may also be used to construct profiles from available data. For example, detailed descriptions of hijackings are gathered in order to establish a "hijacker profile" for airport security; and various tests have been used to construct a "stress profile" to determine how people can cope with stress in their daily lives.

Another use of research is in cost accountability, to evaluate the success of various programs used in rehabilitation. The successes of the program are measured against the cost input. Anticipated projects can be computer-simulated to give some idea of outcomes when large amounts of money are involved. Performance-location studies can be examined and "trended" for the reduction of high-crime areas. Crime reports may be analyzed for the disposition of police services.

Of greater use to the criminologist is research as an aid in the explanation of causes of crime, or as a base for future action.[17] The great value of the researcher lies in the ability to assess, evaluate, and act upon information provided by scientific study.

[17]Currently detailed studies are being made of arson in New York, planned bankruptcies, mortgage rigging, coercion in obtaining government contracts, real estate swindles, major securities, rare-book and art thefts, computer/electronic theft, industrial espionage, and agency/institution fraud. Many of these offenses are "super crimes" and include murder, blackmail, assault, conspiracy, torture, threats, bombings, and disappearances.

No matter how clear the research statement may be, the subsequent actions have to be logical. Criminological research—or any other research, for that matter—must proceed in a logical direction. Logic enables us to bridge the gap between idea and practice, between concept and operationalization, between experiment and conclusion.

The idea or concept begins in the mind—"seeing" in the mind's eye the cause and effect in natural phenomena. These notions or perceptions make us challenge or support existing ideas, or seek change or a solution to a problem, or merely attempt to solve an unexplained event. For the purposes of logical research, these ideas should be clear and concise and have some utility. Our research concepts should be founded upon a search for order, for a possible contribution to theory, and for a base for prediction. Very simply, we begin by observing the general laws of life and challenging some particular facet; we then hypothesize the problem by making a testable statement; then we operationalize,[18] gather data, analyze, make inferences, and possibly make theory; if we are able to replicate consistently, we may make law and thus complete the cycle.

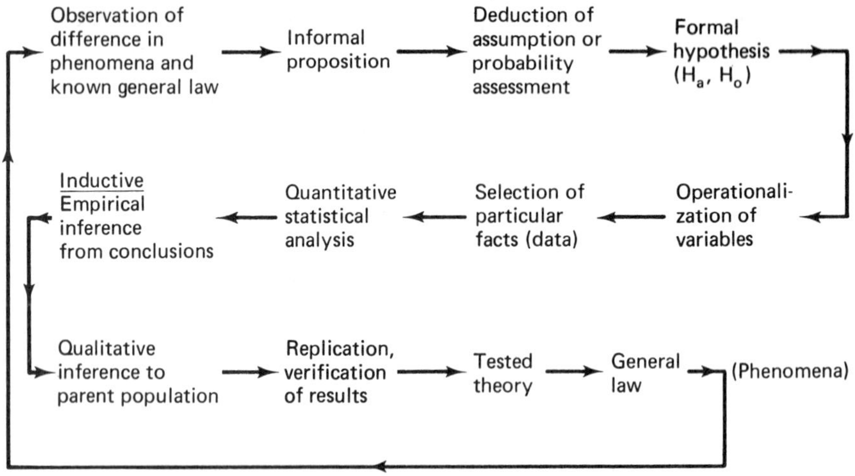

Fig. 1-1 Flow of research logic—the continuity of inquiry.

The cycle implies a continuity of fact, hypothesis, theory, and law. There is an orderly flow, limiting and directing specific inquiry. (See Figure 1-1.) We are following the basic steps in two kinds of logic, *inductive* (taking place in the confines of the mind), and *deductive* (occurring in the mind because of external factors).

[18] Operationalizing is interpretation of the variables, or translation into question form to be used to obtain responses (data) from persons included in the sample.

Inductive reasoning moves from the particular fact or item to the general; deductive reasoning moves from the general law or observation to the particular fact. Most of our reasoning in the research field is inductive; we move from data to theory. However, most of our research ideas begin deductively, seeking a general proposition and then operationalizing to obtain particular facts or data.

The inferential decisions that we apply are based upon statistics. We quantify or measure human behavior, and from the scores or measurements, we are able to analyze those data at an appropriate statistical level. From the conclusions, we may make inferences to the parent population from which the sample or particular facts have been drawn. Quantification places limits on personal opinions and personal judgments; it reduces charismatic events to numbers; it removes the value judgments from research and replaces them with scientific facts. Good examples of this are Charles Goring's study of English convicts, which attacked the concept of the identification of criminality by body type; Dr. Kinsey's famous reports on human sexuality, which exploded myths about human sexual behavior; and statistical research that led to the changing of drug laws.[19]

The decisions we make are based upon a compromise between determinism and probability. The probability of events and of their outcomes is based upon known prior events. We know the direction we are seeking, yet our decisions will be based upon the probability of the outcome we are sure of, rather than that of the one we are less certain of. Our research should flow logically so that in our search for truth we select the outcome probability that leaves us the least room for error.

RESEARCH TERMINOLOGY

In any discussion of research, certain terms are used that must be understood. Terms like *variable, model*, and *hypothesis* arrive on the scene early; most of them are dealt with in the following chapters and are summarized at appropriate intervals. For example, Chapter 3 deals with variables, Chapter 8 with computer terminology. Let us set out a few essential terms here.

Variable = any particular trait or characteristic that can assume a range of values.

The range of values may be *quantitative*, as in height, weight, temperature, distance, speed, age, income, days of illness, number of children; it may rank on a scale such as preference or attitude; it could be IQ or GPA; it may be composite, such as SES (socioeconomic-scale) standing, or a measurement on an alienation scale. Or variables may be *qualitative*, showing such attributes as sex, religion, race, marital status, voting preference, or propensity to commit a crime. Some variables may be

[19] Charles B. Goring, *The English Convict: A Statistical Study* (London: Her Majesty's Stationery Office, 1913); Alfred C. Kinsey, W. B. Pomeroy, and C. E. Martin, *Sexual Behavior in the Human Male* (Philadelphia: W. B. Saunders Co., 1948), and Kinsey et al., *Sexual Behavior in the Human Female* (1953); and *Task Force Report: Narcotics and Drug Abuse* (Washington, D.C.: U.S. Government Printing Office, 1967).

either qualitative or quantitative, such as education, which may be used to find educational status–high school/college/postgraduate (qualitative)–or number of years of schooling (quantitative). A variable is anything that can vary; if it does not vary, it is a *constant*. Variables usually have two or more categories, each completely exclusive of the others, such as sex, which has the categories of male and female.

Relationship = *a connection or association between two or more variables. The variables are incident and are in a particular position to each other. The relationship may be negative or positive, causal or noncausal.*

In a *causal* relationship, one or more variables cause or have an effect upon the other(s), so one cannot be considered without the other. A causal relationship might exist between execution and recidivism if an increase in the number of executions lowered the number of recidivists (criminal repeaters).[20] When an increase in A causes a drop in B, this is known as a *negative* direction. If B rises as A rises, then the direction is *positive*.

A noncausal relationship is a *correlation*. Correlation implies a mutual relationship wherein one variable complements the other or corresponds in the change process. An example of a correlation would be a direct relationship (positive) between education and promotion. For instance, attendance at police academies would not cause promotion, but there could be a significant relationship between the two variables. In positive relationships, both variables rise or drop together; in negative, as one rises, the other drops.

Hypothesis = *a statement of a relationship to be tested; a proposition based upon observed phenomena or prior fact to be used for research; an assumption, or estimate, or guess, that is to be tested; a testable proposition.*

Hypotheses are identified as statements of relationship and are known as research hypotheses, or H_1, or alternate hypotheses, H_a, H_{a_1}, H_{a_2}, and so on. *Hypotheses that are statements of no relationship are known as null hypotheses*[21] and are written H_o, H_{o_1}, H_{o_2}, and so on. (The statistical analysis used in research methodology is particularly suited to test the null hypothesis, as you will see in Chapter 4.) The null or zero hypothesis simply states that there is no relationship between the variables cited in the research statement. Occasionally the statement is called one of "no difference." This is really incorrect terminology, since we are concerned not with differences but with relationship and independence, but the term has come about because of the use of the expressions, "There is no difference in the crime rates of . . .," "There is no difference in attitudes . . .," and the like. It would be more correct to speak of "no relationship," since when variables are used in a model, we are discussing relationships, not differences.

Model = *a representation in diagrammatic form used to show or compare causal*

[20] We are discussing the elimination theory here, rather than deterrence, execution acting as a "final solution" for crime.

[21] We use the null hypothesis for testing and the research hypothesis for constructing the model.

relationships; a construction of causal patterns made from the research statement or research findings.

Arrows are used to show the direction of causality. Models are sometimes called *constructs* or *heuristic devices*. Examples are:

Simple Causal Model (from research hypothesis, H_a or H_1)

$$A \longrightarrow B$$

A causes B, or B is the effect of A, or A influences B.

or

Age (independent variable) ⟶ Decision to commit a crime (dependent variable)

H_a = Age influences one's decision to commit a crime.[22]

Models can become complicated, as in path analysis, but it is always an advantage to keep the model simple so that the thrust of the research may be clearly seen.[23] These terms are expanded later in the text; only brief introductory explanations are given here.

There are two kinds of statistics used:

Descriptive statistics = *numbers or measurements used to describe limits and size, such as populations, samples, and parameters.*

The Uniform Crime Reports are basically descriptive statistics. Most frequency data are descriptive.

Inferential statistics – *numbers used to infer something about the parent population from the sample.*

If, for example, we take from the UCRs the robbery rates for New York in 1975 and 1978, and on the basis of that sample note a 10 percent increase, we could infer that robbery has increased in New York by 10 percent over that period of time. We have used descriptive data to make a statistical inference.

BEGINNING THE RESEARCH STUDY

Research is the discovery of new facts, the verification of old ones, the tracing of logical ideas and sequences, and the formulation of new trends. Prediction is its ultimate goal. All research follows certain precise steps. They are:

1. *The selection of the research topic.* This is the original idea that motivates curiosity, the area of personal or academic interest that generates the driving force. The mind should be so stimulated by the topic that there is a certain sense of compulsion to undertake the research.

[22]The *research* hypothesis would imply a qualitative statement; on the other hand, a *null* hypothesis implies a quantitative statement (i.e., zero relationship).

[23]Models may represent or predict outcomes; they also function to organize variables and suggest modes of analysis.

2. *The decision on a hypothesis.* The research idea must be testable. It is usually put in the form of a null hypothesis, or a statement of no relationship. The original proposition is called the research hypothesis.
3. *The decision on how the variables can be used for data.* All research is dependent upon data. Data are the empirical base for new theory. This step includes the construction of the instrument.
4. *The decision on the research methodology*—where, when, and how data are to be collected and organized. This includes sample size, time limits, cost limits, and technical considerations of data handling.
5. *Statistical analysis.* The method or level chosen decides the sophistication of the study.
6. *Interpretation.* From the organization of systematic data collection and collation, computer printouts, graphs, and tables, conclusions must be drawn that are relevant to the research problem.
7. *Presentation.* This should be in the proper format. It should reflect scholarly style, yet be clear and easy to read. Style should never confuse important findings.

Useful Research Methods

Research in the social sciences may be conducted by any of several different methods, which are generally categorized as historical, experimental, descriptive, and speculative. Table 1.2 shows the most common of the first three categories.

The twelve methods explained in the table by no means exhaust the possibilities; many others exist. And some of the methods are more popular than others. In the social sciences, descriptive methods are used more than experimental, historical, or speculative; and of the descriptive methods, survey research is the most popular.[24] But whichever method is used, keep in mind that *all research methods depend upon control of the variables and precision of measurement.*

The researcher must decide which method to use and if it is the "best fit" for the situation or project. Occasionally more than one method is used, in which case the findings gain in credibility. This is called *triangulation*, and it is a definite advantage in research. For example, survey research may be supported by participant observation and case study. All three methods may be used in a comparative study, thereby giving the advantage of cross-comparisons. The use of more than one method aids in the reduction of research error, and the less error we have, the more precise our conclusions.

The researcher has to decide on how many methods, how many samples, how many people, how much, and how long. The answers should be organized, systematic, and purposeful. In making final selections, bear in mind that too little can be as ineffective as too much.

[24] Journalists prefer case studies: Truman Capote, *In Cold Blood* (New York: Random House, 1965); Vincent Bugliosi with Curt Gentry, *Helter Skelter* (New York: W. W. Norton & Co., Inc., 1974); Gerald Frank, *The Boston Strangler* (New York: The New American Library, 1966). Capote deals with Hickock and Smith, Bugliosi with the Manson family, and Frank with Albert De Salvo.

SUMMARY

Science is the dominant force in our lives. It compels us to examine an orderly universe in which every natural event has an explanation of some kind. The ethics of science teach us that truth is independent of the observer and that it cannot be sacrificed to convenience or expediency. Although science is *applied*—utilitarian and used to solve problems—it is also *pure*, in that it is beyond practical considerations and may provide a future link for other empirical research.

Research is the base for theory, which is the base for general law. In the social sciences, we find that construction of theory is difficult because of the qualitative nature of many areas of our research. We are dealing with human beings, human nature, human situations, all of which vary from day to day.

Research in criminology is fairly recent. Definitions of criminology indicate the areas open to the researcher. The range extends from the etiology (causes) of crime to the social change caused by crime, and includes the criminal justice system. A knowledge of research methodology is needed by practitioners as well as theoreticians. Important decisions often hinge on the understanding of statistical information. For the professional, understanding research can make the difference between the making of decisions for social change and the surrendering of one's power to the technician who supplies the information.

Much that is important to the discipline has been contributed by sociologists, but now several independent schools have been established, and criminology stands as an established discipline. (See chapter appendix.) The American School of Criminology is the last and most recent in a series of developments of such schools.[25]

Because research is so vital in criminology, evaluation of research is just as vital, since it is designed to influence change. As criminological research is concerned with the pathology of crime and the quality of life for society, evaluation of that research will determine the appropriate action to be taken; thus the decision can be made before the event rather than evaluating an ex post facto situation.

Criminological research is designed to investigate ideas, beliefs, and phenomena. In order to do this, it follows certain established rules. It begins with an idea, converts the idea to a proposition that states a relationship between variables, and then operationalizes the variables. The research must proceed in a logical fashion. To ensure this, we use the scientific method of inquiry. However, most of our logic is inductive, in that we constantly move from the data to theory, from particular facts to general law. The nature of the statistical procedure is that we make inferences to the parent population from the sample by using inductive logic.

The proposition that is stated to test the relationship between variables is called a hypothesis. If it is stated in terms of no relationship, it is called a null hypothesis. The research hypothesis may be used for a model that will diagram the variables in causal order, indicating the order of the relationship to be researched. The variables may then be operationalized and a method selected for the actual research study.

[25] Some hold that the Social Defense School is the most recent. See Fox, *Introduction to Criminology*, p. 43.

Table 1.2. Research Methods in the Social Sciences

Research method	Example	Actual study
Historical methods:		
Analysis of existing data: All available data on a problem are researched to support or refute a hypothesis.	Search of all available data on suicide to discover cause.	Emile Durkheim, *Le Suicide* (Paris, 1897); now in *Suicide* (New York: Free Press, 1951). Durkheim used existing data to investigate problems relating to suicide.
Content analysis: The literature is searched for content pertaining to the subject. The search may be made or assisted by computer retrieval, such as Medline, or library retrieval, and the analysis may focus on other research.[a]	Searching the literature for information on drug studies that discuss the use of marijuana.	Mary Lystad, "Social Alienation: A Review of the Literature," *Sociological Quarterly*, Winter 1972, pp. 90–113.
Historical study: Research of a particular time period regarding a subject.	A study of early deviance in the United States from 1750 to 1850.	Rofer M. Williams, *The Super Crooks* (Chicago: Playboy Press, 1973), a short history of super-thieves, 1584–1973; and Henner Hess, *Mafia and Mafiosi* (Lexington, Mass.: Lexington Books, 1970), a history of the Mafia.
Anthropological study: Usually a study of culture and deviance; always includes a history of the group under examination.	A study of deviance in ancient Rome, based upon writings and artifacts.	George C. Homans, *The Human Group* (New York: Harcourt Brace Jovanovich, 1950). Includes several studies.
Case study: Detailed study of a person or persons long dead. (Case studies of living people are descriptive studies.) Research is usually into bizarre behavior and results are used to support a particular thesis.	A murderer is studied to discover his motivation for bizarre crimes, or a family to show hereditary tendencies toward criminal behavior.	Richard Dugdale, *The Jukes* (New York: Putnam, 1877); and Henry H. Goddard, *The Kallikak Family* (New York: Macmillan, 1925).
Experimental methods:		
The controlled experiment: Two or more groups are set up, usually small and of the same size. The control group receives no treatment; for the others, certain variables may be manipulated.	Three groups of 20 inmates are selected at random. Group A is given a "short sharp shock" (intensive correctional treatment); group B is given a relaxed setting with therapy; control group C is left alone. They are studied to determine the effects of punishment.	Carl Hovland, A. Lumsdaine, and F. Sheffield, *Experiments in Mass Communication* (Princeton, N.J.: Princeton University Press, 1949). This classic study showed the effects of film on two groups.

Clinical research: A study of social and psychological factors underlying a problem.	Studies of gang or inmate subcultures, with emphasis on particular personalities and psychological factors.	Richard Cloward and Lloyd Ohlin, *Delinquency and Opportunity: A Theory of Delinquent Gangs* (New York: Free Press, 1960); and Ned Polsky, *Hustlers, Beats and Others* (Chicago: Aldine, 1967).
Descriptive methods:		
Survey research: Results are derived from sample data and used to make inferences regarding the parent population. (This is the most commonly used method; it is dealt with at length in the text.)	A sample is taken from a city, using random techniques; data from a questionnaire are analyzed concerning crime problems; conclusions are presented for the purpose of making inferences based on statistical levels of confidence estimates.	Leo Srole, *Mental Health in the Metropolis* (New York: McGraw-Hill, 1962); David Ward and Gene Kassebaum, "Homosexuality in a Women's Prison," *Social Problems*, 12:2 (1964): and President's Commission on Law Enforcement and Administration of Justice, "Public Attitudes toward the Police," *Task Force Report: The Police* (Washington, D.C.: U.S. Government Printing Office, 1967), pp. 145–49.
Participant observation: The researcher actually becomes involved with the group being researched, in order to examine organization and life-style.	A researcher lives with a gang in order to discover subculture life-styles.	William F. Whyte, *Street Corner Society* (Chicago: University of Chicago Press, 1955); and Laud Humphries, *Tearoom Trade* (Chicago: Aldine, 1970).
Comparative study: Two or more groups or places are compared. Sometimes a "neutral" area is included as a control; sometimes two or more disciplines are compared.	Crime is studied in two or more capital cities simultaneously, for similarities, differences, and possible common causes.	Alex D. Pokorny, "A Comparison of Homicides in Two Cities," *Journal of Criminal Law, Criminology and Police Science*, 56 (1965); and A. Jaffe and Saul Alinsky, "A Comparison of Jewish and Non-Jewish Convicts," *Jewish Social Studies*, 1, 359–66.
Current case study: An in-depth examination of a particular case, sometimes focusing on a specific aspect, and including all environmental phenomena and daily drama.	Case study of abnormal behavior.	Harold Garfinkel, *Studies in Ethnomethodology* (Englewood Cliffs, N.J.: Prentice-Hall, 1967).

[a]Content analysis is sometimes defined as a study of the nature and process of communication, a use of data to measure concepts. See Charles E. Osgood and Evelyn G. Walker, "Motivation and Language Behavior: A Content Analysis of Suicide Notes," *Journal of Abnormal and Social Psychology*, 59, 58–67; and D. Forcese and S. Richer, *Social Research Methods* (Englewood Cliffs, N.J.: Prentice-Hall, 1973), pp. 185–87.

Selection of more than one method or more than one sample aids in the reduction of research error and in the precision and sophistication of the research itself.

This first chapter is introductory and serves to provide the first step in examining the many parts of research methodology that follow.

EXERCISES

1. The purposes and requirements of research and of the researcher were listed early in this chapter. Select three articles on criminology and comment on how these purposes and requirements occur in them.
2. The matters that are inquired into by criminological research were also listed in this chapter. Locate articles on the etiology, epidemiology, and ecology of crime, and identify those matters in the readings.
3. Describe the limits on research. What is meant by "the central position" in research?
4. What are the three main objectives in research? Define *parsimony* (in its research connotation), *specificity, logical sequentiality, verifiability.*
5. Comment on ethics and compromise in research.
6. What are the three divisions defined by Sutherland and Cressey? What are the three basic forms of criminal behavior identified by Mannheim?
7. Outline Elmer Johnson's medical analogy. What is new about Quinney's definition?
8. What common areas are there in Fox, Haskell and Yablonsky, and this author?
9. Comment upon criminology and the quality of life, and upon the evaluation of criminological research.
10. Give an example of a research proposition. Define *variable, relationship, hypothesis, operationalize, phenomena, model.*
11. What is inductive logic? deductive logic? logical development?
12. Give examples of qualitative variables and quantitative variables.
13. What is a causal relationship? a noncausal relationship?
14. What are the functions of a model? What are its parts?
15. Explain the two kinds of statistics; give an example of each.
16. There are two kinds of science; what are they, and what do they do?
17. What is the importance of using more than one method and/or more than one sample?
18. Identify two characteristics of the research imagination.
19. Comment upon how research affects our daily lives.
20. What is "cultural lag"? And what price do we pay for it?

FOR FURTHER READING

Babbie, Earl R., *Survey Research Methods*, Chaps. 1, 2, 3. Belmont, Calif.: Wadsworth, 1973.

Bachrach, Arthur J., *Psychological Research*. New York: Random House, 1972.

Bernstein, Carl, and Robert Woodward, *All the President's Men*. New York: Simon & Schuster, 1974.

——, *The Final Days*. New York: Simon & Schuster, 1976.

Blalock, H. M., Jr., *An Introduction to Social Research*. Englewood Cliffs, N.J.: Prentice-Hall, 1970.

Clark, Robert S., *Fundamentals of Criminal Justice Research*. Lexington, Mass.: Heath, 1977.

Etzioni, Amitai, and R. Remp, *Technological Shortcuts to Social Change*, Chap. 4. New York: Russell Sage Foundation, 1973. Other chapters are also pertinent to criminology.

Forcese, D. P., and S. Richer, *Social Research Methods*. Englewood Cliffs, N.J.: Prentice-Hall, 1973.

Gibbon, Edward, *The Decline and Fall of the Roman Empire* (condensed). New York: Wise and Co., 1943.

Glazer, Myron, *The Research Adventure: Promise and Problems of Field Work*. New York: Random House, 1972.

Greenburg, Bradley S., and Edwin B. Parker, *The Kennedy Assassination and the American Public: Social Communication in Crisis*. Stanford, Calif.: Stanford University Press, 1965.

Johnson, Allan G., *Social Statistics without Tears*, Chap. 1. New York: McGraw-Hill, 1977.

Kerlinger, F. N., *Foundations of Behavioral Research* (2nd ed.). New York: Holt, Rinehart & Winston, 1966.

Nash, Jay Robert, *Hustlers and Con Men*. New York: M. Evans and Co., Inc., 1976. See pp. 251–55 for a brief history of Ivar Kreuger, the Swedish "Match King."

Noggle, Burt, *Teapot Dome: Oil and Politics in the 1920's*. Baton Rouge: Louisiana State University Press, 1962.

Paradis, A. A., *The Research Handbook*. Chicago: Funk & Wagnalls, 1974.

President's Commission on Law Enforcement and the Administration of Justice, *Task Force Reports* (various headings). Washington, D.C.: U.S. Government Printing Office.

Roscoe, John T., *Fundamental Research Statistics*, Chaps. 1, 16. New York: Holt, Rinehart & Winston, 1969.

Rosen, L., and R. West, *Reader for Research Methods*. New York: Random House, 1973.

Shirer, William L., *The Rise and Fall of the Third Reich: A History of Nazi Germany*. New York: Simon & Schuster, 1960.

Smith, H. W., *Strategies of Social Research: The Methodological Imagination*. Englewood Cliffs, N.J.: Prentice-Hall, 1975.

Viano, Emilio, ed., *Criminal Justice Research*. Lexington, Mass.: Heath, 1975.

Zola, Emile, *L'Affaire Dreyfus: La Vérité en Marche*. Paris: Garnier Flammarion, 1969.

Schools of Criminology and Contributors

Geographic School	*Conceptual School*				
	Classical (c. 1765)	**Positivist (c. 1876)**	**Social Defense (1943)**	**Sociologic (1914)**	**Medical, Forensic (1900)**
Italian	Cesare Beccaria (1738–94)	Cesare Lombroso (1835–1909) Enrico Ferri (1856–1929) Raffaele Garofalo (1851–1934)	Fillippo Gramatica	Vilfredo Pareto (1848–1923)	
French	Rousseau (1712–78) Montesquieu (1689–1755) Voltaire (1694–1778) Emile Durkheim (1858–1917)	Gabriel de Tarde (1843–1904) René Descartes (1596–1650)	Marc Ansel	Adolphe Quetelet (Belg., 1796–1874) Auguste Comte (1798–1857)	Alfred Binet (1857–1911)
German	Paul Feuerbach (1775–1833)	Karl Marx (1818–83) Friedrich Engels (1820–95) Hans Gross (Austr., 1847–1915) Gustav Aschaffenburg (1866–1944) Franz Gall (1758–1828)		Max Weber (1864–1920) Ferdinand Tönnies (1855–1936)	Ernst Kretschmer (1888–1964) Sigmund Freud (1856–1939) Carl Jung (1875–1961) Emil Kraepelin (1856–1926)
English	Thomas Hobbes (1588–1679) Jeremy Bentham (1748–1832)	Charles Goring (1870–1919)		Henry Mayhew (1812–87)	Henry Maudsley (1835–1918)

	William Blackstone (1723–80) Samuel Romilly (1757–1818) Robert Peel (1788–1850) John Locke (1632–1704)			
American	Edward Livingston (1764–1836)	Earnest Hooton (1887–1954) William Sheldon Alfred Kinsey Sheldon and Eleanor Glueck	Charles H. Cooley Clifford Shaw Robert Park Ernest Burgess Henry McKay Edwin Sutherland Thorsten Sellin Robert Merton Richard Cloward Lloyd Ohlin Frank Tannenbaum Albert Cohen Walter Reckless Donald Clemmer Gresham Sykes David Matza Richard Quinney Howard Becker Edwin Lemert Daniel Glaser Vernon Fox Donald Taft Paul Tappan Don Gibbons etc.	Isaac Ray (1807–81) Benjamin Rush (1746–1813) William Healy Karl Menninger Vernon Mark Frank Ervin William Glass D. Abrahamsen Eric Berne Ray Jeffreys Alex Bassin Thomas Szasz Edwin Schurr Seymour Halle A. Ellis Benjamin Carp J. C. Coleman M. Guttmacher
Russian Literary School	Nikolai Gogol (1809–52) Fedor Dostoevsky (1821–81) Leo Tolstoy (1828–1910) Mikhail Sholokhov (1905–)			

APPENDIX TO CHAPTER 1

The Schools of Criminology

The schools of thought in the field of criminology can be enumerated in several ways. It is generally conceded that there are four *conceptual* schools: the classical, positivist, sociologic, and social defense. The *geographic* divisions–Italian, French, English, German, and American–although accepted in practice, are not formally acknowledged. Another breakdown is by *method of treatment*: therapy and socio-psychological. And the contributors may be categorized by their *methods of investigation*: medical, correctional, statistical, and legal.

There is some overlapping between the schools; not only are many of the contributors from other disciplines, but the schools may be designated according to the dominance of the nationality of the contributors. For example, the classical and positivist schools are sometimes known as the Italian school, the sociologic as the American.

In the preceding table, no attempt has been made to include all the scholars; the list grows constantly.

2

Beginning Research: The Topic, Application, and Presentation

TOPIC RESEARCH

No research can begin without topic research. It is vital to the experienced researcher and introduces the student to the essentials of research examination.

Certain rules must be followed:

1. A decision has to be made on what to look for, where to look, and when to look.
2. Certain limits are imposed by time, money, and convenience. Therefore, the search should be limited to relevancy, pertinent data, and materiality. There is a temptation to wander and waste time researching interesting side issues, but if the side issues are that good, they should be noted for some future search.
3. Research data must be recorded on cards, in a journal, on audiotape, on videotape, in photos, or on film. The 5″ × 8″ card and a daily journal appear to be the most popular.
4. A plan must be established so that the topic research is methodical and within the researcher's ability.[1]

Although not all research is concerned with field work and empirical study, all research entails reading reports and analyzing them. Prior research in the topic area

[1] John W. Best, *Research in Education* (Englewood Cliffs, N.J.: Prentice-Hall, 1977), p. 21. "The first topic will necessarily be a modest one which can be carried on by an inexperienced researcher in a limited period of time."

has to be examined to see what it contributes to present and intended research. Prior research is a valuable learning tool, in that it shows how to present subject matter in format, illustrates good methodology, and furnishes additional resources.

Analyzing Topic Research

Because prior research is so valuable, it deserves special attention. Any report can be simply read and reduced to conversation; research reports need special treatment.

In reading reports, articles, and monographs, the researcher needs to answer these questions:

1. What is valuable in the report, and what are the concepts used?
2. What methodology and measurements were used to operationalize the hypothesis?
3. Where, when, and how were the data gathered?
4. Who did the research, and did the person's prestige affect the findings?
5. Could the research response have been affected by situation, circumstance, or environment?
6. What errors occurred, what has been omitted, what is redundant or obfuscated, what fallacies are present, and what are the alternatives?
7. How does the reader react to the research, and how would the reader present the research?
8. Is the research ethical, reliable, able to be proved or replicated? Is it truthful, practical, and valid?
9. How can statements such as percentages be converted to real numbers? Can ratios be converted? What do the numbers mean?
10. What is the impact of the research statement—is it emotional, dramatic, an appeal to ridicule?
11. Have diagrams or pictures been used to achieve visual impact? Do visual effects affect the reading?
12. Does the research accomplish what it set out to do?

The researcher is not a critic, he is looking for facts.[2] Some students get emotional while reading certain articles, but emotion is no substitute for research skill, nor are impressive style and format a substitute for content. Experience can be obtained only by reading articles and reports and seriously thinking about them in terms of the twelve guidelines presented.

SEARCHING FOR TOPIC MATERIAL

Scientific investigation is not performed in a vacuum. It occurs in a real world and is used by real people to solve real problems. Criminology, in particular, deals with

[2] The researcher is a critic not in the *fault-finding* sense, but in a *fact-finding* sense. The researcher becomes a critic as skills develop in setting standards and judging criteria.

reality, often at the "gut level." Criminologists research life from the purely theoretical to the seamy practical.[3]

Because we are dealing with life, prior records exist that will enable us to further identify and expand our research study. Once the research topic is selected and an informal statement made of the proposition to be tested, past records should be searched for relevant ideas and related facts.

The Library

The logical place to start is the library. The facilities that the researcher can make use of are listed in the accompanying box. Among the microfiche files mentioned there, most helpful are the National Council on Crime and Delinquency file, with over 2,300 titles, and the ERIC file, which has many titles in crime and delinquency. *The New York Times* files are on microfilm, as are the Nuremberg war trials. Ultrafiche, which contains about 990 pages per 4" x 6" fiche, contains unique collections of old documents; and a good many monographs are on microforms.

LIBRARY FACILITIES AND TECHNOLOGY

The card catalog, under subject heading, author, and book title
Subject headings listed under Library of Congress catalog reference books
The periodical index, and bound and current periodicals
Abstracts
Author and subject bibliographies and dictionaries
Doctoral abstracts, theses, and monographs
New books not yet listed
Unlisted periodicals, journals and magazines, and newspapers
Archives, documents, rare books
Cross-library listings, interlibrary loans
Microforms and microfiche, including ultrafiche
Computer terminals for computer-aided search of relevant materials
Tapes, videotapes, records, films, and slides
Research instructional programs offered by librarians

But the emphasis in any library search should be on the use of card catalogs, using subject headings; the use of dictionaries and bibliographies; the use of encyclopedias; the use of periodicals, especially current journals; and the use of microforms. Research is a routine process in which no stone must be left unturned. *It is recommended that the beginning researcher be guided by the experienced instructor or the experienced librarian.*

[3] Vernon B. Fox, *Introduction to Criminology* (Englewood Cliffs, N.J.: Prentice-Hall, 1976), p. 24: "The problem of the criminologist has become one of defining a sociopolitical event in terms of human behavior and social theory."

Files and Collections

Research of the topic does not stop at the library. Outside the library there are many resources:

1. Some periodicals and trade publications that may be helpful are not available in the library, owing to lack of space. Current magazines often carry articles by scholars in the discipline. Magazines such as *Playboy* or *Penthouse* specialize in using name authorities to write articles. The *National Inquirer* or *Moneysworth* may cite recent studies and references. Trade publications such as airline journals, union journals and travel magazines, are all source material, as are trade catalogs. For example, Sears Roebuck's Fall 1900 catalog lists triple-strength opium at 40 cents for a 2-oz. phial, and the cure for 75 cents.
2. Special-interest files and libraries are available to the researcher. Legal libraries are special law collections that lawyers reserve for themselves but that are open for compatible research. Industrial files can be examined. Certain professional people keep files related to their occupational practice, usually sharing them with other professionals on a strictly ethical basis; but within the limits of invasion of client privacy, these files may be made available on specific request.
3. Media files and libraries, of particular interest to those investigating deviance, are restricted, but upon demonstration of the nature of the research, they are usually made available. Newspaper files contain a wealth of information filed on specific issues. Videotapes are also highly documented.
4. Federal, state, county, city, and local agencies often maintain extensive files that contain masses of information not generally known to the public. Under the new "sunshine" laws, much of this is now readily accessible. The person in charge of the department will usually help find the information one is seeking. Some bureaucrats, of course, resent intrusion into their files, and occasionally, a court order is required to pry information loose. Also, certain information is classified, but this is usually the exception rather than the rule. Many agencies, in fact, issue special reports that are made available for the asking or taking. Agencies of special interest to the criminologist are the FBI; the Department of Justice; the CIA; sheriff's and police departments; the coroner's office; the various departments of corrections; the Department of Health, Education and Welfare; the local agencies for employment, welfare, and taxes; the various courts; probation and parole departments; LEAA and planning departments; juvenile departments; and related agencies. The National Criminal Justice Research Service publishes a yearly document-retrieval index. Many of these resources are listed at the end of this chapter.
5. Many historical and biographical collections found in museums are valuable as a source for comparative period examination. Material not generally well known may be placed in an exhibit on the development of a city or an industry. For example, early crime may be found documented in an exhibit on development of the frontier, the waterfront, stagecoach lines, railways, or medicine. Often, museums and galleries have their own libraries, which are another source for specialized research.
6. Private and restricted-access collections are found in private homes or collections not yet acquired by the public. Examples of these are private collections of artifacts, paraphernalia, personal libraries, items or records of interest, and the like. These collections are usually held either for sentiment or awaiting the highest bid. Old papers are held pending proper scholarly editing. Criminologists

tend to collect items of interest in their occupational field. Access to such collections is usually made by acquaintance with the party concerned, or through some friendly third party.

The University as a Resource

Many university libraries now offer services that are specifically designed to aid the research student. By appointment with your professor, librarians will give an orientation tour and classes in bibliographic research technique. They will not write your project for you, but they will assist you in the fine art of *resource retrieval*. They know how items are catalogued and filed; the reference librarian in particular has specialized training in locating resource material.

You must be able to narrow your search down to titles that will eliminate extraneous material. For example, "crime" is too wide a subject to research, but by specifying "computer crime" or "white-collar crime" or "embezzlement" or "fraud," you limit the area of the search.

The computer-retrieval system works the same way. You feed the computer the titles you want it to locate in its data bank, and the more specific you are, the faster the computer works. The library will also assist you on computer services such as MEDLINE, DATRIX (dissertation search), PAIS (Public Affairs Information Service), and others listed in the resource bibliography at the end of this chapter. Government-subsidized computer services, such as MEDLINE, ERIC, and NCJRS, are less expensive; on-line services cost more and give instant retrieval return; off-line printouts (or searches) are cheaper but take longer, perhaps a few days. Services through a big system such as DIALOG from Palo Alto, California, offer 100 or more data bases.

The cost of services like these is decreasing, and, provided that the number of descriptors is not excessive, the cost is worth the time saved. A descriptor is a name fed into the computer that designates the subject heading to be researched. The computer will search all the books, periodicals, and references in its data bank under that heading and then print out all the listings pertinent to it. *Your descriptors must summarize your topic*. You must be specific. Usually, the librarian will help you write the descriptors.

While books and computers provide information, professors and colleagues provide ideas. You will find your major professor or your advisor very helpful, and it is good policy to talk to colleagues in other departments. Adding an interdisciplinary flavor sometimes improves the final research product.

Remember that *researching current trends demands that you spend time and effort in current periodicals*. Use the indexes and narrow your search to conserve time. Articles in periodicals over six months old are usually indexed; newer ones are not, and you will have to seek them out. Although photostats are excellent, your own *notes with proper references* are the best of all.[4] Take care to enter the complete citation and all pertinent information for future recall.

[4] A 5" × 8"-topic-card file is invaluable for keeping track of bibliography, topics, and book notes.

People

Perhaps the greatest resource of all to the curious investigator is people themselves. By talking to people about your topic—by discussion with *experts* in the field, by discussion with *colleagues* in related disciplines, by the interchange of ideas with the various *librarians and resource people*—your mind becomes enlarged with different aspects of what you yourself are doing.[5] Your subjective viewpoint is merged with the objective viewpoint of others, thus enriching the research topic.

THE NATURE OF RESEARCH

Some nonscientific inquiry, based purely on innovation or imagination, has forced scientific thought into new areas. Speculation on what *is* possible has widened the scientific frontier, whereas the confirmation of what *is not* possible has made science static and in some cases has actually been responsible for its destruction. Research findings are always open to modification; they are a contribution to the discipline, not the final word. Research in the social sciences is restricted not only by its very nature of dealing with society, but in the sophistication of its technology.[6]

Nevertheless, social-science research can and does quantify human behavior. The quantification takes place by using the scientific method, which begins with a scientific statement of the problem—the research hypothesis. The hypothesis states that two or more variables are (causally) related. The null hypothesis, which is used to test the hypothesis, is a statement of no significant relationship between the variables.

Not all research questions, however, are posited in hypothesis form. Some ask

Table 2.1. Informal Research Methods

Type of research	Cause		Effect	
	Known	*Unknown*	*Known*	*Unknown*
Ex post facto		x	x	
Exploration (simulation)	x			x
Ad hoc	x		x	
Serendipity		x	x	
Speculation (long shot)		x		x

[5] Many researchers, especially beginners, are nervous, shy, and easily embarrassed when seeking information from strangers. This is a problem you must learn to overcome by doing. You may even learn not to intimidate others.

[6] Harold J. Vetter and J. Wright, Jr., *Introduction to Criminology* (Springfield, Ill.: Charles C Thomas, 1974), p. 28: "Research is essentially a creative enterprise; no one, except in a very restricted way, can tell another how to do it."

why, some try to find out *if*, and some explore *where*. The types of research without hypotheses are shown in Table 2.1.

The ex post facto inquiry is into such matters as homicide or other crime, accident, disaster, or cause of death. Examples would be the inquiries into the Hindenburg or Titanic disasters; the research is done to find the cause when the effect is already known.

The exploration inquiry is into the unknown–the Arctic, space travel, brain control. Here, we know the means (the cause) but not the effect until it takes place.

The ad hoc inquiry is an examination of what is actually available–who is there, what is there, where it is, and when it can be used. It is a kind of inventorying of previously unknown quantities of known variables–for example, number of arrests, number of lynchings, available computer technology.

"Serendipity" means the happy discovery of something unexpectedly. Examples are the discovery of penicillin, the telephone, and X-rays. In our field, it is research begun by accident, or research whose results are discovered before the investigation explains them. But the odds of such accidents happening are in favor of the trained researcher who is looking for them.

Sometimes when research has exhausted all reasonable possibilities, the chance "long shot" comes home, frequently flying in the face of accepted dictums. Examples of such speculative results are the invention of the airplane, the discovery of oxygen, psychoanalysis, and vaccination. Here, the research is pushed beyond its limits into the realm of discovery.

Formal and Informal Research

Criminology is a comparatively new discipline. The data that are researched are varied, often extremely complex, and relatively unknown. Sometimes we are dealing with facts, but more often with attitudes, prejudices, beliefs, memory recall, past behavior, future behavior, and outcomes.

Because most of the data are conjecture, there is room in the discipline for both formal and informal research methods.[7] Informal research uses observation and organization of data just as formal research does, but it tends to dispense with hypothesis construction as a poor use of time, and it moves directly to law rather than using the intervening step of theory. Formal research is empirical, quantitative, and restricted by scientific method and logical sequence. Informal research is based upon curiosity, inquiry, and speculation; experiments are used to find positive results and to proceed directly toward a law. Refer to Table 2.2 for further comparisons between formal and informal research.

Examples of informal research are crime investigations based upon hunches; investigation of situations that demand answers based upon speculation; trial-and-

[7] Earl R. Babbie, *The Practice of Social Research* (Belmont, Calif.: Wadsworth, 1975), p. 18. Babbie describes science as "an open-ended enterprise in which conclusions are constantly being modified."

Table 2.2. Comparison of Formal and Informal Research

Formal	Informal
Research begins with empirical propositions, statements of fact based upon reality. The phenomena of the real world are observed and translated into statements that can be checked and communicated to others, in a precise, understandable language.	Research begins with similar observation of empirical facts and a statement of the problem relating to those facts, or to the observer's reality. The research is not limited by tangibility or scientific confines.
The research hypothesis is formalized in terms of propositions that are capable of being tested by oneself or others. The formal hypothesis, a statement containing two or more variables, requires precise definition and possible construction of a model.	Investigation is based upon questions to be answered, inquiry, speculation, and informal, tentative hypothesis. The formal hypothesis is considered a delay in the experimental process, and is seldom used.
Operationalization of the variables and organization of data are essential to the research experiment, which details the tests used and the manipulation of the variables in terms of causality for the purpose of acceptance or rejection of the hypothesis. Experiments are carefully controlled, with emphasis on precision of measurement. Guiding principles are economy and the avoidance of fallacy.	Data are ordered and organized for experimentation. The experiments seek positive results. They continue along the question–answer approach. Negative results are often rejected. Experiments are designed to lead directly to formulation of a law.
Findings are presented in a theoretical proposal of statements of causality. The assertions made are logical, consistent, practical, specific, valid, and able to be replicated by others. They act as a bridge between the hypothesis and law. Theory is vital in formal research.	Theory is unnecessary and too formal for consideration. It impedes the direct step from experiment to law.
Law is based upon scientific method proceeding through observation to hypothesis to theory to replication.	Law is based upon observation and experiment.

error efforts in the research of behavior modification; and most psychological and psychiatric research, often made without hypotheses. Such research expands the discipline and opens doors for formal research.

Theory and Research

Some of our research—such as exploratory, practical inquiry into why things work, or the effectiveness of one system over another, or the usefulness of a program—adds to theory only if the empirical data yielded are organized and made part of a wider "theoretical scaffolding."

Theory should encompass the framework in which the empirical data from applied research are to be included. Theory is essentially the formulation, explanation, and prediction of phenomena based upon quantitative research findings.

If, in practice, we can replicate or observe the same result again and again, then our theory, which includes the quantification of our research findings, may be defined as a law. Note that our new law depends upon the same propositions that, by way of theory, were originally research hypotheses, developed in turn from our research topic.

Although we have many theories in criminology, we have few if any laws (in the strictly theoretical sense), owing probably to the fact that we seldom replicate our studies. The trouble is that most research is very difficult to replicate, because we use complex variables—such as self-concept, criminal association, police brutality, and so on—that differ with time and measurement as well as with definition by different researchers. However, if we can overcome all these difficulties, the theory may direct us to further research, and that is its most important quality.

The "research diamond" in Figure 2-1 indicates how law is constructed from phenomena. The observed difference or the challenge of phenomena stimulates the selection of a research topic. Facts gathered about the topic may be tangible or intangible, and the appropriate research methods are used, based upon propositions and hypotheses that they affirm or reject. Theory is constructed on the hypotheses and, if consistent, becomes law. Occasionally, law is created by inspiration or serendipity, accidental discovery. Inspiration tends to be *a priori*, serendipity *a posteriori*.

AN EXAMPLE OF TOPIC SELECTION

If we read in areas motivated by our research interest, we may find that our selection of a topic will lead us to consideration of past theory before we make an informal statement. Let us say that the following articles are required reading:[8]

Stephen Phillips, "Justice for Whom?" *Psychology Today*, March 1977

Nicolas Pileggi, "How a 15 Year-Old Gets Away with Murder," *New York*, June 13, 1977

"Youth Crime Plague," cover story, *Time*, July 11, 1977

Edward Eldefonso, "Santa Clara Probation Report," appendix in *Control, Treatment and Rehabilitation of Offenders* (Beverly Hills, Calif.: Glencoe, 1976)

In this series of readings, the following questions are asked:

1. What is the problem?
2. What is the effect upon the criminal justice system?
3. Is justice served?
4. What can be done to solve the problem?

[8] Taken from the list of readings appended at the end of this chapter.

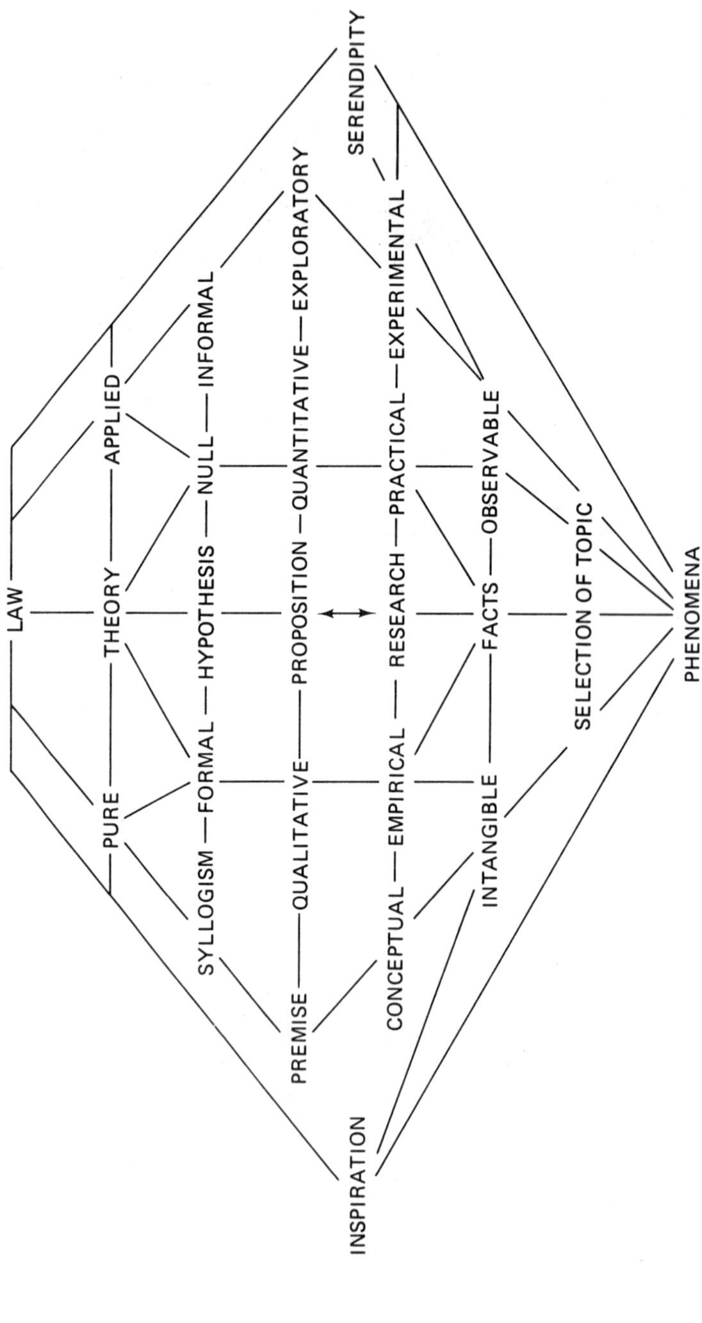

Fig. 2-1 The research diamond.

The answers require the reader to state the problem, identify the variables, set up an informal hypothesis, relate the problem to theory if possible, and identify common threads running through the articles.

The articles introduce the reader to the way others have solved or attempted to solve their problems. The reader learns to order priorities, select relevant variables, and delineate research relationships; to abstract a report, reduce it to a minimum, and apply the facts gleaned to the purpose of his or her own research.

The readings in the crime topic become an exercise in logic, summarization, and presentation. The whole object of topic research is to narrow the field to a specialized study.

Linking the Topic to Theory

The informal statement of the problem is considerably improved if it can be related to prior research or prior theory. The example of teenage crime has been considered by many theorists: Edwin Lemert has discussed primary and secondary deviance and the effect of labeling—that once a delinquent is officially labeled as such, the label is difficult to change, and the delinquent then comes to accept that social role.[9] Cohen has indicated the secondary legal codes that apply to juveniles.[10] Goodman claims that society has failed in offering appropriate alternatives to youth, and thus youth rebels.[11] Lindner maintains that such juveniles become "rebels without cause,"[12] Cloward and Ohlin feel that youth unable to find legitimate opportunity will seek other ways to achieve.[13] David Matza theorizes that youths drift into crime.[14] Each of these and many other theories can be discussed in relation to the required articles.

For example, Stephen Phillips's article, "Justice for Whom?" deals with the complex problem that a D.A. faces when a white teenager has senselessly killed a black teenager. The racial situation is compounded by demands for punishment that goes beyond the meaning of "cruel and unusual." The tragedy of the case is further darkened by family illness and death. Society—and the courts in particular—demands a resolution of the problem.

Because the crime is not unique, it is open to research. In regard to the four questions asked above, the problem is, "Why do teenagers commit murder?" The answer to the second question is that teenage murder is apparently beyond the scope of the criminal justice system. The response to question 3, "Is justice served?" is that justice is frustrated, and the juvenile court (or family court) system was never meant to deal with such crimes; there is no real legal philosophy for teenage

[9] Edwin Lemert, *Social Pathology* (New York: McGraw-Hill, 1951).
[10] B. Cohen, ed., *Crime in America* (Itasca, Ill.: F. E. Peacock, 1970).
[11] P. Goodman, *Growing Up Absurd* (New York: Random House, 1962).
[12] Robert Lindner, *Rebel without Cause* (New York: Grune and Stratton, 1944).
[13] R. A. Cloward and L. Ohlin, *Delinquency and Opportunity* (New York: Free Press, 1960).
[14] David Matza, *Delinquency and Drift* (New York: Wiley, 1964).

murderers. Phillips, Pileggi, and Eldefonso all indicate how they might deal with the problem, but the sum total seems to be that the problem has not been dealt with.

The short discussion above of prior theory indicates that most theories do not fit the circumstances of senseless teenage murder. For example:

Labeling: One is not labeled prior to murder.
Illegitimate opportunity: Nothing is gained by senseless murder.
Drift: If teenagers simply drifted into murder, it would occur far more.

But there does appear to be a bridge in the theories of Lindner and Goodman, with an assist from psychological and psychiatric theory. We now need to make a statement that will enable us to relate to Lindner and Goodman.

A simple research statement focusing on the common problem in the readings would be, as per Lindner:

> There are definite mental characteristics that cause certain teenagers to commit crimes of violence.

A null hypothesis could be:

> There is no relationship between crimes of violence and attitudes prevalent among teenagers.

This latter hypothesis suggests sampling two groups, teenagers without criminal records and teenagers with criminal records. We may also state, as per Goodman:

> Modern society creates situations that cause teenagers to commit crimes of violence.

And the null hypothesis:

> There is no relationship between teenage crimes of violence and social conditions.

This second null hypothesis suggests that we list probable social conditions that could enrage certain adolescents into criminal fury.

We have used our proposition, developed from the readings, to formulate a testable hypothesis. *The hypothesis clearly links the forthcoming research to prior relevant theory*. It creates a link between the topic and operationalization.

Discovering a topic in the readings has led to making an informal statement concerning crime. The informal statement has been compared to prior theory. Relevant theory has indicated that possible formal hypotheses may be proposed. The formal hypothesis can then be written as a testable null hypothesis.

Among the many aspects of the problem in the articles listed are the following:

- How teenage immunity from crimes of violence inflames the public
- How teenage violence obscures other teenage crimes
- How teenagers take advantage of legal definitions, and how experienced criminals train teenagers to do this
- The lack of alternatives in dealing with juveniles
- The spread and ferocity of juvenile crime
- Leadership in teenage gangs and what it entails
- Community fear of teenage assault
- How community fear obscures community responsibility
- Problems of race, and of double standards for rich and poor, old and young, civil rights and social rights
- Overload in the criminal justice system

Each of these factors poses special research problems that can be translated into hypotheses and models. From informal statements, formal hypotheses may be constructed to indicate possible avenues of research inquiry.[15] It helps to write down a few sentences on what one would like to do in the project. The real thrust of topic research is to develop a *manageable* research study.

You must decide upon a specific area of research, to be undertaken within the limits of time, expense, and human effort. Take a concept such as "leadership in teenage gangs." This can be narrowed down still further to items of specific interest. Studies in this area have been done as participant observers,[16] statistical studies,[17] and cultural studies.[18] Items of special interest are:

1. Case studies of gang leadership
2. Rules and rituals used in gang ceremonies
3. Rewards and sanctions applied to gang leaders and by leaders to members
4. Duties and functions of gang leaders; leadership as part of gang structure (the gang as social phenomenon)

The research done here may be statistical, by gathering data on actual performance by gang leaders, showing crimes committed by type and number. Or the gang leader may be studied as a particular case history; the gang itself can be studied from within if one can get accepted as an observer-member. Finally, the gang may be studied as a social phenomenon, with emphasis on gang leadership.[19] The importance

[15] Fred N. Kerlinger, *Foundations of Behavioral Research*, 2nd ed. (New York: Holt, Rinehart & Winston, 1973), p. 23; according to Kerlinger, the ideal hypothesis falls somewhere between the extremes of "generality and specificity," between "vagueness and triviality."

[16] William F. Whyte, *Streetcorner Society* (Chicago: University of Chicago Press, 1943).

[17] Fred M. Thrasher, *The Gang* (Chicago: University of Chicago Press, 1927).

[18] Albert K. Cohen, *Delinquent Boys: The Culture of the Gang* (New York: Free Press, 1955).

[19] M. E. Wolfgang, R. M. Figlio, and T. Sellin, *Delinquency in a Birth Cohort* (Chicago: University of Chicago Press, 1972).

of the research is in the imagination used, the specific interest, the need for the research, and its completion.

The specialization of topic research may be summarized:

1. Find a topic, one that stimulates your interest.
2. Focus the topic into items of specific definability.
3. Set limits on the study—be practical.
4. Consider the actual research method and its completion.

Topics Concerning New Situations

Not all research will have prior research upon which to proceed. Some research is simply to answer the question, *Why*? We may be interested in obtaining a profile of criminal activities, or even of a criminal. Such research, while contributing to our knowledge, does little for theory. Unfortunately, theories on typologies and classifications in criminology are resistant to change, whereas profiles are current, changeable, and often contrary to typologies. Profiles are directed more at problem solving than at making contributions to research theory. Researching a profile has a decidedly *practical* aspect, whereas researching a typology has a *theoretical* intent and is *pure* research as against *applied* research.

A great deal of research in criminology is applied. We seek practical answers for immediate problems, problems that produce crisis situations that demand our immediate attention. Very often, research of problems is limited by either previous theory or prior research that literally forces the researcher into a particular mode of investigation. We also assume that all phenomena are not new, and therefore we need not change our research ways. *These two assumptions—that prior methods are correct and that phenomena are not new—compel us to proceed in the same old way regardless of the fact that our methods may be entirely inappropriate for the research*. To resolve this dilemma, it is proposed that the research imagination seek out new phenomena and devise new methods, in much the same way that the scientific method came into existence.

Using the Topic to Develop a Profile

The collection of data on various specialized subjects lends itself to the construction of a profile. The profile may be of a person, an event, or a community. *A profile is an outline or analysis of specific features revealed by investigation, research, or testing.*

Profiles have been developed from IQ tests, from psychological tests such as the M.M.P.I., and from vocational aptitude tests. Often profiles can be constructed from available data not yet used for that purpose.

A classic example of a study used to profile murder and murderers was that done in Philadelphia by Wolfgang in 1948-52.[20] Contemporary studies have been made to identify hijackers; some research has been incorporated into actually providing a picture profile of a wanted criminal; and frequency data, supported by subfiles and multiple-regression analysis, were used to provide a stress profile.[21] Profiles can be used (1) to identify people or events, and (2) as a basis for prediction. For example, if certain criminals manifest the same characteristics, security officials can identify potential criminality and act accordingly. Profiles may be used to anticipate and frustrate terrorist activities, and to identify patterns of arson and criminal careers.[22]

Use of the Topic for Prediction

When we are able to integrate our findings into practical solutions, we tend to use those findings as the basis for prediction. We are interested in cutting costs, keeping men out of prison, keeping society safe from predators, knowing how effective our criminal justice system will be. On the basis of data gathered from past reports and past performance, we hypothesize that if we apply variable A, then result B will occur; or if we desire result B, we need to find what it is that causes or makes up A, so that we can create A for ourselves. Once we know A, we can then apply it to achieve B whenever we please. For example, if we find out what keeps men out of prison, then applying that remedy should lower prison populations; if we know what elements make a parole a success, we can determine which inmates will be successful in staying outside the walls.

Of course, practice does not always agree with concept, and we do not always achieve what we thought was possible. Unanticipated factors enter into a situation, or the hypothesis is contaminated by prior knowledge, or the situation is confounded by unexpected results. Such results indicate that further research is necessary. (See also Chapter 10.)

The uses of the research topic that we have discussed in this section are illustrated in Table 2.3. Also shown there is its use in cost-benefit analysis, a very important application.

WRITING A PROPOSAL

The *research proposal*, which is the formalization of the topic, is a preliminary to setting out on the project. It is a guide that you design to aid you in your inquiry.

[20] Marvin E. Wolfgang, *Patterns in Criminal Homicide* (Philadelphia: University of Pennsylvania Press, 1958).

[21] Edwin S. Johnson, *Stress Effects in Two Black Community Systems in the Process of Social Change* (Tallahassee, Fla.: Signature, 1976).

[22] Fox, *Introduction to Criminology*, Chap. 13. See also an excellent cross-cultural study by Henry P. Lundsgaarde, *Murder in Space City* (New York: Oxford University Press, 1977).

Table 2.3. The Use of the Topic and Application to Research

Topic Application	*Case Study*	*Participant Observation*	*Survey Research*	*Profile*	*Predictive Study*	*Cost/Benefit Analysis*
Terrorism	Assassination methods and purpose	Hazardous	Attitudes toward terrorists	X	Security, based on profile	Strategy analysis of costs/use/distribution/damage
Crime victim	Victim vigilante	As victim	Crime, based on study of victims	X	Prevention of crime	Analysis of reparations
Arson	Contract arsonist	Immunity study	Survey of causes, damage, and public attitudes	X	Control of arson pattern	Study of insurance payments and fire-risk control
Gambling	Casino owner, gambler	Visit casinos	Attitudes toward gambling	X	Trend studies	Enforcement vs. control (legalization), study of Mafia financing
Drugs	Addict	Test of drug effect, drug culture	Attitudes and sentiment in drug laws and sentences	X	Trend studies of use and traffic	Enforcement vs. control; investigative study of drug financing, manufacture, and distribution
Juries	Juror	Jury service	Survey of jurors, offenders, public on jury response	X	Jury selection	Simulation study
Child abuse	Child, parent	Visit foster homes	Study parent abuse, victim abuse	X	Time and trend study	Community cost
Inmate control	Inmate	Mix with inmates	Public attitude to control and rehabilitation	X	Probability of success of parole	Cost of probation, etc. vs. flat time

The importance of the written proposal is that it is a record of the initial research project. It puts the topic into a formal statement of the intentions of the researcher, translating concepts in the researcher's mind into definitive problems that can be communicated to others. Actual research concepts have to be explained, set out, and defined to give them meaning. Even then, the meaning is limited, since definition in the social sciences is never final.

The proposal will detail how the researcher will seek data from social phenomena; it will set out the variables and tell how they will be quantified; and it will place limits on the research. The proposal should be simple, clear, and brief. It should state:

1. The aims, objectives, and purpose of the research
2. Any underlying theory, describing a model
3. The research and null hypotheses
4. Operational definitions of the variables
5. Methods to be used for obtaining data
6. Statistical levels of analysis
7. Limits on the research in terms of operation, time, and place

SOME SIMPLE RULES FOR PROPOSAL FORMAT

1. The proposal is simply a presentation of the topic for actual research. *It should be easy to read.* Get to the point early, avoiding technical phrases and jargon. State what you want to do, what the purpose of the project is, and what objectives you seek.
2. If there is any underlying theory that motivated the research, state what it is and give references. If you can base a model on your prior theory, do so.
3. When you write your research hypothesis, set it apart, make it brief, and construct it in such a way that you communicate exactly what you are testing. Write your null hypothesis to conform to your research hypothesis, and make your null a statement of no relationship between the variables.
4. The variables in your hypothesis must be defined. They must be made operational, and you must explain how this can be done. Define the variables in time, place, situation, and limits, giving their order and causes. The variables are the key to testing your hypothesis.
5. Describe your proposed methodology. Indicate how you will operationalize your variables and exactly how you will collect your data. Identify the nature of the testing, treatment, control, survey, or any other set of conditions used in the research method.
6. If possible, indicate the statistics to be used in the analysis of data, and the sequence of those statistics. Make a statistical statement of the hypothesis and set limits of retention or rejection of the null. (You will be able to do this after reading Chapter 4.)
7. Set limits on your research in terms of completion, research objective, location, practicality, and size--that is, manageable proportions and specific objectives.

The practical use of the proposal is lost once the research begins. It becomes a record of how it started, complete with notes, discussion, and changes. Therefore, it should have simple sections that clearly show what is to follow:

1. *The title page* should carry an appropriate title that will identify the project and remain the title for the final presentation of findings.
2. *The proposal itself* should use the paragraph headings *Topic, Purpose, Research base, Hypothesis, Variables defined, Methodology, Statistical analysis, and Research limits*. Under each heading should be a brief description with relevant criteria. Three pages should suffice.
3. Attached should be *a question page* containing questions raised by the researcher that are pertinent to the nature of the problem. If there are no questions, a perfect product will be assumed.
4. *Two blank pages* should be added to be used for notes and changes to be made after discussion and further reading.

The proposal is the incomplete map of the research territory. It is the student's or the investigator's personal interpretation of a research idea. It must be refined, modified, and possibly rewritten as progress is made in developing the project. Some of the proposal will be incorporated into the final report.

After discussion of the proposal, the researcher may wish to add the following sections:

Operationalization, describing details of instrument construction, field work, sample size, and data collection.

Pretest, describing possible pretest technique.

Contribution to the discipline, describing use of the research and its practical or theoretical assets.

Review of the literature, a list of books to be read to aid the research project. In the final report, this becomes a survey of the literature.

THE FINAL REPORT

The final report is the completed map of the research process, so even though we have not yet started, we must keep in mind the content of each section that will need completion. Besides the title page, possible table of contents, and lists of figures and tables, the body of the report should contain these headings:

Topic—This heading describes the aim of the research, why it is being done, the objectives, and what the study is about.

Purpose—Here, the hypotheses (H_a and H_o) are set forth and explained.

Variables described—The variables to be used in the hypotheses are explained, defined, described. Methods of selection, causal ordering, and operationalization should be fully set down.

Population, place, and date—The frame of the sampling reference, its place, and date are recorded, as is the type of survey used.

Sampling—The actual details of how the sample is obtained are noted, as is sample size, selection process, and type.

Instrument—The questionnaire is detailed in terms of number of questions, how it is used, how it was constructed, results of any pretest used, any special sections or scales, type of scoring. The questionnaire itself should be attached.

Data collection—The gathering of data is described, and if a team was used, each member's contribution is stated. Controls used, methods of interview, instructions, training, and procedure should all be written up.

Coding—Scales are explained, and all codes used on IBM cards are detailed.

Statistics used—Usually the beginner uses frequencies, scattergram, correlation, cross-tabulations, possibly regression.

Data analysis—Tables are constructed from statistical analysis to set out the results of data collection. The tables are sequential and are based upon computer printouts.

Conclusions—Statements made here concern the rejection or retention of the H_0, possibility of Type 1 or 2 error, internal associations, statistical and substantive significance, and possible inferences to the parent population.

Summary—Here, the researcher may wrap up the project with comments based upon the actual figures obtained. Remember the objective was to test the null hypothesis, not prove anything. State any discoveries you have made and keep to the point—let your facts speak for you.

Acknowledgments—Recognize any help you have received; be ethical and acknowledge people who have assisted you.

Evaluation—This section is for your own benefit and may or may not be included. Here, you may appraise your topic selection, hypothesis, and objectives. You may examine your methodological efficiency, the correctness of your statistics, and the value of your conclusions. You may state possible improvements on your design for future research. In effect, you assess the value of your research project.

Finally, add your bibliography and a transparent cover to complete your final report. Don't forget to include any appendixes. If you are writing a thesis, a *Review of the literature* may be added after *Topic* and will serve to introduce the *Purpose*.

The headings given, and their order, are not definitive; you may adjust headings to suit your own particular research, and you may omit some or add your own. Be brief in your comments; you will discover that *Data analysis* takes up the greatest portion, and you will have a 30-page report before you know it. Even using only one page per heading (most unlikely), you will have 14 pages.

Because tables are so important in the final report, make sure they are properly presented, with variables named, correct data, and attractive design—never crowded, always numbered, and in logical sequence.

These pieces complete the research puzzle. You now know what you are required to complete, and you may plan accordingly. As you read through the text, you will gain information for the completion of each section. It is not an easy task; it requires a great deal of time, effort, and concentration.

USING A RESOURCE BIBLIOGRAPHY

In any research worth the name, the first act is to use a resource bibliography: Library of Congress headings, directories, encyclopedias, dictionaries, handbooks, statistical reports, institutional citations, and bibliography of the research-field bibliographies. (See the resource bibliography appended to this chapter.)

A good preliminary exercise is to "warm up" by reading the lives and times of well-known people in the field, such as Thomas Hobbes, René Descartes, Franz Gall, Benjamin Rush.

The use of the research resource bibliography is a first step in understanding the importance of an underlying theoretical structure. The student also learns style and ethical acknowledgment of former contributors; books cited in bibliographies have their own bibliographies, as well as footnotes and annotations on other sources. The resource bibliography is the beginning of a trail that takes you deeper into the research woods. Seek help from your reference librarian. Take notes on your research, listing all the references you use, including the library call numbers.[23]

SUMMARY

Selection of the topic is probably the most important step in the research journey. The topic should be an idea that captures your interest and motivates your efforts to inquire further.

Before you begin the research, use every resource available to fill gaps in your knowledge and to discover what has already been done in this particular area. Your search should begin at the library but include other resources, such as computer retrieval and discussion with people. Findings must be analyzed, records kept, and important data carefully filed. The topic must be specialized, so narrowed in focus that it is practical, well within your skill to complete.

When you have a topic, try to state a problem in proposition form and then in hypothesis form. Your hypothesis should be a link between past theory and current research. Make a research statement and then a testable null hypothesis. The hypothesis means that you can quantify and *test* your variables; testing means that you can verify them given the same set of circumstances.

Your research should be planned to proceed in a systematic, scientific, orderly flow. Of the several kinds of research, we prefer the scientific method using the testable hypothesis and, if possible, having a theoretical base. The formal approach does make restrictions, but it also aids in theory construction.

[23] Library call numbers are usually pasted on the lower spine of the book: i.e., HV 6787 N87 1976. HV indicates Criminology in the Social Sciences.

The data developed from the research are often used to develop profiles, or for prediction, or for decision making. Thus our research will aid us in gaining control over the outcomes of predicted events.

Before embarking on research, it is wise to write a proposal. This brief outline of the research sets forth the purpose, underlying theory, hypothesis, definition, methods analysis, and limits of the research project. After discussion, it may also include a statement on operationalization, pretest, and a review of the literature, which returns us to the resources of the library and more intensive search for topic material.

The research proposal will be somewhat sketchy at this point, but as you read on, you will gain mastery of the elements you need to include. Keep your early proposal to compare with your later efforts. Remember the construction of the final report, the sequence of its parts, and what you will need to know for its completion.

EXERCISES

1. Define topic research. Why is "focus" important? What is involved in planning topic research?
2. Select a current article relating to research in criminology and analyze it, using the twelve criteria suggested.
3. Detail a systematic plan you would follow in your search for topic material.
4. What resources are available to you outside the library?
5. Describe how you would use "the greatest resource of all."
6. Discuss the importance of theory to research and the possible limitations it places on research.
7. What can you gain from using resource material?
8. Describe several different kinds of research. Define *ex post facto; ad hoc; a priori; serendipity; quantify*.
9. Informal research lacks the restrictions of formal research. Discuss the advantages and disadvantages of formal versus informal research.
10. What is meant by the "direction" of the research?
11. What is the *central element* of theory construction, what is provided by "linkage of the hypothesis," and what is "theoretical scaffolding"?
12. Why are there many theories but few laws in criminology?
13. Read the four articles mentioned on teenage crime and discuss your findings about (a) the problem, (b) the effect, (c) the result, and (d) resolution.
14. Write hypotheses for the lack of alternatives in dealing with juvenile crime. Can you test your hypotheses?
15. What is DATRIX? PAIS? DIALOG? ERIC?
16. Define *profile, prediction, social change, descriptor, retrieval*.

17. How does the proposal differ from the final report? What are the parts of a proposal?
18. What are the parts of the final report? Describe each one.
19. What are two assumptions that limit research?
20. Write a proposal on teenage crime and keep it for future reference.
21. After reading the resource bibliography that follows, decide which reference work you would use for the following topics; you may use more than one.

- Crime statistics for the state of New York
- The first police force
- The Haymarket Affair
- The life of Clarence Darrow
- The "climatic theory" of crime
- The history of the "insanity plea"
- Comparative data on prisons
- A list of articles on tax fraud
- The implications of intelligence on crime
- The success of women on parole
- Prison argot
- Number of arsons in Los Angeles, 1970–1975
- Date of John Dillinger's death
- The contribution of physiognomy
- The Descartian Dichotomy
- List of members of the Italian school of criminology
- Data on child abuse
- Recent abstracts on victimization
- The case reference and details of *Gideon* v. *Wainwright*
- The last execution by firing squad in the United States
- The largest swindle in history
- Brain control of prison inmates
- The latest on computer crime
- The history of heroin traffic
- Sex crimes and body typologies

A SHORT RESOURCE BIBLIOGRAPHY FOR CRIMINOLOGY

Directories and Indexes

American Society of Criminology. Members, organizations.

City Directory of Services. Available for each city.

Lankes, George A., *A Directory of Selective Correctional Films*. Buffalo, N.Y.: Erie County Community College, 1971.

Latka, Brenda J., *Directory of Law Enforcement and Criminal Justice Associations and Research Centers*. Washington, D.C.: National Bureau of Standards, 1973.

Mannheim, Hermann, *Pioneers in Criminology*. London: Stevens, 1960.

Marcus, Marvin, *Criminal Justice: Bibliography* (2nd ed.). Atlanta: School of Urban Life, Georgia State University, 1976.

Scott, Sir Harold R., *The Concise Encyclopedia of Crime and Criminals*. N.Y.: Hawthorn Books, 1961.

Sellin, T., and L. D. Savitz., *A Bibliographical Manual for the Student of Criminology*. Washington, D.C.: National Council on Crime and Delinquency, 1965.

Wolfgang, Marvin E., et al., *Criminology Index: Research and Theory in Criminology in the United States*, 1945–1972. New York: Elsevier Scientific Publishing Co., 1975.

For Computer Search and Retrieval

MEDLINE. Search of medical literature, government subsidized.

ERIC (Educational Resources Information Center). Search of all educational research documents, government subsidized.

NCJRS Document Retrieval Index. Not commercially available. Searches all research on criminal justice, subsidized.

Child Abuse and Neglect. Available through NCJRS and LEAA.

Current Awareness Service. Available as above.

PAIS (Public Affairs Information Service). Available through DIALOG.[24]

DATRIX. Dissertation search. Available through DIALOG.

Social Sci Search. Search of social-science research. Available through DIALOG.

The New York Times Information (Service) Bank.

Bibliographies, Guidebooks, Abstracts

American Jurisprudence. Rochester, N.Y.: Lawyers Co-Operative Publishing Co., 1975.

Black's Law Dictionary (rev. 4th ed.). St. Paul, Minn.: West Publishing Co., 1968.

Bloch, Herbert A., and Gilbert Geis, *Man, Crime and Society*. New York: Random House, 1962. Contains extensive bibliography.

Cheney, Frances N., *Fundamental Reference Sources*. Chicago: American Library Association, 1971.

——, *Sources of Information in the Social Sciences*. Chicago: American Library Association, 1973.

Corpus Juris Secundum. New York: American Law Book Co. See index for appropriate heading.

Crime and Delinquency Abstracts. Rockville, Md.: National Institute of Mental Health, 1966–72.

Crime and Juvenile Delinquency: A Bibliographic Guide to the Basic Microform Collection. Washington, D.C.: The National Council on Crime and Delinquency, 1976. Consists of over 2,300 titles on microfiche, constantly updated.

[24] DIALOG system offers over 100 data bases.

Document Retrieval Index. Washington, D.C.: Department of Justice, LEAA, NCJR Service, yearly.

Encyclopaedia Britannica.

Encyclopedia Americana.

Encyclopedia of Social Work. New York: National Association of Social Workers, 1965 to date. 2 vols.

ERIC Educational Documents Index. Washington, D.C.: National Institute of Education, 1966 to date. Contains many items on delinquency.

Fox, Vernon, *Introduction to Criminology*. Englewood Cliffs, N.J.: Prentice-Hall, 1976. Contains extensive bibliography and tables.

Gates, J. K., *Guide to the Use of Books and Libraries* (3rd ed.). New York: McGraw-Hill, 1974.

Glaser, Daniel, *Handbook of Criminology*. Chicago: Rand McNally, 1974.

Index to Legal Periodicals, 1952 to date.

International Encyclopedia of the Social Sciences. New York: Macmillan, 1968. 17 vols.

Lindzey, G., and E. Aronson, eds., *The Handbook of Social Psychology* (2nd ed.). Reading, Mass.: Addison-Wesley, 1968. 2 vols.

Psychological Abstracts. Washington, D.C.: American Psychological Association, 1927 to date.

Social Science Index, 1927 to date. An index to periodicals.

Sociological Abstracts. New York: Abstracts, 1952 to date.

Statistical Abstract of the United States. Washington, D.C.: U.S. Government Printing Office, 1879 to date.

Tompkins, Dorothy C., *Administration of Criminal Justice*. Montclair, N.J.: Patterson Smith, 1970. A selected bibliography compiled at the Institute for Governmental Studies at the University of California.

Ulrich's International Periodicals Directory. New York: R. R. Bowker, 1966 to date. 2 vols.

Winchell, C. M., *Guide to Reference Books* (8th ed.). Chicago: American Library Association, 1967.

World Almanac & Book of Facts. New York: Newspaper Enterprise Association, 1968 to date.

Statistics

Biderman, Albert D., et al., *An Inventory of Surveys of the Public in Crime, Justice and Related Topics*. Washington, D.C.: U.S. Department of Justice, 1972.

Sourcebook of Criminal Justice Statistics, 1973 to date.

Uniform Crime Reports for the United States. Washington, D.C.: U.S. Federal Bureau of Investigation, 1954 to date.

The United States Book of Facts, Statistics and Information, yearly.

Walker, N., *Crimes, Courts, and Figures: An Introduction to Criminal Statistics*. New York: Peter Smith, 1973.

Journals

American Criminal Law Review
American Journal of Corrections
American Journal of Sociology
American Sociological Review
British Journal of Criminology
Canadian Journal of Criminology and Corrections
Corrections Digest
Crime and Delinquency
Crime and Social Justice
Criminal Justice Newsletter
Criminal Law Digest
Criminal Law Quarterly
Criminal Law Reporter
Criminology
FBI Law Enforcement Bulletin
Federal Probation
International Journal of Offender Therapy and Comparative Criminology
International Police Academy Review
Journal of Correctional Education
Journal of Criminal Law and Criminology
Journal of Police Science Administration
Journal of Radical Criminology
Journal of Research in Crime and Delinquency
The Police Chief
Prison Journal
Social Case Work
Social Forces
Social Problems

READINGS IN CRIMINOLOGY TOPICS

The following list of readings is designed to promote problem awareness and to stimulate further research inquiry.

Teenage Crime

Eldefonso, Edward, and W. Hartinger, *Control, Treatment and Rehabilitation of Offenders*. Beverly Hills, Calif.: Glencoe, 1976. See appendix, pp. 303–31, "Santa Clara Probation Report, James Smith."

Phillips, Stephen, "Justice for Whom?" *Psychology Today*, March 1977, pp. 70–88.

Pileggi, Nicholas, "How a 15-Year-Old Gets Away with Murder," *New York*, June 13, 1977, pp. 37–50.

"The Youth Crime Plague," *Time*, July 11, 1977, pp. 18–27.

Ethics in Research

Fields, Cheryl M., "A Growing Problem for Researchers," *The Chronical for Higher Education*, 14, no. 10 (May 2, 1977), 1, 15.

Fromm, Erich, *The Anatomy of Destructiveness*. New York: Holt, Rinehart & Winston, 1973, pp. 47–61.

Milgram, Stanley, "The Behavioral Study of Obedience," *Journal of Abnormal and Social Psychology*, 67, no. 4 (1963), 371–78.

Zimbardo, Phillip, "Pathology of Imprisonment," *Society*, Vol. 9 (April 1972).

Behavior Modification by Brain Control

Friedberg, John, "Let's Stop Blasting the Brain," *Psychology Today*, 9, no. 3 (August 1975), 18–25.

Russell, Dick, "The Unsavory Business of Mind Control," *Argosy*, November 1975, pp. 29–36.

"State Court Bars Experimental Brain Surgery," *Prison Law Reporter*, 2, no. 9 (August 1973), 433–80.

The Problems of Mass Murder

Campbell, Colin, "Portrait of a Mass Killer," *Psychology Today*, May 1976, pp. 110–14.

Hellman, Peter, "58 Killings in One Week," or "Seven Days of Killing," *New York*, August 28, 1972, pp. 24–29.

"Slaughter at Random," in *Crimes and Punishment*, ed. Jackson Morley, 87–96. New York: Symphonette Press, 1974.

Whitman, Alden, "Murder on Our Minds," *New York*, October 3, 1977, pp. 27–41.

Getting Away with Crime

Glenn, Gary F., "Crime *Does* Pay," *The Police Chief*, January 1976.

"Why Criminals Go Free," *U.S. News & World Report*, May 10, 1976.

Wilson, James Q. "If Every Criminal *Knew* He Would Be Punished If Caught . . .," in *Readings in Criminal Justice, 77/78*. Guilford, Ct.: Dushkin, 1977.

Crime and Sentencing

Allen, Harry, and Clifford Simonsen, "Correctional Ideologies and a Changing Clientele," in *Corrections in America: an Introduction*. Beverly Hills, Calif.: Glencoe, 1975.

"Crisis in the Prisons: Not Enough Room for All the Criminals," *U.S. News & World Report*, November 28, 1977, pp. 74–79.

Doleschal, Eugene, "Rate and Length of Imprisonment," *Crime and Delinquency*, January 1977, pp. 51–56.

Evans, Robert, Jr., "Changing Labor Markets and Criminal Behavior in Japan," *Journal of Asian Studies*, 36, no. 3 (May 1977), 477–89.

Fox, Vernon B., "Criminal Career Patterns," Chap. 13 in *Introduction to Criminology*. Englewood Cliffs, N.J.: Prentice-Hall, 1976.

Organized Crime

Anderson, Jack, "The Shadow of the Mafia over Our Government," *Buffalo (N.Y.) Courier-Express*, August 7, 1977.

Gage, Nicholas, "Has the Mafia Penetrated the FBI?" *New York Times Magazine*, October 2, 1977.

Hammer, Richard, "The Heat's On" (Part VI) and "The American Nightmare" (Part XII), in *History of Organized Crime*. Chicago: Playboy Press, 1976.

Kuehn, Lowell L., "Syndicated Crime in America," in *Deviants: Voluntary Actors in a Hostile World*, ed. Edward Sagarin and Fred Montanino, Glenview, Ill: Scott, Foresman, 1977.

Political Crime

Auletta, Ken, "Should These Men Go to Jail?" *New York*, December 1, 1975, pp. 34–41.

"Public Officials for Sale," *U.S. News & World Report*, February 28, 1977, pp. 36–38.

Sykes, Gresham M., "Governmental Lawlessness," in *Criminology*. New York: Harcourt Brace Jovanovich, 1978.

Police Corruption

Hayes, Frederick O'R., "Patrick Murphy on Police Corruption: An Interview," in *Crime and Justice*, ed. Jerome Skolnick, Martin Forst, and Jane Scheiber, DelMar, Calif.: Publisher's Inc., 1977.

The Knapp Commission Report on Police Corruption. New York: George Braziller, 1972.

Souryal, Safwat, "Stages of Police Corruption," *The Police Chief*, 42, no. 2 (February 1975), 63–65.

Future Crime

"New Tactics in Battle against Fires for Profit," *U.S. News & World Report*, September 5, 1977, pp. 31 ff.

"Now It's a Wave of Thefts in Historic Documents," *U.S. News & World Report*, September 5, 1977, pp. 51 ff.

"Ways Con Men Cash In on the Energy Crisis," *U.S. News & World Report*, August 8, 1977, pp. 58, 59.

FURTHER AIDS TO RESEARCH AND RESEARCH WRITING

Bachrach, Arthur J., *Psychological Research: An Introduction*, pp. 1–83. New York: Random House, 1966.

Barzun, Jacques, and Henry F. Graff, *The Modern Researcher* (rev. ed.). New York: Harcourt Brace Jovanovich, 1970.

Batten, Thelma, *Reasoning and Research: A Guide for Social Science Methods.* Boston: Little, Brown, 1971.

Becker, Howard S., *The Outsiders: Studies in the Sociology of Deviance.* New York: Free Press, 1963.

Best, John W., *Research in Education* (3rd ed.). Chap. 3, "The Use of Reference Materials." Englewood Cliffs, N.J.: Prentice-Hall, 1977.

Borg, Walter R., *Educational Research: An Introduction*, Chap. 3, "Reviewing the Literature." New York: D. McKay, 1963.

Campbell, William G., and Stephen V. Ballou, *Form and Style: Theses, Reports, Term Papers.* Boston: Houghton Mifflin, 1974.

Emberger, M. R., and Marian R. Hall, *Scientific Writing.* New York: Harcourt Brace Jovanovich, 1955.

Fowler, H. W., *A Dictionary of Modern English Usage* (2nd ed.). New York: Oxford University Press, 1965.

Funk & Wagnalls Standard College Dictionary. New York: Funk & Wagnalls, 1968.

Glazer, Myron, *The Research Adventure.* New York: Random House, 1972. See pp. 59–72, "Reacting to Social Injustice."

Hammond, Phillip, ed., *Sociologists at Work.* New York: Basic Books, 1964.

Hauser, Phillip M., "Delinquency and Crime," in *Social Statistics in Use.* New York: Russell Sage Foundation, 1975.

Hull, Helen, ed., *The Writer's Book.* New York: Barnes & Noble, 1956.

Johnson, Ellen, *The Research Report: A Guide for the Beginner.* New York: Ronald Press, 1951.

Kerlinger, Fred N., *Foundations of Behavioral Research* (2nd ed.). Chaps. 1 and 2. New York: Holt, Rinehart & Winston, 1963.

Lester, James D., *Writing Research Papers* (2nd ed.). Glenview, Ill.: Scott, Foresman, 1976.

Levine, Samuel, and F. F. Elzey, *A Programmed Introduction to Research*, Part 1. Belmont, Calif.: Wadsworth, 1968.

Levitt, Eugene E., *Clinical Research Design and Analysis*, pp. 3–26. Springfield, Ill.: Charles C Thomas, 1961.

Lewis, Norman, *The New Roget's Thesaurus.* New York: Garden City Books Edition, 1961, by arrangement with G.P. Putnam's Sons.

Lucas, F. L., *Style* (2nd ed.). London: Cassell, 1955.

Miller, Delbert C., *Handbook of Research Design and Social Measurement*, Part 1. New York: D. McKay, 1970.

Oxford English Dictionary. New York: Oxford University Press.

Perrin, Porter G., *Writer's Guide and Index to English.* Glenview, Ill.: Scott, Foresman, 1968.

Publication Manual of the American Psychological Association. Washington, D.C.: The Association, 1974.

Strunk, William, Jr., and E. B. White, *The Elements of Style*. New York: Macmillan, 1962.

Trelease, Sam F., *The Scientific Paper: How to Prepare It, How to Write It* (2nd ed.). Baltimore: Williams and Wilkins, 1951.

Turabian, Kate L., *A Manual for Writers of Term Papers, Theses, and Dissertations*. Chicago: University of Chicago Press, 1973.

Webb, Eugene J., et al., *Unobtrusive Measures: Non-Reactive Research in the Social Sciences*, Chap. 1, "Approximations to Knowledge." Chicago: Rand McNally, 1971.

Weil, Benjamin H., ed., *The Technical Paper: Its Preparation and Processing and Use in Industry and Government*. New York: Van Nostrand Reinhold, 1954.

Williams, Roger M., *The Super Crooks*. Chicago: Playboy Press, 1973. Case studies.

Wolfgang, M. E., "Uniform Crime Reports: A Critical Appraisal," *University of Pennsylvania Law Review*, 3 (1963), 408–38.

Wollan, Laurin A., Jr., "Coping with Crime in Tomorrow's Society," in *Readings in Criminal Justice, 77/78*. Edited by Donald E. J. MacNamara. Guilford, Ct.: Dushkin, 1977.

Wright, Burton, and Vernon Fox, *Criminal Justice and the Social Sciences*. Philadelphia: Saunders, 1978.

3

Variables in Research Design

DEFINING VARIABLES

Variables are the basic building blocks of any research design. They are the substance of the hypothesis and the tangibles of testable propositions. Simply, variables are used to quantify; they translate concept into reality.

Variables have been defined in several ways:

1. Those characteristics or properties that can vary
2. Logical groupings of attributes or characteristics
3. A set of mutually exclusive characteristics
4. A means of quantifying (or counting) variation
5. Those attributes or characteristics that have difference and no magnitude (qualitative), or that have difference and magnitude (quantitative)
6. Those properties that may be used in constructing models for cause and effect, relationship, association or prediction
7. The basic units of statistical analysis, providing levels of measurement based upon groupings of differences (variations)

As opposed to the variable, that which does not vary is called a *constant*. For example, sex, which is a qualitative variable, varies as to gender–male or female; if there were only one sex, it would be a constant, and thus meaningless in terms of measuring differences. Similarly, IQ, which is a quantitative variable, varies from person to person; if everyone had the same IQ, or the same IQ characteristic or intelligence trait, then lack of variation would make research of no effect.

With variables such as sex, race, or religion, one can see clear grouping of variations in attributes. Sex varies into the two characteristics of male and female; race into clear groupings of white, black, Indian, Oriental, and so on; religion into Protestant, Roman Catholic, Jewish, or whatever other religious group is included; color of eyes into blue, brown, green, and so on.

Such groupings are mutually exclusive, with the attribute or characteristic peculiar to the group. In the Uniform Crime Reports of the FBI, the groupings are also mutually exclusive; the index offenses in 1975 were listed as murder, forcible rape, aggravated assault, robbery, burglary, larceny-theft, and motor-vehicle theft. However, murder, for example, is broken down into subgroups (variables) of age, weapon used, crimes cleared, race, and sex, each of which contains mutually exclusive characteristics. And each is quantifiable—it can be counted. The categories of a variable must be mutually exclusive, i.e. items must fall into one or the other *never* into both.

MEASURING VARIABLES

Variables are *qualitative*, varying in quality—race, sex religion, or *quantitative*, varying in quantity—age, income, weight, number of arrests. The difference between qualitative and quantitative variables is that of magnitude. There is no difference in magnitude between male and female (qualities), but there is between ages, incomes, IQs, and the like. One is older or younger, earns more or less, is of greater or lesser intelligence, and so on. The difference of magnitude is either limited (discrete) or it is unlimited and can take on any value (continuous).[1] Qualitative variables such as sex, political preference, or game outcome have limited values and so are discrete variables with no magnitude; some quantitative variables, such as preferential ranking and family size, are also discrete. All continuous variables are quantitative, and some discrete variables may be quantitative.

It is important to note that there are *levels of measurement* of variables. We are not just measuring numbers in the arithmetic sense of the word; we are using levels or scales of measurement. Variables are measured in four basic scales: *nominal, ordinal, interval*, and *ratio.*

Nominal Scale

Nominal measurement is discrete and qualitative. Most nominal variables may be dichotomized. Some—such as sex, the toss of a coin, an outcome of true or false, an answer of yes or no, a gradation of high or low—are already composed of two categories; others may be dichotomized by arbitrary division. Other examples of

[1] Discrete variables can take on only finite sets of values; continuous variables may take on infinite values, fractional values, or any range of values. See Figure 3-1.

nominal variables are social class, religion, education by school, crime by type, degree of offense, and location of occurrence. Whenever a nominal variable is dichotomized, it may be treated as a binary variable.[2] This type of variable is extremely useful in statistical analysis such as regression and chi-square, the former being parametric, the latter nonparametric. Nominal qualitative dichotomous variables are always found in background data in the behavioral sciences and are easily manipulated in nonparametric analysis. Nominal qualitative discrete variables are somewhat similar.

Ordinal Scale

When there are scales or orders among nominal variables, such as the ranking of high, medium, and low, the variable is measured as an *ordinal variable*. Ordinal variables indicate rank order among categories. Class may be ordered as upper, middle, and lower; judges may be ranked as severe, average, and lenient, or in order of competence—1, 2, 3, 4, and so on; types of offenses may be classified as first, second, and third degree; security may be ranked as maximum, medium, and minimum; escape risk may be ranked on a scale of 1 to 10. Ordinal variables are discrete and continuous, as the ranking implies. If there is a number ranking, a continuous variable is indicated. Ordinal variables lend themselves (as do nominal variables) to nonparametric analysis.

Higher-Order Variable Scales

Interval and ratio scales are higher-order variable scales and are used with parametric statistics. They are both truly quantitative and very useful, in that there are equal intervals between the units of measurement. However, there is an important difference between them. The IQ scale is an interval scale, but we cannot say that a person with an IQ of 140 is twice as bright as one with 70. Placing a score for esteem on a scale of 1 to 20 is an interval placement, but a score of 20 would hardly indicate twenty times more esteem than a score of 1. The Fahrenheit system is an interval scale, but a temperature of 40°F. is not "half as cold" as 80°F. The interval score does give us fixed intervals, however, and thus lends itself to easy arithmetic calculation.

Ratio scales are the most powerful of all those used in variable measurement. Ratio scales such as height, weight, and age give us not only all the advantages of interval scales, but also an indication of magnitude of difference. For example, a 300-pound man is twice as heavy as a man weighing 150 pounds, a person 80 years old is twice as old as one 40 years old, and a man 6 feet tall is twice as tall as a boy 3 feet tall. Similarly, a person with 50 arrests has been arrested five times as often as a person with 10 arrests, and a released felon who returns to prison after one

[2] In a binary variable, one category is assigned the value of zero, the other the value of 1. Sometimes 1 and 2 are used for the categories.

year has obviously four times the recidivism of one who stays out for four years. In other words, a ratio scale has a meaningful zero and also indicates magnitude.

Combined and Summated Variable Scales

Another type of variable, which is widely used in survey research but rarely included in the textbooks, is the variable based upon the combination of two variables. The *combined variable* scale is based upon the division of one variable by another. A good example of this is the density given by dividing the number of people by the number of rooms to get the number of people per room:

$$\text{Density (people per room)} = \frac{\text{Number of people in household}}{\text{Number of rooms in house}}$$

This has also been used for describing age and weight ratios for measurement of obesity and premature aging in stress research.

$$\text{Weight (or age) factor} = \frac{\text{Estimated weight}}{\text{Actual weight}} \quad \text{or} \quad \frac{\text{Estimated age}}{\text{Actual age}}$$

The closer the scores are to unity, the less the obesity or premature aging, with corresponding reduction of stress symptoms.

The combined variable is a valuable tool in research and should be utilized whenever possible.

Occasionally, several variables are accumulated to produce a single or *summated variable*. This often occurs when clusters of variables focus upon a single issue. It is convenient to sum the variable scores and use a mean or index of the entire cluster:

$$\text{Variable mean score} = \frac{\text{Cluster of variable scores}}{\text{Number of variables in cluster}}$$

If several such clusters exist, a ranking may be made of the hierarchies in the several clusters.

Summing up variable scales:

A *nominal variable* measures only differences.

An *ordinal variable* measures differences and shows rank order.

An *interval variable* measures differences, and shows order and equal units.

A *ratio variable* measures differences, and shows order, equal units, and magnitude of difference.

Nominal and ordinal variables are qualitative.

Occasionally, ordinal variables are both qualitative and quantitative.

Interval, ratio, combined, and summated variables are quantitative.

Tables 3.1 and *3.2* summarize the properties and functions of variables described in this chapter.

Table 3.1. Variable Qualities

Type of variable	Quality				
	Category label	*Rank or order*	*Equal-units scale*	*Scale indicates magnitude*	*Scale gives precision*
Nominal	+	–	–	–	–
Ordinal	+	+	–	–	–
Interval	+	+	+	–	–
Ratio	+	+	+	+	–
Combined	+	+	+	+	+
Summated	+	+	+	+	∓

Table 3.2. Mathematical Functions of Variables

Type of variable	Mathematical function	Scale	Data
Nominal	Equal to or not equal to (= or ≠)	None	Discrete, often dichotomous
Ordinal	Greater than or less than (> or <)	Units not equal	Discrete or continuous
Interval	Add or subtract (+ or –)	Equal units	Continuous
Ratio	Add, subtract, multiply, divide (+, –, ×, and ÷)	True zero Equal units	Continuous
Combined	Same as ratio	From negative to positive	Continuous
Summated	Same as ratio	Develops hierarchy	Continuous

The Nature of Variable Measurement

Variables, then, are essential in the quantification of data. They are the indispensable components of research design; all variables lead to data and all data lead to variables. *Figure 3-1* indicates the nature of the measurement used for variables. Discrete data are primarily used in nonparametric analysis, and continuous data are used in parametric analysis.

It can also be seen from the diagram that traits may take on a range of values and thus be continuous; height and weight, years of education, and recidivism are traits. Attributes, on the other hand, represent limited variation among categories

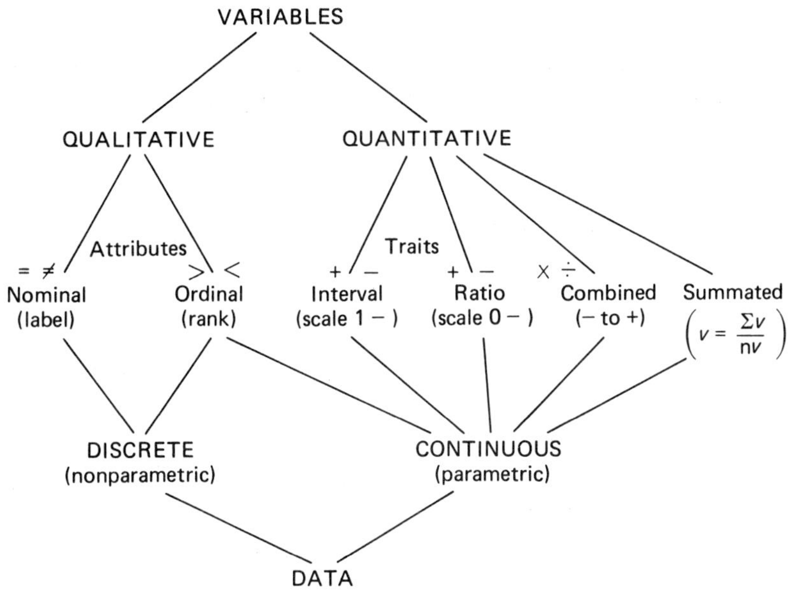

Fig. 3-1 Relationship of variables to data

such as sex, race, religion, level of stress, and so on.[3] Characteristics may be traits or attributes. Variables, then, are defined as having mutually exclusive characteristics that may be traits or attributes. Nominal variables permit only equality or non-equality; ordinal variables permit less-than or greater-than comparisons; interval variables permit addition and subtraction; ratio variables permit addition, subtraction, multiplication, and division[4] (as do combined and summated variables).

In dealing with people as we do in the social sciences, and in criminology in particular, we are inclined to deal with attributes more than traits, with discrete data more than continuous data. However, it should be noted that the higher the order of the variable, the more sophisticated the statistical technique. More can be done with ratio than with nominal variables. The statistical technique used for analysis is limited by the nature of the variable. The primary and basic point concerning a variable is that *it lends itself to statistical description, and the quality of that description determines the outcome of the statistical analysis.*

TYPES OF VARIABLE ANALYSIS

Research in criminology explores the associations or relationships between two or more variables. Examples are race and crime, handguns and homicide, parental education and wife abuse, judges and sentences. Often, several variables enter into

[3] Attributes are sometimes called *qualities.*

[4] Ratio scales have a true zero; i.e., Number of Arrests: O = No arrests.

the picture, as with attitudes and gun control, or community response and casino gambling. In the former, several different aspects of attitude may be explored; in the latter, age, race, sex, religion, and education are background variables that would enter into community response.

The study of just one variable is called *univariate analysis*; of two variables is *bivariate analysis* (the most common); and of three or more variables, *multivariate analysis*. The multivariate approach is often a combination of several bivariate analyses, as in the use of the elaboration paradigm, which will be described later.

Bivariate analysis is particularly suitable for testing nominal variables using discrete data, frequency data—sex and delinquency, race and homicide, religion and recidivism. Bivariate analysis lends itself to contingency tables and chi-square analysis, as in Table 3.3 for homicide samples taken from different cities. Counting the number of people in a particular category describes that category statistically. This count in categories, called frequency data, would appear in cells A, B, C, and D of Table 3.3.

Table 3.3. Frequency Data Model

	Race	
Homicide	*White*	*Black*
Low	A	B
High	C	D

Discrete data lend themselves well to frequency counting. In fact, bivariate analysis used in contingency tables depends upon the use of nominal variables with frequency data. All that frequencies do is describe the number of people, events, or occurrences in a particular category. *Frequencies simply state how many times a particular characteristic, attribute, or quality occurs in a sample population.*

Note that in this type of bivariate analysis, only dichotomous variables are used in a 2-by-2 table. Of course, in some bivariate analysis, more than two categories will exist in one or both variables, in which case there will be a 2-by-3, 3-by-3, 3-by-4, or 4-by-4 table, and so on, depending upon the actual number of categories in each variable. But for simplicity and exploratory work, the 2-by-2 table is invaluable.

Often, continuous variables can also be broken down by *dividing along the mean* into a high/low dichotomy. For example, a list of convictions—5, 7, 8, 6, 4, 3, 2, 5, 4, 6, 6—could be dichotomized along the mean of 5.1, with those scores below 5.1 being categorized as "low," and those above as "high." If necessary, an arbitrary level can be set as appropriate to the situation—in the example above, six are low and five are high.

Frequency data are simply the number of events in a particular category. The frequency may be expressed as a percentage or a proportion; percentages always

Table 3.4. Frequency-Data Example

Drug abuse	Race: *White*	Race: *Black*	
Low	A 90	B 40	130
High	C 50	D 20	70
	140	60	200 = *n*

total 100, proportions always total unity, or 1. For example, in *Table 3.4*, we see two variables, race and drug abuse. Race has two categories, white and black; drug abuse has two categories, low and high—or little use and heavy use. A sample of 200 people has been taken for these hypothetical data ($n = 200$). Percentages may be totaled down, across, and of the sample total.

In this table, the frequencies appear:

For the variable *race* (each category)	White	= 140
	Black	= 60
For the variable *drug abuse* (each category)	Low	= 130
	High	= 70

These frequencies appear in the margin and are known as *marginals*. The frequency data in the internal cells is calculated from questionnaires or data fed into the computer:

The frequency of white low drug abuse = 90 for this category, Cell A
The frequency of black low drug abuse = 40 for this category, Cell B
The frequency of white high drug abuse = 50 for this category, Cell C
The frequency of black high drug abuse = 20 for this category, Cell D

Notice that for each cell, the number of events or characteristics is exclusive of the other cells; each event can fit into only one cell, or one category. And each frequency can be expressed as a percentage of three category totals; for example, Cell A is 64 percent of the white column total, 69 percent of the low-drug-abuse row total, and 45 percent of the sample total.

Two variables are also used in measures of correlation. *Correlation does not show cause and effect*; it shows the relationship of one variable to another. For example, there may be a high relationship between inner-city residence and high crime, but this does not show that living in the inner city causes high crime or vice versa. Correlation is a very useful statistical tool to show the strength of relationship between two variables and is essential if we go one step further, into prediciton of one variable based upon the other. For instance, correlating work habits and recidivism, it may be shown that it is possible to predict a man's return to prison from his work habits. In correlation, continuous or interval/ratio data are preferred.

Later in the book, the statistical methods mentioned here will be explained; at present, it is sufficient that we understand the nature of variables.

As more and more variables are used in analysis, the statistics used become more complex, and the research method often enters what is called the elaboration paradigm. Hierarchies of variables are established, paths between variables are computed, interaction and additivity are examined. We move from the simple to the advanced, depending upon the level of analysis required. Because the variables assume a certain order during analysis, it is necessary to know the rules that determine that order.

VARIABLES AS THE KEY TO RESEARCH DESIGN

From the very outset, it should be clear that variables are the key in grasping the three essentials of all research. Variables aid us in the following processes:

Exploration—what it is that we are examining
Description—where and how (and when)
Explanation—why an event is occurring

Variables are essential in:

Reliability—the ability to identify phenomena accurately
Validity—the truth and substance of the research
Replication—the continuing proof of the research design (theory)

Variables aid in model building, in the formalization of theory, and in the determination of inaccuracies and error. We cannot count without variables, we cannot measure without variables, there are no data without variables and consequently no statistical quantification or analysis.

As stated earlier, the research design is based upon the relationship or cause and effect of two or more variables. *We are looking for the systematic interconnection of relationships.* As the relationships become more (or less) determined, the variables assume particular names so we may place them in the schematics of cause and effect. We have already determined the level of measurement and to some degree the nature of the variable. Now we need to determine the order of the variables, the nature of the relationship, and the statistical method that is applicable.

The exact order of the variables is determined from the hypothesis or the proposition that is being tested and is subject to certain specifications. Let us consider some basic models in research.

Variables in Models

Order in variable placement in model construction depends on the nature of their relationship. Most research design is concerned with why a certain variable has an effect upon another—for example, the effect of TV programs on children, acceptance of casino gambling by a community, attitude of male police officers toward female police officers. In every case, it is necessary to establish which is the independent variable and which the criterion or dependent variable.[5] *It is the criterion or dependent variable that we are interested in.* In a simple model:

$$A \longrightarrow B$$

or, "variable A causes/has an effect upon variable B," A is labeled the *independent* variable and B the *dependent* variable. The problem is to decide which is which. Three rules aid in this decision:

1. If the variable comes first in *time order*, it is independent.
2. If it is *least likely to change*—if it is *dominant*—it is independent.
3. If it *influences* or *has effect* on the other, it is independent.

Conversely, the variable that is last in time order, most likely to change, and subject to influence is the dependent variable. In the statement, "There is no difference in arrest rates between sexes among juvenile delinquents," the I.V., or independent variable, based upon time order, is the sex of juvenile delinquents. The D.V., or dependent variable, is the arrest rate, which is more likely to change. The model becomes:

Sex of juvenile delinquents ⟶	Arrest rates
Independent variable	Dependent variable

This could be analyzed by a 2-by-2 contingency table, *Table 3.5*, with arrests being dichotomized along the mean. The resulting chi-square analysis would determine the retention or rejection of the proposition.

This simple model is the basis for all survey research design. We must have an independent and a dependent variable. Very often, there is more than one of each—especially of independent variables. In the example above, the number of arrests could be influenced by the ages and races of the delinquents. The model would then change, but still in keeping with the basic rules. Race and age are independent

Table 3.5. Frequency Model–Sex by Arrests

Arrests	Sex of juvenile delinquents *Male*	*Female*	
Low	A	B	Total low arrests
High	C	D	Total high arrests
	Total male	Total female	Total = n = Sample size

[5] The name "criterion" is usually reserved for experimental situations where the independent variable can be manipulated.

variables, since they are in prior time order, are least likely to change, and do exert effect. In such a case, the model now becomes:

Race		Sex of		
Age	⟶	delinquent	⟶	Number of arrests
Antecedent variable		I.V.		D.V.

Age and race are called *antecedent variables* because they come prior to the sex of the delinquent. (Actually in this model, findings may well determine that race and sex should be antecedent to age.) Antecedent variables are prior to independent variables and exert effect upon the dependent variable through the independent variable, as the causal arrows indicate.

Occasionally, a variable may intervene and cause either intensification or mitigation of effects. This type is called an *intervening variable*. In the model, education might well be an intervening variable. That is, the number of years or level of education may well influence the number of arrests of a juvenile delinquent. The model then becomes:

Age		Sex of		Level of		Number of arrests
Race	⟶	delinquent	⟶	education	⟶	
Antecedent		Independent		Intervening		Dependent

Remember that variables that are not dependent are independent. Both the antecedent and intervening variables are independent, although they are in special relationships. The importance of this fact is that *in test or control situations, we never control for the dependent variable*. All other variables may be subjected to test or control statistics. Should the model be changed, changing the dependent variable, *the rule still applies*. The new dependent variable is *never* controlled.

Some models become remarkably complex, particularly with emphasis now being placed on multifactor solutions. Other variables we use are *extraneous, component, conjoint, conditional, distorter, suppressor, spurious, reciprocal, contingent*, and *symmetrical.*[6] The variables most used are *asymmetrical*.

The variable, then, receives its name from its place in the causal order we are investigating. We are most interested in the dependent variable. It is clear that one cannot explain or prove the cause-and-effect relationship; the causal statement is too limited and can only approach the truth. The behavioral sciences differ in this way from the physical sciences. For example, the law of gravity is an irrefutable truth; the link of lung cancer to tobacco smoking, on the other hand, affects only some people, is prevalent only in some areas, and is practically unknown in others. Many of the propositions tested in criminology resemble the tobacco → cancer causal link. They simply do not have the validity of claims like the law of gravity.

The strength of the causal model lies in its imagination. All too often, complex models have been constructed as an intellectual exercise rather than an attempt to

[6] Morris Rosenberg, *The Logic of Survey Analysis* (New York: Basic Books, 1968), Chaps. 1–7. Variables may also *contaminate* or *confound* outcomes.

solve a problem. Social research must be taken seriously, and if it is, the statements to be tested will have value in the real world. Variables selected from those hypotheses should be based upon serious reflection and consideration of the nature of the work being performed. Criminology is a science dedicated to survival, so we should use no less than maximum effort in producing quality research work. We are dealing with an exercise in logic that becomes sterile unless it is also an exercise in imagination.

The Importance of Variables

In research, we are looking for theory. Theory is in essence an explanation of events, phenomena, or observable facts. The research design rests upon the model, and the model is based upon the operationalization of the variables selected. Moreover, most models that are constructed are based upon previous successful research designs. Theory is, in practice, an accumulation of successfully tested research findings.

The logic at this point may be seen as:

Informal proposition → Formal hypothesis → Selection of variables → Model

It is assumed that the variables selected can be operationalized, and thus the model can be tested. The testing of the model then leads:

Model → Research findings → Replication → Theory → Informal propositions → Formal
Verification hypothesis
Inductive Deductive

The reasoning is then complete, as we move from inductive to deductive reasoning,[7] from the particular to the general, and then from the general to the particular. In effect, we are moving from a lower to a higher order of conceptual thinking. (See Figurc 3-2.)

Cause of Errors

Certain errors may creep in or accumulate at any stage of the research. These errors may be due to personal bias or prejudice, faulty reasoning, the nature of the problem, various social pressures and influences, or incomplete knowledge of the research. More specifically, errors arise in the research design in connection with the following elements:

Informal proposition (research idea): too general for practicality; influenced by personal feelings; designed to be investigative rather than to meet research-design commitments; not based on logical search for order in the real world; metaphysical, tautological, or not provable; based on wrong perception of events.

[7] Some say we move from deductive to inductive reasoning. It depends upon whether one is Newtonian or Baconian. I believe both are equally important in research.

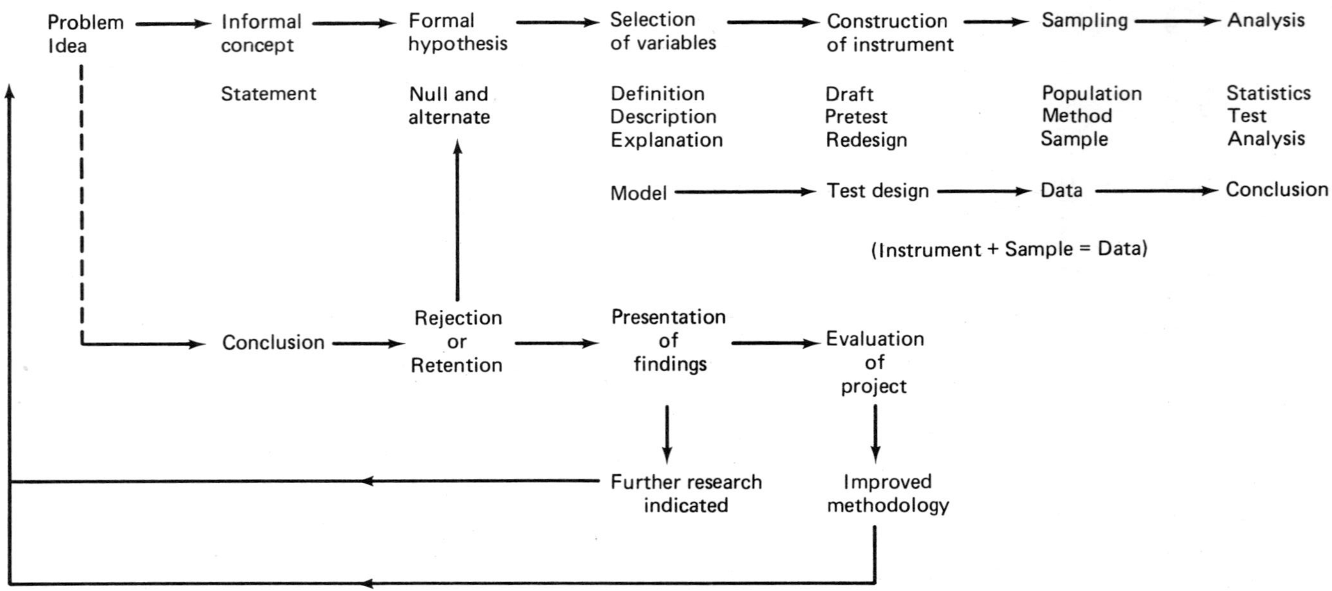

Fig. 3-2 Flow of research methodology

The purposes of research are: 1. Exploration—a search for differences; 2. Description—inferences about a population; 3. Explanation—resolution of difference.

Formal proposition (hypothesis): lacks order, cannot be set in a model; has not been tested; contains bias; is not based on prior theory; contains confused, ambiguous, impractical, or untestable concepts; cannot be stated as a null hypothesis; lacks ethical consideration.

Variable selection: variables cannot be operationally defined; ambiguity of definition limits use; no prior definition exists for application; definition used is confusing; variables do not test the proposition; use of certain variables slants the research; variables contain inadequate gradations; variable measurement does not meet situational requirements; key variables have been overlooked.

Model construction: is poor and does not state testable proposition; model is too limited, omits important variables; model is stated in wrong logical order; model does not permit adequate analysis; model suggests finality; model is "cooked" to coincide with research findings.

Research findings: wrong statistical analysis; emphasis on statistical rather than substantive significance; conclusions based on wrong use or wrong order of variables; hypothesis error (Type 1 or 2), resulting from faulty operationalization; personal or computer error, resulting in wrong conclusions; sampling errors; instrument errors; lack of controls; unknown factors.

Operational Definition of the Variable

The idea, concept, proposition, or research hypothesis to be examined begins in the mind of the scientist and must then jump the gap to the real world. It can do this only by being operationalized as a variable:

Mind of the Scientist	*Variable*	*Reality*
Research idea	⟶ Element to be tested ⟶	The world in which the element exists

If the variable is not correctly defined, the research is useless. The operational definition of the variable is the ground rule by which the research proceeds. The definition must be (1) easily understood, (2) easily applied to a proper sample for testing, and (3) able to be replicated for verification.

For example, intelligence is conceived of as one's score on an IQ test; psychological characteristics may be measured on an MMPI scale; GPA can be calculated from accumulated test scores; age or income is easily defined, as is race or religion. These definitions are now fairly standard and are accepted. The seven categories of the Uniform Crime Reports are also standardized; we know what is meant by the number of homicides, robberies, burglaries, and so on. But in using a variable to define attitude, or a behavioral trait, or anxiety, or esteem, we must first carefully define the limits of the category.

The definition of the variable decides the nature of the questions to be asked and the sample to be used. The definition must be such that the characteristic does indeed exist in the population, and that people asked for responses can make them. The definition of the variable also decides its operational use. Some variables are so defined that a scale is used in testing for them, as in prejudice, view of community leaders, attitude toward an event or fashion, degree of feeling on a subject, perception of events and change, and so on. Such scales will be discussed under the heading of instrument construction.

Variables are by necessity limited and are often subject to refinement. In a sense, we move from primitive to sophisticated definitions by trial and error; but we cannot advance without a trial and the recognition of error.

Because variables are the stepping stones in our journey from concept to practice, they should be clearly identifiable, definable, and utilitarian. Therefore, the variables to be tested should be prominent in the research (formal) hypothesis. They must be written out with suggested alternatives,[8] synonyms, and associated nouns. From this list, key variables can be selected that best fit the practicality of the project. From that point, the variable can be defined, operationalized, and used in the field test.

For example, for an examination of the idea that rehabilitation programs prevent return to prison, let us take the null hypothesis:

> No relationship exists between recidivist rates of those felons who have participated in rehabilitation programs and those who have not.[9]

The variable selection is:

Dependent variable: Recidivist rates
Independent-variable categories:
- Felons
- Those in programs
- Those not in programs

Categories for the D.V. would reflect return to prison after one, two, three, four, and five years; or it could be split into high and low categories.

In this easy example, the definitions are not difficult to discern. A table could be constructed, and a simple test would show if there was indeed a relationship. But if we examine the type of programs that felons are involved with, a totally different picture may emerge. By definition of the type of program to be examined—educational, vocational, religious, athletic, or nonprogram—the categories could reflect a totally different interpretation of the hypothesis. We might find that only certain programs have an effect upon the return to prison. Again, our research might lead us to inquire into prisoner attitudes toward programs, in which case questions would be set up that reflected a scale of attitude from positive to negative. *The nature of the research depends entirely upon the operational definition of the variable.* Even the variable "prison" can be defined as one or two or more prisons.

[8] This method often identifies components of the main variable.

[9] The null could be expressed as "no difference between," but here we are using the concept of "no relationship."

Not only is order important in deciding on a logical model, but the order often depends on the nature of the relationship of the variables. Three types of relationship occur in models: reciprocal, symmetrical, and asymmetrical. Most social-science research deals with asymmetrical relationships.[10]

Reciprocal relationships are those that influence each other equally. Like the chicken and the egg, it is difficult (and unnecessary) to decide which comes first. However, the union of reciprocal relationships can influence other variables in a conjoint relationship. In the commission of a crime, the situation is often reciprocal with the intent:

$$\text{Reciprocal} \quad \begin{matrix}\text{Situation}\\ \updownarrow \\ \text{Intent}\end{matrix} \quad \longrightarrow \text{Criminal act}$$

Generally, reciprocal relationships are seen somewhat like heart and lungs, eye and brain, authority and power: One cannot function without the other; they reciprocate and are interchangeable in terms of importance.

Symmetrical relationships exist where neither variable has any effect upon the other. The relationship between the variables is accidental, occurs by chance, and neither has any particular priority in time order, dominance, or influence. The relationships are spurious, occasionally parts of commonality, and sometimes alternative causes of the same effect. Here are examples of symmetrical relationships:

> Revenge and reward are both causes of homicide, yet they are unrelated and have no clear priority over each other.
>
> It was felt for a long time that the full moon caused violent crime. One does not have to be a scientist to see that these phenomena are unrelated and that, if they do occur together, it is coincidental.[11]
>
> In a prison system are found felons and guards, but one does not cause the other; they are merely parts of a common system.
>
> Many black people drink cocoa, but it would be folly to say that drinking cocoa is related to blackness. The association is accidental.
>
> A recent study attempted to relate rock-and-roll music to unwed mothers. Again, the association was accidental.

There can be no cause and effect in symmetrical relationships. One variable does not cause or influence the other.

Asymmetrical relationships are the central core of research. In these relationships, the dependent variables arise out of, or are influenced by, the independent variables.

[10] Rosenberg, *The Logic of Survey Analysis*, Chap. 1.

[11] The fact is that some researchers are looking into "lunar effects," but the point to be explained is why not everyone is affected by them, the way the oceans are. And even the tides tend to vary.

The causal forces can be readily identified. One variable (the I.V.) is responsible for, or causes, or has an effect upon—produces change in—another (the D.V.). It is in causal relationships that we have one component of understanding in science, which is an explanation by laws and not by causes.

As shown in *Table 3.6*, most asymmetrical relationships fall into the following categories:

Stimulus-response, as used in psychology. A stimulus is used to create a response. The response is the dependent variable.

Behavior-response. Attitudes, abilities, habits, values, drives, traits, characteristics, and powers are used to determine a response in a certain way under designated circumstances.

Background variable-behavior. This central type of relationship is the one most used in social research. The background variable is one that is not dependent on circumstances and that changes very little. Sex, age, race, religion, residence, education, and height and weight are used as independent variables to observe change in such dependent variables as deviance, alienation, political preference, mental health, and attitude toward sentencing. Often, the background variable is made up of components in the person's life-style that vary but little.[12]

Condition-consequence, or *phenomenon-prediction*. If a certain condition exists, then a certain result will follow: Overcrowding will cause riots; more handguns will cause an increase in homicide rates. The result is somewhat hypothetical; for instance, hard work will lead to success. The results may indicate that further research is necessary.

The real problem in any asymmetrical relationship is to locate the order of the variables—what is causing or changing what, and what the effect is—and then define them prior to operationalization. The validity of the research design depends on definition of the variables that are selected from the asymmetrical relationship for the purpose of gathering data on the phenomena mentioned.

STATISTICAL NOTATION FOR VARIABLES

Statistical notation is used to save time when entering calculations. A raw score or a score that is taken directly is usually referred to as x or, if there is another variable, as y. The sum of all those scores is written as Σx or Σy, (Σ = sum) meaning total of all the scores in x variable or of all the scores from y variable. A frequency is indicated as f; thus, fx means multiply the x score by the number of times it occurred: 3×10, 6×8, and so on. Be careful when you see Σx^2, which means sum *each score after it is squared*; do not confuse it with $(\Sigma x)^2$, which means *sum all the* x *scores, then square the total*. Sample size is noted as n; or $n = 100$ if there were 100 people in the sample. For statistical reasons, we use $n - 1$ to obtain an unbiased estimate in our calculations.

[12] Rosenberg (*The Logic of Survey Analysis*, p. 17) would call this relationship "property-disposition," which is somewhat limited in sociological definition.

Table 3.6. Variable Relationships

Relationship	Independent variable	Dependent variable
Simple model (A causes B)	A	B
Statistical model (correlation/regression)*	X or x	Y or y
Behavior–response	Behavior/Attitude/Ability	Response or consequence of behavioral influence
Stimulus–response	Stimulus or motivating effect	Response or reaction to stimulus
Background variable–behavior	Characteristic in respondent's background that is dominant, varies little, and influences behavioral outcomes	Behavior, attitude, choice, habit, ability, values, or traits of client
Condition–consequence	Prexisting or predetermined condition such as test, program, or social institution	Consequence or result expected from prior condition
Phenomena–prediction	Existing or known facts of phenomena	Predictive outcome or planned outcome
Controlled experiment	Experimental or manipulated variable	Criterion (or measured effect) variable
Ecological (interrelationships in social system)	Predisposing or precipitating factor	Specific outcome of I.V. effect

*For the purposes of correlation, variables x and y are presumed equal in status.

The single most important measure is the *mean*, without which we cannot calculate the variation or standard deviation. We need to know the mean before we can measure dispersion of the scores. The mean, or x-bar ($\overline{x}$), as it is called, is found by simply adding up all the scores and dividing by the sample size:

Mean $= \dfrac{\Sigma x}{n} = \overline{x}$, or $\overline{x} = \dfrac{\Sigma fx}{n}$ (Note, $\Sigma f = n$)

Mode = The score that occurs most
Median = The midpoint in a list of scores; easily obtained by simple arithmetic
Range = The interval from the lowest to the highest score, or $x_{max} - x_{min}$. As a rule of thumb, the range is usually six times the standard deviation.

The *variation* is the averaged squared deviation of scores about the mean. It indicates the distribution of the scores. The sample variation is used to estimate the population variation. It may be calculated:

$$s^2 = \frac{n\Sigma x^2 - (\Sigma x)^2}{n(n-1)}$$

The *standard deviation* is the square root of the variation. It is vital to inferential statements, is expressed in the same units as the original measure, and, when used as a constant or a standard measure, will determine the proportions of scores between the deviations. It is an average measure of dispersion about the mean and may be calculated:

$$s = \sqrt{\frac{n\Sigma x^2 - (\Sigma x)^2}{n(n-1)}}$$

These formulas may be punched directly into most calculators. Be careful when you are substituting, and remember to watch the brackets. For example, in the variable *age*, where $n = 14$, scores are given: 18, 24, 26, 28, 34, 37, 41, 44, 46, 52, 56, 61, 65, 70.

The *mean* $= \Sigma x/n = 602/14 = 43$ yrs.
The *median* = 42.5 yrs. There is no single *mode*.
The *range* $= x_{max} - x_{min} = 70 - 18 = 52$ yrs.
The *variation* $= \dfrac{14 \times 29{,}304 - 602^2}{14 \times 13} = 263$
The *standard deviation* or square root of variation = 16.2

(See the discussion on statistics and standard deviation in Chapter 9.)

Means assume that we are dealing with continuous data, with quantitative results. Qualitative data only become qualitative when frequencies are introduced.

The *Pearson Product Moment* (PPM) is used to show correlation between two variables. A *moment* in mathematics is simply a mean of products of variables in a distribution. The PPM is an average of two variables obtained by measuring the covariation of variables x and y and the variation of x times the variation of y:

$$\text{PPM} = r = \frac{\text{Covariation of } x, y}{\sqrt{(\text{Variation } x)\,(\text{Variation } y)}}, \quad \text{or} \quad \frac{\text{Cov } x, y}{(\text{s.dev } x)\,(\text{s.dev. } y)}$$

The calculator formula for this is:

$$r = \frac{n\Sigma xy - \Sigma x \Sigma y}{\sqrt{(n\Sigma x^2 - [\Sigma x]^2)\,(n\Sigma y^2 - [\Sigma y]^2)}}$$

(These formulas and their meaning will be explained in a subsequent chapter.) It can be seen that the standard deviation of the variable provides the major part of the equation (denominator). The PPM is used for parametric analysis of continuous interval data.

Chi-square is used as a measure of association in bivariate analysis for non-parametric discrete data. This test of independence is based upon the assumption that observed values will equal expected values if there is independence between the two variables. In other words, if the null hypothesis is to be retained, the observed values will be close to the expected values. Chi-square is given as:

$$\text{Chi-square} = \chi^2 = \frac{\Sigma(O - E)^2}{E} \quad \text{where} \quad E = \frac{R \times C}{N}$$

where

E = the expected value
O = the observed value
R = row value in contingency table
C = column value in contingency table
N = number of cases in the sample

Again, this formula will be dealt with in later chapters. The apparent difficulties with formulas resolve very quickly when they are converted into matrices or into calculator formulas.

These two formulas, Pearson r and chi-square, are the most used in exploratory research design and analysis. The actual steps to analysis begin with a frequency analysis, which is a univariate analysis of each variable. Thus, the variables are now translated into numerical form, and quantification can proceed to analysis of collated data. The variables must be able to be counted and scored. The data must be accumulated and transposed to formula.

The simple steps to variable analysis can then progress to more complex analysis of results, and the hypothesis now becomes scrutinized mathematically and statistically.

Variables, once selected and defined, become operationalized and then subject to statistical analysis. The measurement of the variable selected determines the level of the statistical analysis. Interval and ratio variables subject to parametric analysis are under much more stringent assumptions than are discrete nonparametric data. But any analysis should be related to the real world and the substance of what is being tested. Figures in complex statistics often seem overwhelming until one realizes that they are merely statistical manipulations.

SUMMARY

Any grouping that may fluctuate or vary is called a variable; if it does not vary, it is a constant. Measurement of variables is by scales rather than arithmetic. The four basic scales are nominal, ordinal, interval, and ratio. The first two are qualitative and discrete, the last two continuous and quantitative. Ordinal variables may be either qualitative or quantitative, depending upon the type of ranking.

All variables are designed to yield data. Common to variables is their order in research design. They may be classified as independent or dependent, according to which affects the other. Time order, dominance, and influence are criteria for separation of independent and dependent variables.

Models become more complex as more variables are added, and the names given to the variables depend upon where they fit in the model. Variables are essential to hypothesis construction; they are the building blocks of new theory, bridging the gap between concept and practice and aiding in the quantification of an idea. Variables need exact definition for operationalization. Once operationalized, they may be used to collect data and yield them for statistical analysis.

Variables are subject to various form of relationship. The one we are most concerned with is called asymmetrical, the relationship of behavior to background variables. Although we are mostly concerned with bivariate analysis, we are also aware of multivariate analysis and complex statistical use of variables. Bivariate analysis of variables enables us to explore relationships of qualitative variables. We may see very quickly what is happening by a chi-square analysis. As more and more variables are introduced into the model, the more complex it becomes, and thus the more selective we are in terms of statistical analysis. However, all complex designs are really based upon the simple two-variable model.

Most of our early research will be descriptive—that is, using the method known as survey research. In order to select variables for this kind of research, we must be very careful how we explain and define our variables. The operationalization, or the testing of the variables in practice, depends upon our definitions. We must be certain that the variables we select actually test the proposition we are stating. The most tested type of asymmetrical relationship, background-behavior, requires that we carefully define such dependent-variable concepts as stress, alienation, deviance, and other ambiguous behavioral qualities. Validity depends upon a secure definition. Statistical analysis can be performed only when quantification of the variable has been defined.

1. What is a variable? What is a constant? Give examples.
2. What are the two main categories of variables?
3. Describe the four levels of variable measurement. Why can ordinal measurement be considered in two categories?
4. Explain a summated variable; a combined variable.
5. What variables are used in parametric analysis? in nonparametric analysis? Why?
6. Define: *trait, attribute, characteristic, dichotomize, statistic.*
7. What type of variable data is used in a contingency table? What is this method of analysis called?
8. How would you dichotomize parametric data? Why do this?
9. Variables are essential in three things and they aid us in three others. What are these six key points?
10. What are the three basic types of variable analysis? Explain *mutually exclusive, frequency, magnitude.*
11. What is a model? Construct a simple model. Name the parts.
12. What are the criteria for determination of the independent variables? What variable is never controlled?
13. What errors may creep in during variable selection?
14. There are three basic rules for variable definition; define a testable variable and apply the rules.
15. What is a null hypothesis?
16. Cite illustrations of symmetrical relationships; of asymmetrical relationships.
17. Background data or the property that is least likely to change influences behavior. Why is this so important?
18. Univariate statistical analysis of a variable can tell you several things. Name them.
19. Describe measures of location, disperson, association, and prediction.
20. What is the difference between chi-square and Pearson Product Moment correlation?
21. Cite a few reasons why variables are so important.
22. For each of the following, define the variables, rewrite it as a null hypothesis (no relationship between x and y), and tell how you would test it.
    (a) Men are more likely than women to go to prison.
    (b) More handguns than any other weapons are used in homicide.
    (c) The longer a felon stays in prison, the greater the likelihood of his return.
    (d) Computer crime is the most profitable.
    (e) Capital punishment deters crime.
23. Construct simple models for the statements above and name the parts. If a

2-by-2 analysis is warranted, draw the table with hypothetical figures.

24. Look at some Uniform Crime Reports and see if you can find a frequency, a mean, a mode, a median. Can you calculate a standard deviation?
25. How do variables figure in the logic of theory construction?

FOR FURTHER READING

Blalock, Hubert M., Jr., *Social Statistics.* New York: McGraw-Hill, 1972.

Bradley, J. I., and J. N. McClelland, *Basic Statistical Concepts.* Glenview, Ill.: Scott, Foresman, 1978.

Byrkit, Donald R., *Elements of Statistics* (2nd ed.). New York: D. Van Nostrand, 1975.

Davis, James A., *Elementary Survey Analysis,* Chaps. 1–3. Englewood Cliffs, N.J.: Prentice-Hall, 1971.

Leonard, Wilbert M., *Basic Social Statistics.* St. Paul, Minn.: West Publishing, 1975.

Lieberman, Bernhardt, *Contemporary Problems in Social Statistics,* Section 1. New York: Oxford University Press, 1971.

Rosenberg, Morris, *The Logic of Survey Analysis,* Chaps. 1 and 2. New York: Basic Books, 1968.

Schaumberger, N., and G. Marshall, *A First Course in Statistics.* New York: Macmillan, 1978.

Schutte, Jerald G., *Everything You Always Wanted to Know about Elementary Statistics,* Sections 1 and 2. Englewood Cliffs, N.J.: Prentice-Hall, 1977.

Selltiz, C., et al., *Research Methods in Social Relations* (3rd ed.). Chaps. 1–5. New York: Holt, Rinehart & Winston, 1976.

4

The Hypothesis: Concept and Practice

MAKING A RESEARCH STATEMENT

Research scientists are primarily involved in finding order in the universe. Social scientists in particular are concerned with identifying social problems. They tend to create data from social phenomena for the purpose of studying observed differences, problems, or whatever motivates the research mind. From the very moment that a problem is identified, the researcher is aware that he is limited:

1. Social problems have general meaning but no final definition. It is difficult to define precisely because of the intangible nature of many social concepts.[1]
2. The research problem exists in the mind of the researcher and must be explained in order to be generally accepted. At best, "general acceptance" is an approximation and is obtained by a consensus of varying opinions.
3. The study of surrounding social phenomena is limited by what is obtainable, what is practical, and the level of the sophistication of measurement.
4. The very nature of measurement of qualitative variables, such as the qualities, attitudes, or attributes of people, is limited by social and environmental change. Exact replication (and therefore verification) is almost impossible because of changing circumstances. Time, growth, change in life-style, fluctua-

[1] Earl R. Babbie, *Survey Research Methods* (Belmont, Calif.: Wadsworth, 1973), p. 27. Babbie writes, "Ultimately, social regularities persist because they tend to make sense for the actors involved in them." Concepts exist because of "logical expectations."

tion from original response, and memory decay all affect the accuracy of repeated measurement.
5. The researcher's own prejudices, bias, personal judgments, and social values tend to enter into the research and subtly affect the subjective observation of sociocultural differences. The formulation of the research statement, consciously or unconsciously, becomes or tends to become personal rather than general, subjective rather than objective.
6. No matter how carefully the researcher controls for error, it is always present in a greater or lesser degree. The final statistical finding will be only a close approximation based upon probability and logic.

Any research statement is also subject to limits:

1. It is made from reality that can be checked by others, and thus must be communicated precisely.
2. It contains specific statements of relationships that are subject to replication.[2]
3. The statement of the problem in definitive terms limits both fallacy and causal error.
4. Definition of the problem determines the level of the sophistication of measurement.
5. The deterministic nature of the research limits the research statement to retention or rejection of the research hypothesis.
6. The hypothesis is a specific statement aimed toward understanding networks of causal relationships among interrelated phenomena. *No phenomenon exists by itself.*

The statement of the problem is an attempt to develop propositions to explain what is actually happening about us. It is a hypothesis of cause and effect, a delineation of testable variables, a designation of variable definition, and a means for operationalizing the project. We are looking for the systematic connection of facts—the greatest number of facts from the smallest number of hypotheses or propositions.[3] We assume that no more causes are to be stated than those that account for the problem or phenomenon. We assume that there is an underlying theoretical base, that we have logical development, and that we have not limited our investigative imagination.

The Direction of the Research

Perhaps the most important concern is the philosophical question of the direction of the research—what it does for criminology, its application, and its consequences. Although the formal hypothesis is mainly a testing of theoretical propositions, it

[2] Fred N. Kerlinger, *Foundations of Behavioral Research*, 2nd ed. (New York: Holt, Rinehart & Winston, 1973), p. 25. Kerlinger sees the hypothesis as man's most powerful research tool; as conjectural, testable, speculative; as explanative and predictive; as minimizing fallibility, especially in the determination of positive and negative evidence.

[3] The principle of Occam's razor—a guide to parsimony in research.

is the central element of theory construction.[4] By applying the scientific method to testing the hypothesis, we are assuming that it can and will be subject to replication that results in verification. Concern for the direction of the research also ensures the underlying theoretical base upon which the research is built. *The hypothesis should be a bridge between past sequential development and future research, between past theory and new theory. It should also be a link between abstract concepts and the reality of life–concept and measurement.*

The hypothesis should show the relationship between the research problem and the theory upon which it is based. The academic restraint of a formal hypothesis is imposed for the sake of order in the research process. In the case of a series of hypotheses, they should be set out in a sequential hierarchy. In effect, *the hypothesis is the arrow indicating the direction of the research.*

THE RESEARCH HYPOTHESIS

A research hypothesis is simply a statement of the problem in qualitative terms. In order to test the problem—and testing is implied in the research statement—a quantitative statement is made, called the null hypothesis. Although in testing we are measuring differences,[5] in essence our final conclusions concern the relationships stated in the research hypothesis. Therefore, the null hypothesis is really a statement of no (null) relationship between the variables mentioned in the research hypothesis.

To put this complex concept in simpler form, let us look at a simple qualitative statement made in the form of a research hypothesis, then made as a null hypothesis, measured, and finally written as a conclusion.

1. *Simple Research Hypothesis: A causes B; relationship of A and B.*
   Sensational crime causes fear.
2. *Simple Null Hypothesis: A does not cause B; no relationship.*
   There is no relationship between sensational crime and fear.
3. The variables are: Independent variable = Sensational crime
   Dependent variable = Perception of fear

   Measurement of the differences perceived by people in the sample indicate that people do fear sensational crime more than any other (i.e., Jack the Ripper, Boston Strangler, Zodiac, Manson family, etc.).
4. Although we have measured differences, we have shown there is a relationship between sensational crime and fear. We would thus reject the null hypothesis at the limits we have set, and we would retain the research hypothesis.
5. If we had stated that there was no difference between one's perception of fear and sensational crime, the statement would not have been as accurate as the

[4] Kerlinger, *Foundations of Behavioral Research*, p. 21: "The relations expressed in the hypothesis tell the investigator, in effect, what to do. . . . Hypotheses advance scientific knowledge by helping the investigator confirm or disconfirm theory."

[5] R. J. Senter, *Analysis of Data* (Glenview, Ill.: Scott, Foresman, 1969), pp. 164-67. "When differences . . . are being evaluated, the particular hypothesis used is the null hypothesis."

> statement of no relationship. *We are measuring differences to determine relationships.* If the variables are independent, then there is no difference and no relationship, and A does not cause or influence B.

In an actual study, legislators wished to know why so many escapes were occurring at a state home for delinquent boys.[6] The task force doing the study listed not only all the variables that might contribute to escape but also those that were background variables. The research statement was taken from the informal problem, "Why do so many boys seek to escape from the State Detention Center?"[7] The research hypothesis, or H_a, stated:

> There are factors that influence attitudes toward escape.

The null hypothesis stated:

> There is no relationship between (factors) variables and attitudes toward escape.

The research hypothesis is stated as qualitative, the null as testable and quantitative. If the null is correct, then we must abandon the research hypothesis. Since the null is set out in testable form, it is apparent that we will try to prove it wrong. Note that we do *not* directly test the research hypothesis. *We test the null, because of the quantitative statistical assumptions that are implied in its formal mathematical description.* In the actual writing, we set limits for the rejection or retention of the null. We do not set limits or design statistical procedures for the research hypothesis.

Errors in Stating the Hypothesis

The most frequent error committed in stating the research hypothesis is that of ambiguity. *Confusion will arise if the statement does not permit the exact definition of the variables to be tested.* The actual hypothesis may be general, but the details of the proposition cannot be general; *they must be precise.* If, for example, in the problem on escape, the contributing factors had not been carefully thought out, the project would have reached an erroneous conclusion based upon the nature of the offense rather than the factor of recreation. In another research project, in which attitudes to physical punishment were examined, the clientele were not defined. As a result, a sample was taken from two Catholic schools with a high ratio of boys to girls, and the project lost all meaning. In a project investigating attitudes toward the death penalty, there was complete confusion on the rating of attitudes because of scoring different crimes. Very simply, the problem tested had never been discussed; it was pasted together in a hurry and suffered the usual frustration of being completely unworkable.

[6] Nadine Young, "Attitudes of Youths at Industry towards Escape," an unpublished paper under the author's direction, State University of New York, 1978.

[7] William J. Goode and Paul K. Hatt, *Methods in Social Research* (New York: McGraw-Hill, 1952), pp. 68–73. "The formulation of *usable* hypothesis is of central importance."

The research statement depends upon research of the problem itself, the discussion of that problem, and the detailed definition and explanation of every variable used in the statement.[8] Most failures in research occur because they are rushed and nobody takes time out to think the problem through. Certain guidelines may be helpful.

Once the problem has been identified, ask:

1. What are the components of this problem? What are the variables? Can they be defined? Can they be explained in their relationship to one another? Can they be operationalized?
2. What is the purpose of the research? Where are we going? What are we doing? What is the result of this research? Is it feasible? Can it be done in time? What is the cost in time and energy? What is the financial cost?
3. Does this research make sense? Can it be verified? Can it be duplicated? Has it been done before? What can we do with the results? Are we solving problems or creating problems? *Are we basing our assertions on evidence?*[9]
4. Have we avoided ambiguity, confusion, fallacy, and metaphysics (We cannot test God, justice, love, hate, death, etc.) Can we communicate our findings to people?
5. Can truth be found independently of ourselves, or is it only in the eye of the beholder? Are we logical? Will our research explain causal relationships? Any relationships? Does it really do anything?
6. Have we used simple language, or have we hidden the garbage in scientific jargon?

Error creeps in when truth lies sleeping. It is much better to work over the research statement several times than have the entire project wasted. Many a confused and frustrated research team has wasted time, energy, and funds because someone started on the wrong research foot. Some classic examples of statements are:

People who have many birthdays tend to live longer.

Eating rice causes one's skin to go yellow.

The high birth rate in the Low Countries is caused by storks.

The more fire engines there are at a fire, the greater the damage.

Drinking cocoa causes homosexuality.

Such examples are obvious; but the problem is not so laughable when the ambiguities are hidden. Classic examples of this are the constant research endeavors into body-type theories in criminology—that certain body types are crime-prone. Other theories have been that criminals have inferior IQs and peculiar cranial shapes; that black skin is caused by a unique form of leprosy, and that any intelligence in blacks is due to white intermarriage; that divorce causes juvenile delinquency; that TV violence can precipitate murder.

All these ideas have been tested by serious criminologists and other social

[8] J. A. Davis, *Elementary Survey Analysis* (Englewood Cliffs, N.J.: Prentice-Hall, 1971). Davis gives variables four parts: name, definition, categories, and sorting procedure.

[9] Jacques Barzun and Henry F. Graff, *The Modern Researcher* (New York: Harcourt Brace Jovanovich, 1970), Chap. 7, "Truth and Causation."

scientists. They had hosts of believers and often influenced the legal codes of the day. That is why error in the research statement is so important. *Error in a survival science can create havoc in people's lives.* Had the research statements been carefully thought out, a great deal of misery could have been avoided. Such research statements may be the result of dishonesty—an apology for a very insecure status quo; but more often they are the product of misguided and misplaced intentions based upon inadequate research of the problem itself.[10] Current research in criminology should remember past errors and not repeat them.

Definitive Strength of the Hypothesis

It is difficult to understand how such dangerous ideas were actually put into practice. We know that at one time, saying the earth was round was heresy against the church and punishable by death; that if blacks in early America attempted to learn how to read, they committed a serious crime punishable by flogging; and that for many years it was believed that the full moon produced criminal behavior. The errors appear to occur more from a lack of science than of common sense, although both are indicated. Contemporary researchers are no less human, and on occasion we see the same old mistakes couched in technical jargon.

The advantage of the dual statement, the research hypothesis and the null hypothesis, is that it can withstand assault because it is designed to test its own validity.

> *The initial statement—the research statement, or the research hypothesis, or H_a—indicates our research objective, states the relationship of the variables, and usually indicates the effect or influence of the independent variable upon the dependent variable.*
>
> *The dependent variable is that variable that is changed, influenced, or causally affected by the dominant, less changeable, precedental independent variable.*
>
> *The second statement—the null statement or null hypothesis, or H_o—indicates the testability of the research statement and is so stated to disprove the research hypothesis. It states the independence of all the variables by indicating no relationship between them—that is, that any effects of one upon the other are entirely due to chance.*

Stating the Reverse Hypothesis

It is a good idea to state the research hypothesis in reverse (change the order of the variables) to see if the reverse carries more weight than the original. This is not the same as the null hypothesis. Take, for example, the assertion, "Black genetic

[10] Morris Rosenberg, *The Logic of Survey Analysis* (New York: Basic Books, 1968), pp. 197–201. Rosenberg points out that while there is a strong mutual dependence of data and theory, data do not *prove* a theory, they only support the findings. Even if the hypothesis is confirmed, the relationship may possibly be spurious.

intelligence will improve by intermarriage with whites." The null would simply state, "There is no relationship between intelligence and racial intermarriage." Intelligence or IQ would be the dependent variable and racial intermarriage the independent variable.[11] However, the reverse hypothesis would state, "White genetic intelligence will deteriorate with intermarriage with blacks." The conclusions point to the futility of proceeding further with the research.

Another form of reverse hypothesis can also indicate the incorrectness of a research statement. Take this example:

H_a: Stiffer penalties will cause a drop in drug traffic.

H_o: There is no relationship between penalties and drug traffic.

R_a: Leniency in drug offenses will cause an increase in drug traffic.

Comparing the H_a and R_a, we see that, from experience, whereas penalties may have a great deal to do with social control, they have little to do with control of drug traffic.

The statement of a reverse hypothesis often indicates the error of the research:

H_a: Criminal man can be identified by atavistic stigmata.

H_o: There is no relationship between criminality and atavistic stigmata.

R_a: Noncriminal man can be identified by civilized characteristics.

Would that we could indeed identify the civilized man, especially on election day! And a good many innocents have been found guilty because they looked criminal. Notice how the reverse hypothesis goes beyond the null.

H_a: A person becomes a communist by association with communists.

H_o: There is no relationship between communism and association with communists.

R_a: A person can become a noncommunist by associating with communists.

The implication here is that one becomes something else by associating with other people. Senator McCarthy called such people "fellow travelers."[12] A reverse hypothesis points out at once that this is extremely doubtful, or, as one person put it, "Sleeping in a can doesn't make you a sardine."

Stating the research in alternative ways can indicate the strength or weakness of the research and certainly reveal flaws in the research hypothesis. The reverse, opposite, or alternate-null hypothesis is very useful. Remember that the only answer to "The earth is flat" was, "The earth is round." By reversing the variables we obtain:

R_{a_1} = The reverse, or B causes A.

[11] Arthur J. Bachrach, *Psychological Research: An Introduction* (New York: Random House, 1966), pp. 21–25. Bachrach defines "hypothesis myopia" as ignoring facts that are clearly in view, because of preconceived notions.

[12] Sen. Joseph McCarthy, *Hearings of House Committee on Investigation of Un-American Activities* (Washington, D.C., circa 1950). The McCarthy hypothesis held the country in the grip of anticommunist hysteria.

By using terms or variables in opposition we obtain:

R_{a_2} = The opposite of A causes the opposite of B.
R_{a_3} = The opposite of A causes B.
R_{a_4} = A causes the opposite of B.

Using terms in opposition, or using a variation of variable concepts is a means of testing hypothesis construction and research objectives.

THE NULL HYPOTHESIS

Possible Outcomes

We would prefer to reject the null hypothesis and thus be in a position to assert the "truth" of the research hypothesis.[13] The results, however, may be contrary to our preference and must be reported objectively and accurately. The outcome of the statistical analysis is compared to the statistical statement of the null and the limits we have set. It is upon this comparison that we must make a decision. There are six choices:

1. Reject the null when it is true.	Incorrect
2. Reject the null when it is false.	Correct
3. Retain the null when it is true.	Correct
4. Retain the null when it is false.	Incorrect
5. Fail to reject; neutral	No decision
6. Fail to retain; neutral	No decision

If the probability is such that our final statistic meets the criteria of the limits we have set in terms of confidence levels and intervals, then we make our final decision on the null based purely on probability.[14] The meaning of our decision is:

Rejecting the null means the relationship does exist, does have scientific meaning, can be (possibly) verified, and has occurred because of cause and effect, not chance. We can never explain away all the error, but we can be reasonably sure of our results. We also assume the null is false.

Retaining the null, or not rejecting the null, means that any relationship we have observed has occurred purely by chance, that the variables are independent, and

[13] Gene V. Glass and Julian C. Stanley, *Statistical Methods in Education and Psychology* (Englewood Cliffs, N.J.: Prentice-Hall, 1970), pp. 271–79. "We have given up any hope of making either of the decisions, 'H is true' or 'H is false,' with certainty. Such certainty is impossible without knowing the entire population."

[14] Jerald G. Schutte, *Everything You Always Wanted to Know about Elementary Statistics* (Englewood Cliffs, N.J.: Prentice-Hall, 1977), pp. 118–19. Schutte sets out four steps for testing the hypothesis.

that no scientific meaning is attached to the relationship, which is spurious, accidental, or fortuitous.

Failing to reject or being unable to retain implies that no decision is made because of the closeness of the results. Further research is indicated, since slight changes in the level of significance or the sample size would swing the decision one way or the other.

Hypothesis Testing

The null hypothesis is that statement of the problem that is to be tested. Its retention or rejection is the make-or-break of the project. Therefore, assuming we begin with testing a null hypothesis of no difference between the variables, two possibilities exist when we reject, and two possibilities exist when we retain. Rejection of the null hypothesis is written statistically as *R*:, which means, "Reject the null hypothesis when . . .," and certain conditions are then given to complete the statistical statement of limits.

Two possibilities exist when the H_o is rejected:

1. The H_o is true. Here, we have rejected a true finding. The error we have committed is known as a *Type 1 error*, or α (alpha). We have concluded that there is a difference between the variables, when in fact there is none. Rejection of a true null hypothesis, A $\not\rightarrow$ B, is the assumption that one variable is related to or influences another when it does not.

Prevention of Type 1 error: The rejection of the true finding occurs when there is an inaccurate estimation of the population parameters by the sample statistic; the level of significance that was chosen was too loose, and thus too restrictive. The error may be corrected by *tightening the significance level*—which is the probability of making this error—moving from $\alpha = 0.1$, or a one-in-ten chance of error, to $\alpha = 0.05$, a one-in-twenty chance.

2. The H_o is false. Here, we have rejected a false conclusion, and this is what we set out to do. By rejecting what is false, we are more likely to retain what is true.

When the null hypothesis is retained, two possibilities exist:

1. The H_o is true. This, of course, is desirable. We always wish to retain the truth in our research conclusions.[15]

2. The H_o is false. Here, we have kept a false finding and reported it as truthful. We have assumed no relationship between the variables when in fact there is one. This is a *Type 2 error*, known as β (beta).

Prevention of Type 2 error: We cannot always control for Type 2 error as well as we would wish; but we can reduce the probability of error by *increasing the sample size*—keeping samples over 30, preferably close to 100. When samples are small, there is grave danger of retaining a false finding of no relationship.

Remember that *rejection of one hypothesis implies acceptance of another.*

[15] The "truth" is, of course, our probability assumption based on the statistical test.

Strength and Weakness of the Null

The null hypothesis, precise as it is, does have an inherent weakness, in that it is subject to Type 1 and Type 2 errors.[16] The cost and time expended in research that is subject to Type 1 error can be limited by setting the probability of error at 0.05 or lower, providing less chance of rejecting a correct null. But solving the problem of Type 1 error creates another problem. Retaining a false hypothesis, Type 2 error, becomes more likely when we take precautions against a Type 1 error.[17] In other words, the more we guard against rejecting a true hypothesis, the more likely we are to retain a false hypothesis, and this is the greater error.

A consideration of the points raised earlier, under "Hypothesis Testing," will indicate the logic of this situation, which is illustrated in Table 4.1. As we seek to report the facts, we tend to move into a grey area of error, and this can cause the loss of an idea that is potentially useful to society.

Table 4.1. How Type 2 Error Develops from Prevention of Type 1 (and Vice Versa)

Decision made

	Reject null hypothesis		*Retain null hypothesis*	
Possible error	None	Type 1	Type 2	None
Possible outcome	False	True	False	True
Actual error	–	Alpha	Beta	–
Findings stated	Relationship	Relationship	No relationship	No relationship
Actual existing facts	Relationship	No relationship	Relationship	No relationship
Evaluation	Correct	Incorrect	Incorrect	Correct
Prevention of error	–	Tighten significance level	Increase sample size	–

Although the null statement has an inherent weakness, it also has inherent strengths. The moment it is used, it implies possible replication. No one may use the null hypothesis without making it available to others for testing. Its simplicity is its virtue. The null assumes a "zero-statement"–that no differences exist, that no relationships exist, that any apparent effects exist only by chance, and that we start from zero in measuring any possible effects of the independent variable upon the dependent variable.

[16] H. W. Smith, *Strategies of Social Research* (Englewood Cliffs, N.J.: Prentice-Hall, 1975), pp. 68–70.

[17] It is also true that when we guard against a Type 2 error, we may commit a Type 1 error.

Another strength is that the null does not assume "fixed" or "crooked" situations, or "runs of luck," or even "honest" situations. Certain statistical calculations may assume honesty in coins and dice, but this weakness is not present in the design of the null.

The null also enables us to test situations that are not directly testable. For example, if a car stops and the hypothesis is, "The vehicle is out of gas," this may be tested directly. To ascertain the effects of rehabilitation on prison inmates, however, involves indirect testing and therefore the use of the null hypothesis.

We cannot ensure infallibility in any one method or any combination of methods. The most powerful test we have is the use of the null hypothesis. It lends itself to statistical quantification, analysis, and scientific decision making. Even though it may be used to present findings that appear controversial, it can also be used to examine those findings and determine their validity.

The Statistical Statement of the Null Hypothesis

The previous discussion of hypotheses has been with emphasis on the descriptive statement, the statement of the relationship between two or more variables in an either/or situation.[18] To avoid repetition in the statistical section of the findings, the null is written in statistical abbreviations. These notations include reference to the type of statistical analysis, the table value of acceptance or rejection, the level at which rejection of the null can occur,[19] the number of degrees of freedom, and any other pertinent statistical information. *The interval* (or table value) that is set for rejection of the null *is a function of the confidence level.* This will become clearer as you read the section on the normal curve.

The statistical statement is designed to present outcomes of the null hypothesis:

1. It is a statement of no relationship (difference), sometimes accompanied by an alternate expression.
2. The rejection of the null hypothesis is significant because we are looking for the effect of the independent variable upon the dependent variable, or statistical difference.
3. The null is a statement concerning the population that is being examined; it explains limits. However, its rejection or retention is based upon the sample statistics, not the parent-population statistics.
4. Selection of the proper statistical analysis determines outcomes. Level of analysis is based on assumptions for data.
5. The null hypothesis will be rejected if its probability of being correct is very low. This probability is arbitrary and is selected by the researcher. It is usually

[18] Smith, *Strategies of Social Research*, pp. 44–53. Smith gives nine rules for "constructing good hypotheses."

[19] Significance level is affected by sample size, difference between means, scores within samples, and directionality.

0.05 or less; i.e., the chances of being wrong are one in twenty or better. The probability, 0.05, is the significance level, or alpha (α).[20]

6. *Rejection of the null hypothesis is regarded as statistically significant at the specified level.*
7. Nonrejection of the null is nonsignificant and is generally regarded as somewhat inconclusive.
8. Nonrejection or retention of the null indicates that there is no difference in the means of the variables, that the tested populations are separate populations, and that at the specified significance level, no relationship exists. The variables are independent, and the effects, if any, are due to chance, sampling or instrument error, and/or insensitivity.
9. If the level of significance is changed—say, from 0.05 to 0.1, depending upon the risk the researcher wishes to take (0.1 = 1-in-10 chance of error)—then the interval of rejection may also change.
10. The researcher must decide upon the direction of the research in order to select the proper statistical test for rejection of the null hypothesis. (The H_0 does not indicate direction; the test statistic does.)

Item 10 mentions statistical direction. If variable x varies according to variable y—that is, as x goes up, y goes up, or as x goes down, y goes down—x and y move in a *positive direction*. If x goes up as y goes down, or vice versa, then x and y move in a *negative direction*. Also, *"greater than" or "less than" is positive*; "equal to" or "not equal to" may be either or both. Positive tests are usually one-tail; negative tests are usually two-tail. One-tail tests are directional, because the result can be anticipated; two-tail tests are nondirectional and not anticipated, as in "equals" or "does not equal."

The statistical statement consists of the following parts:

1. Abbreviation *R*:, which means, "Reject the null hypothesis"; then the conditions under which the null will be rejected.
2. An abbreviation designating the statistical analysis or test used, such as:
   (a) χ^2 = chi-square
   (b) r = Pearson correlation coefficient
   (c) F = F ratio (analysis of variance)
   (d) t = student's t-test
3. A sign indicating "equal to," "less than," or "greater than" a particular tabled value (=, <, >, ⩾) (test direction).
4. The tabled value, showing the point of rejection based upon 5 and 6. (Two values for a two-tail test.)
5. The level of significance, known as alpha or α, followed by the level set, usually arbitrarily 0.05.
6. The number of degrees of freedom permitted by the sample size, sample design, or statistical analysis (df =).

[20] The significance level is also the probability that the relationship is due to sampling error (chance). The lower the significance level (0.05 or less), the less chance that factors affect the stated relationship. We reject the null if the statistical value is less than 0.05.

7. The actual sample size.[21] This gives the reader some idea of the scope of the research and its expected validity. It relates the statistical to the descriptive null (N =).
8. If an alternate hypothesis is included, then only the null is tested. Alternates are usually included in an "equal to" or "not equal to" hypothesis. The null comes first.
9. At the conclusion of the analysis, the calculated sample statistics may be compared with the statement.[22]
10. Finally, the decision to reject or retain the null hypothesis may be added; i.e., "Reject the null hypothesis."[23]

The statistical statement is related to the descriptive statement by setting the test criteria for the null hypothesis. Its significance comes about by the rejection of the null.

MAKING THE STATISTICAL STATEMENT

1. After the descriptive statement has been made, the null hypothesis may be stated statistically:

$$\text{R:}\quad \chi^2 \geqslant 3.84,\ \alpha = 0.05,\ \text{df} = 1 \qquad \text{N} = 100$$

This statistical statement reads:

R: = Reject the null hypothesis
$\chi^2 \geqslant 3.84$ = if the calculated value of chi-square equals or exceeds the table value of 3.84
$\alpha = 0.05$ = at the level of significance of 0.05
df = 1 = with one degree of freedom (in a 2 × 2 contingency table)

Or:

$$\text{R:}\quad r < 0.35,\quad \alpha = 0.001,\quad \text{df} = 98 \qquad \text{N} = 100$$

Reject the null hypothesis if the Pearson correlation coefficient (r) is less than 0.35 at a significance level of 0.001.

Or:

$$\text{R:}\quad H_o\text{: } \mu_1 = \mu_2 \qquad H_a\text{: } \mu_1 \neq \mu_2$$

Reject the null when population mean 1 equals mean 2. Retain if mean 1 does not equal mean 2.

Other, similar statements are used for t-tests, regression, analysis of variance, covariance. Pearson r and chi-square are the most-used test statistics in this text.

2. Because the degrees of freedom are determined by sample size or

[21] Hubert M. Blalock, Jr., *Social Statistics* (New York: McGraw-Hill, 1972), pp. 155–66, "Steps in Statistical Tests."

[22] Marshall Gordon and Norman Schaumberger, *A First Course in Statistics* (New York: Macmillan, 1978), pp. 99–104, "Hypothesis Testing."

[23] The statistical statement sets the mode for decision making. The final decision should recognize the possibility of Type 1 or Type 2 error.

frequencies developed from sample size, it is useful to specify the sample size in the statistical statement; i.e., N = 100. State also the correct df.

3. Specify the level of significance *and* the table limits for rejection of the null hypothesis. No statement is valid without a confidence level *and* a confidence interval.

4. Assuming the analysis is complete and the data have been computerized, compare the calculations with the tabled values in the statistical statement and complete the test by making the appropriate decision.

5. Be certain that if your data fit the assumptions for your choice of statistical analysis based upon your perception of data patterns; i.e., extremes, distribution, and linearity.

6. Inferentially, the statement includes the possibility of Type 1 or Type 2 error; check your final decision accordingly.

Significance

When significance is found, reject the null, but consider also the question of substantive significance versus statistical significance. *We are searching for substantive significance that has meaning in the real world.* Statistical significance may occur in the mathematical and statistical calculations, and we may be overwhelmed with computer printouts, but numbers in themselves are meaningless unless related to the research statement.[24] A small significance in a large sample may be more important than a large significance in a small sample. The latter may be striking, but it may also be limited to that sample, that location, and even the experimenter's own bias. Large samples in actual social research yield small significances, but such findings are still important, particularly if they are substantive.

A good example of substantive significance occurs when we are investigating epidemics. It is important to note exactly when a case occurs, and the number and location of the cases. Let us say that two cases of "Legionnaire's Disease" are reported in Maryland. Statewise, we have a statistical significance of 1:50; populationwise, a significance of 1:110,000,000, or 0.9^8. The significance is almost infinitesimal. Yet since the disease may increase fatalities geometrically, we have to consider the possibility of its doubling itself every day, and thus wiping out every living soul in the United States in 27 days. The substantive significance of the rapidity of disease spread takes precedence over the statistical significance of only two cases.

Another example is the number of cigarettes one may smoke before cancer is terminal. The question really is, how much cancer is needed to terminate a life? The answer is very little. It is rather like asking what size bullet is needed to kill a man; numbers become academic, it is the substance that counts. The greater danger is the retention of a false hypothesis—the assumption of no relationship when in fact there is one—a Type 2 error.

[24] Blalock, *Social Statistics*, p. 163. It is always possible to avoid a Type 2 error, but large numbers are not proof in themselves.

The Lombrosian error was a Type 1 error, in that Lombroso rejected the true null hypothesis of no difference between body measurements of criminals and noncriminals. Actually, he moved from observation to theory without the intervening steps of hypothesis construction. But it is certain that he did proceed upon some informal hypothesis. The substantive findings in his numerous autopsies led him astray regarding substantive findings in actual society.

Research statements must be designed to prevent error, not accumulate error.[25] The hypothesis should be:

1. Observable–discernible and discoverable
2. Logical–reasonable and justifiable
3. Possible–practical and feasible
4. Repeatable–verifiable by duplication

The second point, logicality, can be tested by asking if the hypothesis is sequential, if it can be understood, and if it is scientific.

Finally, hypothesis testing involves a fact often overlooked. In social science, perhaps especially in criminology, the most we can do is approximate cause and effect. There is always some part that is not examined, some factors that are overlooked, some causal influence that has been omitted because we do not have the sophistication to measure it. *We restrict the number of events that are related.* This is a necessary but limiting factor in understanding the chain of causality.

In a way, we select facts to suit ourselves and the nature of our research. Each researcher attempts to choose from a variety of observations those facts that can best be fitted into intelligent organization, creating a unique pattern with his investigations like a thumbprint on the page of progress. Research is an alphanumerical world in which concepts are translated, separated, and analyzed. Guided by intelligence, common sense, and probability, we assess the hypothesis as true or false based upon science and our own critical judgment, realizing that there still remain contradictory evidence that has not been explained, ideas that have not been explored, and scientific truths not as yet comprehended. Even common sense may be used to cover deficiencies when verification involves detailed, routine research labor. All research findings are open to modification, and the final conclusion based upon the hypothesis is by no means the last word on the subject. As social scientists, we cannot create absolutes, we can only make a contemporary assessment.

APPLYING HYPOTHESES TO ACTUAL RESEARCH

Consider, for example, the examination of the public's attitude toward the imposition of the death penalty. This favorite topic has been investigated many times, with varying results. The purpose of the research is to discover how people react because

[25] Richard J. Larsen and Donna Fox Stroup, *Statistics in the Real World* (New York: Macmillan, 1976), pp. 10–26, "Characterizing Variability." The authors simplify hypotheses to "objectives."

of their different backgrounds–education, age, race, sex, religion, occupation, and marital status. The independent variables are already present in the background data of people being questioned. The dependent variable is attitude toward the imposition of the death penalty, and this has been stated in the informal hypothesis.

The research hypothesis, or H_a, would state:

> There is a relationship between a person's background and his attitude toward the imposition of the death penalty.

The null hypothesis would state:

> There is no relationship between one's background and one's attitude toward the imposition of the death penalty.

Table 4.2. Differences between Research and Null Hypotheses

Research hypothesis, H_a	Null hypothesis, H_o
States causality of variables, relationships or differences	Nullifies causality by stating no relationship or difference
States influence or effects of independent variable upon dependent variable, or between two or more variables	States all variables are independent, all effects are due to chance; nullifies causal order
States samples are from diverse populations, with differences between the means	Samples are from one population, with no differences and identical means
States relationships are intentional, planned, or asymmetrical	Relationships are spurious, coincidental, accidental, or fortuitous
Is predictive	Is not predictive
Is quantitative or qualitative	Is quantitative, never qualitative
States positive or negative direction of relationships (or both, or none)	Technically does not state direction, although the statistical statement of H_o may indicate direction
Is descriptive	Is explanatory
Is not testable	Is testable
Has no statistical statement. Used for model construction	Statistical statement is basis for test criteria
Acceptance needs verification	Significant when rejected
May be useful for theory	Eliminates non-useful hypotheses
Is stated formally for testing by null hypothesis	Is derived from the research hypothesis
Cannot be used for decision making	Is extremely useful for decision making
Is subject to theoretical and construction errors	Is subject to sampling, analysis, and test errors
Is used for inferences to parent population	Is not used for inferential statements

Note that, even though the null is derived from the research hypothesis, there are many differences between these two statements. (See *Table 4.2*.) Awareness of these differences will enable you to write hypotheses that are easily understood. In the statement of causality, the variables are identified, and the next step is the description, definition, and explanation of those variables. Construction of a model based upon the research hypothesis helps in organizing the variables and in representing them in a causal diagram. We can then proceed to the prime task of ascertaining the effects of the independent variable(s) upon the dependent variable(s).[26]

The Variables Described

In the description of the variables, each category must be entered. For example, under *Age*, each grouping must be described, unless the age of each person is entered separately. Age may be described in the following categories: 18-28 yrs., 29-39 yrs., 40-50 yrs., 51-61 yrs., and over 61 yrs. Categories like this are easy to code. Note that each is sequential upon the last and does not overlap; after 18-28, the next category starts at 29 but also includes an equal interval or span of years. Such groupings also lend themselves to dichotomizing—here, into *under 40 years* and *over 40 years*. (Most nonparametric data are dichotomous. Age, of course, is parametric, but when put into categories, assumes nonparametric qualities.) The intervals may be set wherever the researcher desires, but they should be equal and they should be sequential. Overlapping, as in 18-28, 28-38, 38-48, and so on, with ages 28 and 38 occurring in two categories, is the kind of error that confuses frequency data.

For the purposes of nonparametric analysis, five groups are considered the maximum; larger numbers extend analysis into unwieldy tables. As a simple rule of thumb, do not carry more categories than are absolutely essential, with five the limit.

Race may be described as white, black, and other, or extended if the ethnic quality is a feature of the research, in which case Indian, Chicano, or Oriental may be added. Occasionally, as in voting-pattern research, ethnic origin is important, and white is broken down into British, Greek, Italian, German, Irish, Italian, Polish, Russian—or whatever groupings there are. *Sex* is simply dichotomized into male and female. *Religion* is usually answered in terms of Protestant, Catholic, Jewish, and Other. *Marital status* may be answered as married, single, living together, divorced, or widowed. *Occupation* can be described as white-collar, blue-collar, professional, unemployed, retired, and housewife. *Political preference*, which is sometimes added to background variables, can be described as Republican, Democrat, Independent, or Other. The list of background variables varies with the researcher's choice, but in most social-science projects, the variables are fairly standard, changing only to suit

[26] Allan G. Johnson, *Social Statistics without Tears* (New York: McGraw-Hill, 1977), pp. 239-40, "What Are Hypothesis Tests Good For?" "All the technical competence in the world can't make up for poor judgment and hasty or arbitrary decision."

the nature of the survey. *The background variables are properties or characteristics of the individual respondents, and we are most interested in the nature of the asymmetrical relationship by which those characteristics influence, cause, or stimulate acts, attitudes, and behavior.* This relationship determines the model in *Figure 4-1*. This simple model describes and explains the most-used and most important relationship in survey research. It shows how certain variables will influence others.

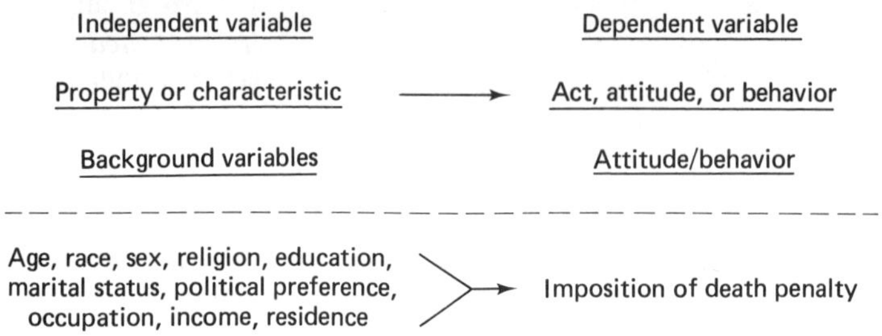

Fig. 4-1. Hypothesis model

Source: Moritz Schlick, "Causality in Everyday Life and in Recent Science," in *Publications in Philosophy*, vol. 15 (Berkeley, Calif.: University of California Press, 1932).

We do not test the research hypothesis or the model. We do test the null hypothesis, to see if relationships shown in the model (or stated in the research hypothesis) have occurred by chance. If we reject the null hypothesis, then the research statement and the model, the visual presentation of that statement, stand. *The model described* (except for the actual variables that are named) *is the core of survey research*. No matter what modifications are added, or by how many variables it is extended or elaborated, the relationship of a person's characteristics and behavior is the basic building block, the central theme of social research.[27]

In this model, education, income, and residence have been added to the list of background variables. *Education* may be listed as elementary school, high school, college, or by years or grade level; *Income* may be listed in categories such as, below $5,000, $5,001-$10,000, $10,001-$15,000, and so on, or it may be listed individually; *Residence*, which is becoming more and more important, may be listed in actual coded locations or in quadrants (N, E, S, W) or by districts. These variables change little and have great influence on a person's thinking and behavior; they need only definition for the categories used.

Another factor influencing one's attitude toward the death penalty would be the fact of having been a victim or involved in a crime. In the list of variables, names would be given to these two variables, such as *Victim of Crime* and *Involved in Crime*, and each would be defined and explained.

The dependent variable appears simple; it seems that all we need to know is

[27] Colin Bell and Howard Newby, *Doing Sociological Research* (London: Allen & Unwin, 1977). It is this central theme that sparks the controversy in the social sciences.

whether or not people believe in the imposition of the death penalty.[28] Certainly this question should be asked, and the variable would be named (D.V.) *Belief in the Death Penalty*. The categories are a simple yes or no; shades of grey are not important. However, in view of the seriousness of crime and its current juvenile ramifications, it is necessary to create another dependent variable, attitude toward imposition of the death penalty on juveniles. This variable would be called (D.V.) *Death Penalty for Juvenile Delinquents*. The categories here are 14-, 15-, 16-, and 17-year olds; it could also be extended to male and female juveniles.

Again, the gravity of the death penalty is such that it has been imposed only for certain crimes. The variable here is (D.V.) *Death Penalty for Listed Crime*, and the categories are premeditated murder, kidnap/ransom murder, forcible rape, killing of law-enforcement official, assassination, hijacking, terrorism, contract murder, child murder, abortion, and arson-murder. The categories divide into simple yes/no responses.

The variables have now been described, defined, explained, and set in logical order. This model can be fitted to reality. It can be tested and the end results interpreted. It is easy to explain and communicate, and the results will be easy to analyze even though there are ample data. Suppose, for example, that there are 20 responses for 20 variables, and that a sample of 200 is to be taken; already there are 20 x 200 responses, or 4,000 entries, to be made.[29] This is a minimal study, a practice effort. Therefore, it must be noted early that too many variables will create overwhelming data. This is fine if one has the time, as data analysis is time-consuming, but in a beginning research situation, the objective is to learn how to do it. The project should be the size a student group can cope with.

Experience shows that 100 surveys per member of a team using 20 variables can overpower any new researcher. The resulting computer printouts are quite unreasonable. Excessive numbers of variables create computer "fishing expeditions," in which students develop more and more statistical data without comprehending what they are doing. It is vital that success be achieved on a reasonable project. Four-member teams are the best project units. The project should be real, contemporary, important, and should generate the motivation to get out and do it. Before any of this can happen, the research statement has to be thoroughly discussed.

Differences between Concept and Practice

No matter how well put the research hypothesis is, the simple fact is that it must be able to be operationalized—that is, translated into reality. In the classroom or the

[28] There may be more than one dependent variable; the model is limited only by logical construction and practicality of completion. There is no single "correct" model, or any "correct" single dominant variable influencing or causing a single dependent effect.

[29] Robert S. Clark, *Fundamentals of Criminal Justice Research* (Lexington, Mass.: Heath, 1977), pp. 43–45. Clark points out, as does Blalock, that large samples may not constitute quality research even if they give statistically significant results.

office, the world is presented in a neat textbook format, or in the careful charts and tables of a two-dimensional report. But the real world is not a tidy place. People live in an "ordered society" (based upon routine and habit) that borders on dysfunction. It is one thing to develop a remarkable project conceptually; it is quite another to put it into practice.[30]

As social scientists, we deal with other human beings. We must be aware of the limitations imposed by that fact, or we will approach our research in an unreal, idealistic manner. Putting our research into practice often requires modification for completion, since unknown factors enter into field work that were invisible until the project was started.[31] The research should be flexible enough to incorporate change when it is necessary. If the research statement is to be modified, it should retain its original intent and still aim at its original goal. If variables have to be changed to accommodate new situations, they should still relate to the research statement.

There is no rule of thumb for field work; each situation requires its own resolution.

WHY USE HYPOTHESES AND FORMAT?

The bulk of this chapter has been a presentation of how to write a good hypothesis, how to relate it to the real world, and how to look beyond it. The format was stated as trying to prove ourselves wrong by stating the null hypothesis clearly, then setting out to test it. The questions then arise, Is research limited to this style of format? Must we begin this way? Does it apply to every occasion? The answers are that this is one method, a very powerful method, but it is not the only way to do research.[32] It is certainly one of the best ways to do social research.[33]

Is it always necessary to state the null hypothesis in the form of no difference between variables? Some research cannot be stated this way; it may involve a simple expression of satisfaction or dissatisfaction, win or lose, improvement or deterioration, survival or death. Such either/or research examination should be stated as hypotheses 1 and 2, or H_1 and H_2. An explanatory note aids in setting the reader clear on what is being researched. However, if, in the course of the statistical analysis, a null-hypothesis situation arises, it ought to be stated as such and in the frame of reference to which it applies. Examples are (H_1 and counter H_2):

[30] Stanley Cohen and Laurie Taylor, "Prison Research: A Cautionary Tale," *New Society*, V. 31, no. 643, 253–55. After signing the Official Secrets Act, the researchers are in danger of becoming "subjects."

[31] Some of the problems are legal restrictions, ethics, language, mobility, sickness, the weather, conflicting events, and the like.

[32] Some current methods are ethnomethodology, neo-Marxism, game simulation, and even no-method. See also E. Webb et al., *Unobtrusive Measures; Non-Reactive Research in the Social Sciences* (Chicago: Rand McNally, 1966).

[33] John T. Roscoe, *Fundamental Research Statistics* (New York: Holt, Rinehart & Winston, 1969), pp. 144–46. We overcome the hazard of ignorance by calculated risk.

H_1 People of city X are dissatisfied with police performance.
H_2 People of city X are satisfied with police performance.
H_1 Candidate Doe will win the election for mayor.
H_2 Candidate Doe will not win the election.
H_1 There is no improvement in the county social services.
H_2 There is improvement in the county social services.
H_1 There is no relationship between arrest rates and convictions.
H_2 There is a relationship between arrest rates and convictions.

In the hypotheses above, the formal null form is avoided in order to state the gist or thrust of the research, which is a clear issue of yes or no. We are not considering the independence of the variables or the differences of the means.

The same kind of problem arises when we wish to create a ranking of issues or persons. The hypothesis simply states that there is or is not a ranking of issues. *The hypothesis should get to the point of the research*, not twist it to suit a statistical pattern.[34] The research statement should state precisely what we are interested in doing. Of course, we could state that:

H_o = There is no difference in the selection of candidates.
H_a = There is a difference in the selection of candidates.

But what we want to know is if Candidate Doe will win! And this is the point that should be stated if that is what we are seeking.

We seek to quantify our results, but we are not limited by the statistical design and the research format. This is but one method, albeit a very good one, for research methodology. There are nonreactive measures that will be discussed later—participant observation and case-study methods that add credibility to survey research. Also, some social scientists oppose the use of any method, claiming that methods inhibit inquiry. They feel that the most important point of research is the examination of research itself. Another method, already referred to, is the statement of objectives rather than hypotheses.

The purpose of the hypothesis is really implicit in its translation. The word, which comes from the Greek, means "a sub-statement" (hypo-thesis), or an underlying proposition (to theory). The hypothesis is the basis for the model, and the model is the road map for our research.[35] The hypothesis enables us to push further into uncharted knowledge.

We make an assertion based upon differences that we have observed, or some evidence that we wish to challenge; or even to hazard an opinion upon some future event. Then, by nullifying that statement, we establish a null hypothesis for statistical testing. In view of the fact that the physical sciences began this way, and

[34] Eugene E. Levitt, *Clinical Research Design and Analysis* (Springfield, Ill.: Charles C Thomas, 1961), pp. 39–43. "The primary purpose of the hypothesis is to stimulate research, not to be true or false. . . ."

[35] Hubert M. Blalock, Jr., *Causal Inferences in Non-Experimental Research* (New York: W. W. Norton & Co., Inc., 1964), p. 172. "Causal laws are working assumptions of the scientist, involving hypothetical statements. . . ."

still operationalize their hypotheses, it is clear that the social sciences have to compress several hundred years of progress to catch up.

SUMMARY

The research statement, which is a formal construction of a research proposition, states variable relationships that may be tested. The objective of research is to explore those relationships. The formal research statement becomes the research hypothesis, which is the basis for the quantitative testable null hypothesis. The research statement must describe precisely the variables in the relationship and the effect of one upon the other, developing the idea of causality expressed in the original proposition that challenged some existing phenomenon.

Whereas the research hypothesis is descriptive and predictive, the null hypothesis is not; it seeks to prove the research hypothesis incorrect.[36] The null is the testable hypothesis, the one subject to stringent statistical analysis. As the null is derived directly from the research hypothesis, it is important that the research hypothesis be written correctly. After finding a suitable topic for research and setting out the problem to be investigated, we must clearly state the variables and their relationships. The statement should be clear, pertinent, and free from ambiguity. The null hypothesis is written as soon as possible after the research statement. The variables to be used in the test are listed, defined, explained, and set out in the categories that are needed for the research. No variables may be used that are not specified in the research statement or defined in the variable list under "Variables Described." The operationalization of the variables determines the responses that will meet the definitions you have stated (or that are required for the questionnaire).

It is easy to slip into error if precision is lacking in the initial stages of hypothesis construction. The hypothesis must be feasible and within the researcher's power to complete. The variables must be translated into reality. One way to test your hypothesis is to state its reverse; if the reverse statement is not ridiculous, then examine your original carefully.

Testing implies that once the results are in, the research is complete. It is not that easy. Hypothesis testing is subject to error, and we need to be aware of the errors that can destroy the research findings. The rejection of the null hypothesis is significant, but if we reject a true finding (Type 1 error), then we report incorrectly. Further, if we take precautions to avoid a Type 1 error, we may retain a false finding—a Type 2 error, the most troublesome and the most difficult to avoid.

The statistical statement of the null is a statistical shorthand for its test criteria. The outcome of the statistical statement determines its use for decision making. Although the decision to retain or reject is based upon statistics, the final decision to use the findings for inference to the parent population should be based upon the statistical outcome *and* the substantive content of the findings. Even then, the decision is a combination of human endeavor and science.

[36] We never *prove* the research hypothesis, we *disprove* the null. We fail to prove there is no relationship. If there is no relationship, the research hypothesis cannot stand.

Examples have been given of the operationalization of variables for research design, with the variables shown as parts of a model, a visual diagram of the research hypothesis. We do not test the model; we test the null hypothesis, and upon that test, the model becomes credible or invalid. In construction of our model, we aim to get the greatest number of facts from the least number of variables, stating our ideas in simple language. Describing the variables places them in testable categories, which aids in formulation of the questions we will need for responses. Most important in the operationalization process is the thorough discussion of *all parts* of the model.

Use of the null hypothesis, although preferred, is not the only method. The null has weakness as well as strength, but at present is the best research tool we have.

We cannot arrive at the exact truth, but we can arrive at an approximate plausibility, or a reasonable explanation of the truth.

EXERCISES

1. What are the limitations on the researcher after identifying the problem? Discuss the effects of change and time on variables.
2. What is entailed in "a statement of the problem"?
3. What is the difference between the research hypothesis and the null hypothesis? Why is the null important?
4. Discuss "no difference" and "no relationship."
5. Explain why the use of the null is the most favored method.
6. What are the rules for writing a good hypothesis?
7. Why is discussion of the hypothesis important? What is "content"?
8. Why should you use only variables that are included in your hypothesis? What is the principle of "Occam's razor"?
9. Discuss alternatives to the formal hypothesis.
10. What are some errors in writing hypotheses?
11. How would you set about examining propositions concerning body typologies?
12. Where would you find the research objective? the testability of that objective? the outcome of the test?
13. We never "prove" the hypothesis; what exactly do we do?
14. Explain Type I and Type II errors. How would you control for them?
15. What is the statistical statement of the null? What are its parts?
16. What is the 0.05 level of significance? Why 0.05?
17. What is substantive significance? Which is the more important, statistical or substantive significance?
18. What is the difference between propositions, hypotheses, theories, and laws? Are there such absolutes as laws?

19. Discuss the selection of operational variables in the idea, "Most drugs should be decriminalized." Make a practical H_a and H_o, and select variables.
20. Make a simple model based upon your hypothesis in exercise 19.
21. If your findings were "nonsignificant," what would this mean?
22. Discuss the limits on testing your hypothesis. How would you exercise parsimony? economy? control for Type 1 and Type 2 errors?
23. Describe your variables for testing the H_a, "There is a relationship between age and attempts to escape from prison."
24. With a team of four, how would you set about making your research project practical?
25. Suppose that in your research on escape, you discover during field work that other variables contribute to escape. What would you do?
26. Describe some major obstacles in research.
27. Comment on the differences between concept and practice.
28. Define *spurious, extraneous, independent variable, inferential.*
29. What is meant by "As we correct for a Type 1 error, we move closer to a Type 2 error"?
30. What are the advantages of using the null hypothesis? What are some weaknesses of the null?

FOR FURTHER READING

Babbie, Earl R., *The Practice of Social Research*, Chaps. 3, 4. Belmont, Calif.: Wadsworth, 1975.

Barzun, Jacques, and Henry F. Graff, *The Modern Researcher*, Chaps. 5, 7. New York: Harcourt Brace Jovanovich, 1970.

Bachrach, Arthur J., *Psychological Research*, Chaps. 3, 4. New York: Random House, 1966.

Festinger, L., and D. Katz, eds., *Research Methods in the Behavioral Sciences.* New York: Holt, Rinehart & Winston, 1966.

Paradis, A. A., *The Research Handbook*. Chicago: Funk & Wagnalls, 1974.

Rosenberg, Morris, *The Logic of Survey Analysis*. New York: Basic Books, 1968.

Roscoe, John T., *Fundamental Research Statistics*, Chaps. 15, 16. New York: Holt, Rinehart & Winston, 1969.

Ross, R., *Research: An Introduction*. New York: Barnes & Noble, 1974.

Smith, H. W., *Strategies of Social Research*, Part II. Englewood Cliffs, N.J.: Prentice-Hall, 1975.

Steele, H. C., *How to Motivate and Direct Students in Science Research.* Huntsville, Ala.: Strode, 1970.

Tamur, Judith, et al., eds., *Statistics: A Guide to the Unknown*. San Francisco: Holden-Day, 1972.

Thorwald, J., *Crime and Science*. New York: Harcourt Brace Jovanovich, 1967.

5

Other Methods, Triangulation, and Validity

METHODS AND VALIDITY

The previous chapters may lead the reader to assume that the survey method of research is the only one that need be used. The survey method is very good, but it becomes even more sophisticated when used in combination with other methods. Not only can we quantify and control for sampling error, but we can also maintain control of the quality of the data and can process it in a logical and statistical sequence. *The use of other methods, such as nonreactive methods, acts as a check on reactive methods.*[1] Survey methods, excellent as they may be, are best examined in the light of the way they are obtained. They are basically statistical computations, taken from a complex social situation without consideration of *all* the many dynamic factors that may bear on them.

The use of other methods aids in the control of error caused by factors affecting internal and external validity. *Internal validity is dependent upon the correctness and accuracy appropriate to the research design and the measuring instrument.* If the differences that one seeks to measure can be explained away by inaccuracies in the design or measurement, then internal validity is lacking. The use of other methods can assist in correction of this serious error.

[1] Eugene Webb et al., *Unobtrusive Measures: Non-Reactive Research in the Social Sciences* (Skokie, Ill.: Rand McNally, 1966), Chap. 1, "Approximations to Knowledge."

In other words, if we reject the null hypothesis because of faults in our design or instrument, then we have committed a Type 1 error (rejection of a true hypothesis) because we lacked internal validity. No matter how much we tighten our level of significance, we will continue to commit this error until we correct for or establish internal validity. We can best correct this situation by using other methods in addition to survey research: case study, participant observation, examination of physical evidence, investigation of sources, a check on language differences, redesign, pretest, and further discussion and elaboration of the aims and purpose of the research.

External validity is dependent upon factors affecting the inference made from the sample to the parent population. If the differences or relationships measured in the sample cannot be inferentially applied to the parent population, then external validity is lacking. If we reject the null, assume a relationship exists because of faults in the sampling method, and apply it to our parent population, we have committed a Type 1 error because of lack of external validity. External validity can be corrected for by randomization and representation in the sampling procedure.

Many factors affect project validity.[2] People change, they become "survey-saturated," surveys sometimes create artificial situations, and often the interviewer interjects his or her own bias in selection and testing of the sample.

Errors caused by internal and external validity (see *Table 5.1*) affect the interpretation of the results based upon the sample. For example, suppose we were dealing with a group of inmates who had been the subject of many tests. If our research failed to account for the fact that our respondents (1) were test-saturated; (2) were not representative of a larger world of inmates; or (3) were preoccupied with other matters of importance, like survival, parole, escape, riots, punishment, food, visits, and so on (extraneous variables)[3]—then our results would suffer from internal-validity defects. If we also had (1) a small sample size, not randomized; (2) a biased selection of that sample; or (3) distrust of a previous testing situation—then our results would also show defects, these due to lack of controls for external validity. The results obtained from the sample would only reflect conditions in the sample and not be applicable to the larger parent population from which the sample was taken. If we did make inferences, the chances are that serious errors would be made, almost certainly because our findings were due to error that could be explained by lack of proper controls. The relationships (if any) that were reported would be by chance and not due to the effect of the independent variable upon the dependent variable.

Although external and internal validity have usually been applied to experimental design, that type of design is now part of a wider setting. Formerly, experimental design was conceived as taking place in a laboratory under controlled conditions.

[2] Donald T. Campbell and Julian C. Stanley, *Experimental and Quasi-Experimental Designs for Research* (Skokie, Ill.: Rand McNally, 1963).

[3] John W. Best, *Research in Education* (Englewood Cliffs, N.J.: Prentice-Hall, 1977), pp. 95–108.

Table 5.1. Control of Internal and External Validity

	Decision made			
	Reject null hypothesis		*Retain null hypothesis*	
Possible error	Type 1	Type 1	Type 2	Type 2
Possible outcome	True	True	False	False
Actual error	Internal	External	Internal	External
Findings stated	Relationship	Relationship	No relationship	No relationship
Actual facts	Only in sample	Only in sample	Only in sample	Only in sample
Evaluation	Incorrect	Incorrect	Incorrect	Incorrect
Due to:	Faulty design Faulty instrument Stimulation Maturation Saturation	Sampling error Representation Treatment effect Subjectivity Bias/Prejudice	Design Questions Effects Change Repetition	Sample Selection Testing Carryover Ecological fallacy
Definition	Differences reported or not observed are due to design or instrument error = Errors due to internal validity		Differences reported or not observed are due to sampling procedure = Errors due to external validity	
Prevention of error	Correct design, careful construction of instrument, proper statistical level of significance, avoidance of overtesting, check for change and stimulation		Randomization, representation, large sample size, avoidance of interviewer effect, pretest, use of substantive and statistical significance	
Caution:	Control for Type 1 and Type 2 errors as well as for internal and external validity. Control for all errors at the same time. Use other methods (triangulation) for control of internal validity, more than one large random/representative sample for control of external validity. Use the correct statistical analysis.			

The ultimate aim of such research was its application to the outside world. Experimental design has now come to include research in the classroom, the institution, and virtually any closed setting that can be seen as situational or in which the variables may be controlled.

However, the use of other methods, employing triangulation, lends itself to the correction of errors caused by faults in internal design and defects in instrumentation.[4] Triangulation is a control on the quality of validity. The use of other methods, which also implies the use of controls to ensure validity, is particularly applicable for survey research, since it enhances the credibility of the findings.

The research progression is a constant awareness of error and of means to limit and control that error, in order to produce as exact a finding as is humanly possible.

NONREACTIVE MEASURES

Survey research is one of the most important quantitative tools we have. However, the method has built-in error, in that it is a *reactive* type of research.[5] Some errors, such as hypothesis error and sampling error, have been touched on; others, such as instrument error and interview error, are discussed in other chapters.

Because the survey method is reactive—that is, demands reaction from the respondent—it is prone to many inaccuracies. It is *obtrusive*; it seeks a personal response, often by direct confrontation. Because it is widely used, it becomes subject to the abuse of *familiarity*. Because it is administered by people to people, it is subject to *bias, prejudice, and set*. The continual use of surveys has made them subject to *manipulation* by clients.

The use of surveys under certain circumstances becomes highly questionable. For example, in a survey on weight loss and diet control, the clients may very well show what is expected, especially if they are paid for the survey. In any case, the survey will probably be invalidated a few months later when the situation returns to normal, or to noncontrol. A similar situation can occur when we tell people that on a second survey or posttest, we expect an improvement. We tend to create a self-fulfilling prophecy; test results will indeed improve, not only because of respondents' expectations, but also from their practice at taking the test.

The serious business of obtaining valid data is also affected by "survey saturation." Some major accessible areas have been literally overworked by pollsters. Most surveys look alike even if the contents are different; thus, respondents tend to assume that the same questions are going to be asked again, and they become tired of "doing the same thing."

A further limitation on survey methods is the assumption of population stability. Not only do people move from one place to another, but the composition of the

[4] H. W. Smith, *Strategies of Social Research* (Englewood Cliffs, N.J.: Prentice-Hall, 1975), pp. 271–76.

[5] Earl R. Babbie, *Survey Research Methods* (Belmont, Calif.: Wadsworth, 1973), pp. 50–52, "Is Survey Research Really Scientific?"

population changes in terms of age, race, sex, education, religion, and political preference. If these changes are not observed, it will be wrongly assumed that sample inferences apply for an unlimited period to an unchanging population.

If we use only one method of measurement, we tend to limit our view of the phenomena we are examining.[6] If there are errors in the reactive research, we should use nonreactive methods to correct and control our research product. Any method that does not confront or personally interact with the client is nonreactive. Some methods, such as case study and participant observation, use both reactive and nonreactive measures.

Nonreactive measures are *contrived* or *hidden observations*, in which the person is unaware that he is being observed; *participant observations*, of which there *is* awareness; the *searching of records* and archives; the *examination of physical evidence; the systematic checking of items or events; simulations; examination of audiovisual tapes and films; impersonal key response; secondary analysis*; and *systems analysis*. These ten nonreactive or unobtrusive measures cover a variety of ways to support and extend the research method. In combination with survey research, they add validity, credibility, and corroboration. Much that is qualitative is omitted in survey data, and the use of other methods gives depth to the research. The only rules for combination are these:

1. The methods should be linked (either causally or structurally).
2. They should enlarge and substantiate the inquiry.
3. Limitations and errors should be subject to control.

Observation

When a researcher becomes part of the local scene, a native, and is not known to be an observer, the observations are *contrived*. If, for example, the observer wished to study hospital reaction and posed as a staff member, or prison reaction and posed as an inmate, the observations would be contrived.

In *participant* observation, the observer, although part of the local scene, is usually identified and known. The results are somewhat biased and lack control because of the nature of qualitative observation. Such observations are useful for making strategic decisions for field work, for checking sample availability and representation, and for checking responses to survey data. The validity of such studies depends entirely upon the factuality of the observations and supporting logic. Several important studies have been made of street gangs, police corruption, Mafiosos, and other subcultures that are hard to locate and use for survey research.

Hidden observations are somewhat simpler. They take place behind two-way mirrors, through peepholes or keyholes, or any other place in which the observer is hidden from view. The ethics of such methods leave a lot to be desired.[7] How-

[6] Webb et al., *Unobtrusive Measures*, p. 34.

[7] Filming people without their consent raises a critical ethical issue, as does tape-recording. There are legal restrictions on these "invasions of privacy."

ever, psychologists and educators claim that they do produce valuable data. "Candid Camera" uses this type of observation for TV entertainment.

Hidden observations are subject to a peculiar type of error. Most of us live two lives, a public and a private one. Thus, behavior that is presumed to be observed may in fact be secret or nonsocial behavior (nonsocial meaning not in society; not meaning asocial). For example, if we observe a group of children from behind two-way mirrors and make notes on the "learning process," that is not the same learning process as when the relationship is adult-to-child; what we see is child-to-child. Similarly, in making hidden observations in society, we are observing behavior between ingroups rather than between the group and a stranger (the observer) or outsider. The error lies in the fact that as adults in the one case or as outsiders in the other, we will impose our own thinking or stereotypes on what we see or think we see going on. The reality between the children or the ingroups may in fact be totally different from what we perceive. Our perceptions will be based on our own level of experience rather than that of the observed group. It is clear that we should record only what is fact and avoid conclusions on such data.

Hidden observations—and even *simple observations*, where the observer is present—are fraught with misinterpretation; cultural customs, mannerisms, and language are all subject to change and shift in interpretation over time. Personal observations for operationally defined situations can be objective, but without definition, such observations become opinion and value judgment.

Searching the Records and Archives

As a means of research, this is really a form of secondary analysis, in that it is an ex post facto review of former or prior research. Often it involves a review of previous data and a search of the literature on a particular topic. In nonreactive research, this method may be:

1. A search of records and archives, documents and journals, for new material on a particular issue.[8]
2. A search for the frequency of certain specific items, publications, occurrences of events, behavioral responses, or attitudinal patterns.
3. A search for previous research in a specified area.
4. A search of ancient material (archival search) for the purpose of learning what is *not* recorded rather than what is—and why it was omitted from the record. (The omission or deletion may have been ordered.)
5. A search of the current record—such as Uniform Crime Reports and federal statistics—to investigate contemporary styles and trends.
6. A search of journals, diaries, business records, old newspapers, sales catalogs, examination results, and the like for episodic events, much like historical search. A search of old police files, "Wanted" posters, training manuals, and court and county files can reveal how the criminal justice system used to operate.

[8] This should include microforms.

Examination of Physical Evidence

Examination can reveal what are known as trace measures, or wear and tear, the accretion or erosion of time. Comments have been made on the wearing of office stairs, the wear on books that are continually checked out at libraries, the number of Bibles stolen from motels, and so on. A famous trace measure was the toe of the statue of St. Peter in Westminster Abbey; the toe had been literally kissed smooth by the faithful as they entered the abbey. Other trace measures are the number of potholes in certain roads in Pennsylvania and New York, ads cut out of magazines in waiting rooms, graffiti on the walls of restrooms, garbage at rock concerts, the number of Christmas cards received, and the number of beer cans scattered along the beaches. Accretion can be measured by the growth of art collections, libraries, unique collections of memorabilia, music collections, the explosion in the paperback industry, the increase in the demand for higher education, the rapid increase in crime.

Physical evidence is not limited by trace or accretion; it is the observation of hard physical facts.[9] We can observe and measure weight, height, age, body type, head size, body temperature, the number of tattoos on a person, the length of hair, the size of the feet, deformities, and abnormalities. We may also observe the physical phenomena of left- and right-handedness, eye movement, body language, and physical gesture. Physical evidence also encompasses fingerprints, footprints, body wounds, types of weapons used in crimes, crime-scene evidence, crime-preparation evidence, and abandoned vehicles. It also involves physical groupings, measurement of game strategies, social distance—in fact, physical evidence involves anything measurable that can be touched, tasted, smelled, seen, or heard, has time duration and impact, and occupies space. Such physical measurement is *hard data*, and hard data that support our research findings are always worth introducing into the research presentation. Often physical evidence is overlooked because it is taken for granted, too immediately obvious, and assumed to be known to everyone. But someone has to make the statement of the obvious. Physical evidence is rather like Mount Everest—it needs to be surmounted because it is there. It is a matter of observing, using the research imagination, and putting it all together.

Systematic Checking of Items or Events

This is, in effect, the making of the current record. It is the nonreactive, unobtrusive measure of what is happening, the simple counting of things as they occur. It could be the number of people in a bar or at a football game, the frequency of male visits to houses of ill-repute, the number of first-offender appearances in court, the

[9] Jacques Barzun and Henry F. Graff, *The Modern Researcher* (New York: Harcourt Brace Jovanovich, 1970), pp. 146–47. The authors divide physical evidence into "verbal" and "mute." Verbal evidence carries writing or inscription.

number of offenders on death row, the frequency with which a patrol car visits a high-crime area, the number of porno establishments in a given location, the different sentences handed down by judges for the same offense, the ratio of guards to inmates in a county jail, or the number of inmates who report sick and their complaints. Contrasting facts make interesting comparisons.[10]

Systematic checking may take time if the events occur over a considerable period. On the other hand, some events can be counted spontaneously. It is a matter of choice.

Simulations

Simulations can be made three ways: with people, with computers, and with a combination of both. In a simulated situation, the observer is usually standing to one side, watching the reaction. Some simulations produce definite reactive effects, but they are caused by the situation and not the observer. Zimbardo's prison simulation and Milgram's behavioral study of obedience were people simulations. On the other hand, the limits-of-growth studies were computer simulations of what would happen to society if resources were used up.[11]

The danger in people simulations is the problem of ethics: Can we use people for experiments? How far can we go in extending the frontiers of human knowledge? Should we attempt to duplicate conditions of real life even though they represent the worst in human nature? Obviously, if we want to study lying, cheating, stealing, sadism, cruelty, and cowardice, we are taking ethical risks. The researcher has to resolve the conflict between his own conscience and the possible benefits to humanity of such a study. All scientific progress involves some risk, and some studies involve more risk than others. To understand such problems demands the courage of one's convictions, a willingness to take personal risk, and an ability to face caustic criticism from colleagues. Certain experiments cannot be simulated because they are irreversible. But as long as simulation with people is reversible, the ethics of the situation appear to resolve in favor of the researcher, provided of course that the clients know the nature and consequences of the experiment and participation is voluntary.

Game simulation is fraught with error, since the study usually degenerates into a game. The tendency is to encourage the "monopoly syndrome," wherein the cleverest game player will try to take all. Game playing is in effect the imposition of our rules (societal rules as game rules) on what we think takes place in someone else's situation. Another defect of game simulation is the fact that it *is* a game, and

[10] It is easy, for example, to find the number of *subscriptions* to a publication, but one might ignore the number of *submissions* to the same publication. The latter often exceeds the former, which makes a very interesting observation.

[11] Phillip Zimbardo, "Pathology of Imprisonment," *Society*, Vol. 9 (April 1972); Stanley Milgram, "The Behavioral Study of Obedience," *Journal of Abnormal and Social Psychology*, 67, no. 4 (1963), 371–78; and Donella H. Meadows, *Limits to Growth* (New York: Universe Books, 1972).

the results can be repeated. In real-life situations, many results are final, irreversible, and perhaps terminal to the "players." No two life situations are ever exactly alike, even though they may appear similar. Shakespeare said, "All the world's a stage, and all the men and women merely players," but the fact is that life is neither a repeat performance nor a game. Game theories are limited by the three restrictions already cited: They tend to become games, they impose our rules on other people's situations, and they are repeatable. Games and simulations are strictly ordered by (1) input, (2) rules, and (3) the number of players. The input is further circumscribed by situational circumstances.

Games are approximations of real-life social situations.[12] In restricting the social situation to game size, we exclude many variables so that the game or simulation is manageable for two or more players. For instance, in Zimbardo's prison simulation in Stanford, California, time itself, an essential element of incarceration, was severely curtailed in order to complete the experiment. Also, the simulated conditions did not permit the development of an administrative culture and an inmate subculture, both of which affect role reaction. Third, since the conditions were determined by the researchers and applied specifically to the experiment, they only loosely approximated real prison conditions. Conclusions drawn from the experiment, however dramatic, apply to the experimental sample; caution must be exercised in making inferences to a wider general prison situation.

However, simulation can be quite useful. It is an exercise in hypothetical research, seeking to reach beyond the researcher into a future world, for possible solutions to social problems that may occur or alternative solutions to problems that have already occurred.[13] Simulation tests probable hypotheses in possible situations under defined game rules. Such tests are useful for setting up strategic forces for riot control, deciding on the tactical use of patrol cars, examining the efficiency of police administrative operations, and detecting flaws in operational procedure. Simulation is an aid to decision making in that it presents alternatives.

Computer simulations permit the manipulation of vast numbers of variables to simulate the observer's view of the research problem. Again, however, computer simulation telescopes time, and time is the very essence of many social situations, determining the effect of future variables that may be left out of the computer equation. We have a very limited ability in predicting future events, but the computer has none at all, only the formula we feed into it. Thus, the simulation on the computer is at best hypothetical, mathematical conjecture, educated estimation that is most likely subject to a wide degree of variation. The computer may be right purely by accident, and its calculations may coincide purely by chance, in that if we are using probability at the 0.05 level, it could be "correct" at least 5 percent of the time.

[12] See Smith, *Strategies of Social Research*, Chap. 11, "Simulation and Gaming."

[13] Richard E. Barton, *A Primer on Simulation and Gaming* (Englewood Cliffs, N.J.: Prentice-Hall, 1970), pp. 1–9. Barton writes, ". . . what is simulated may never come into being." Simulation is used for trying out designs before actual production.

Forecasting by computer[14] or simulation depends upon:

1. Stability of events, situations, and environment and implied consistency of data
2. Assumptions used being verified and logical
3. Data that are accurate and that fit the assumptions used for forecasting
4. Possible verification by replication (or near replication)
5. Extraneous variables (and effects) being identified
6. Time and future referents included as variables
7. Control for personal error

To be scientific, prediction must, as a minimum, conform to these rules. It is exceedingly difficult to make our model fit those assumptions.

The modern complexities of many simulated games grew out of two concepts:

1. *Zero-sum* games are those in which someone loses and someone wins. The games are competitive. War games are basically zero-sum. Chess, the most famous of war games, is the oldest board game and, incidentally, represents advanced computer technology. Newer board games are Battleships, simulating naval strategy, and Star Wars, simulating spaceship maneuvers. Most sports eventually boil down to a zero-sum game.

2. *Non-zero-sum* games are those in which the players are partly competitive, partly cooperative. There are no set winners or losers, and outcomes are unpredictable. The most famous of these is Prisoner's Dilemma. Two offenders are locked in separate rooms and informed of their Miranda rights. The possible outcomes, shown in *Table 5.2*, are predicted on the consequences of the crime and freedom for turning state's evidence. The game indicates that there is no way of knowing the final outcome for the "suspects"—it depends on their own rationale for confessing or remaining silent, and the external pressures forced upon them. Note that the

Table 5.2. The Prisoner's Dilemma

		Suspect 1	
		"Cops out"	Remains silent
Suspect 2	"Cops out"	Both get 5 yrs.	1 gets 10 yrs. 2 gets immunity
	Remains silent	1 goes free 2 gets 10 yrs.	Both get 2 yrs. (charges reduced)

Source: Attributed to A. W. Tucker

[14] Rein Turn, *Computers in the 1980s* (New York: Columbia University Press, 1974), pp. 18–43, "Forecasting Methodology." The author identifies two models, exploratory (present to the future) and normative (future back to the present).

game is still an approximation of real life: It does not take into account alternative sentencing procedures, leniency or tyranny of the judge, corrupt law practice, plea bargaining, illness, escape, postponement, or external intervention.

Non-zero-sum games infer that winners may be losers and losers may be winners. A real-life situation involving many people can hardly be represented in a game. As the number of people is increased, the number of possible outcomes becomes astronomical. If there are ten variables to one person, the permutations are already $n! = 3{,}638{,}800$; for ten people with ten variables each, the number goes clear off the paper. Of course, selective combinations may be used, but even then, the numbers run into the millions and we haven't begun to quantify. Computer simulation is limited by the information fed into it.

To achieve any real research value:

1. Simulation must closely approximate a real-life situation, in that it will resemble and be identified with the *variable* named.
2. Computer *programs* must be representations of real life. Often, a great deal of time is spent on programming that is indefinite, contains many "bugs," and yields only simple results. Limits must be defined.
3. Time spent on simulation should not exceed the input. All too often, simulators become obsessed with the game, and it begins to absorb inordinate amounts of time and energy that could be better utilized observing the real thing.
4. The structuring of progams should not become the construction of a closed system, thus leaving little room for unstructured social behavior, as in Prisoner's Dilemma.
5. Interpretation of data must include interpolation of qualitative results, since computers only make decisions on quantitative data. And in translating data results, or translating quantitative results into qualitative ideas, even more care is needed.

Examination of Tapes, Films, and Photographs

This is a valuable tool of the researcher. Tapes can be played back at leisure; audio tapes can be edited and transcribed; photos may be enlarged, examined carefully, and documented. In examination of recorded conversations, a voice-stress analyzer could be used to indicate the validity of the comments made, although stress analyzers, like lie detectors, are much overrated, since stress is produced under a variety of circumstances, not just lying.

Examination of tapes is a way of rating various behavioral responses. A great deal of information may be gained by taping or filming events and then reviewing the product later. One is not under pressure and can calmly and objectively observe the research data. The tape is a permanent record, and TV or A/V tapes are virtually a total record. The instant playback provides another very useful device for correction of error.

Impersonal Key Response

This method is used when there is no personal confrontation, either by sight or by voice, between the observer and the client. Key-response devices are used for selected respondents to rate TV programs directly to program raters, for checking on ESP responses, and for keeping clients unknown to each other.[15] The key is like a small calculator hooked up to a telephone line; there is no contact other than electrical impulse.

Secondary Analysis

As the name implies, secondary analysis is the going over of prior research analysis. The purpose is to either prove or disprove that research, or discover evidence that has been overlooked. Unlike a review of the literature, secondary analysis is the examination of data. Fortunately, most research is now reproduced on microforms and carefully indexed. One index, the NCCD microform index, is set up by subject, author, geographic area, and category. A great deal of time and effort is saved by using microfiche. Microforms also have vast quantities of research not generally found in the library itself.

Systems Analysis

This is the investigation of the relationship of the research project to the social system in which it belongs, and also the investigation of subsystems within the project. An investigation into the operation of probation would see probation as a subsystem of the criminal justice system of arrest/appearance/trial/sentence/disposition. Within the system of probation itself is sentence/community alternative/supervision/placement/rehabilitation. Such an examination of relevance is observational rather than reactive in the survey sense.

Systems are related to simulation, since simulation techniques attempt to represent social systems. The advantages are that the researcher sees the macro and micro, the overview and the focus of what is happening. Systems analysis extends the observer's range, in that it shows both external and internal factors in the causal chain of events.

Table 5.3 tabulates this and the other nonreactive research methods described in this section.

[15] Also used by consumer-market product raters to test the impact of TV commercials and product appeal.

Table 5.3. Nonreactive, Unobtrusive Research Methods

Method	Type	Purpose
Observation Case study*	Personal Contrived Hidden	Participant observation Deceptive observation Secret observation
Search of records	Archives Journals Microforms Documents	Investigation of past for new material, specific items, trends, historical perspective, patterns, and omissions
Physical evidence	Trace Accretion Phenomena Hard evidence	Data on wear and tear The collection of items or events through time Record of people's physical characteristics, geographical data, and obvious facts Criminalistic or scientific recording of discovered physical data
Checking of events	Counting	Keeping the current record of people, occurrences, items
Simulation	Social Games Computer	Using people to stimulate a social event or pattern; making an operational model with humans Using rules, techniques to approximate social conditions Using a program to permit rapid prediction of an estimated social model; occasionally combines people, games, and computers
Media examination	Films TV or A/V tapes Audiotapes Photographs	Examination of the audio or visual record without pressure of the actual situation
Impersonal key response	Rating	Rating of issues without the presence of the observer
Secondary analysis	(Microforms)	Reexamination of prior research
Systems analysis	Any of the above	Overview and focus of research project; study of external and internal systems and of subsystems

*Without interview.

TRIANGULATION—PRECISION IN USE OF RESEARCH METHODS

Triangulation is a navigational concept. In aeronautics, the idea is to get three lines bearing upon each other so that the location of the craft is pinpointed. (See *Figure*

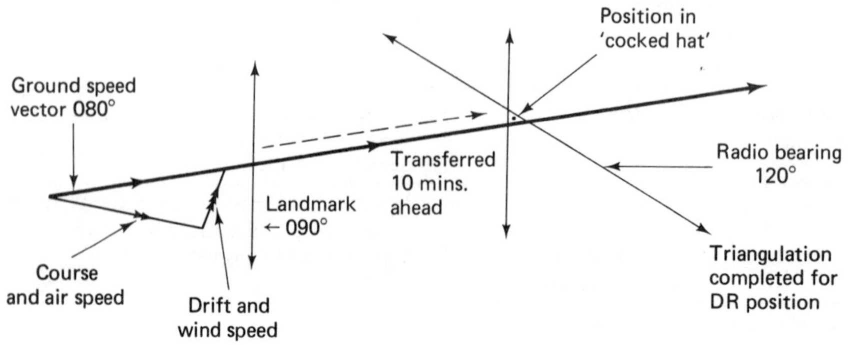

Fig. 5-1 Navigational triangulation

5-1.) Usually, the ground speed is a known vector from wind or wave drift; then, a bearing is taken on a known landmark, and finally a radio or astro bearing is used to complete the "cocked hat." During the navigational process, each bearing is moved ahead in time. The process is called dead-reckoning or DR navigation.

Navigational triangulation is based upon the assumptions:

1. That no single measurement is accurate of itself
2. That during the measurement process, position has changed, owing to travel speed and time elapsed
3. That the final bearing is still an approximation but the estimated location of the craft is more certain than by use of a single method, since it is somewhere within the triangulated area

For research methodology, the assumptions for triangulation are:

1. That no single method is precise
2. That the measurement process involves a shift over time in scoring that reflects social change
3. That the hypothesis is substantiated when tested under more than one theory, more than one scoring method, and more than one sample

The use of other methods in triangulation improves the research and acts as a control on the survey validity.

Internal validity can best be taken care of by using more than one method for scoring, or more than one test for the same variable, or by using tests to determine variable validity and honesty of response–pretest, test, and retest. For example, in a measurement of stress (anxiety), one scale used could be based on the mental concept of anxiety, and another on the physical manifestations of anxiety; the client could be asked for a self-rating on a stress line from zero (no stress) to 9 (extreme stress); also, the client could be rated by the observer, using a stress scale based upon observed anxiety reactions. The measure of stress is then validated by alternate responses to the same variable.

Internal validity is also achieved by back-translation[16] and by making every effort to overcome language problems. To ignore language problems is a major error; in fact, all research should state specifically if it is in the language (or dialect) known to the client. The classic case is that of Chicano and black children's being classified as retarded because they could not comprehend the language used in IQ tests. Pretesting would have revealed this problem.

The researcher looks *inside* the research design to correct deficiencies and uses clues developed from other methods to improve the design. A good research design usually involves a comparison group (sample) and a neutral group composed of people from the other two groups. In an ideal study of crime patterns in two cities, City A and City B, triangulation would be effective in the design (see *Figure 5-2*). If

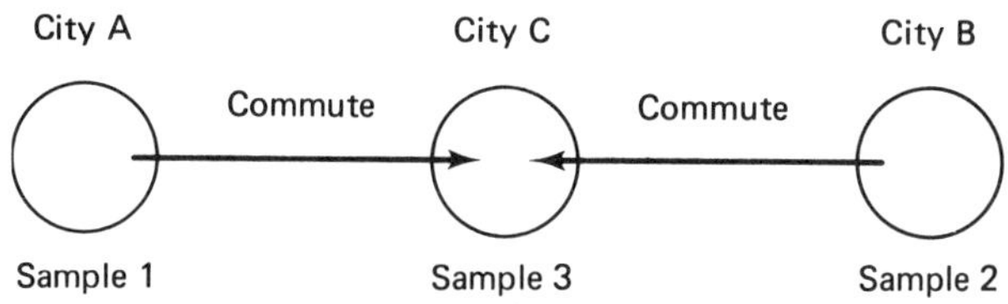

Fig. 5-2 Using triangulation in a study of comparative crime patterns

the sample from City C contained equal numbers of commuters from Cities A and B, we would have an almost perfect design. We could then determine through the design any defects that occur within it. We could determine if crime-pattern differences were consistent or existed only because of the defect in design. One serious defect in such a design, a single-test cross-sectional survey, is corrected by using more than one test location. We are now in a position to compare locations, and also to determine the importance of residence as a variable, which we could not do with only one sample. Not only has internal design been improved, but the increase in the number of samples, in sample size, and in representation has improved *external validity*. As a rule of thumb, internal validity depends upon the control of variables in the design used to get data; external validity depends upon control of the sample and sampling procedure. (See *Table 5.4*.)

If we ask, "What variables should we use to get our data, and how can we include them?" the chances are that the design will reflect improvement. Using other methods will aid in getting the answers we need. Testing in more than one area may be complemented by testing over more than one time period. Do not forget to ensure that all samples taken are representative of the parent population. The survey gains further if there are several investigators, or if team research is used. Finally, use more than one method of analysis.

[16] Richard Brislin, "Back Translation for Cross-Cultural Research," Ph.D. dissertation, Pennsylvania State University, 1969.

Table 5.4. The Use of Triangulation for Research Validation

Validity	Method
Internal validity	Select variables that can be included by categories and are applicable to the research. Use pretest, test, and retest.
Variable	Use more than one method to score, such as question format, scale, self-rating, client rating, Likert-type response, ranking, physical manifestations, hard-evidence measures.
	Use back-translation–check the comprehension of the questions, the time of response, the method of response.
External validity	More than one sample More than one location More than one time
Sample	Use comparative samples. Use cohort or panel studies. Use survey, telephone survey as well as interviews. Use random methods, but do not be bound by them; make sure the sample represents the parent population.
Interviews	Use interview teams.
Analysis validity	Use more than one level–but be sure to use appropriate analysis to fit the assumptions of that method. Analyze carefully the significance levels, both the statistical significance and the qualitative substantive significance.
Model and hypothesis	Substantiate the model and the hypothesis by looking for alternative explanations or suggesting other forms of research. Use other theories to prove or disprove your hypothesis.
Report	Keep your report to the point. Research that is backed up by more than one method has more logical validity (and substance) than one that uses only one method.

Triangulation of methods, data, and interviewers adds to research validity. It is, in effect, an averaging process of getting us to the most probable position. We might hit the right conclusion on our research the first time with a single cross-sectional study, but triangulation verifies our position with alternative data, acting as a check on chance occurrence, coincidence, and fortuitous circumstances.[17] We also attempt to locate our research in time and space, thereby giving it a more secure frame of

[17] Earl R. Babbie, *The Practice of Social Research* (Belmont, Calif.: Wadsworth, 1975), pp. 283–94, "Other Modes of Observation."

reference. Journalism demands answers to the questions, who? what? when? where? and how?; we cannot settle for less in the scientific world.

The aim of research is to control error (we cannot eliminate it) and arrive as close to the truth as possible. Any method, any evidence, any ethical means that will aid us should be used.

THE USES OF OTHER METHODS FOR PROBLEM SOLVING

To the beginner, research has more meaning if it is shown to accomplish something. And it does have distinctly practical uses aside from the search for knowledge for its own sake. Here are a few examples of what research can be used for.

The serious problems in criminology and criminal justice are so complex that the researcher should focus upon a particular part rather than the entire field. Maxwell Atkinson concentrated upon suicide research rather than the sociology of deviance. Following his attempts to scan some 6,300 works on suicide (there are probably over 7,000 now), he was forced to narrow his interest to coroners and the categorization of deaths as suicides.[18] He also discovered that someone else (Jack Douglas) had already researched a problem he was interested in.[19] Dr. Atkinson used survey research, participant observation at the coroner's office, case study, and review of the literature and existing records. Each part of his research caused changes that he had not previously anticipated. For example, he had been unaware that his survey had to be approved by the Coroner's Society (the work was done in England), and during the resulting delay, he collected qualitative data that changed the course of the research. His research was "subject to competing perspectives"; the methods he was using demanded that choices be made.

The quantity of data, the selectivity within methods, and the imposition of time, circumstance, and money all place demands on the researcher. We must make decisions to complete the project, to remain within focus of the original objective, and to settle for the best available compromise. To be too rigid or too idealistic in the matter of field work may mean that the project is never completed. We never get *all* the available data, we are never satisfied with the methodological or analytical outcomes, and we never seem to have enough time. In dealing with social problems, we do the best we can under very difficult circumstances. Dr. Atkinson's journey appears typical of the problems we face.

Even when we are given vast amounts of data prepared by others, the analysis into a problem-solving strategy is still ponderous. The National Advisory Commission on Criminal Justice Standards and Goals was requested to devise a strategy to reduce crime. The body of statistics the commission used was the 1971 Uniform

[18] J. M. Atkinson, "Suicide and the Social Organization of Sudden Death," Ph.D. dissertation, University of Essex, England, 1977 (London: Collier Macmillan, 1979).

[19] J. D. Douglas, *The Social Meanings of Suicide* (Princeton, N.J.: Princeton University Press, 1967).

Crime Reports. The objective was a 50 percent cut in the rate of "high-fear" crimes by 1983 and in five other crimes (homicide, forcible rape, aggravated assault, robbery, and burglary) by 25 percent. Trends in crime rates were analyzed from 1960 to 1971. A simple "eyeballing" of the UCRs will show that crime rose faster during that period than the population increase. For example, homicides almost doubled—from 9,030 to 17,630. If the population had kept pace with the homicide rate, by 1972 the U.S. population would have been 364 million.

By analyzing the UCR tables, the commission noted that violent crime:

1. Occurs in the cities
2. Is committed by males
3. Is concentrated in the 15–24 age bracket
4. Is committed by the poor and unemployed
5. Stems from the black ghetto slums
6. Is committed by people who are like their victims
7. Is usually committed by repeaters

The objectives based upon this analysis were:

1. Reduce juvenile crime by the use of diversionary programs, (a) removing status cases (truancy, etc.) from the courts, and (b) diverting nonstatus cases from institutions.
2. Improve social services for the poor and unemployed by developing career education programs.
3. Reduce delays in the criminal justice system—speed up the court process.
4. Increase citizen participation to prevent crime.[20]

The methods used by the commission were analysis of the record; discussion of the issues with experts, as in the Delphi technique;[21] and experience based on prior participant observation. The drop in 1976 from the peak of 1975 may well indicate some accuracy in the forecast.

If the forecast of the NACCJSG fails, it may well be due to its lack of theoretical underpinning. The issue of crime prevention is an area of research in itself. One content analysis of the theory on crime prevention has been done by Lamar T. Empey. Dr. Empey has examined the various theories of crime prevention and reluctantly decided that crime prevention is a "fugitive utopia" that we grope for but never grasp.[22] After studying in at least 78 books and articles such matters as

[20] National Advisory Commission on Criminal Justice Standards and Goals, *A National Strategy to Reduce Crime* (Washington, D.C.: U.S. Government Printing Office, 1973).

[21] The Delphi technique, developed by the Rand Corporation in 1950, is basically a poll of a panel of experts who have been supplied with information upon which they make a forecast. Usually, the members are unknown to each other, to prevent pressure, influence, and intimidation. Information is fed back to the experts as the forecast is developed. See Juri Pill, "The Delphi Methods: Substance, Context; A Critique and an Annotated Bibliography," *Socio-Economic Planning Sciences*, 5:58 (1971), 57–71.

[22] Lamar T. Empey, "Crime Prevention: The Fugitive Utopia," in Daniel Glaser, ed., *Handbook of Criminology* (Chicago: Rand McNally, 1970), pp. 1095–1123.

the labeling approach, conflict and consensus, interactionism, opportunity theory, alienation, gang formation, behavior modification, differential treatment, reference group theory, repression, and diversion, he concluded that "an emphasis upon repression or diversion fails to account for the means by which a person acquires a legitimate identity and a stake in conformity." He suggests that:

1. The penal code should be changed to eliminate nonpredatory, victimless crimes.
2. Prevention programs should be adapted to bring changes into illegitimate as well as legitimate socializing institutions.
3. The police should be freed to concentrate upon predatory and organized crime and should use citizen participation.

Empey's brilliant analysis is based upon extensive examination of the literature, the existing records (UCRs), government reports, and many prior experiments, including simulation. The analysis is really an examination of the research methods previously used, a research of the researchers.

The commission thought that the police are hampered by attention to juvenile status crimes, truancy, drinking, and running away; Empey felt that attention to crimes such as drunk offenses, drug addiction, and other nonpredatory, victimless crimes—gambling, prostitution (excluding organized crime)—also limits police in their activities to control predators and protect person and property in society.

Suppose we want to investigate the hypothesis, "There is a relationship between the work efficiency of the police and the type of duties they perform." In our research we would have to distinguish between the types of crime that police should deal with and the types they should not—and decide who will do the jobs that we propose to give to someone else. We would also have to examine the expected role of the police in public life. Their duties have not suddenly come into being; they have evolved from the requests of the people. In fact, we expect and demand more and more from our police force—not only the investigation of organized crime, but disturbances of the peace, child abuse, vehicle accidents, crowd control, emergency distress calls, right down to leading funeral processions and opening locked doors for people who lose their keys.

Our research could easily create a problem rather than solve one. The point is that the use of other research methods will bring up issues not seen in the simple construction of a questionnaire. Case study and participant observation add depth to the research. In fact, the common thread in the research examples cited is that they all seek a better way, having been conducted in order to improve the quality of life. None of them were specious or superficial; they were dedicated, ethical, and professional efforts made with considerable personal introspection and reflection on what path to take. The fact that no immediate answers were forthcoming indicates the complexity of the subject.

When dealing with concepts concerning people and social or behavioral problems, we do not have the tangibility of evidence such as fingerprints. Some use, however, may be made of the polygraph. The polygraph measures chest and abdominal respiration, galvanic response, sweating or dryness of the skin, muscular tension, pulse, and blood pressure. Even with the use of other methods, this apparently scientific instrument is not infallible;[23] in a test of polygraph records, the results were shown to be accurate 91 percent of the time, certainly demonstrating a relationship between the polygraph and its detection of deception. But the researcher is looking for evidence that the suspect is either innocent or guilty, and that margin of error is too great for legal decision. However, a polygraph would be of assistance when used with other methods. Other technical measures for detecting deception are voice-stress analyzers and observation of the eye retina.

A great deal of criminological research in the drug area has been used to make a case for or against drug use. Good research does not need to argue the point, it can stand on its merit. A good study on drug abuse was made by Bates and Crowther,[24] using a survey of present research, interviews, and observation. The authors presented the facts without judgment, pointing out that research should "present data on the use of these substances or their effects . . . without arguing for their use or their prohibition."

The use of more than one method enables us to define the research, look at other perspectives, and bring a better measure of credibility into our research methodology.

SUMMARY

Survey research is one of the best research methods we have, but it is not the only method. Used with other methods, its validity improves. Most other methods are nonreactive—that is, they do not cause a reaction from the respondent, they do not confront the respondent, they are largely observational or search methods.

Validity in research consists of internal validity, which prevents the explanation of differences by defects in the design itself, and external validity, which permits us to make inferences from our sample to the parent population. As with Type 1 and 2 errors, we need to control for both types of validity. Errors in internal validity occur because of faulty design, failure to note the effects of extraneous variables, change in the respondents in the sample, or failure to include the proper variables or the proper questions in the survey instrument. Errors in external validity occur because of poor sampling procedure, poor selection of the sample (size and stratification), treatment effect, interviewer bias, or oversubjectivity (involvement with the research).

Control of these errors may be exercised by using other methods—such as case

[23] Frank S. Horvath and John E. Reid, "The Reliability of Polygraph Examiner Diagnosis of Truth and Deception," *Journal of Criminal Law, Criminology and Police Science*, 62 (1971), 276–81.

[24] William Bates and Betty Crowther, "Drug Abuse," in Edward Sagarin and Fred Montanino, *Deviants: Voluntary Actors in a Hostile World* (Morristown, N.J.: General Learning Press, 1977), pp. 260–325.

study, participant observation, simulation, search of the literature and records, examination of physical evidence, and back-translation—to improve the survey design itself so that the proper variables are used to gain the information needed for research analysis. The use of other methods makes us aware of extraneous factors that could affect the outcome: prior testing and its effects, the nature of the sample itself, and environmental and situational effects. By the use of more than one method, called triangulation, we are able to place our research in a wider frame of reference with more points of reference.

Two major errors inherent in the survey method are maturation and saturation. Maturation implies change, mobility, and lack of stability; saturation implies over-familiarity with surveys and manipulation by the client and the interviewer. The use of other methods can control these errors.

The use of other methods may also be appropriate for problem solving. Often the research in the field requires their use because of unknown events or unforeseen difficulties. Knowledge of other methods then permits the adaptation of the research to these special circumstances. In addition, the use of other methods makes the researcher aware of factors (variables) not previously considered but vital to the project.

Research in criminology and criminal justice is somewhat complex. We do not have the certainty of methods like fingerprinting or forensic chemistry, but we do "come into our own" when we test the validity of lie detectors, formulate a strategy for prevention of crime, or look scientifically at drug abuse. Further, we can examine deficiencies in statistics themselves by observing the way they are made and how they are kept by the officials in charge—coroners, police, and elected politicians.

We must record our observations without judgment, presenting data as they are and not as we would like them to be. When commission members or peers express suggestions on future outcomes, research scientists should test those forecasts for feasibility. The use of several methods implies that we are using systematic and organized common sense in conjunction with the scientific method. The methods we use depend upon the circumstances, the nature of the research, and the imagination of the researcher. Our only restraint is an ethical conscience.

EXERCISES

1. What is validity in research? Explain internal and external validity.
2. What controls would you use for internal and external validity? Use as an example research of drug use in a high school.
3. Explain triangulation of data, method, interviewer.
4. What is meant by, "The credibility of findings is enhanced by the use of more than one method."
5. Explain nonreactive measures. What are they, and what do they do?

6. Contrast survey research and unobtrusive methods.
7. What are "cues and clues" in trace and accretion measures?
8. Why are ethics involved in some nonreactive measures?
9. What is a polygraph? How would you describe this technically? What information can you get from it?
10. Research on racism often ignores the written record because a written record invokes the concept of documents and books. Explain how you would use graffiti in restrooms, tattoos, underground papers, and private correspondence.
11. Name some kinds of research that have used the eyes as part of the research method.
12. How would you account for the apparent success of Milgram's "obedience experiment"?
13. What was the value of Zimbardo's "prison simulation"?
14. In a forecast to reduce crime, could the computer calculations be "correct"? Discuss.
15. What are "zero-sum games"? the Prisoner's Dilemma? "non-zero-sum games"?
16. How could impersonal key response be used in criminal justice research?
17. What is back-translation? How would you use it in a survey in a ghetto district?
18. What were some of Dr. Atkinson's problems?
19. What are the "high-fear crimes"? Discuss the aims of the National Advisory Commission.
20. How would you propose testing a polygraph?

FOR FURTHER READING

Anderson, Ralph, and Irl E. Carter, *Human Behavior in the Social Environment: A Social Systems Approach*. Chicago: Aldine, 1974.

Barton, Richard E., *A Primer on Simulation and Gaming*. Englewood Cliffs, N.J.: Prentice-Hall, 1970.

Bureau of the Census, U.S. Department of Commerce, *The U.S. Book of Facts, Statistics and Information*. Washington, D.C.: U.S. Government Printing Office; and New York: Essandess (special edition). Published annually.

Campbell, Donald T., and Julian C. Stanley, *Experimental and Quasi-Experimental Designs in Research*. Skokie, Ill.: Rand McNally, 1972.

Cavan, Sherri, *Liquor License*. Chicago: Aldine, 1966.

Chambliss, William J., "Vice, Corruption, Bureaucracy, and Power," *Wisconsin Law Review*, 1971, pp. 1150–73.

Davis, M. D., *Game Theory: A Non-Technical Introduction*. New York: Basic Books, 1970.

Douglas, Jack, *Research on Deviance*. New York: Random House, 1972.

Etzioni, Amitai, *Modern Organizations.* Englewood Cliffs, N.J.: Prentice-Hall, 1964. An excellent primer.

FBI, U.S. Department of Justice, *Crime in the United States: Uniform Crime Reports.* Washington, D.C.: U.S. Government Printing Office, annually.

Feldman, Saul D., ed., *Deciphering Deviance.* Boston: Little, Brown, 1978. An excellent reader, particularly Part II, "Techniques of Studying Deviant Behavior."

Garfinkel, Harold, *Studies in Ethnomethodology.* Englewood Cliffs, N.J.: Prentice-Hall, 1967. See Chapter 5.

Glazer, Myron, *The Research Adventure: Promise and Problems in Field Work.* New York: Random House, 1972.

Goffman, Irving, *Asylums.* New York: Doubleday, 1964.

Ianni, Francis A. J., with Elizabeth Reuss-Ianni, *A Family Business: Kinship and Control in Organized Crime.* New York: Russell Sage Froundation, 1972.

Inbar, M., and C. S. Stoll, *Simulation and Gaming in the Social Sciences.* New York: Free Press, 1972.

Kaplan, L. J., and Dennis Kessler, *An Economic Analysis of Crime.* Springfield, Ill.: Charles C Thomas, 1976.

Luft, Joseph, *Group Processes.* Palo Alto, Calif.: Mayfield, 1970.

McCall, G. J., and J. L. Simmons, *Issues in Participant Observation: A Text and Reader.* Reading, Mass.: Addison-Wesley, 1969.

Matzner, Dorothy, and Margaret English, *Victims of Justice.* New York: Atheneum, 1973. A detailed case study of a murder.

Nash, Jay Robert, *Hustlers and Con Men.* New York: M. Evans, 1976. Detailed records of men and methods.

National Research Council, Panel for the Evaluation of Crime Surveys, *Surveying Crime.* Washington, D.C.: National Academy of Sciences, 1976.

Polsky, Ned, *Hustlers, Beats and Others.* Chicago: Aldine, 1967.

Szasz, Thomas S., *The Manufacture of Madness.* New York: Harper & Row, 1970. A study of fallacy as applied to mental health.

Webb, Eugene J., Donald T. Campbell, Richard D. Schwartz, and Lee Sechrest, *Unobtrusive Measures: Non-Reactive Research in the Social Sciences.* Skokie, Ill.: Rand McNally, 1971.

Whyte, William F., *Street Corner Society.* Chicago: University of Chicago Press, 1955.

Winslow, Robert W., ed., *Crime in a Free Society* (3rd ed.). Encino, Calif.: Dickenson, 1977. Selections from reports by the President's Commission on Law Enforcement and Administration of Justice, the National Advisory Commission on Civil Disorder, the National Commission on Causes and Prevention of Violence, and the Commission on Obscenity and Pornography.

6

Design and Data

SELECTION OF A RESEARCH DESIGN

In earlier chapters, advantages and limitations of various types of design have been mentioned. Before proceeding to the techniques of survey research, we should consider further problems in selection that affect human qualitative judgment rather than quantitative statistical decision.

All research is a study of samples of one kind or another, whether it be objects, events, or people. No behavioral research can encompass all the people on the earth—or, for that matter, all the people in particular locations. We do not have the time, energy, or resources to conduct comprehensive and exhaustive census-type surveys, and even if we had, the data would become dated owing to population change and instability. The very best we can hope for is a representative sample, taken from a parent population and containing all the characteristics of that population, including the limitations of dating and change. *Anything that occurs within the population should occur within the sample*, if our sample is truly representative.

Census data are commonly taken for granted as accurate.[1] But census takers are human beings, and therefore, human error occurs in compiling census data as it does in any other research. Error occurs in the gathering of the data, transference

[1] Claire Selltiz et al., *Research Methods in Social Relations* (New York: Holt, Rinehart & Winston, 1976), pp. 513–14.

of the data to computer language, typographical errors in entering data in final reports, and mistakes in computations. *We must be alert for error in the use of any data.* Statistics are not always what they appear to be. Even crime statistics are subject to criticism.[2] The best we can achieve in the face of such extreme difficulties is an approximation of actual phenomena.

Since the drawing of a sample that is perfect in randomness and representation is almost impossible, almost all samples contain error. Statistical techniques enable us to estimate error and to generate our inferences from the sample within a given confidence statement. We use very limited data from a small part of the parent population, the sample, to form a conclusion concerning the whole. No matter how good the statistical technique is, the error in the sample and the probability in the technique means that hazard is a necessary part of our scientific existence. Our final conclusion is based upon the statistical *probability* of error in the sample—the certainty of chance.

This acceptance of the existence of error or chance in our calculations is the very reason why we never prove our hypothesis,[3] but rather fail to prove the null hypothesis. We demonstrate that the relationship, if it exists, occurs because of the effect of the independent variable upon the dependent variable *and chance.*

With this in mind, *the main consideration in the selection of a research design should be whether it is suitable in meeting your research objective.* Your next consideration should be whether you have sufficient training and experience to complete your project. The design must be within the limits of your practicality, ability, and expertise. Practicality means taking into account your own limits and considering the end work of analyzing data, writing reports, and evaluation of the project. Moments occur in most projects when we wonder whether it is worth it. Having a clear perspective of the final result enables the researcher to overcome frustration and seek the rewarding finish. Practicality is the estimation of one's ability to overcome delays and obstacles, and the allowing for unexpected and unanticipated holdups.

Finally, consider the time element and your resources. You must have the time and the resources necessary for completion of the project. Resources include transportation, typing, keypunching, computer work, and so on.

RESEARCH DESIGN WITH ASSIGNED VARIABLES

Figures 6-1 and *6-2* show two designs—one a suggested student pattern, the other an advanced design. The simpler design, Figure 6-1, implies that in a single cross-sectional survey, only a few variables will be tested and the data will be analyzed as

[2] Marvin Wolfgang, "Uniform Crime Reports: A Critical Appraisal," *University of Pennsylvania Law Review*, 111 (April 1963), 708–38.

[3] Robert S. Clark, *Fundamentals of Criminal Justice Research* (Lexington, Mass.: Heath, 1977), p. 47: "The point is not to prove the hypothesis is *correct*, but to *find out* something."

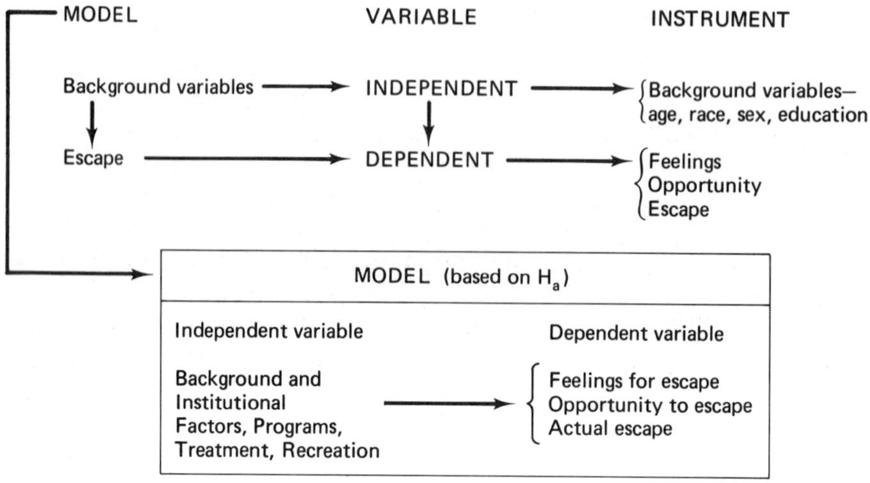

Fig. 6-1 Student's research design (cross-sectional survey)

simply and effectively as possible. This is in fact an exploratory design, intended to get to the point quickly. It decides how the variables are affecting each other and can be used for three main types of statistical analysis: frequencies, Pearson correlation, and chi-square.

Figure 6-1 is based upon the formal hypothesis, "Escape is motivated by a number of institutional factors."

H_a = There is a relationship between institutional factors and escape.

H_0 = There is no relationship between institutional factors and escape.

The model or research hypothesis is expressed vertically, and the variables are then related horizontally to the instrument. In a larger diagram, all the variables are related to items on the questionnaire.

The conclusion of the survey was that of the 17 background and institutional variables tested, the strongest association was between recreation (or lack of it) and escape.

The advanced design, Figure 6-2, includes by inference the use of the elaboration model.[4] It is given to show how the basic building block of the student design is elaborated, and how the same format is used to position the variables on the instrument. This type of format enables the researcher to visualize the pattern of research before the actual field work. It tells him what kind of data he may anticipate.

The diagram is based on the hypothesis, "Criminal behavior is determined by one's perception of life—which is influenced by environment and heredity—and is mitigated or intensified by life opportunities."

[4] Although a major function of design is to reduce or eliminate other explanations or hypotheses, we should consider other alternatives in its construction. See (for use of other theories) L. Berkowitz and J. Macauley, "The Contagion of Criminal Violence," *Sociometry*, 34 (1971), 238–60.

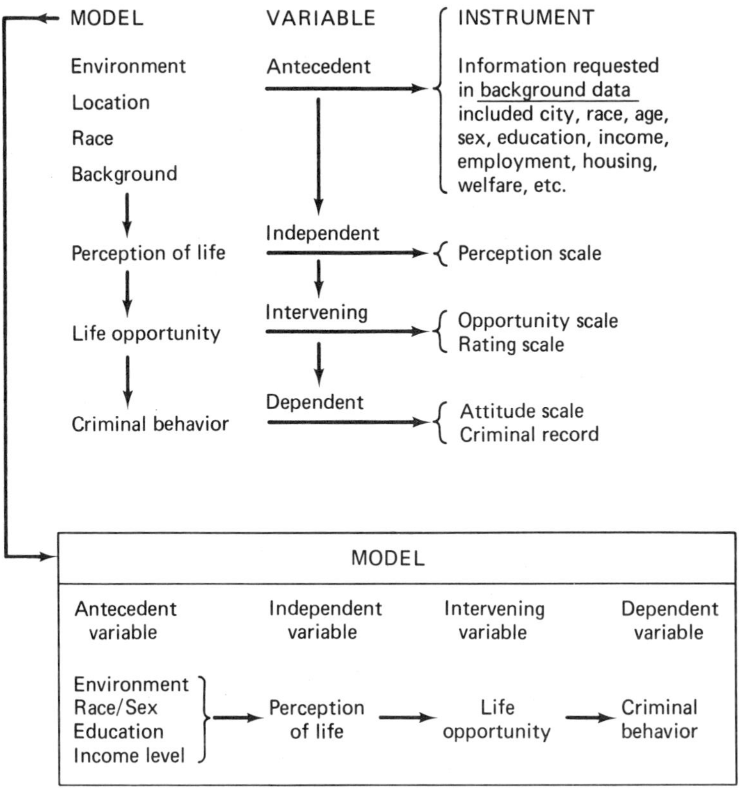

Fig. 6-2 Relation of variables to research design (cross-sectional survey/comparative survey)

H_a = Criminal behavior is influenced by one's perception of life.

H_0 = There is no relationship between one's perception of life and criminal behavior.

The model is expressed vertically in the table, and each section of the model is then related horizontally to the instrument. In complex models, this format is most useful. Each variable is then noted as to the form of it to be used—question, scale, or record. Alternatives used are also noted, and any supplemental measures or backup scales are appended.

The research design is based upon the methods you will use in your project, and also upon the clear statement of the problem, its testability, and its practicality. We would like the problem to be current, critical, and contributive to the discipline. Analysis of concepts in the problem should provide the opportunity for inferential statements to be made to the parent population.

The design should, if possible, include a questionnaire that provides the data for analysis and can be used again for possible replication. It should also include linkage to theory, the hypothesis to be tested, sampling procedure, collection of data, and anticipated analysis of data.

The use of more than one method is preferable. And since error is cumulative, the design should include caution and controls as well as flexibility in adjustment when error is detected.

Pretest

Pretest is a must in design. This cannot be stressed enough, since pretest not only indicates error before it affects the main study, but points out improvements that can be made.[5] It will indicate sampling defects, language errors, procedure errors, format errors, and analysis errors. Pretest is what one might call a transistorized version of the main model. In its capsule form, it gives an estimate of the cost, time, and difficulty that will be involved in the study. Its use is well worth the time and effort.

Pretest is the prior testing of the survey instrument on a smaller sample taken in a neutrally selected area. Its object is to find out if the questions proposed for the survey questionnaire will work—that is, if the responses will give the desired data for analysis. By using the proposed questionnaire on a smaller sample, the researcher gets some idea of the practicality of the project in terms of selection of the sample. sample representation, interviewing or sampling procedure, gathering of the data into workable sequence for analysis, and actual analysis of the data.

After the questionnaire or sampling method is decided upon, the next decision is where to select a small testable sample that will not affect the outcome of the main study. We do not want to test respondents twice in the same population, so using people in the pretest would exclude them from the main sample. The ideal small sample is from a neutral location that contains a population with virtually the same characteristics as the population to be tested.[6] A sample of approximately 30 will yield the results necessary to correct any errors. The instrument itself is usually subject to the most correction, since pretesting invariably reveals that certain questions are not getting the expected results. The questions will have to be rephrased, put into simpler language, corrected for methodological errors (double questions, negative questions, and leading questions), and improved in terms of scoring procedure. A major improvement in most questionnaires is reduction in size, which means a saving in time spent on interview or other-procedure.

The running of the survey in capsule form is the equivalent of a laboratory test or a trial run prior to the major research.[7] It gives the researcher a view of actual

[5] Earl R. Babbie, *Survey Research Methods* (Belmont, Calif.: Wadsworth, 1973), pp. 205–11.

[6] The population for pretest should resemble the main testable parent population in terms of composition, stratification, and distribution of variable characteristics.

[7] C. A. Moser and G. Kalton, *Survey Methods in Social Investigation*, 2nd ed. (New York: Basic Books, 1972), pp. 47–52. "[Pretest] is to try out systematically all the various features of the main inquiry."

SUMMARY OF THE USE OF PRETEST

1. Pretest should consist of testing the proposed final instrument on a neutral population with approximately the same characteristics as the proposed parent test population.
2. A smaller sample should be used so that results are gathered quickly. Spontaneity and speed are essential for success in putting the findings into effect before there are changes in the proposed test population or before any outside events interfere with the research.
3. The findings of the pretest should be examined in terms of:
   (a) The time the instrument took to administer
   (b) The readability of the questions and dialect translation
   (c) Comprehension of the test by the respondent
   (d) The nature of nonresponses, missing values, contradictory responses, and spoiled questionnaires
   (e) Whether the responses given provide data for testing the objectives of the research
   (f) Whether the sample is representative
   (g) The suitability of the method used
4. During the pretest, the possible effects on outcomes of any other variables should be noted. Controls may be proposed for inclusion in the final research design. Be alert for unexpected events.
5. The use of other methods should be considered to give meaning to the research. Consider alternative perspectives.
6. Any clue or information that will add to the refinement of the final test instrument should be used. *The purpose of the pretest is to give precision to the final research analysis*. Note carefully any discrepancies or problems.
7. A statistical analysis of data gathered will indicate weaknesses in the methods used that need correction.
8. Besides revealing field and operational difficulties, the pretest will give an estimate of completion time and cost. It also creates a climate for the final project.
9. The object of the pretest is to determine the workability of the research method; the testing of the hypothesis is secondary at this point.
10. Any adjustments to the research design made from pretest findings must be in line with the objectives of the research.

field conditions and problems to be encountered during operationalization, revealing difficulties not anticipated in previous discussion or non-test situations. *The pretest enables the researcher to objectively test the research method, as against the test of the research hypothesis.*[8] It becomes clear during pretest that unless the method (and the research design) is suitable for the research, the testing of the hypothesis will be imprecise, erroneous, and inaccurate.

[8] Hans Zeisal, *Say It With Figures*, 5th ed. (New York: Harper & Row, 1968), pp. 172-75. While we *test* the method, we should *probe* the hypothesis.

Pretest will permit an estimate of the time to be spent in the field and the approximate cost, and it will also be a trial run for data analysis. Again, it is the method that is being tested, and the object is simply to see if the method will work.

The pretest has other advantages. It introduces the researcher to other methods, such as case study and participant observation. The composition of the population can be observed and the response rate and the form of the response checked, and thus we can adjust the questions asked.[9] The accessibility of the client, the safety of the interviewer, and the efforts of co-members can be checked. The way data are collected and scored can be examined to determine its efficiency. Pretesting is also valuable in identifying extraneous variables that may or may not have an effect on the research.[10] This means that controls may be introduced to give precision to the research.

The whole purpose of a preliminary study such as a pretest is to discover and correct problems before the main study begins, not at the end when it is too late. A more sophisticated study preceding a major project, such as an investigative feasibility study, is called a *pilot study*. A pilot study usually follows pretests and tries to resolve major problems prior to a large undertaking.

The value of pretest cannot be overemphasized. Pretest findings can improve definition, operationalization, procedure, sampling, the instrument and techniques used, and statistical analysis.

DATA

The Production of Data

Pretest is the preliminary search for data, a testing of the research design, and an examination of practicality. The search for data, which is based upon the research method, yields the information necessary for analysis and decision making. The data ought to be diffused fairly evenly throughout the parent population from which the sample is taken. This assumption of equal variance is called *homoscedasticity.* It is the equal variability, spread or scatter of the characteristic in the population. There should be a *normal distribution*, which follows a pattern similar to a bell-shaped curve.

Our search for data follows three main assumptions:

1. Randomness—that the sample selected will be random
2. Homoscedasticity—that there will be equal variances of the data
3. Normality—that there is normal distribution

We are looking for every member of the sample to have equal chance of selection, be part of equal representation, and have no extreme characteristics that would not

[9] John A. Sonquist and William C. Dunkelberg, *Survey and Opinion Research* (Englewood Cliffs, N.J.: Prentice-Hall, 1977), pp. 7–8: "Many serious errors can be avoided by taking time to make an adequate pretest."

[10] When ranking items, pretest aids in early selection.

normally be found in the population from which the sample is selected.[11] The data we seek are on social phenomena, pertinent facts that can be recorded as statistics. They are the quantification of reality. We gather data on the disposition—acceptance or rejection—and the behavioral characteristics of social concepts. We can quantify social behavior, criminological concepts, and criminal justice hypotheses. We select our survey design to meet the measurement expectations of the variables and gather data with as much sophistication and precision as possible (See *Figure 6-3*). All data are dependent upon the precision of observations made.

The data we are seeking from the parent population are seldom factual, a matter of hard physical laws. Only background data conform to those requirements. Most of our data are based upon memory recall, beliefs, prejudices, past behavior, and some anticipated future behavior. Most are nearly true, and a lot are personal conjecture. Nevertheless, we can replicate our studies, verify our findings, and predict future trends. The ultimate goal of research is prediction.

Using Crime Data

The Uniform Crime Reports (UCRs), published annually by the FBI, represent a systematic effort to collect data on national crime statistics. Information is supplied to the FBI by various state reporting and local agencies, but the data on criminal offenses are based upon FBI definitions of those offenses, since the states' definitions may differ.

Certain offenses, such as murder, forcible rape, robbery, and aggravated assault, are defined as crimes of violence. Burglary, larceny-theft, and motor-vehicle theft are property crimes. These seven offenses make up the *crime index*, which in 1976 comprised 11,304,800 crimes. There has been no reduction in the crime-index total in the last twenty years; although murders, robberies, and burglaries have decreased, there has been an increase in rape, assault, and larceny-theft.[12]

Larceny-theft, or stealing property, includes shoplifting, pocket-picking, purse-snatching, theft of parts from cars, and the taking of property without force, violence, or fraud. There were some 6,270,800 cases of larceny-theft in 1976—three cases for every 100 people in the United States. And these are only the reported statistics, which are estimated to be less than half the actual number of crimes.[13]

The University of Chicago's National Opinion Research Center in 1965 gathered data from households and queried the victims of crimes, many of whom said they had not reported the crimes to the police because of inconvenience, apathy, fear,

[11] Theoretically, each sample should be the same, but it never is because of various errors. Therefore, most of our calculations are based upon the averaging of "infinite samples."

[12] FBI, *Crime in the United States, 1976: Uniform Crime Reports* (Washington, D.C.: U.S. Government Printing Office, 1977), Table 2.

[13] Phillip H. Ennis, *Criminal Victimization in the United States: A Report of a National Survey* (Washington, D.C.: U.S. Government Printing Office, 1967).

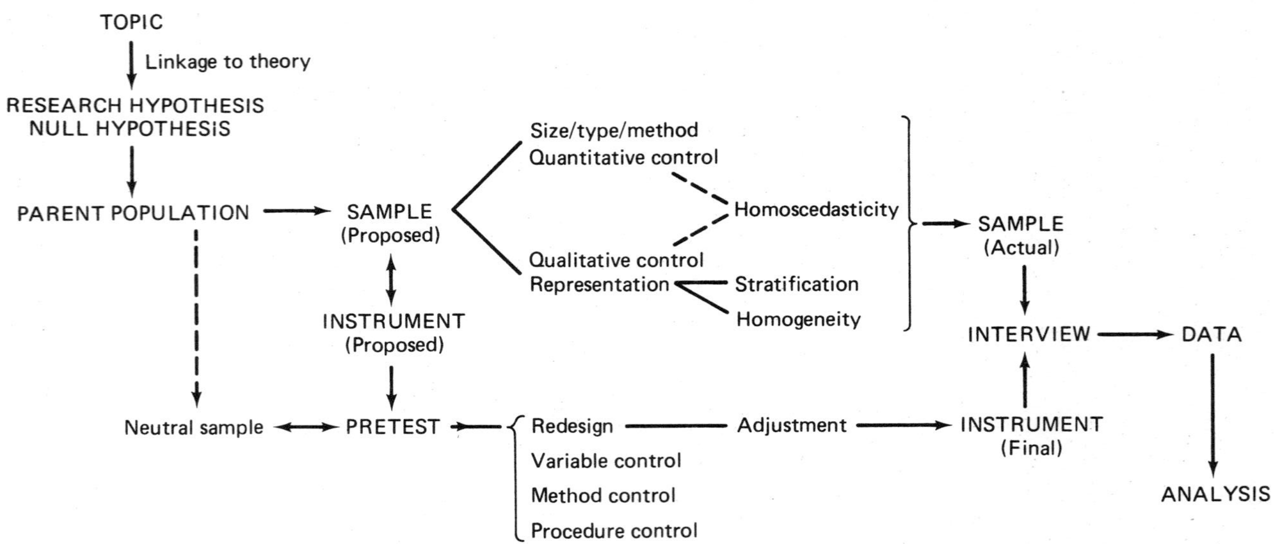

Fig. 6-3 The production of research survey data from the parent population

distrust, sickness, family obligations, risk, or the like. This and other follow-up surveys indicate that crime is indeed twice as high as reported statistics.[14] The conclusions reached on the Uniform Crime Reports will certainly have to be revised in the light of the NORC and other victimization studies.

The outstanding difference in the collection of data on the same issue (crime in the population) by the two methods is that the FBI definition is based on the offense (*crime*), whereas the NORC survey was concerned with the *population*, the victims and nonvictims. We are not always faced with dichotomies such as this, but as the statistics indicate, we do need to be aware of what kinds of data we are collecting.

Gathering data on crime presents problems in research design in terms of (1) internal and external validity,[15] (2) sampling and procedure, and (3) analysis and editing. It would appear that at the very beginning of survey research, we have difficulties interpreting data and controversy on how they should be obtained. Forecasting and the interpretation of trends depends upon the accuracy of the data used in the calculations. No matter how impressive the numbers become, it is the quality of the data and the research design that determines the outcomes.

There is no doubt that data reported in from various police agencies carry the weight of fact, authority, and credibility. On the other hand, data obtained by survey research (field work) and supplemented by other methods and other strategies are technologically more sophisticated, and closer to an accurate picture of the phenomena. This may be seen in *Figure 6-4*.

The design of the research should indicate how the data are to be used. Like the design, the data must fit the objectives of the research and must be appropriate for the analysis. It would also appear that both methods of gathering data can be combined for certain types of research.

Care must be taken in using data when interpreting frequencies for profiles or for building models for trends. If a controversial issue such as race is being analyzed from statistical data and the data are incorrect, the following errors may occur:

1. Race may be overemphasized in criminal participation.
2. Race may be minimized in criminal offenses.
3. Race may be entirely misinterpreted as being of no significance.

The first error will probably result in bias and prejudice, the second in minimizing the importance of social correction, and the third in ignoring the problem altogether. From the UCRs, it would appear that the greatest number of crimes are committed by young blacks in the black community.[16] If this is so, we have a social problem

[14] LEAA news release, 1974: see also *Crimes and Victims: A Report on the Dayton–San Jose Pilot Survey of Victimization* (Washington, D.C.: U.S. Government Printing Office, 1974).

[15] Bettye K. Eidson Penick and Maurice B. Owens, eds., *Surveying Crime* (Washington, D.C.: National Academy of Sciences, 1976). See Chaps. 5 and 6 on definition and method.

[16] FBI, *Uniform Crime Reports, 1976*, Tables 41, 47, and 53.

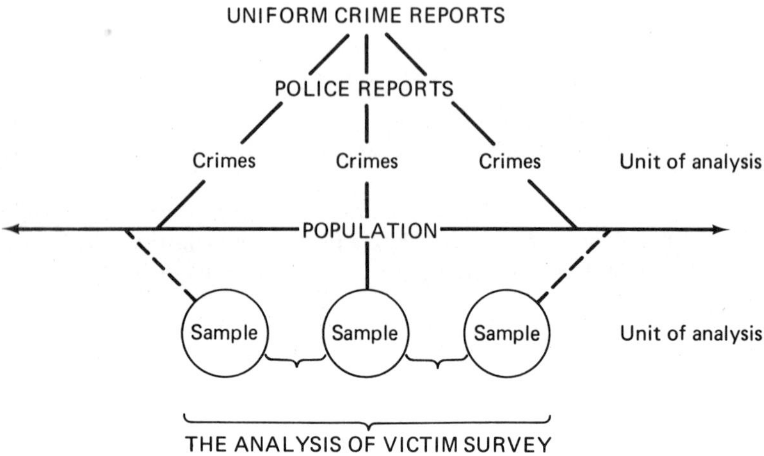

Fig. 6-4 Two methods of reporting crime

of the first magnitude; but if the data are in error, we are in danger of creating a statistical stereotype with consequent harm. Building a profile based upon inadequate or incorrect data will lead to error in identifying our objective, or to a completely false objective; it may result in incorrect forecasting, leading to major errors in decision making. The use of more than one method and alternative strategies in the collection of data cannot guarantee perfect accuracy, but it will act as control for more obvious errors that occur with the use of only one method.

Other uses of crime statistics are the study of the causes of crime—its *etiology*—the characteristics of the offender, the spatial distribution of crime, and the *ecology* of crime.[17] Again, a word of caution concerning the type of data used. The UCRs do provide an enormous fund of data to be used in these studies. They give age, race, arrest patterns, location, type and time of offense, value of property stolen, and disposition of the crime. It is a simple matter to fill in the gaps with other government or agency data on education, family life, employment, housing, physical environment, and personal characteristics. But we also need to gather data on social organization, crime patterns, cultural expectations, and developing opportunities for deviance. The more we understand the factors contributing to the cause of crime and its spread, the better able we are to propose control and prevention.

The phenomenon of crime is so complex that even the collection of data becomes a problem. Its importance cannot be overestimated. Our data determine the direction in which we move, either identifying the problem correctly or following a trail of error.

[17] Robert W. Winslow, *Crime in a Free Society*, 3rd ed. (Encino, Calif.: Dickenson, 1977), Chaps. 4 and 5, pp. 105–65.

Data, Instrument, and Sample

As we have seen, data may be accumulated from direct reports, from the simple counting of defined events, or from client response in a population segment or sample. The selection of a sample from a parent population implies that the sample will be like, but not identical to, the parent population. The difference between the characteristics of the sample and those of the parent population is error that we find in the sample. We never know exactly how much error will occur. Therefore, our calculations are based upon estimation of error, and our conclusions are based upon those calculations. We are continually faced with the problem of eliminating error, or at least controlling for or reducing the proportion of it, to bring the sample into line with the parent population. This calculation is known as the proportional reduction of error, or PRE.

When we are dealing with hard data—age, income, height, weight, or other continuous measures—the sophistication of statistical techniques enables us to calculate error to mathematical precision; with soft data—attitudes, preferences, behavior, or other discrete facts—we must be aware that something will be lost in the translation into numbers. The more steps that are added, the greater the risk of accumulating error. Sampling theory is basically a discussion of sampling error and how to overcome it.

In addition, when we ask questions that require recall, second thoughts, subjective answers, and difficult personal response, we add response error to sampling error. Let us return to the basic schematic of research design, *Figure 6-5*. The only error that enters in at A is a conceptual error. In the selection of variables, B, the error that occurs is omission, poor description, or poor definition. On closer inspection, it can be seen that all data are developed at C and D. At D, the instrument is tested on the sample. We now have:

Instrument + Sample = Data

No data are obtainable without applying the appropriate questionnaire to the sample, so in order to generate data, we must generate a sample. We know that error occurs because of differences between the sample and the parent population, and we know that with the use of soft facts, more error will occur. The equation now becomes:

Instrument error + Sample error = Data error

It is upon data error that our calculations are made and our conclusions are posited. The instrument is quite meaningless without the sample, and the sample is meaningless without data; one depends upon the other. We can control for sample error by sampling techniques and strategies. We cannot estimate instrument error, control

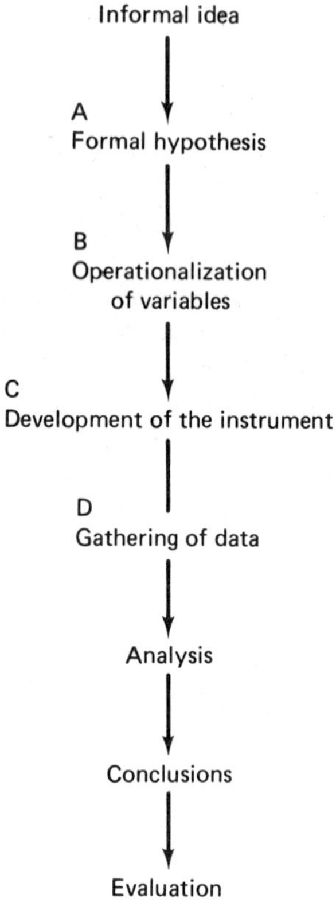

Fig. 6-5 Research design

for which depends upon definition, operationalization, and refinement from pretest. A poor sample or a poor instrument will break the research.

Data generated by the instrument are as in *Table 6.1*. Questions 2-9 all involve error. Even when the questions are asked precisely, the client may not perceive the question accurately, answer it truthfully, or even be representative of the population. When we add these errors to the facts that we may not have an ideal sample and that our sampling procedure may not be suitable for the research design, we can see that survey research can produce some very dubious conclusions because of the accumulation of sampling and nonsampling error.

Every control possible must be exercised on sampling procedure and refinement of the instrument. Even when facts are reported as they occur, their tabulation may not be reliable *unless* they are suitable for the research objectives. In fact, the reported facts may become used to support spurious objectives, as when they are reported as complete when incomplete, or reported as representing the total population when they do not.

UCRs, for example, are reported as representing 96 percent of the U.S. population, yet they appear to be at variance with other surveys. Thus, if we are examining

Table 6.1. Instrument Response

1.	Hard background facts	Age, race, sex, income, education, etc.
2.	Recall or memory	Answers to factual questions
3.	Attitudes (past/future)	Responses to questions on issues
4.	Feelings	Answers to questions on personal matters
5.	Prejudices	Responses to questions on beliefs
6.	Biases/Moods	How respondent feels at the time
7.	Self-ratings	Client's rating of own performance
8.	Observer rating	Interviewer's rating of client
9.	Dummy questions/verification	Tests of truthfulness

crime statistics for the purposes of studying homicide, the UCRs would be quite adequate, since the reported rates would vary little from the incidence of murder in the population. If we study drug abuse, however, we may find a wide variable between UCR statistics and actual abuse. And even in a homicide study, we need to be cautious about police definitions, coroner's definitions, and social definitions, which might produce three different sets of statistics, although they would be reasonably close. On the other hand, definitions of larceny-theft would give a considerable range of values, especially in reported and unreported crime.

In the determination of crimes of fear or the ranking of crimes by importance, there would be disagreement. The crimes causing greatest fear or concern are listed by the FBI and the NAC as murder, forcible rape, robbery, aggravated assault, and burglary; and the FBI adds larceny-theft and motor-vehicle theft to its crime index. But recent observations show that crimes causing the greatest fear are murder, assault (mugging), rape, arson, and vandalism.[18] And Kaplan and Kessler list crimes of importance in order of economic impact as (tentatively) gambling, loan-sharking, narcotics, and arson.[19] None of these appears in the crime index, and most of them are committed by organized crime.

The UCRs do point out how overburdened the court system is by giving the number of offenders prosecuted against the number of offenses committed. Each year, as crime increases are shown in the UCRs, the number of offenders prosecuted appears proportionately smaller. There were 9,608,500 arrests of offenders in 1976; the number of crime-index offenses reported was 11,304,800.[20] Of those arrested, 36 percent were found guilty, and 33 were referred to juvenile proceedings. But in spite of the numbers involved—3 million, or 1.5 percent of the population—it would appear that the odds of criminals going unpunished is being increased by the sheer impact of numbers on the system.

The UCRs offer a special challenge to those who can see the economic and social advantages of coping with crime. Their data may not be the best, but they are good data if they meet the research objectives.

[18] Author's observations in New York, 1976–78.

[19] Lawrence Kaplan and Dennis Kessler, *An Economic Analysis of Crime* (Springfield, Ill.: Charles C Thomas, 1976).

[20] FBI, *Uniform Crime Reports, 1976*, Table 24.

A survey can be conducted in many ways: by mail, telephone, interview, panel, cohort study, cross-sectional study, comparative study, longitudinal study, and multistage survey. But whatever the form, all surveys involve risks, owing to certain assumptions that:

1. The questions are exactly pertinent to the information required to explain the variables as they have been defined.
2. The sample is exactly representative of the parent population (random, homoscedastic, normal distribution) and is the right size.
3. No outside forces (extraneous variables) will affect or confound the outcomes or the collection of data.
4. The right level of significance within the correct df (degrees of freedom) and confidence interval has been selected for the appropriate statistical analysis, for rejection (or retention) of the H_0.
5. Controls have been properly established for internal and external validity and to avoid contamination.
6. The data leave no room for ambiguity in final computer analysis and analytical conclusions. The findings will have substantive and statistical significance.

These assumptions are made for an ideal result from an ideal survey, which will probably never exist. From the very beginning, we cannot be certain the right questions have been asked; and if we use only one sample, the chances are that, even if it is extreme, it can fool us 5 percent of the time. Thus, we are never certain we are asking the right question of the right person. Nor do we know the effect of outside variables, and we can set a degree of significance only arbitrarily. Further, any controls we may make for validity are really controls on estimates rather than on statistical performance. And last, when using soft data, we never entirely remove ambiguity. Final definition is an elusive utopia for the social sciences.

Because all data are collected by human beings, the ultimate error—the human error—persists to the end; and when we collect data from human beings and let other human beings interpret them, we compound the error. A good example of this was the *Literary Digest* prediction in 1936, from data collected from more than 2 million readers, that Landon would beat Roosevelt in the presidential election.[21] The sample simply did not correspond with the total characteristics of the parent population. The list, drawn from people with cars and telephones, was not representative, and although it was a massive sample, it was an extreme of the type that can fool us 5 percent of the time. Another example was the 1948 Gallup poll, also based on incorrect sampling, that concluded that Dewey would be elected in a landslide. But Truman was elected by over 2 million voters who had been "undecided" right up to polling time.

[21] Moser and Kalton, *Survey Methods in Social Investigation*, p. 79. The actual sample was 10 million, with over 2 million replies.

Modern polling techniques do have surprising accuracy, but they can also be surprisingly wrong. Polls conducted by politicians with a vested interest do attempt to create a "bandwagon" effect, and surveys conducted by scientists do tend to create an "iatrogenic effect." A political poll may use leading questions and insert political propaganda against the opponent.[22] Medical or scientific surveys tend to make people measure themselves by prior findings, as in deciding how normal one is as against the results of the Kinsey survey.[23]

An Example

The serious business of data collection is restricted by the method used, which can affect the final outcome. For example, telephone surveys are notoriously unreliable on issues of personal preference, but they work well for consumer interests. Consumer interests are usually group interests, implying that the use of telephones on group issues might well be successful.

This issue was tested by David LiBassi, who came to me after a lecture on methods and said he would like to test the error in telephone survey against the error in interview survey.[24] He felt that there would be a great discrepancy and wanted to research the difference. In western New York State, where nearly everyone has a phone, this seemed reasonable, because the large numbers did not appear to cancel out errors inherent in phone surveys. Rather, the large number of unlisted phones, the nonresponses, and the mobility of the population intensified the problem of getting accurate phone data.

The research design was planned to test the data obtainable from telephone surveys and interviews on the issue of attitude toward casino gambling in western New York State. It was theorized that if the questionnaire was held constant, any differences in data would be due to the method used, since telephone data are usually considered inferior to interview data.

The issue of casino gambling was contemporary, had generated a great deal of comment in the area, and would get a maximum response. Because this was a high-stress ethnic area, the relationship of stress to gambling would be measured, and since elections were close, political preference would be requested.

The research design in its informal stage now looked like *Table 6.2*, which indicates several methods of comparison for checking on the variation in the data obtained. LiBassi's team was now ready to test the attitudes of city residents toward gambling. As a formal hypothesis, his H_{a_1} stated:

> There is a relationship between age, race, sex, religion, education, income, marital status, and political preference and attitude toward casino gambling.

[22] During a mayoral campaign, threats and abuse were added to the polling techniques (western New York, 1977).

[23] Harry Hopkins, *The Numbers Game* (London: Secker & Warburg, 1973), pp. 14 and 36–41. The iatrogenic effect is unwittingly induced by the statistician, based upon the findings.

[24] The survey is shown in detail in Appendix 3.

Table 6.2. Informal Comparative Design

Test	Proposed research design		
Method	Interview data	◄—►	Telephone data
Attitude	▲ Casino gambling	◄—►	Casino gambling
Behavior	│ Stress	◄—►	Stress
Preference	▼ Political preference	◄—►	Political preference

Arrows indicate comparisons.

H_{a_2} stated:

> There is a relationship between stress and attitude toward casino gambling.

H_{a_3} stated:

> There is a difference between telephone data and interview data concerning attitudes toward casino gambling.

The null hypotheses for testing stated "no relationship" for H_{a_1} and H_{a_2} and "no difference" for H_{a_3}. The last null hypothesis, like the others, was expected to be rejected.

The next step was to operationalize the variables into an acceptable and workable questionnaire that could be used in interviews and over the telephone. The background variables were easily identified as age, race, sex, religion, marital status, political preference, education, income, and ethnic background. Stress was measured on a stress line that was self-rating.[25] Attitude toward gambling was to be determined from totaling the answers to seven questions, giving a range from 0 to 28—zero indicating indifference, 1 the lowest attitude toward gambling, and 28 the most favorable attitude. After four questions concerning legalization and participation were added, the questionnaire was pretested and adjusted on the basis of the pretest findings. The final questions were based upon discussion of the issues and items discovered in the pretest that could influence outcomes. For example, the question on ethnic background was added because the ethnic composition was mixed. Answers to this question were commented upon by LiBassi in his conclusions.

Upon completion and rewrite, the instrument needed to be tested. This meant the selection of two samples, one for interview and another for telephone. Four members of the team were each given 70 surveys to complete, 35 of each; the other two each got 60 surveys, for a total of 200 surveys of each type. For the interviews, the city was divided into equal zones, with each interviewer taking every fiftieth person until 35 responses were complete (making 1,750 people represented in each zone, for a total frame of 10,000). For the telephone survey, each member was

[25] Copyrighted by Edwin S. Johnson, in *Stress Effects in Two Black Community Systems in the Process of Social Change* (Tallahassee, Fla.: Signature, 1976), p. 55.

assigned 132 pages of the directory and selected every 1,003rd residence. Upon no response, the nearest name was chosen. The surveys were completed and the data computerized and analyzed using frequencies, correlation, and chi-square. The findings were somewhat surprising, as you will see in Appendix 3.

This survey was conducted primarily to check differences in data; the issue of casino gambling was secondary, and stress and political preference were minor issues. As it turned out, the data from the telephone surveys did not differ significantly from those from the interviews. They were not determined by the method so much as by the particular issue. Also, there was no significant relationship between the background variables, or between stress and political preference, and attitudes toward casino gambling. The null hypotheses were retained in all cases.

This research design tested an idea and motivated an interesting study, a comparison of interview and telephone data. It opened the way for a comparison of group issues versus individual preferences, or why polling by telephone is often so unreliable. The study also pointed up the testing of methods to gather data and the strategy of using more than one method. Perhaps more important is the fact that the design was not to *prove* the hypotheses, but to *use* the hypotheses to discover something.[26]

Challenging Data by Observation

The marijuana controversy has been carried on for some years now, and much data have accumulated on its use. The opponents say that marijuana smoking:

1. Irreversibly damages brain cells with premature aging
2. Lowers body resistance to disease and cancer
3. Damages chromosomes (increasing birth defects and disease)
4. Causes lung cancer and abnormal sperm cells
5. Leads to sterility, impotence, or both
6. Causes hormonal deficiencies[27]

Apparently, marijuana smokers are due to become extinct, since they become sterile, suffer an early death from disease, or go insane. Such scientific findings were published by the Senate Internal Security Subcommittee in 1974. Item 1 was backed up by Dr. A. M. G. Campbell in a 1971 study; item 2 by Dr. G. Nahas in 1974; item 3 by Dr. Akima Morishima in 1974; item 4 by Dr. Cecile Leuchtenberger in 1974; and item 5 by Dr. Robert Kolodny in 1974. The impact of all this medical and scientific data could not but influence the direction of decision making in Congress.

For some reason, the committee did not review findings concerning long-time

[26] Clark, *Fundamentals of Criminal Justice Research*, pp. 50, 51. Clark points out the importance of research objectives.

[27] Edward Brecher and editors, "Marijuana: The Health Question," *Consumer Reports*, March 1975.

marijuana smokers. Such a study had been in progress in Jamaica in 1970, and the report was finished in 1972; it was finally published in 1975.[28] (Why it was delayed raises some interesting questions.)

The Jamaica study of the long-term effects of marijuana smoking reported "no significant physical abnormality" in any of the groups. Two other field studies produced similar results—one at the University of Pennsylvania under Dr. Igor Grant, and another, involving almost 1,000 students, under Dr. Normal Quill at UCLA in 1972. Dr. Melvin Silverstein, also at UCLA, investigated the loss of immunity to disease and found no evidence to suggest such a conclusion; several doctors found no evidence to support the conclusion of chromosome damage;[29] and finally, Dr. Jack Mendelsohn of Harvard Medical School found no relationship between low testosterone levels and marijuana intake. It appeared that the limited data from laboratory studies could not stand up under replication or comparison to field studies on large groups of long-term users.

The value of any data is the ability to be replicated. If for any reason the conditions prevailing cause distortion of data, or the data are gathered from nonrepresentative populations (such as monkeys) or from small or extreme samples, the conclusions will be based upon erroneous calculations.

Some Uses of Factual Data

The UCRs' table on stolen property uses monetary data—the value of property stolen and property recovered. In the 1976 table, over $4 billion worth of property was reported stolen and only 29 percent recovered. We do not have estimates for unreported losses, but we may safely double the amount. The UCRs' preceding table gives average values for each crime. For example, of the 1,165,686 thefts of property from cars, the average value was $216. But the loss in an average homicide, reported at $81, does not include loss of future earnings or future contributions to the community.[30]

The UCRs do aid in getting a factual estimate of how much crime there is and how costly it is. But many economic crimes are not reported. Corporations and banks do not like the publicity associated with prosecutions, which can cause a loss of public confidence. Many employers do not like to lose time in court appearances, and many feel that they can handle the situation better than the police can. Some avoid police inquiries for personal reasons. And computer fraud, which is usually large, is generally kept concealed. Thus, the UCRs do not as yet deal with the economic impact of crime on the nation, since those crimes with the most monetary value are not reported as such. We really need an index of economic crime to illustrate its enormous damage to American society.

[28] Dr. Vera Rubin and Dr. Lambros Comitas, *Ganja in Jamaica* (The Hague: Mouton, 1975). Dr. Rubin is the director of the Research Institute for the Study of Man; the study was commissioned by the National Institute for Mental Health.

[29] See citations in Brecher, "Marijuana."

[30] FBI, *Uniform Crime Reports, 1976*, Tables 18 and 19.

An index of economic crime would include:

1. The narcotics industry, easily the largest business in the United States in the sale of hard and soft drugs
2. Manipulated gambling, probably the second largest crime industry
3. Theft of securities and manipulation of bank records
4. Loan-sharking, bankruptcy scams, holding-company manipulation
5. Real estate manipulation and fraud, the selling of phony property
6. Computer fraud and computer embezzlement
7. Arson, probably the fastest-growing and most profitable crime
8. Pornography, smut, and prostitution, still a major source of profit to organized crime
9. Price fixing and rigging for criminal intent, bootlegging
10. Political bribery, labor-union and bureaucratic corruption, including kickbacks, contract default, manipulation of taxes

Thefts of art works, documents and major forgeries would appear lower in the list above.

The economists have barely entered the research of crime, but they are progressing.[31] Crime data compiled by economists appear to operate on three levels:

1. Totals showing the impact of crime (as in the UCRs)
2. Analysis of the financial operation of a criminal business
3. A cost/benefit or cost analysis of the effects of crime or of applying sanctions

The last item has been used to analyze rehabilitation efforts and court procedure techniques. Using monetary statistics to quantify crime is useful in showing economic impact, but it can do little to find causes or solutions.

The Value of Data to Research Objectives

The use of data for survey research has been questioned for several reasons. Critics say:

1. Interviewers get too many informed answers from such a large percentage of uninformed people. (20 percent are estimated uninformed.)
2. The samplers appear to get very few refusals; they seem to complete surveys by a "compulsory process"—by virtually compelling people to answer by virtue of social-role expectations of the interviewer–client relationship.
3. People often express one view in public and another in private, particularly on many personal matters, such as race, sex, income.
4. People change their views with public opinion—the bandwagon effect now known as "momentum"—or fluctuate with the charisma of some public

[31] The income from crime, probably between $50–$100 billion per annum, deserves the attention of economists.

figure, especially when scandal is involved or when they are outraged at a public crime, such as assassination or corruption.

5. Votes supposedly indicating a "pro" position may actually be votes *against* another issue. Votes *for* abortion may actually be votes *against* children or juvenile delinquents or welfare cases. Votes *for* pornography may be votes *against* women, marriage, or harsh penalties for unacceptable sex, and vice versa.
6. Mostly young people and students are surveyed or are respondents, and this represents the younger, inexperienced tail wagging the older social dog.
7. There are people who like to say yes, and there are people who like to say no, and there are people who will always be indecisive and have no opinion.[32]
8. Many questions on surveys are confusing, open-ended, or leading, or represent a combination of error, and may never meet the research objectives.
9. The objectivity of the survey implies that all parts of the research blueprint are carefully numbered and included, when in fact they are not.
10. The quantitative statistical quality of data overwhelms the client with a sense of numerical powerlessness—a statistical anomie—and the qualitative attributes of life are lost in scientific calculations.

In the face of such a list of data errors, one may well wonder why statisticians, and research methodologists in particular, persist. The answer is that, on the whole, reliable data properly gathered are responsible for most of modern progress. The advantages of the use of research data in social science are these:

1. Research data represent a scientific approach to measuring differences and relationships, understanding causal associations, and eliminating spurious beliefs and pseudoscientific conclusions. The use of the hypothesis motivates research that generates data for the testing of the null hypothesis.
2. Social-science sampling procedures save time and money, and in their present sophistication are surprisingly accurate.
3. The use of statistical analysis of data aids in decision making and to a great extent eliminates judgmental values and decisions based upon uninformed opinion.
4. Sampling and analytical techniques aid in the prevention of error, ensure industrial safety, point up flaws in budget expenditures, are invaluable in epidemiological studies, and are useful in the examination of crime from interdisciplinary viewpoints.
5. Human behavior, when quantified, can be better understood for the purpose of improving the quality of life, the control of crime, and the correction and rehabilitation of offenders.
6. Data used for the quantification of behavior can be qualified by other data—the use of other methods to give the research validity. The study of crime data is enhanced by interdisciplinary approaches.[33]
7. *Only* by the use of data are we able to obtain frequencies, percentages, proportions, means and averages, ranges, variations, deviations and distributions, correlations, and analysis.

[32] Hopkins, *The Numbers Game*, pp. 102–21.
[33] Zeisal, *Say It With Figures.*

8. Data from survey research are particularly valuable in assessment of critical situations when a crisis decision must be made. They can eliminate many wrong decisions and, while not guaranteeing the correct one, may indicate it.
9. Survey data permit the population being sampled to participate in the decision making process. This is the best use of survey data. Data may also be used for prediction.
10. No proof exists without data, no discovery can be confirmed without data. *This is as true in the social sciences as in the physical sciences.*

SUMMARY

Research design, which includes the research method, depends upon the generation of data for its success. The research design must meet the aim of the research objectives. Correspondingly, the method used must generate data that supply the information for statistical analysis. In the past, many surveys were made that were cross-sectional, "one-shot," single-factor analyses. Surveys now are expected to produce data that can be supported by other methods and by and through other disciplines.

The generation of data depends upon two things, the sampling procedure and the appropriateness of the instrument. We would like the sample to represent the population, and we would like anything that occurs in the parent population to occur in the sample. Data on human beings are collected by human beings and therefore subject to human error. The science of survey research, or any research, is a science of the control of error. Even in our final conclusions, the decision is made upon the *probability* that the relationship does not happen by chance; but even so, chance still enters into the equation. The design does much to eliminate error by incorporating the proper procedure and proper controls. The design must be within the practicality and experience of the researcher.

Another "must" in the construction of the research design is pretest. The findings from pretest invariably add sophistication to the final instrument by revealing many problems not foreseen in nonfield conditions. Pretest is mainly a test of the workability of the method as well as the practicality of the hypothesis.

In the final test or survey, the sample should possess randomness, representation, and homogeneous variances; otherwise, our data will not represent the parent population.

Computers aid in processing data, but they will only process what is fed into them. For example, the UCRs are an invaluable source of data, but the methods used to gather them are determined by the offense rather than the actual crime rate in the population. If we use such data for decision making or prediction, we must be careful that we understand the limitations, since error will accumulate from inaccurate definitions in the operationalization of the variables and the method used to gather data (sampling). The data we use in the social sciences are already suspect because of ambiguity in the definition of behavioral concepts. To counteract the errors in soft data, we need confirmation by other methods. The ideal type of design will try to check its own method and will certainly use other methods. Data must be challenged by life observation as well as by statistical analysis.

EXERCISES

1. What is meant by making the sample "truly representative"?
2. Define *parent population, randomization, inference, probability*.
3. Explain, "We never prove the hypothesis." Why do we seek test results rather than "truth"?
4. What are some important factors in your consideration of a research design?
5. Comment on the sentence, "The research design must meet the aims of the research objective."
6. What are some of the factors in pretest? Describe how you would prepare for and give a pretest. What are you testing? What will your findings include?
7. What is instrument response? How would you check for question comprehension? What are some points to check for method suitability?
8. Samples should conform to three main assumptions. What are they?
9. Data in the social sciences are "nearly true, and a lot are personal conjecture." Why is this?
10. What are the UCRs? Upon what kind of data are they based? What is the weakness in this data base? What are victim surveys?
11. If data are used for research and research findings are used for decision making, what errors can occur if a wrong data base is used?
12. Define *etiology, ecology, epidemiology, epistemology*.
13. How does data error occur? How would you control data error?
14. What are some of the risks in using surveys? How could an extreme sample be used to fool the researcher?
15. How could apparently scientific data gathered under laboratory conditions be misused? Were such findings used inadvertently by the Senate subcommittee's publication regarding marijuana?
16. Construct a potential index based upon police performance.
17. How would you combat "statistical anomie"?
18. Comment on the errors and advantages of the use of data in the social sciences.
19. How can common sense aid science, and vice versa?
20. Why should we use data as a base for action?
21. Development of scales for measurement is a useful practice, as we shall see in the next chapter. Try developing a scale for jury selection, using a plus or minus, or a weighted score whose total determines acceptance or rejection of the juror. Include background factors as well as general demeanor.

FOR FURTHER READING

Bailey, Kenneth D., *Methods of Social Research.* New York: Free Press, 1978.

Barzun, Jacques, and Henry F. Graff, *The Modern Researcher,* Chaps. 3–7. New York: Harcourt Brace Jovanovich, 1970.

Clark, Robert S., *Fundamentals of Criminal Justice Research,* Chaps. 3–6. Lexington, Mass.: Heath, 1977.

Feldman, Saul D., *Deciphering Deviance.* Boston: Little, Brown, 1978. See Parts I and II, especially articles by Richard Fox, Anthony Starr, David Phillips, and Shirley Angrist.

Hopkins, Harry, *The Numbers Game.* London: Secker and Warburg, 1973.

Inciardi, James A., and Harvey A. Siegal, *Crime: Emerging Issues.* New York: Praeger, 1977.

Johnston, Norma, Leonard Savitz, and Marvin E. Wolfgang, *The Sociology of Punishment and Correction* (2nd ed.). New York: John Wiley, 1970. There are many excellent examples in this reader; Section VI, "Prediction," contains several famous studies. Cf. Hopkins, Chap. 6.

Kaplan, Lawrence, and Dennis Kessler, *An Economic Analysis of Crime.* Springfield, Ill.: Charles C Thomas, 1976. This reader covers many of the economic aspects of crime.

Larsen, Richard J., and Donna Fox Stroup, *Statistics in the Real World.* New York: Macmillan, 1976.

Levitt, Eugene E., *Clinical Research Design and Analysis.* Springfield, Ill.: Charles C Thomas, 1961. A neat book (160 pp.) that discusses clinical designs.

Penick, Bettye K. Eidson, and Maurice B. Owens, eds., *Surveying Crime.* Washington, D.C.: National Academy of Sciences, 1976. An academic evaluation of the victim surveys by NCS.

Reichard, Robert S., *The Numbers Game.* New York: McGraw-Hill, 1972.

Rosen, Stephen, *Future Facts.* New York: Simon & Schuster, 1976. Read about the future of society in Chap. 5.

Sagarin, Edward, and Fred Montanino, eds., *Deviants: Voluntary Actors in a Hostile World.* Glenview, Ill.: Scott, Foresman, 1977. Discusses contemporary problems.

Senter, R. J., *Analysis of Data.* Glenview, Ill.: Scott, Foresman, 1969. A statistical look at data.

Sonquist, John A., and William C. Dunkelberg, *Survey and Opinion Research.* Englewood Cliffs, N.J.: Prentice-Hall, 1977.

Turn, Rein, *Computers in the 1980s.* New York: Columbia University Press, 1974.

Vetter, Harold J., and Jack Wright, *Introduction to Criminology.* Springfield, Ill.: Charles C Thomas, 1974. See Part III, "Patterns of Criminal Behavior."

Winslow, Robert W., ed., *Crime in a Free Society* (3rd ed.). Belmont, Calif: Dickenson, 1977. Read the FBI Uniform Crime Reports with this book.

Zeisal, Hans, *Say It With Figures* (5th ed.). New York: Harper & Row, 1968. Prof. Zeisal uses various topical situations to develop data, such as a data score for jury selection, or selection of a trial with or without jury.

7

The Instrument, the Sample, and the Method

It would be presumptuous to attempt to summarize all the books that have been written on the three subjects of questionnaire design, sampling, and sampling procedures.[1] The points raised in this chapter are set out simply as guidelines for the student in the hope that you will read further on these subjects. Of course, while reading is very important, true knowledge of survey research comes from experience in the field—real-life research of controversial social problems.

Conditions in criminology and criminal justice are changing so rapidly that data previously gathered often become obsolete before they can be used again, and long-range forecasts are very difficult. We need to get solutions for problems very quickly, so our methodology must respond to the challenge of the times; we need to be faster, more accurate, and technologically more efficient.

In politics, the response of the voters has been analyzed to such a fine art that predictions of election outcomes can be made with very small samples. But political outcomes are usually win-or-lose situations; the issues in criminology and criminal justice are more complex. We are dealing with crime, punishment, law, sanctions, protection, and resocialization.

The instrument—the questionnaire—is the tool that, in conjunction with the sample, actually generates the data essential for the statistical calculations. The

[1] In the bibliography list, "For Further Reading," at the end of this chapter, each book contains further bibliography for specialized reading.

instrument is the means by which the variables are operationalized. The variables are set forth in question or statement form; the respondent answers the question or states agreement or disagreement with the statement. How the question is designed determines the response.

The questionnaire should be simple, easy to answer, and uncluttered, and take as little time as possible. Questionnaires with too many questions are not only complex

REQUIREMENTS FOR QUESTIONNAIRE DESIGN

1. The questions must be precise, easily understood, and easy to answer. Questions that are brief and to the point are best.
2. Directions should clearly indicate where and how to respond to questions. Scoring should be neat, easy to code, and placed on the right.
3. Questions should motivate the respondent to answer; they should capture the interest of the client. Avoid excessive recall.
4. Do not use complex questions such as "either/or," "this or that," double-barreled questions, and questions using technical phrases. Avoid double negatives.
5. Unlike census forms and tax returns, which have a particular format and use, questionnaires are generally best kept simple, short, and straightforward. Unless asking for specific information from a specific person (i.e., people who have been arrested, drug users, victims of crimes, etc.), do not use complex questions such as, "If yes, answer the following; if no, go on to question 23."
6. As a beginner, try to limit the questionnaire to one page. It saves time, effort, and worry. If you must extend it, each section should be separate. If your questionnaire is long, you will tire your client–and yourself. A short questionnaire enables you to keep the variables in sequence, each question leading to the next.
7. If the questions contain personal information, make sure your respondent is protected by *not* recording name, address, telephone number, Social Security number. Protect the anonymity and confidentiality of your client.
8. Questions should not be offensive, attack the client's privacy, or result in incriminating information. All responses should be voluntary.
9. If clients are handicapped, blind, or illiterate, help them answer the questionnaire, but do not respond for them. Write the answers exactly as given.
10. Design the questionnaire format so that it can be completed in the least possible time. Don't waste your time or your respondent's time with foolish questions. Use common sense, experience, and pretest findigns to improve your questions. Do not crowd your questions; leave space for answers. Your questionnaire should have five parts–title, statement to the client, questionnaire, appreciation, and special observations by the interviewer. Correct for grammar, typos, and spelling.

Source: H. W. Smith, *Strategies of Social Research* (Englewood Cliffs, N.J.: Prentice-Hall, 1975). See Chap. 8, "Surveys: Use and Misuse of the Interview and Questionnaire."

to answer, but complex to analyze. Usually each variable becomes a question or a response; thus, the more questions there are, the more variables must be analyzed. When the variable is designed as a scale, even more work is involved. As a rule of thumb, the number of variables equals the number of questions.

The questionnaire should be divided into at least two parts, questions on the independent variables and on the dependent variables. Again as a rule of thumb, the number of parts should be the same as in the projected research model. It is wise to draft a rough design for the instrument before it is put into final form. Good questionnaires do not just happen; they are the result of hard work. *The guiding principle in questionnaire design is to ask, "Am I writing questions that will show the effect of the independent variable upon the dependent variable?"*

QUESTION DESIGN

Questions may be set out in dichotomous form, in category form, Bogardus form, Likert-type response, scale form, single response, and open end.

Dichotomous Form

This calls for a yes/no, true/false, male/female type of response. The client has to be one or the other (This form should be avoided if there is a category of *No answer, Independent, Not applicable*, or *Don't know*.)

Example: Have you ever been arrested for a felony? Yes____ No____

Category Form

This question requires the respondent to fit himself into a select category from a choice of several, as in religion, political preference, and education. The categories give the design the necessary ingredient of stratification.

Example: What is your religion?
Protestant____ Catholic____ Jewish____ Moslem____ Other____

Bogardus Form

This type of series of questions is ideal for scaling attitude or prejudice, and it actually rates itself by the graduated responses.

Example:

1. Do you approve of work programs for felons? Yes___ No___
2. Would you like a work program in your district? Yes___ No___
3. Would you work with a felon? Yes___ No___
4. Would you have a felon living in your home? Yes___ No___

The last question would be significant and would score the same as the total for questions in that group.[2]

Likert-Type Response[3]

This type of response is now most favored, since it gives the client a chance to rate his own answer. The scoring box is usually set to the right, with abbreviations explained on the questionnaire form. Coding gives a rating scale of five intervals (0-4, 1-5), and the choices run from "easy" to "impossible," "strongly agree" to "strongly disagree," "extremely satisfied" to "extremely dissatisfied," and "rarely" to "frequently"—the last of which takes the time element out of the question and puts it in the response box. The choices in Likert-type questions run from extreme to extreme, giving greater choice of selection in the response but also increasing the number of cells for statistical analysis and thereby inviting error if the sample or cell total falls below a required number.

Example: The death penalty should be reinstated.

SA___ A___ U___ D___ SD___

(The form has explained that SA means "strongly agree," A means "agree," U means "undecided," D means "disagree," and SD means "strongly disagree.")

Sometimes a series of Likert-type questions is arranged to give a total that may be used as an attitude scale. Coding on a single question, such as the one above, may run from 1 through 5, with 5 being most opposed to the death penalty. If six questions were used, totals would range from a low of 6 to a high of 30. The advantage of using a series of questions to total is that if the questions are logically related, the resultant scale gives a wider range than does a single response; indeed, each characteristic tested sums into a more complete picture of an attitude, a belief, an opinion, a value, or the life-style of the respondent.[4]

[2] E. S. Bogardus, "A Social Distance Scale," *Sociological and Social Research*, 17 (1933), 265-71.

[3] R. Likert, *A Technique for the Measurement of Attitudes* (New York: Columbia University Press, 1932).

[4] Fred N. Kerlinger, *Foundations of Behavioral Research*, 2nd ed. (New York: Holt, Rinehart & Winston, 1973), Chap. 29, "Objective Tests and Scales."

One caution: *Coding scores are best omitted from the questionnaire*, since they may influence the respondent to "do well" by scoring as high as possible.

Rating Scales

Respondents are asked to rate themselves on lines, ladders, or graphs indicating their response. The scales indicate scores of 1 through 10, 0 through 9, low to high, or none to extreme. In other scales, a client may be requested to score a series of events against a standard score given for a common event such as marriage. He may be asked to rate a birth, a death, an accident, unemployment, etc. against a standard value or average score, i.e. marriage = 100. Scales are a relief to the general format and are interesting for the client. They may also be compared and correlated with other measures used in the survey. An example:

Rate your present fear of vandalism (Circle one number)

0 1 2 3 4 5 6 7 8 9 10
None Some Average Great Extreme

The scale will describe the method of scoring and also indicate values appropriate to the scores.

Single Response

These items are usually age and income, cited in actual figures. They may also be categorized by recoding, which is a computer form of regrouping or rescoring values. Answers to single-response items, because of the personal nature of such questions, may not be entirely accurate. For example, people may overstate or understate their incomes, depending on whether they are applying for a credit card or replying to the IRS. Age is also a delicate factor, since it can affect insurance, retirement, job status, marriage status, and medical status. A better alternative is to offer a category with a range in which the respondent may fit with others of the same group. Ten-year and $5,000 groupings are acceptable. For example:

Age:
- 18–28 yrs. ______
- 29–39 yrs. ______
- 40–50 yrs. ______
- 51–61 yrs. ______
- 62+ yrs. ______

Income:
- Under $5,000 ______
- $5,000–10,000 ______
- $10,001–15,000 ______
- $15,001–20,000 ______
- $20,001–25,000 ______
- $25,001 or over ______

Notice that the groups do not overlap, each category continues where the preceding one stopped. In this way, the respondent must fall into one or the other, not into both.

Open-End Response

This category is an inquiry into personal opinion, habit, or values; answers are expressed in writing. They can be most informative, but they are almost impossible to score. Space for the reply should be adequate.

Leading Questions and Other Devices

Construction of a questionnaire appears to be a simple task. It is, but only if you are prepared to do your homework. If you rush at it, you may find that your final instrument is not exactly what you had in mind. The questionnaire is designed to furnish as much unbiased data as is obtainable.[5] If the questions are poorly designed, problems accumulate. The easiest and costliest error is that of poor wording, which can lead the respondent to give the answer he believes is required rather than the information needed for the survey research. For example:

1. The police are not doing an effective job. Yes___ No___
2. Do you agree with the president's action on the enforcement of drug laws? Yes___ No___
3. Are you satisfied with the present corrupt political administration? Yes___ No___
4. Would you support higher standards for judge selection? Yes___ No___
5. Are you satisfied with your present income? Yes___ No___
6. Would you support the death penalty for juveniles? Yes___ No___

These six questions lead the respondent to answer as the interviewer sees fit. Certain key words are used—*not . . . effective, agree with the president, corrupt, higher standards, satisfied, juveniles*—to persuade the respondent to come out on "the right side." The first question is negative, leading to a "no" answer; the second leads to a "yes," to show agreement with the president; the third is clearly prejudicial; the fourth appeals to higher standards; the fifth is obvious—most people want more; and the sixth calls for a "no" from anyone who does not want to be thought of as a child abuser. The respondent is tricked into answers that are fixed. All such questions should be avoided; the question should offer a free choice.

Keep the questions brief and to the point. If you are asking your respondents to rank items or issues, do not overload them with long lists; a list of ten items is sufficient. And make sure the items have been carefully selected on the basis of

[5] C. A. Moser and G. Kalton, *Survey Methods in Social Investigation*, 2nd ed. (New York: Basic Books, 1972), Chap. 13, "Questionnaires."

pretest. Although you shouldn't use too many personal questions, questions at "gut" level get more responses than impersonal ones do. For example:

Juvenile delinquents should receive heavier sentences. Yes___ No___

was changed to:

I think juvenile delinquents' sentences should be
More severe___ The same___ More lenient___

The revised question will get more responses; it demands personal attention.

There are ways of greatly improving the questionnaire. With a little imagination, the test question can elicit a surprising amount of information. Take the question:

Are there times you use police services? Yes___ No___

This can be greatly improved by taking the time out of the question and extending it on the right:

Do you use police services: Often___ Sometimes___ Rarely___

If there are several time questions, they can be put together; for example:

	Often	Sometimes	Rarely
Have you been bothered by strangers?	___	___	___
Are you troubled by TV crime reports?	___	___	___
Do you go out alone at night?	___	___	___

Not only can this type of response be easily coded—by 1, 2, 3, or 3, 2, 1—but the related items on a scale may be totaled, thus giving a score for each client.

Some investigators purposely include in their scales verification items to prevent the client from "fixing" the results. And dummy items can be inserted to counter the tendency of some people to answer the questions in a definite pattern. Of course, this can give rise to some dummy items getting more responses than the variables![6]

The objective of the questions is the *discovery of facts*, not manipulation of the client. Therefore, we need to know the pitfalls and avoid error.[7] False questions will generate false outcomes. *The research is only as good as the questionnaire, and the questionnaire is only as good as the words you choose and the format you use.* You generate the instrument that generates data.

Back-Translation in Practice

Questions should always be understandable. It is a mistake to think that the people in the sample will understand them because you do. If there are racial, educational,

[6] Leo Srole, *Mental Health in the Metropolis* (New York: McGraw-Hill, 1962). See Srole's anomie scale.

[7] Earl R. Babbie, *The Practice of Social Research* (Belmont, Calif.: Wadsworth, 1975), Chap. 5, "Questionnaire Construction"; and John W. Best, *Research in Education*, 3rd ed. (Englewood Cliffs, N.J.: Prentice-Hall, 1977), pp. 157–76, "Improving Questionnaire Items."

occupational, or any other cultural language differences, the researcher should endeavor to write the questionnaire in the language familiar to the sample to be tested. One way of doing this is by back-translation. In this technique, a person who is a member of the parent population or who knows its language well is asked to *translate the question* into language acceptable to the proposed sample. The translation is then given to another member of the parent population, who is asked to *translate the question back* to standard English.[8] If it can be returned to its original form, or near it, the translation is acceptable for testing.

For example, a question from a survey in a black community read:

I think I am no good at all. Often___ Sometimes___ Rarely___

The first translation, made by a black from the community, read, "I am down on myself." The back-translation read, "I feel like I am no good." The translation, "I am down on myself," was acceptable. It was then pretested and found to be valid.

This is one sample of how questions may have to be changed by back-translation.

STEPS IN BACK TRANSLATION

1. The proposed question for variable data is set up in its original form.
2. A member or members of a neutral or the parent population are selected who are conversant with both forms of the question, original and translated.
3. The first translation is made—of the original question into suitable form for the parent population.
4. The translated question is given to other members to translate back to the original. These members are unaware of the first translators.
5. Corrections are made if needed, and the question is adjusted or put through the same process again until the back-translation equals the original question.
6. The new form is pretested.
7. Adjustments are made if required.
8. The new form of the question is now ready for final survey on the sample.

Words in the culture of educated native Americans can have quite different meanings in other cultures, and grammar may differ greatly. For instance, normally we avoid double negatives, but in some forms of speech they are acceptable. The pretest will reveal the workability of the question, and it may lead to clues for other questions. The form of English used must be appropriate to the local dialect and the educational level of the community.

[8] R. Fink, "Interviewer Training and Supervision in a Survey of Laos," *International Social Science Journal*, 15 (1963), 21-34.

Sampling Theory and Sampling Practice

Error can be controlled by selecting a sample of the appropriate size.[9] Size may be statistically determined, but as a rule of thumb, small samples should not be less than 30, and large samples not less than 100. Other factors in sample size are the number of cells (categories) used and the method chosen. Sample size, as we shall see in the discussion on the normal curve, determines how closely we approximate the parent population. The theory of sampling is valid for all practical purposes, is more precise than other methods, gives us an approximation of the real world, and is based upon statistical logic. We use logically defined constants, logical calculations, and a logical decision-making process.

The errors in sampling stem from the fact that sampling theory is just that, a theory, and as such is not technically practical. We have to adjust the theory to put it into practice, because its assumptions seldom apply. For example, the theory is based upon infinite populations and infinite samples; it is mathematically based upon probability sampling with replacement, and the use of continuous data. We cannot replace our sample, nor are we always fortunate enough to have continuous data. In addition, extremes in the population may affect the calculations and thus the final decision on the hypothesis; for instance, two millionaires in a sample could seriously affect the mean for income.

Applying the Rules in Practice

In practice, as many methods as possible are combined to give the desired results. *Convenient systematic-stratified samples based upon judgmental considerations are often used.* Judgmental sampling is sampling that is based upon the researcher's own understanding of the population to be surveyed. It really falls under the heading of nonprobability sampling—that is, it lacks random design; however, in many cases it can indicate the best possible survey selection without a waste of time in testing areas known to be not applicable.

The combination of methods helps reduce error.[10] I cannot emphasize enough that *the objective of sampling is to obtain as representative sample as is humanly possible*, and any method or combination of methods that achieves this purpose is acceptable. These rules will help:

1. *Keep the sample size large*—certainly above 30 and preferably closer to 100. A maximum size under most conditions would be 1,500.

[9] Hubert M. Blalock, Jr., *Social Statistics*, 2nd ed. (New York: McGraw-Hill, 1972), pp. 529–30.

[10] L. Kish, *Survey Sampling* (New York: Wiley, 1965). For example, Kish indicates that quota samples used in selected areas are more efficient than judgmental samples alone.

2. *Stratify the sample* to reduce error. Use whatever available categories are pertinent to the research project.
3. *Use a combination of methods* to obtain your sample. Systematic-stratified samples that are chosen intelligently and are convenient are often appropriate.
4. *Always inject the idea of probability sampling* in favor of quota and non-random methods.
5. *Be innovative* in getting your sample. Do not be distressed because one method does not work; try another.
6. *Aim to be as representative as possible*. This is the best way to reduce sampling error.

Sampling in practice involves taking what is available as far as time and cost will allow.[11] For example, if a total universe is available, such as an entire institution, the researcher is in luck. If the sample is not too large and the community is small, samples are taken by random numbers. If the population—say, of a city—is large, involving many thousands who cannot be assigned numbers for reasons of time or practicality, then a systematic sample may be developed—either by using the multi-stage cluster method, or by developing quadrants, or by taking the most populous buildings or shopping malls.

A team of researchers, used at different times and locations, may obtain a very good representative sample. For example, in a student study of issues, the campus was divided into quadrants and the population was sampled in each quadrant. This was followed up by sampling the largest and busiest building complexes. The sampling was taken at different times, including peak hours. Thus, a 10 percent representative sample was taken, with no person being sampled twice. A sampling team of 50 was used, divided so that members went to each section of the sample design, with each member obtaining 25 samples. Normally, sampling teams are not that large. Student teams vary from four to six members; four-member teams appear to be more efficient.

For students to sample a city population, I recommend the following design.

Random Sampling

Random sampling became a "science" some years ago.[12] By this method, in order for everyone, every event, or every object to have an equal chance of selection, *it must first be numbered*. Then a list of random numbers is generated by the computer, and the selection process begins by starting at an arbitrary place in that list and selecting the number that corresponds to the list. For example, assuming that 100 items have been numbered (addresses, names, students) from 0 to 99, and assuming also that ten of those numbers are to be selected randomly, so that every

[11] Moser and Kalton, *Survey Methods in Social Investigation*. Read Chapters 4, 5, 6, 7, and 8 for a comprehensive view of sampling, pp. 61–210. The authors deal with basic sampling, sampling problems, techniques, and national random designs.

[12] R. Fisher, *The Design of Experiments*, 6th ed. (New York: Hafner, 1951).

item shall have an equal chance of selection, the researcher will turn to a *table of random numbers*. These tables may be found in most statistical books and are available in indexes or appendixes in some others. They may be generated by programmable calculators by entering the range and "seed" numbers, or obtained from computer programs. To use them, one may start anywhere as long as horizontal or vertical movement is consistent. Let us take a hypothetical table:

81465	97643	40215	67842	71054	86432	69544	04783
10580	15012	04011	82647	91656	14273	94360	30156
12368	46673	65491 →	32679 →	97852 →	01235	85566	47321
81342	89043	68345	17543	23868	55692	90832	31486
43286	57403	95348	17392	28360	47651	91287	41395

We start in the third block at row 3, column 1. The starting digit is marked and the direction is indicated. Since we need two-digit numbers, reading across our ten selections we have 65, 49, 13, 26, 79, 97, 85, 20, 12, and 35. Had the page been longer, we could have gone down or up, we could have skipped every second number or every three spaces; there is no set rule but consistency.

In a small universe or population, containing only a few hundred people, the use of random numbers may be wise. But when the situation involves thousands, as it often does, or even tens or hundreds of thousands, using random numbers becomes less practical. It takes too much time, and it is not very reliable as numbers become larger. For example, in the case of, say, 500 prisoners in the same medium-custody classification, an independent random sample could be obtained using random numbers. However, in a city with a population of 400,000, or even in a university of 10,000 students, the use of random numbers is precluded by the time and effort required. Some numbers selected may not be currently resident, some may be in the hospital, some may be temporarily out of town, some may have moved or died. Such a list, unless it is absolutely current (highly improbable), will produce errors.

Other means can be used to obtain just as effective a sample. One of these means is a *systematic random sample*. Again, this involves counting the population, but beginning at an arbitrary point, every *n*th member is selected. For example:

1 (2) 3 4 5 6 (7) 8 9 10 11 (12) 13 14 15 16 (17)

Here, in the numbers 1 to 17, starting at 2, every fifth person has been selected.

Using Multistage Sampling

Several important elements enter into actual sampling:

1. In a multistage procedure, the city (or total population under examination) is divided into precincts, zones, quadrants, or residential areas, then into locales, and finally into sampling areas.
2. Systematic random sampling is usually used in each.

3. Representation is maintained by stratification.
4. Team training and uniform procedures and techniques reduce error; i.e., uniform interviewing, scoring, and coding.
5. Changing interviewers, times, and places helps in reducing set.
6. Discretion should be balanced by experience and methodological considerations when using judgmental, convenience, or quota samples.

To obtain a perfect random sample in a city is almost impossible, and the cost/benefit ratio may well indicate that it is not worth it. The method above does produce a very reliable estimate of the parent population from the sample. Remember, we are dealing with a city of many hundreds of thousands. However, we will not include people under 18, those in institutions and hospitals, the shut-ins, and the very old. Now the sample must be representative. It must include a ratio of sex,

STUDENT SAMPLE DESIGN

1. In a large city, or section of that city—say, with a population of 400,000—the area should be divided into population zones of approximate equal size—say, eight zones of 50,000. Usually, this follows residential patterns or compass quadrants.
2. Usually in each zone, there is a busy area where masses of people interact, such as a large bureaucracy, industrial concern, or shopping mall. Shopping malls are preferred because of the weekend traffic and the variety of people who go there.
3. Assuming that a sample of 400 is required (this could easily be 800 for four students), the ratio is now 50 per zone, or one in 1,000. This ratio is too high to be practical. A practical ratio is one in 50, or one in 100. Such a sample in each zone is now of every fiftieth person out of a sample population of 2,500.
4. The team member will now sample every fiftieth person in the two zones—a total of 100 people out of a total population of 5,000.
5. The total sample of 400 represents a population of 20,000, or 5% of the total city population. This is a considerable, convenient, and good sample.
6. Judgmental considerations in most surveys will eliminate children, very old people, and tourists. Stratification will balance the sexes, and the age, occupational, and racial groups.
7. This sampling can be backed up by a random sample from the telephone directory, based on a 1:1,000 ratio. The samples may be compared.
8. Several teams may be used to triangulate, increasing the sample validity. The large size of the sample—400 or more—reduces sample error, particularly when the sample is truly representative. Size and homogeneity act to reduce error. Precinct sample based upon this approach may be used to predict election outcomes when sample sizes of 1,500 are triangulated.
9. The final sample will reflect data from all over the city, from almost every walk of life. Such samples are usually very representative; and the method gives the student a worthwhile survey experience and results in worthwhile data. The results are surprisingly accurate.

race, age, occupation, politics, and religion that conforms to the parent population. We can take care of the sex, race, and age balance in the systematic random interviews. Political preference is taken care of by using the precinct system; occupation and religion by moving into known areas of occupational and religious preference, since most cities are subdivided by subcultural preference.

Figure 7-1 shows the actual progression of the sample selection. Only one precinct is shown there, for the sake of simplicity; in practice, several would be used, with each subdivided and subject to third-stage rules.

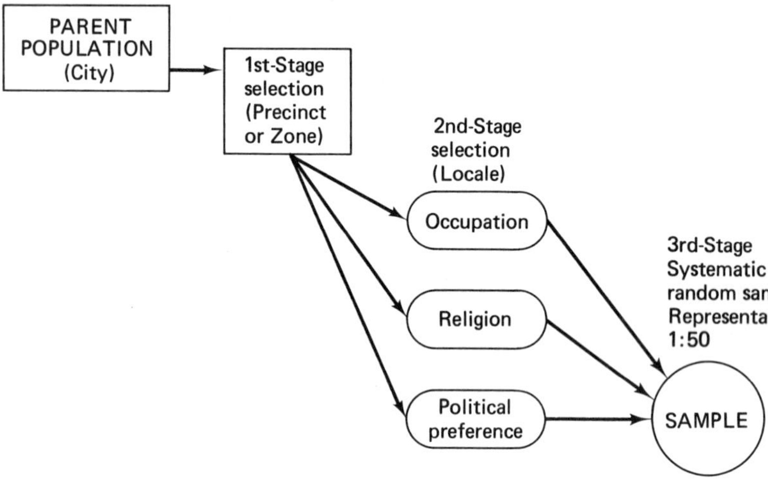

Fig. 7-1 Three-stage sampling process

In effect, the validity of the process is based upon:

1. *Statistical precision*, by using large samples from different areas
2. *Proportional representation*, by successively dividing the parent population into representative areas for sampling
3. *Homogeneity* in the sample as represented in the parent population, by the use of maintaining known stratified ratios
4. Use of *qualitative and quantitative control*, by combining sampling and statistical techniques to reduce sampling error
5. Use of *triangulation*, in using more than one area, more than one time period, and more than one interviewer

The final selection of clients from the multistage process conforms to the rule that as the number of clusters increases, the number of sample elements decreases. The final sample, which is in reality a collection of samples, is truly representative of the parent population.

SAMPLING METHODS

Sampling theory hinges on two main ideas, randomness and nonrandomness, also known as probability and nonprobability sampling respectively.[13] Sampling methods are shown in *Table 7.1* and their uses in *Table 7.2*.

Table 7.1. Sampling Methods

Probability	Nonprobability
Independent random sample (I.R.S.), in which every unit in the parent population has an equal chance of selection. This ideal seldom occurs in practice.	*Quota sampling*, selected without probability. Small quotas are fallacious; e.g., "3 out of 5 doctors . . ." Directory sampling is often used with quota sampling.
Systematic random sampling from available items. The sample is selected at regular intervals on a ratio of population to sample size.	*Convenience sampling.* A large sample, based upon any method, is taken at the best possible locations at the best possible times, at the best possible convenience.
Stratified sample, based on percentages of of categories that occur in the parent population. Sampling for each category is carried out as above.	*Judgmental sampling.* The best available sample is used, based upon the most intelligent choice, using personal judgment. Such a sample is limited by haste, experience, and choice. It also lacks randomness.
Cluster or *area sampling*. Areas are divided into zones or clusters, which are selected at random and subdivided; the method is repeated, each unit becoming smaller. This is sometimes called *multistage cluster sampling*. The chance of a cluster's selection is proportionate to its size; this is known as *PPS sampling* (probability proportionate to size). Each element has a probability equal to the number of selected clusters times elements per cluster/population size. If cluster size is increased, element number must be decreased.	*Availability sampling* has inherent bias but may be useful for pretest or exploratory survey. Client is accepted as available.
Directory sampling, taken randomly from telephone or city directory, or from utility, license, or mail-order lists. Sampling is by phone or mail. Directory sampling may involve any or all of the methods above.	Also included with nonrandom designs are content analysis, historical study, case study, participant observation, controlled or laboratory experiments, and nonrandom panel studies.

[13] Blalock, *Social Statistics*, p. 509. Blalock identifies four kinds of probability sampling–random, systematic, stratified, and cluster–and four kinds of nonprobability sampling–available, judgmental, convenient, and quota. Directory sampling is often systematic random sampling by page or letter.

Table 7.2. Uses of Sampling Methods

Probability	Nonprobability
Panel samples. A panel of people is randomly selected from a parent population, preferably for a time study of the effects of the independent variable on the dependent variable. The panel remains the same even if the parent population changes.	*Panel samples* such as those seen on TV are *nonrandom* and are not truly representative. In any case, the longer the study goes on, the more any panel loses its random quality.
Cohort sampling involves using the same population or cohort over a period of time. The sample may change, but the general locus of the parent population does not.	*Cohort studies* over 5- and 10-year periods are extremely useful; they increase the random factor, decrease nonprobability.
Comparative sampling. This method involves taking samples from two or more communities on a random basis, then comparing them. This eliminates a great deal of error that is not visible in single-area samples.	*Comparative sampling* has been done *with quota samples*, as have many designs. The main difference is that because the selection of the quota is left to the field worker, it usually ends up as those people closest to the interviewer.
Cross-sectional samples, easily the most popular, are taken at one time at one location. Unfortunately, many errors occur that are not visible, such as the effect of time and place upon the sample. The use of comparative studies has reduced much of this error.	*Cross-sectional samples* approximate nonrandom studies in terms of time and place.
Multiphase sampling. The main sample is subdivided for inquiry into selected questions, resulting in greater economy.	*Nonprobability is in essence the lack of representation in the sample as compared to the parent population.*
Master samples. For the purposes of selected results, voting outcomes, TV ratings, or consumer usage, samples are carefully selected from key areas and maintained as rating centers or panels.	*Master samples* become quota samples when they cease to represent the parent population. They need replacement with time and location.
Triangulation sampling. More than one method or one area is used to confirm or deny results of a single study. The better combination of methods aids in reducing or controlling sample error. This type of design becomes *contextual* if the environment and milieu are also examined.	More and more researchers are using a combination of methods for sampling, including combinations of random and nonrandom methodology, seeking the best from both worlds. Survey is combined with participant observation and case study.
Longitudinal sampling. The data are collected over a period of time. This aids in studying trends, changes in attitude, patterns of behavior, etc. Whereas cross-sectional studies are made at one point in time, cohort and panel studies are usually longitudinal.	*Time studies* are made with quota samples to save the expense and effort of large research designs.

Table 7.2. Uses of Sampling Methods–cont.

Probability	Nonprobability
Parallel samples are taken when studying comparative groups, such as faculty/students; clergy/congregation; officers/ranks. Equal samples are compared.	*Nonrandom parallel samples*, such as star players and audience, are used for TV ads to show similarities.
Preference sampling, such as with Likert-Bogardus, or Guttman-scaled responses, when used randomly gives very good indicators of social behavior.	*Sociometric sampling* is basically nonrandom and has fallen into disuse. It was widely used in educational studies to explain interaction based upon cumulative preferences.
Controlled sampling takes place in real-life situations, with random samples taken from two or more groups. Occasionally, two entire groups or universes are compared–one with a treatment, the other without. This is a form of comparative study.	*Controlled or laboratory studies (experiments)* are not random and take place under set conditions in which the researcher can manipulate the variables, which are not subject to chance, have a fixed value, and are therefore nonstochastic (have no probability).
Census sampling, data collected to verify census data. This has been found to be necessary to check on poor survey work.	A large nonresponse item or inadequate training of census workers can actually invalidate a census, reducing it to nonrandomness.
Pretest sampling is usually taken in a neutral area that does not affect the main sample design. It is probably the most important type of sampling, as it determines the final draft of the instrument that in turn determines the final data.	*Pretest samples* are sometimes nonrandom, as results are used to gather information for improvement of the final draft of the test instrument. This is discussed in the text.

Three Ways to Sample–A Comparison of Survey Methods

In survey research, three methods are most used by behavioral scientists to collect data. The best is *interview*, a personal interaction with the client; the second is *telephone*, an impersonal interaction with the respondent; and the third is the *mail-out*, an impersonal interaction with an impersonal reactor.

Telephones are convenient for conducting surveys, a fact well known among circulation managers, consumer rating polls, and TV polls. But the telephone survey has built-in error as well as built-in efficiency. See *Table 7.3*.

Interviews are preferred to the other two methods because of the relative success of this method. It has a high degree of accuracy and sophistication. Interview surveys have medium to high costs, moderate work demands, high control of data, high motivation and spontaneity; they are convenient and widely used. They are easy to pretest and to administer, and not too much time is expended in completion. There is also the advantage of actually being in the field and observing background

Table 7.3. Errors and Advantages in Using Telephone Surveys

Errors	Advantages
Not all people have phones. Poor people who lack phones (15%) are left out, causing economic bias in the sample.	Most people have or share phones; 85% of the population is accessible by telephone.
Many people have unlisted numbers–about 16% in the entire country and 33% in the cities. [AT & T, 1977.]	Most people can be reached by sequential dialing or from lists supplied by credit companies. The large numbers provide convenience.
Many who are called do not answer; people refuse to disclose information over the phone for various reasons; others can't be bothered.	Many people, even though rushed, will talk for a few minutes. The phone is an excellent way to reach shut-ins and widen the sample spectrum.
Many listed have moved or died, are on holidays, are sick, or are not available.	The large numbers reduce sampling errors.
New phones are unlisted for some time, owing to listing procedures. Repairs affect lines.	Cost of a local survey is low, and it is easy to train telephone interviewers.
Some people have two, three, or more listings, giving them more than one chance of selection.	Randomness versus nonrandomness becomes a matter of individual versus group interest in phone surveys.
Commercial offices are listed. This increases nonresponse and affects randomness.	There is a rapidity of response on key issues. People like to give opinions on current issues.
Sampling by names may involve cultural bias.	Group issues and consumer issues tend to be fairly accurate.

data and the effect of any extraneous variable or other unanticipated effects. It is easy to train interviewers, and one is able to handle special cases (infirm and illiterate) quite well. Nonresponse is usually low and completion high. On the other hand, interviews do suffer from interviewer effect, halo effect, and reactive effect.

Mail surveys take more time to prepare and more time to complete. There is usually a large number of nonrespondents,[14] people who do not have the time or inclination to reply even when an SAE (self-addressed envelope) is provided. The mail-out is best for the inaccessible person, the shut-ins, and the elderly. They are also great for issues that should be decided in the privacy of one's own home. But mailed questionnaires do take time in sending out and waiting for the return. To be returned, they must invite the respondent to participate, and that means the questionnaire must be short, attractive, vital, and pertinent to a current issue.

[14] Blalock, *Social Statistics*, p. 528. See also D. Wallace, "A Case for and against Mail Questionnaires," *Public Opinion Quarterly*, 18 (1954), 40–52.

ERRORS IN SURVEY RESEARCH—THE METHOD ITSELF

Reactive Effect (Method Effect)

If you put a rat in a box and give it electric shocks, the rat will react. Pavlov eventually had his dogs salivating at the ringing of a bell. Tigers can be made to jump through rings of fire. By operant conditioning, reward reinforcement, and other, dubious methods such as aversive behavior modification, animals learn or react to certain things. Survey research methods have been likened to such experiments. The analogy is stretched, but it is not entirely untrue.

EXAMPLE: If the client is exposed to media conditions, such as cameras, lights, microphones,and exciting personalities, the abnormality of the situation creates a reactive effect that in turn produces a change in the client response. Inviting people into a university for an interview, introducing yourself as an important person—even just measuring a person in an interview—sets the stage for a reactive effect.

CONTROL: The interview should be pleasant and comfortable, with as few distractions as possible. Your appearance should be normal and as equal to your client's as circumstances permit. Your demeanor should be pleasant and agreeable. Preferably, the client should be unfamiliar with the survey, unknown to you, and interviewed for as brief a time as possible. Do not coach, persuade, coerce, intimidate, or otherwise "train" your client. The responses should be spontaneous, honest, and voluntary. Using any kind of influence or manipulation destroys the objectivity and impartiality of the result. Do not inject prejudice or your personal opinion into the conversation. The client does not need your value judgments.

SPECIAL COMMENT: The interview, unless specifically designed, is not an investigative exposé or a medical diagnosis. Nor does it function as a dating service or "crisis clinic" for free advice. The aim is to complete the survey as quickly and as smoothly as possible. Keep free from client involvement.

Interviewer Effect

Not only does appearance affect the interview, but the age, race, sex, educational level, and mannerisms of the interviewer also produce a reactive effect that may cause change in the response and subsequent error in the survey.

EXAMPLES: *Age* can produce a definite bias. The older people grow, the more conservative they tend to become, and response may change owing to personal experience. The age of the interviewer also affects the respondent. If the interviewer appears too young and inexperienced, the client may not respond. On the other hand, a young person may have great success with his own age group.

Race, for obvious reasons, produces bias. A white woman in a black district will have little luck, and may be exposed to ridicule and hazard. Usually, the same ethnic type is preferred in conducting interviews, or one of each kind in pairs in a multiracial situation. In a southern black community, a white interviewer would have to be extremely well known to produce any kind of a result. The reverse is also true; a black would get nowhere in a white residential district. Some ethnic groups are more closed than others and will not respond other than to one of their own kind.

Sex has all the built-in errors of liberation and chauvinism. Opposite sexes tend to "put each other on." Males invariably do better with males, women with women. The age of the interviewer sometimes mitigates the effect of sexual bias.

Educational level can intimidate the less-educated client or entertain the more-educated. It is wise to cultivate an appearance of average intelligence when interviewing.

Mannerisms, accents, fidgeting, and lack of interest can completely ruin an interview. Avoid picking, scratching, sneezing, sniffing, knuckle-cracking, hair-twiddling, and "psychiatric" comments such as, "Hmmm, I see . . . and? . . . Go on . . . ." If you have an accent, minimize it. Do not monopolize the conversation with your own wisdom and explanations. Pay attention to your client; do not look off into the distance during the conversation. Not only is this very rude, but you bear the responsibility for the next researcher in this location—it could be yourself!

CONTROL: It is impossible to match interviewers with clients, but is possible to approximate. If you are in a team, select the area and location that you will do best in. Older people do better in an area with a higher concentration of the elderly; young people do well in student-dominated areas. Cities tend to divide into specific areas where people of certain ages, races, and occupations are concentrated. Do not get into racial arguments; accept the fact that blacks interview blacks better than whites do, and vice versa. Try and cultivate the "average education" approach; do not overwhelm your client with your intellectual brilliance. Your client will be friendlier if you stay away from sex, politics, religion, and medicine—and any other areas in which you think you are expert. *Just keep to the point.*

SPECIAL COMMENTS: During the interview, be patient and polite. If the client has forgotten his glasses or is illiterate, you will have to go through the questionnaire a step at a time. If he is handicapped, be helpful without being offensive, showing pity, or overreacting. Treat people as normally as you can. You will be surprised at how many people have survived without an education, with handicaps, or with many other social disadvantages. Survey research interviews are an education in life itself.[15]

SPECIAL WARNING: Be careful of thieves, muggers, rapists, and other criminals; take precautions accordingly. Be prepared to be propositioned, insulted, sworn at, and asked for money. You may also be shown out or thrown out. On the other hand, life may be uneventful.

[15] Claire Selltiz et al., *Research Methods in Social Research* (New York: Holt, Rinehart & Winston, 1976), pp. 563–72: "The first requisite . . . is to put the respondents at their ease."

Role and Response Set (Client Effect)

Just as Jello sets in a mold, so selection of clients and their responses set in a particular way. In some surveys, there is a demand for a certain clientele. In voting patterns by precinct, the respondents might be all adult Irish, aged 18 to 65; in an inmate sample, they will all be inmates of a certain ID. These are deliberate selections chosen for special purposes. However, role set can occur accidentally if the sample representation is not watched. If this happens, the same distortion that occurs in specialized populations will occur in a supposedly "true" sample.

Response set occurs in the questionnaire when the questions are too limited, leading, or familiar to the respondent, or when the respondent is ignorant of the requirements. The result is a pattern of response.

Poor sampling procedures and poor instrument construction result in role and response set. Regardless of the methods used, the sample must be representative by observation, not merely by pure statistical procedure. If the sample is small and biased (all of one kind), role set will occur. If the questionnaire is so impoverished that familiar questions are used and sequences occur, the chances are that response set will ruin the project.

EXAMPLE: If the first few questions produce *yes* or *true* responses, the client may form the pattern of positive answers, or vice versa. If the questions call for an *agree* or *disagree* response, a respondent may prefer to *agree*. Strong statements particularly tend to produce agreement; sequences often call forth sets of responses; and leading questions invariably produce biased answers.

CONTROL: Representative sampling, using a combination of sampling methods, will avert role set. A large sample will preclude bias, if the choice is stratified. Avoid small samples, unless taking an entire group. Watch the sample returns closely and check the percentages against actual estimated figures for the parent population.

Construction of the instrument either creates or prevents response error. Avoid sequences of standardized questions that produce *yes-no, true-false* responses. Vary the position of the questions. Vary the format if you are using more than one method of testing the same variable. Select questions that will provide verification of others. Use dummy questions to break sequences—but do not score them. Make your questions interesting, brief, to the point, and easy to answer.

SPECIAL COMMENT: Do not encourage role set by becoming so familiar with the instrument that you tire after the routine use of it many times in one day. Any changes in your voice or presentation, or changes in the wording itself, could produce a role set induced by the interviewer.

Make sure your questionnaire indicates *why* the answers are requested. A respondent who does not know what he is doing may give bizarre responses. This can happen accidentally if your client is bizarre; but if your questionnaire is bizarre, it will happen every time.

Remember: If the sample or the questionnaire is distorted, the data will be in error and inferences made from the sample to the general population will also be distorted. Role or response set will provide that kind of distortion.

Measurement Effect (Instrument Effect)

This effect occurs when the instrument sets out to do one thing and ends up doing another. The constant use of an instrument breeds familiarity, and the respondent will get better by practice. The original test or survey becomes a broken code, and the client now plays a game to "beat the house." This happens in IQ tests, GRE, LSAT, MMPI, and even Rorschach tests. Surveys fall into the same category. Client spontaneity and honesty are lost in game playing.

EXAMPLE: In repeated surveys, the client learns or thinks he or she has learned the test objective. The responses become scores and expectations, rather than new data—as in IQ, weight-control experiments, ranking, and political outcomes.

CONTROL: Avoid the repetitious use of surveys in the same sample area. Devise a questionnaire that will give the same results with a different format.

People Effect

It happens that people do lie, cheat, steal, and commit other human errors. Not only respondents, but occasionally workers, do dishonest things. Some respondents cheat and lie on the questionnaire, others play games, some are blatantly dishonest. Some researchers are the same way; they "cook the books." The research is fabricated, manipulated, the conclusions are made after the data are changed.

Fortunately, deliberate manipulations are infrequent; the accidental happen more often. Accidental manipulation occurs when the data are poorly handled or adjusted to meet deadlines; when, consciously or unconsciously, prejudice influences the findings; when clients are permitted or encouraged to lie; when workers hand in fabricated data and the boss is unaware of it; when the boss mixes up the findings, irretrievably changing the order of the results; when programs are selected that accidentally fix the outcome.

EXAMPLE: If respondents lie on questionnaires, or if the responses are fabricated by the workers or the project director, the outcome will be useless. If a program is selected that ensures a high correlation, a high chi-square, by fixing sample size, the results are also fixed. The choice of frequency data to ensure a positive known outcome is deliberate, unethical practice, and is in effect lying. Such practices are self-destructive and academically irresponsible.

CONTROL: There are already too many errors present in the survey method; we must not induce more. Only the highest ethical standards, the most precise work, the most responsible performance will do. One never knows when the work that is done will be reexamined, or used as the basis of newer research. All our conclusions, all our research should be to improve the quality of life, not degrade it.

THE WORLD OF NONRESPONSE

If anything can kill a survey and the resulting conclusions, it is the nonresponsiveness of the sample population. Nonresponders have fooled not only pollsters, but consumer researchers, census takers, and social scientists who have sought to inquire into people's private and secret lives. Some people simply do not talk about what they do.

Nonresponse is so important that it must be reported in the survey. For example, in voting patterns, where they can decide an election, the nonrespondents have sometimes been the largest single group. They must be considered in determination of sample error, to give us that much more control over estimates. If we simply ignore the nonrespondent and go on to the next person, we are in danger of passing over a very important part of the sample population and we run the risk of fixing the results.

Research is not like a horse race in which we select the horse we want. We must carefully report what is actually in the sample. If we wish to reduce the number of nonrespondents, we can reduce the sample size—if we are prepared to accept that risk. It is also important to include nonresponse items in the questionnaire, so that the respondent has the opportunity of stating that he is independent, is undecided, or doesn't know.

For example:

Will you vote in the election? Yes___ No___ Undecided___

Would you vote for the death penalty? Yes___ No___ Don't know___

Questions on religion or political preference should include the category *Other*, for those who are not specified. It is important that room always be left for the nonrespondent, or the person who doesn't wish to or cannot fit in a specified category.

The nonrespondent can often be identified by the interviewer in terms of sex, approximate age, race, and other identifiable background characteristics that may help fill in the blanks as to independent variables. A careful observer gets to know much about the client before the interview even starts. This is a matter of training and experience in the field; the researcher learns what to look for. In this way, the nonrespondent can be partially identified without having said a word, and the questionnaire can be filled in in the proper sections even though some gaps may exist and will be noted as nonresponse. And regardless of how the survey is answered by respondents, the actual number of nonrespondents should be reported.

Mortality and Attrition

Akin to missing values is the missing person. Often in random or even telephone surveys, the person needed is simply not there. For all practical purposes, the sampling continues until the number of cases decided upon is complete. The attrition rate, the number of no-answers, is noted. If the rate is too high, especially in a small sample, obviously it can kill the research. In a large sample, the sample size reduces the error and the completion of the sample compensates for the nonrespondent.

The term *mortality* originally arose from mail-out surveys, when the no-answer was presumed dead for statistical purposes. In real life, the no-answer, nonrespondent phenomenon must be handled differently. In a random sample, the number of nonrespondents can be decided upon by estimation—say, 10 percent, 20 percent, or whatever the arbitrary figure. The sample size is then increased by that number. For example, if the sample was set at 100, with an anticipated nonresponse of 20 percent, the actual sample selection would be for 120 people in a random or a systematic random sample. Then, after the first twenty interviews, if the twenty-first were missing (no answer, not available, refused, moved, sick, too old, mute, illiterate), the next random number or systematic random sample would be selected. The researcher simply goes on to the next client. Remember, we want our sample to be representative as well as statistically accurate. We want to balance theory with practice.

SUMMARY

Research is only as good as the questionnaire. The instrument is the tool that actually yields the data, and its construction determines the quality of the data in the survey method. Therefore, to gain precision during the measurement process, we want the instrument to be exact. It should be simple, uncluttered, asking questions that can be answered directly. There are many types of questionnaire. The type used depends on the objective, the educational level of the respondents, and differences in dialect and occupational status.

Most questionnaires have five parts: the title, statement, questionnaire, appreciation, and interviewer's observations. The instrument should be neat, not too long, and presented in an interesting format. Scoring may be done on the right-hand side of the questionnaire or on a multiple-response sheet. Scoring the answer should be geared to coding for IBM cards. When designing an instrument, consider the time it takes, the cost, and the work involved.

Questions may be asked in different ways. Eliminate ambiguity by asking simple questions. Choose your words carefully. Avoid double-barreled, leading, and negative questions. Used properly, a series of questions may be used to form a scale. Questions may also be set out in scale form. Break the pattern of the questions to avoid response set, and insert "dummy" questions. Use pretest and back-translation to improve your questionnaire. A five-point response is better than a two-point response, so try to keep your *yes/no* and *true/false* items to a minimum.

When you design your instrument, set out the variables according to their position on your model. It will help you see the sequence of what you are doing.

After pretest, the instrument needs to be tested on the main sample. Any proposed sample should be representative of the parent population. Ideally, each sample would have randomness and representativeness and would reflect equal variances of the characteristics of the parent population. The characteristics would also be normally distributed. Seldom do such conditions prevail, and we are fortunate in having sampling theory at our disposal to correct prevailing conditions.

There is quite a difference between sampling in theory and sampling in practice. Even when we use random numbers, there is a chance that our sample will be less than random. If it contains extremes, those extremes will affect the outcome of the calculations. Modifications of random sampling may be used with discretion. The researcher may use systematic random sampling, systematic convenience random sampling, multistage cluster sampling, and judgmental random sampling, which is closer to nonprobability or nonrandom sampling but may be used for some surveys. All sampling is improved by the use of stratification—that is, obtaining in the sample the same proportion of characteristics as in the parent population. If the parent population is 50 percent black, 50 percent white, 50 percent male, and 50 percent female, those proportions should be obtained in the sample, but this does not mean that the sample should contain 50 percent black men and 50 percent white women.

Sample size is important in the control of sampling error. It is reasonable to assume that a large sample is more representative than a small one, but it is more accurate to use proper procedure in selection of a sample, so that it conforms to the best possible choice under the prevailing circumstances. The sample size should be not less than 30, and should be representative, preferably random, and in line with the proposed research problem.

Three methods are very popular with survey researchers: interview, telephone, and mail. The most used is the interview, which involves confrontation and reactive effect. Interview procedure must be uniform to reduce error in obtaining data. As the final step in generating data, the interview should be controlled to reduce interviewer effect, halo effect, and reactive effect. Courtesy and patience are vital.

Not all people will respond to surveys. Many do not wish to discuss their affairs or to proffer opinions. These nonresponses, like the undecided or independent in a voting poll, can affect the outcome of the survey, especially if they constitute an unusually high percentage. Not only should provision be made within the questionnaire itself for those who have no opinion, but the number of nonresponses should be reported.

Survey methods are never easy. They require a great deal of thought and constant alertness to detect error and make adjustments. Good questionnaires are the results of practice and pretest. A good questionnaire will generate the information needed for concluding the research. It is at the heart of the research, yet it needs the interview to bring out its full import. Good research is the culmination of selection of a good problem, a good design, proper selection of the sample, a redesigned pretested instrument, correct interview procedure, and appropriate statistical analysis. Each step of the way needs to be checked until it is the best possible choice.

EXERCISES

1. Comment on general principles concerning the construction of a questionnaire. What is a guiding principle?
2. There are three popular types of survey questionnaire. What are they?
3. There are at least two parts to the questionnaire itself, and five parts to the whole format. What are they?
4. Comment on the design of the questionnaire, on scoring, crowding, word use, length, observations by the interviewer, voluntariness, use of trivia, educated phrases.
5. How would you handle an illiterate, a blind person, a mentally retarded person in an interview?
6. What are two ways of scoring? What is a multiple-response sheet?
7. You should consider three points when designing a format. What are they?
8. Explain: dichotomous form, category form, Bogardus form, Likert-type response, rating scales, single response, open-end response.
9. Design a self-rating scale for safety on the streets.
10. Rewrite:
    (a) When was the last time you smoked pot? And how much?
    (b) The death penalty cures recidivism among juveniles and adults.
    (c) Sirhan Sirhan, Lee Harvey Oswald, and James Earl Ray should have been executed for capital crimes.
11. Write a questionnaire to test acceptance of police brutality and corruption.
12. What is a dummy question? When is it used?
13. Rewrite:
    (a) Sometimes I feel like breaking the law. Yes___ No___
    (b) It's nobody's fault there's no law enforced. True___ False___
    (c) Jurors should not argue with the judge. Yes___ No___
14. Select two questions from any survey of the white middle class and back-translate them for the black ghetto.
15. Construct a simple research model and outline it as per the student's research design.
16. Explain three points to consider when selecting a sample.
17. From a table of random numbers—or a programmable hand calculator—generate a sample of 30 from 200 cases, assuming they are all numbered.
18. Now generate a systematic sample based upon a ratio of population divided by sample size.
19. Using the letter *S* in the telephone directory, generate a systematic sample based on the formula above.
20. Is there an ethnic bias in using the telephone directory?

21. What is wrong with taking the first 100 students in a campus survey?
22. Explain the difference between homogeneity and heterogeneity as far as stratified samples are concerned.
23. Develop a multistage-cluster sample for 400 from a city area of many thousands. Develop another sample of 400 from the telephone directory. How would you develop a sample for mail-out?
24. Would you eliminate children, tourists, the elderly, the sick, prison inmates? If so, why?
25. How would you triangulate?
26. If, while interviewing, you suddenly find a few millionaires responding (it does happen), how would you handle the extremes if your survey included income research?
27. Why inject the idea of probability sampling over quotas?
28. Sampling hinges on two ideas. Comment on them.
29. Define: *panel, cohort, longitudinal, cross-sectional, comparative, multiphase, parallel, master sample, sociometric.*
30. Compare the three methods–interview, telephone, and mail-out.
31. Comment on the rules for interviewing. Which is the most important? Why?
32. What is reactive effect? interviewer effect? client effect? instrument effect? people effect?
33. What is nonresponse? Describe two kinds.
34. How would you correct for missing people in your survey?
35. Comment upon sampling in theory and sampling in practice.

FOR FURTHER READING

Atkinson, J., *A Handbook for Interviewers: A Manual for Government Social Survey Interviewing Staff, Describing Practice and Procedure on Structured Interviewing*, #M 136. London: Her Majesty's Stationery Office, 1967.

Babbie, Earl R., *Survey Research Methods*. Belmont, Calif.: Wadsworth, 1973.

Blalock, H. M., Jr., and A. B. Blalock, eds., *Methodology in Social Research*. New York: McGraw-Hill, 1968.

Bock, R. D., and L. V. Jones, *The Measurement and Prediction of Judgment and Choice*. San Francisco: Holden-Day, 1968.

Borgatta, E. F., ed., *Sociological Methodology*. San Francisco: Jossey-Bass, 1969.

Cochran, W. G., *Sampling Techniques* (2nd ed.). New York: John Wiley, 1963.

Festinger, C., and D. Katz, eds., *Research Methods in the Behavioral Sciences*. New York: Holt, Rinehart & Winston, 1953.

Geddes, Donald Porter, ed., *An Analysis of the Kinsey Reports*. New York: New American Library, 1954.

Glock, Charles, ed., *Survey Research in the Social Sciences*. New York: Russell Sage Foundation, 1967.

Gordon, Raymond L., *Interviewing: Strategy, Techniques and Tactics*. Homewood, Ill.: Dorsey, 1969.

Greenwood, P. W., and J. Petersilia, *The Criminal Investigation Process*. 3 vols. Santa Monica, Calif.: Rand, 1975.

Hyman, Herbert H., et al., *Interviewing in Social Research*. Chicago: University of Chicago Press, 1954.

Kahn, Robert L., and Charles F. Cannell, *The Dynamics of Interviewing*. New York: John Wiley, 1957.

——, "Interviewing," in G. Lindzey and E. Aronson, eds., *Handbook of Social Psychology* (2nd ed.). Vol. III. Reading, Mass.: Addison-Wesley, 1968.

Kerlinger, Fred N., *Foundations of Behavioral Research* (2nd ed.). New York: Holt, Rinehart & Winston, 1973.

Kish, Leslie, *Survey Sampling*. New York: John Wiley, 1965.

Lofland, John, *Analyzing Social Settings*. Belmont, Calif.: Wadsworth, 1971.

McCall, George, and J. L. Simmons, *Issues in Participant Observation*. Reading, Mass.: Addison-Wesley, 1969.

Miller, Delbert C., *Handbook of Research Design and Social Measurement* (3rd ed.). New York: D. McKay, 1977. The classic work on instrument construction. See especially pp. 163–390.

Morris, Peter, *Prisoners and Their Families*. London: Allen & Unwin, 1965.

Moser, C. A., and G. Kalton, *Survey Methods in Social Investigation*. New York: Basic Books, 1972.

Moursond, Janet, *Evaluation: An Introduction to Research Design*. Monterey, Calif.: Brooks/Cole, 1973.

Parten, M. B., *Surveys, Polls and Samples*. New York: Harper & Row, 1950.

Phillips, B. S., *Social Research: Strategy and Tactics* (2nd ed.). New York: Macmillan, 1971.

Rosen, L., and R. West, eds., *Reader for Research Methods*. New York: Random House, 1973.

Runkle, P. J., and J. E. McGrath, *Research on Human Behavior*. New York: Holt, Rinehart & Winston, 1972.

Selltiz, Claire, et al., *Research Methods in Social Relations* (3rd ed.). New York: Holt, Rinehart & Winston, 1976.

Smith, H. W., *Strategies of Social Research*. Englewood Cliffs, N.J.: Prentice-Hall, 1975.

Torgeson, W., *Theory and Methods of Scaling*. New York: John Wiley, 1958.

Vallier, I., ed., *Comparative Methods in Sociology*. Berkeley, Calif.: University of California Press, 1971.

Wilmer, M. A. P., *Crime and Information Theory*. Edinburgh: Edinburgh University Press, 1976.

Yamane, Taro, *Elementary Sampling Theory*. Englewood Cliffs, N.J.: Prentice-Hall, 1967.

Young, Pauline V., *Scientific Social Surveys and Research*. Englewood Cliffs, N.J.: Prentice-Hall, 1966.

8

Coding, the Program, and the Printout

Coding is an introduction to the technical side of methodology—to the hardware, the computer, the keypunch, and the processing of the IBM card. The computer will do many things for you if you follow the rules *precisely*. There is absolutely no room for error. The classic slogan is "GIGO"—if you put garbage in, you get garbage out. Any mistakes you enter into the system will result in great frustration. You are now translating the concepts of research into tangible form, holes punched in a card, making the ideas you started out with quantified and machine-measurable.

After scoring your interview results on the questionnaire or on multiple-response sheets, you are ready to keypunch your data into a computer batch, complete with computer program. I have concentrated on the SPSS system, since that has occurred more widely in my travels than any other.[1] It is not difficult, and it can handle both simple and complex programs.

The technical side of research methodology begins at the keypunch, goes through the computer in a programmable deck of IBM cards, and if correct, generates a computer printout containing an analysis of your research data. The hard work of statistical analysis is done for you by the machine. Nevertheless, you must analyze the statistical results and decide on the logic of the findings.

[1] Other systems are DATA-TEXT, IMPRESS, STATJOB, BASIC, BMD, and LISP. New systems are created with new program languages. SPSS uses FORTRAN.

It is much simpler to enter data by a coding system than to use words. Thus, we can enter answers *yes* and *no* as 1 and 2 or 2 and 1 respectively, according to whether we wish *yes* to be high or low. Keep in mind how you wish your answers to be valued. For example, *strongly agree* may be 1 or 5 on a five-point scale, depending on what you wish it to represent. All answers except open-end questions can be coded numerically. The code is then punched into the data card.

If you are using scales, you may use two- or three-digit numbers or even decimals. Your code manual will tell you how to enter them. Try to keep your coding simple; even on a low number of variables (say, 20), the coding can get confusing. As you will see, every variable has a place on the card and every number has its column.

Numeric coding is preferred to alpha (letter) coding. It is faster and saves computer time. Continuous numeric coding—that is, keeping all the fields together without spacing—provides more data space on the card and also saves computer time.

All the data on your response sheet for only *one case* should be entered on *one card.* Although we sometimes have two or more cards for one case, we never have two cases on one card. If you design your coding neatly, you can get up to 80 bits of information about one individual on one card.

The Data Card

Coding simplifies the entry of data on IBM cards for computer analysis. The data deck is usually done first, and the program instructions added later. The data deck is exactly what it says it is—a deck of data cards. These are the simplest to do.

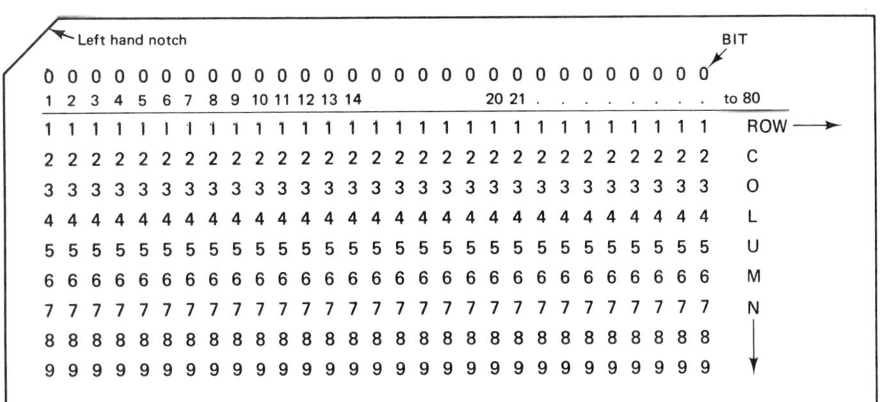

Fig. 8-1 Section of IBM card

The IBM card is shown in *Figure 8-1*. Note that it contains columns and rows, The columns descend from 0 to 9, the rows go across from 1 to 80. There are also two rows above the zeros that can be used. Thus, there are 12 x 80 spaces on the card, 960 "bits" of information, that can be punched by the keypunch machine. For our data, we are concerned with the 800 printed "bits." Note that on the card, all the numbers in the zero row are zeros, all of row 1 are 1s, all of row 2 are 2s, and so on down to 9s. Each column, or combination of sequential columns, called a "field," may represent a variable.

The card is often represented on a large green form, a computer score sheet, called an *IBM FORTRAN coding form*. The coding form will represent 24 single cards on one sheet.

Now, what exactly do we enter on the IBM card? Every variable that is put in question form on the instrument should be able to be coded numerically.[2] Numeric coding is easy and fast and saves time in programming. For example, "Sex: Male___ Female___" resolves itself into 1 for a male response, 2 for a female response. In fact, on the questionnaire it may be entered as:

Sex of respondent: (1) Male___ (2) Female___

Race may be entered as:

Race: (1) White___ (2) Black___ (3) Other___

If age is to be entered by category, it may be entered as:

Age: (1) 18–28 yrs. (2) 29–39 yrs. (3) 40–50 yrs.
(4) 51–61 yrs. (5) Over 62 yrs.

Entering age this way avoids later recoding. Similarly:

Religion: (1) Protestant___ (2) Catholic___ (3) Jewish___ (4) Other___

Notice that each category is given a number. *Coding is simply numerical ordering of categories*. If there are no categories and the entry is in numbers, then no code is used; the actual numbers are entered on the IBM columns that are used for that variable. Similarly, scale totals are entered directly.

Coding of questions raises a special issue of how the computer works. For example, the computer scales from low to high unless ordered otherwise, so that in *Race* as above, "White" would be low and "Other" high. Remember this in looking at direction on the signs in correlation.

[2] All coding must be uniform, you may never change codes once you have started entering data, and you may not change variable order; the variable response must correspond with the variable order.

If the question, "Do you commute? (1) Yes____ (2) No____," were scaled against race, it would look like *Figure 8-2*. Assuming that more whites than any others commute, the nature of the scoring would indicate a positive correlation. Had the scoring been changed for one category, the result would have been a negative correlation. It is worthwhile to keep an eye on end outcomes so that consistent results are obtained; otherwise, one spends time figuring where the direction of the relationship is. It is convenient to draw a diagram like *Figure 8-2* to anticipate how the question should be coded.

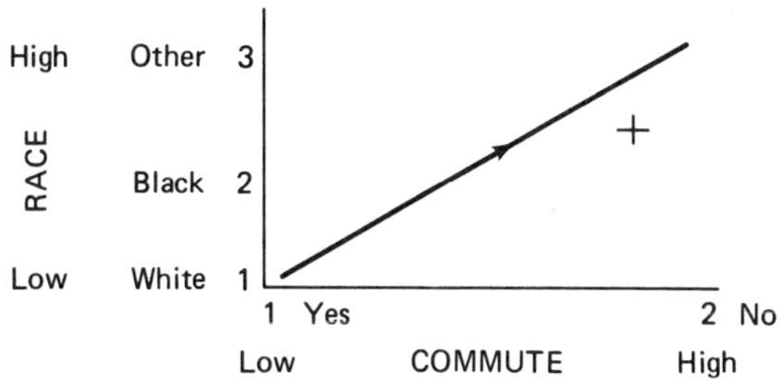

Fig. 8-2 Direction shown by scoring (positive correlation)

If the answer is a simple yes or no, decide whether the scoring should be 1, 2 or 2, 1. Similarly, when the question calls for a Likert-type response, an opinion from "Strongly agree" to "Strongly disagree," decide whether the coding should go from 1 to 5 or from 5 to 1. If "agree" is the more important response, it should have the higher coding number. As a rule of thumb, the greater the importance, the higher the number.

Keypunching

Punching the cards immediately will break the task up and also record the information before any questionnaires or coding sheets are lost. Keypunch machines occasionally suffer from abuse, wear and tear, and jamming. Various controls on the machines are used to clear them. Whenever a machine is used, it is always wise to first check the printout on the card against the actual punch marks. A test card can be punched with the numbers 1 to 0, or if ALPHA (letters) is used, the letters may be checked.

There are certain do's and don'ts:

Never use a defective machine

Never attempt to unjam a machine; let the technician do it.

Never use old, bent, torn, spindled, or mutilated cards.

Never go back over a mistake; use another card and clear the bad card.

Never try advanced techniques until you have mastered the simple ones.

Be relaxed. Be prepared to make some mistakes. Even though your companions may be typing up a storm on the keypunch, remember that they too had to start on Day 1, and often they will help you if you get in a jam.

Have your data ready. Sometimes it is helpful if one person reads the data while the other punches the cards. Coding sheets are extremely useful. Check each card.

Find out what the keypunch will do. Get familiar with the machine. Discover what happens if you do not hold down the NUMERIC key when you feed in numbers. Discover each symbol on each register. Learn how to duplicate, backspace, set the printer to column 16, release, and clear. Do not abuse the machine.

Be neat. Throw old cards in the recycle can. Keep your own work together and keep your cards in a box. Handling them spoils them. Keep them together with a proper-size rubber band, preferably one at each end.

Scoring and Coding

Two types of scoring are widely used, marginal or edge coding and multiple-response sheets. The former is scored directly on the questionnaire and is seen in *Figure 8-4*. The latter, shown in *Figure 8-3*, is extremely useful for telephone surveys and saves time and cost. On multiple-response sheets, many clients may be scored on one page; the scores may be entered directly in code; and the master sheet is easy to store for record keeping. A disadvantage of the response sheet is that the interviewee does not have a chance at self-rating or self-scoring, whereas the questionnaire does ensure personal attention.

Variable Item	Respondent Number														
	1	2	3	4	5	6	7	8	9	10	11	12	13	14	15
Age	18				1										
Race	B				2										
Sex	M				1										
Education	HS				2										
Religion	P				1										
Marital status	S				1										

Fig. 8-3 Multiple-response sheet

On the sheet shown, the client response has been entered as given under column 1. In column 5, the same data are coded. In practice, the coded data may be entered directly for the respondent, in this case for respondent 1 under column 1. The response sheet enables the interviewer to operate without the need for supervision. A disadvantage is that it does lend itself to "curbsiding."[3]

[3] Fabricating the responses (while sitting on the curb).

Marginal coding on the questionnaire is usually entered right after the interview. The client should not be aware of coding scoring, since some clients will respond to obtain the highest score or highest code.

Coding a Project for Data Analysis

The best way to see the computer in action is to follow a project through the coding process. A project on the city police is used here to show the methods used. It begins with the instrument (the questionnaire), proceeds to the data cards, then to the program cards, and finally to the computer printout and the data analysis of the FREQUENCIES program used. The questionnaire is a one-page format with the

Group # 33
Client # 003

Please circle one option in each of the following questions:

1. AGE:	(1) 18-28	(2) 29-39	(3) 40-50	(4) Over 50	2
2. RACE:	(1) White	(2) Black	(3) Other		2
3. SEX:	(1) Male	(2) Female			2
4. RELIGION:	(1) Catholic	(2) Protestant	(3) Jewish	(4) Other	4
5. POLITICAL PREFERENCE:	(1) Republican	(2) Democrat	(3) Independent		2
6. FINANCIAL STATUS:	(1) $0-8000	(2) $9000-17000	(3) $18000-25000	(4) $26000+	2
7. Are the police courteous?	(1) Yes	(2) No			2
8. Do the police respond to emergency calls?	(1) Yes	(2) No			1
9. Are the police neat in appearance?	(1) Yes	(2) No			1
10. Do you feel the police are corrupt?	(1) Yes	(2) No			1
11. Are police patrols adequate for safety?	(1) Yes	(2) No			2
12. The city police have kept up with developments in crime detecting.	(1) Strongly agree	(2) Agree	(3) Disagree	(4) Strongly disagree	1
13. Police response to calls is quick and efficient.	(1) Strongly agree	(2) Agree	(3) Disagree	(4) Strongly disagree	4
14. The police get along well in the community.	(1) Strongly agree	(2) Agree	(3) Disagree	(4) Strongly disagree	1
15. The police should not enforce laws relating to gambling, minor narcotics, prostitution, alcoholism, and pornography.	(1) Strongly disagree	(2) Disagree	(3) Agree	(4) Strongly agree	4
16. Budget cutbacks have reduced police effectiveness.	(1) Strongly agree	(2) Agree	(3) Disagree	(4) Strongly disagree	4
17. Sexual attitudes of the community are of no concern to the police.	(1) Strongly disagree	(2) Disagree	(3) Agree	(4) Strongly agree	4
				CITYATT	18

Thank you for your time and participation in this survey.

This survey is conducted by the Task Force Team from City University with the express purpose of examining city police relationships with the community.*

*In the original questionnaire, the coding was omitted; it is included here only to show how marginal coding is quickly completed from actual scoring. In questions 12–17, a low of 6 is pro-police, a high of 24 is anti-police. This questionnaire is neat, gets to the point, is easy to complete and easy to code. Actual code reads 3300322242222111214144418 for the IBM card.

Fig. 8-4 Survey measuring the effectiveness of the city police department, conducted by city university task force

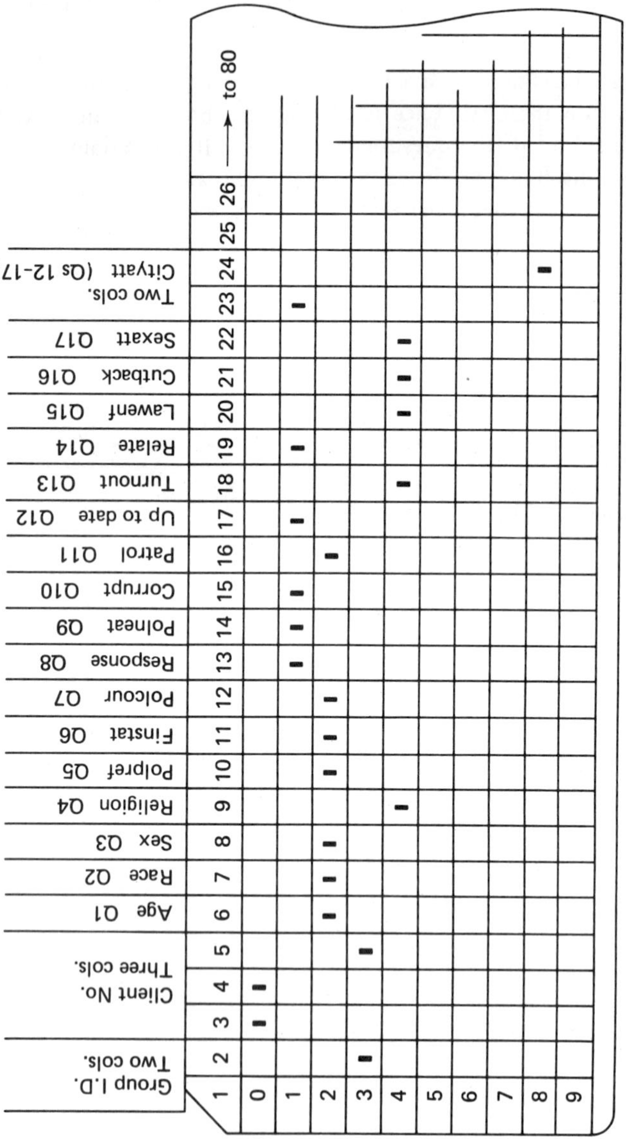

Fig. 8-5 IBM card showing coding of variables

coding set right into the questions. The data deck was rapidly punched and checked for errors against the client responses. Of the 450 cards, a sample is given in *Figure 8-5*. Each data line represents a data card. The data deck was punched first. It was checked for response agreement and for actual count of the sample size ($n = 450$).

This survey was conducted in the nine councilmanic districts or voting precincts of a particular city. The locations selected were important ones where people could be contacted on weekends. One week was devoted to the collection of data. Every fiftieth person was selected, with care taken to keep the sample representative. Thus, the actual sample size was 50 x 450 = 22,500, about 17 percent of the total population. In effect, it was a convenience sample, but it did contain some randomization and representation and thus had considerable validity, as it was taken from nine different locations. Note how multistage sampling was used, as per Chapter 7.

In the questionnaire, there are 17 variables listed as questions. If we include the client number for the purposes of counting the cards, 18 variables are to be listed. If we sum the totals for questions 12 to 17, the last six questions, and call this variable *Attitude toward the City Police* (Cityatt, for short), the total is 19 variables. Thus, the data card would read as in *Figure 8-5*.

Variables have been abbreviated to show the exact FORTRAN language used on the VARIABLE LIST card. Notice that no variable name exceeds eight letters. Sometimes the variables are numbered and the list reads, "VAR1, VAR2," and so on. I prefer the actual name, to help in the detection of error and give direction to beginners. Notice that "Cityatt" has been added as a scale made up of the last six questions on the instrument.

Control and Specification Fields

Up to this point, I have emphasized one-variable analysis in order to show basic building blocks. If you can handle a single variable, you will soon be able to handle two or more. The first program you will learn to write for the computer is one that deals with each variable on an item-by-item basis. It is called FREQUENCIES, and it computes the frequency data of each variable on the data card. Once you have run this program successfully, you will be able to run others dealing with two-variable relationships.

Before you write the program, there are several things you should know about the use of the IBM card. You are already aware of the 80 columns and the ten numbered and two unnumbered rows. Now the card divides into two parts for programming, the control field and the specification field. The first 15 spaces are the control field, and spaces 16 through 80 are the specification field (see *Figure 8-6*.) Thus, if the computer reports an error in the control field, you will know it occurs in the first 15 spaces on the IBM program card; an error in the specification field occurs after space 15. (These rules do *not* apply to the data deck.) It becomes clear that 16 is a key space; it is often referred to as the starting point for the specification label.

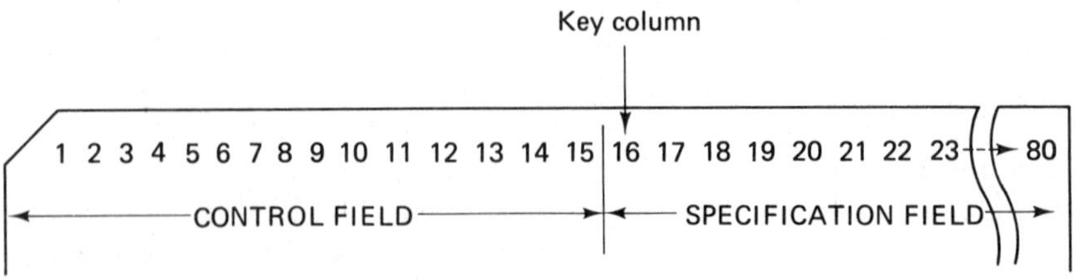

Fig. 8-6 IBM card showing control and specification fields

The Deck

Any IBM card deck is divided into at least five parts: (1) job definition cards, (2) data definition cards, (3) task definition cards, (4) data cards, or the data deck, and (5) end cards. Later, you may add certain sections, but there will always be at least five parts in the IBM deck.

1. *Job definition cards* enable you to get into the computer. These are access cards that enable the computer to recognize you and to set limits on what you need in the way of space and time and to give your job a program. There are three basic cards:
   (a) *Run card*, or access card, which is usually orange and is often preprinted so that all you have to do is enter your access code number and space and time.
   (b) *Program card*, which tells the computer which program you will select for your job.
   (c) *Pagesize card*, which instructs the computer to print so many lines per page—usually 80.
2. *Data definition cards* define the data deck for the computer. A name is assigned, the variables are defined and designated. Variables are given values, the number of cases is set, the format of the data deck is explained, and the printout that you need is set up. Each type of data definition card has a special purpose; the principal ones are these:
   (a) *Run name*. This is simply a name given to the project to identify it at a later date.
   (b) *Variable list*. A list of all the variables used is set forth under certain rules and explains every piece of data on the data card and how it occurs.
   (c) *Input format*. The computer is told how to read the data card and each variable on it.
   (d) *N of cases* is the number of cases in the sample, which must correspond to the number of cards in the data deck.
   (e) *Input medium*. This tells the computer that you are using cards, as against any other form of input medium.
   (f) *Variable labels* explain the variable more fully than the short name or mnemonic used in the variable list.
   (g) *Value labels* describe the values assigned to each variable.
   (h) *Missing values* are assigned to special cases where data are missing or are to be omitted from the calculation.
   (i) *Subfiles* tells the computer to enter data into files set up by the user.
   (j) *Recode* is a special case of changing the value of the variable.

3. *Task definition cards* define the task set for the computer to solve:
   (a) *FREQUENCIES* is the program used for analyzing the data into actual count, frequency, and percentage in each category of each variable.
   (b) *PEARSON CORR* is used for correlation.
   (c) *CROSSTABS* is used for chi-square analysis.

   There are several other programs. Each program must have:
   (d) A *statistics* card to determine the statistics to be used.
   (e) *Options.* Occasionally an options card is used to set up special analysis or to speed up the analysis.
   (f) The *READ INPUT DATA* card, which tells the computer to read the data deck.
4. The *data deck* follows the READ INPUT DATA card.
5. *End cards* end the operation; usually, there are two:
   (a) *FINISH*, which ends the run
   (b) /*, which completes the run

Some Rules for SPSS

There are several variations on the IBM deck, but the basic format is that given above. Details may be found in the SPSS manual, the manual for the *Statistical Package for the Social Sciences.* This once-small paperback has grown to a manual of many programs, with new ones added regularly. The language used is FORTRAN; the programs are peculiar to the social sciences and involve a great deal of statistical expertise.

Several programs may be run on one input when you become more sophisticated. There are certain limitations that must be observed:

1. The control field has fixed name values, and their use must be as designated, in the proper order without a single error. *You must be absolutely precise.*
2. The specification field has only six kinds of entries:
   (a) Names, limited to 8 characters only
   (b) Values, limited to 20 letters
   (c) Keywords: TO, BY, THRU, WITH
   (d) Labels, limited to 40 letters; must be a single element
   (e) Delimiters: =, (,), /, blank
   (f) Operators: +, –, *, /=, **, =

   Names, keywords, values, labels must be separated.
   There must be NO spelling errors, NO spacing errors.
   There can be NO alterations, overtyping, or bent cards.
   No words or elements can be split on two cards.

Every time a variable is used, it must be identified with the name used in the VARIABLE LIST. It cannot be changed. For example, if *education* (which has nine letters) was abbreviated to EDUCAT in the VARIABLE LIST card, it must always be EDUCAT when explaining the label and explaining the value, or when used in a task definition card.

Table 8.1. Program Setup for FREQUENCIES for Survey on City Police

RUN CARDS:	
Job card (Red)	//BSCLASS5 JOB '33344455', 'ESJOHNSON', REGION=320K, TIME=(0000,10)
	The class number decides the order of processing; the digit after CLASS *must* be the same as the last digit in the 8 digit access number. The access number that comes after JOB is given by the computer technicians. Then comes a nine-letter personal ID. The calculation space or work space is usually set but may be enlarged for big jobs. Time is set to accommodate the run; in this case, ten seconds is ample. On a shared line, the smaller jobs appear to be run faster. Most job cards are red or orange, but this is only to help the card reader separate the many decks he or she has to handle. Most job cards are also preprinted, with only the access number and ID to be filled in. Check the time setting, you may have to fill that in. This is the first card in the deck, and it must be perfect. The time used will be recorded against your access number. All control cards start at the margin in column 1.
Program card	// EXEC SPSS
	This card calls the SPSS library into operation for your run. SPSS is one of many libraries used. EXEC is abbreviation for "execute" or "put into operation." Some libraries use SPSSH; check the coding at your computer center.
	16
Procedure card	PAGESIZE 80
	Under column 16, the number 80 is entered (8 in 16, 0 in 17) This tells the computer to limit printing to 80 lines per page. Most computers run at 55 lines per page. There are other limitations in the SPSS procedure cards. (See the SPSS manual.)
	16
Run-name card	RUN NAME PUBLIC ATTITUDES TOWARD CITY POLICE
(Total = 4 cards)	Again the actual name starts at column 16, in the specification field. Note that PAGESIZE is one word, while RUN NAME is two. Please write these control labels carefully. If the file is to be saved for later use, a FILE NAME card may be used after the RUN NAME card, with an appropriate file name in the specification field. The file name is eight characters in length and may be followed by a 64-character label.
DATA DEFINITION CARDS:	
VARIABLE LIST	16
	CLIENT, AGE, RACE, SEX, RELIGION, POLPREF, FINSTAT, POLCOUR, RESPONSE, POLNEAT, CORRUPT, PATROL, UPTODATE, TURNOUT, RELATE, LAWENF, CUTBACK, SEXATT, CITYATT

Three cards are required to list these variables. (Each line is a new card.) Elements are never divided. *Variables appear in the same order as they are entered on the data cards.* The names are unique, cannot change, and are limited to eight letters. Occasionally the format "VAR1–VAR19" is used. Notice that the group ID is omitted, and this will be skipped in the reading format instruction to the computer. Notice that the control field is omitted on the second and third cards.

```
               16
INPUT MEDIUM   CARD
```

The input medium is IBM cards. Other mediums used are TAPE, DISK, and OTHER. In this case, the program and the cards are entered together.

```
               16
N OF CASES     450
```

The number of cases, N OF CASES, must correspond to the number of cards in the data deck, unless there are other specific instructions.

```
               16
INPUT FORMAT   FIXED (2X, F3.0, 17F1.0, F2.0)
```

The reading instructions are to skip the first two columns (2X–X means skip); then read a single variable of three columns, F3.0; read 17 variables of one column each; and finally, read one variable of two columns. There are many ways of entering input format, but it is best to keep the data numerical, keep the format simple, and keep it brief. If you keep in mind that F can also mean field, then you will place your variables exactly in their proper fields. Also, the total of all the columns used inside the FIXED brackets should equal the number of columns used on the card–in this case, 24. The computer can be instructed to read whatever you choose, but first master the simple formats. Notice how commas are used as delimiters in this card and the VARIABLE LIST card.

(Total = 6 cards)

MISSING VALUES This card is optional. It is entered to show its place in the deck. It is defined later in the text.

RECODE
This card, defined later in the text and entered to show its position in the deck, is optional but is used on runs for chi-square and is usually based upon division of the categories by dichotomizing along the mean into high/low categories. All recoding must be based on original entry in the variable list and value labels. RECODE changes value labels, and thus new value labels must be entered.

(Number of cards needed may vary)

```
               16
VAR LABELS     POLPREF POLITICAL PREFERENCE/FINSTAT FINANCIAL STATUS/
               POLCOUR POLICE COURTESY/RESPONSE RESPONSE TO EMERGENCY CALLS/
               POLNEAT POLICE APPEARANCE/CORRUPT POLICE CORRUPTION/PATROL
               ADEQUACY OF POLICE PATROLS/UPTODATE POLICE TECHNOLOGY/TURNOUT
               POLICE RESPONSE TO CALLS/RELATE POLICE COMMUNITY RELATIONS/
               LAWENF LAW ENFORCEMENT OF MINOR CRIMES/CUTBACK EFFECT OF BUDGET
               RESTRICTIONS/SEXATT POLICE ATTITUDES TO SEX/CITYATT PUBLIC
               ATTITUDE TO POLICE
```

Table 8.1. (cont.) Program Setup for FREQUENCIES for Survey on City Police

The slash is used as a delimiter and the next label is placed up against it. However, at the end of the statement, the slash is not used, as the next control field takes over. Each line is a new card, but the control field VAR LABELS is omitted, even though the specifications start at column 16. No word or element is split.

```
VALUE LABELS  AGE (1)18-28 (2)29-39 (3)40-50 (4)OVER 50/RACE (1)WHITE (2)BLACK
              (3)OTHER/SEX (1)MALE (2)FEMALE/RELIGION (1)CATHOLIC
              (2)PROTESTANT (3)JEWISH (4)OTHER/POLPREF (1)REPUBLICAN
              (2)DEMOCRAT (3)INDEPENDENT/FINSTAT (1)$0-8000 (2)$9000-17000
              (3)$18000-25000 (4)OVER $26000/POLCOUR TO PATROL (1)YES (2)NO/
              UPTODATE, TURNOUT (1)STRONGLY DISAGREE (2)DISAGREE (3)AGREE
              (4)STRONGLY AGREE/RELATE (1)STRONGLY AGREE (2)AGREE (3)DISAGREE
              (4)STRONGLY DISAGREE/LAWENF (1)STRONGLY AGREE (2)AGREE
              (3)DISAGREE (4)STRONGLY DISAGREE/CUTBACK (1)STRONGLY DISAGREE
              (2)DISAGREE (3)AGREE (4)STRONGLY AGREE/SEXATT (1)STRONGLY AGREE
              (2)AGREE (3)DISAGREE (4)STRONGLY DISAGREE
```

(Total = 19 cards)

All values are listed in order, and variable names are used as they appear in the VARIABLE LIST. Values are taken from the instrument. Note the use of /, and the use of spacing. The line should not extend or be split at column 80.

TASK DEFINITION CARDS:

```
              16
FREQUENCIES   GENERAL=ALL
```

The task definition card in this case is FREQUENCIES. Others are explained as needed, such as PEARSON CORR and CROSSTABS. All task definition cards are followed by a STATISTICS card, and on occasion, an OPTIONS card is used.

```
              16
OPTIONS       1,3,9
```

These options, available from a choice of nine, mean: 1, missing values will be excluded when a missing values card is used; 3 specifies an 8 × 11 format for tables; 9 causes a reference dictionary to be printed for the printout. It is wise to find out first if these options are available in the computer program. Computer programmers have a tendency to change programs without warning. This card is optional, and you should read the SPSS manual before exercising options in your run.

16

STATISTICS ALL

A statistics card must follow the task definition. While the options card may be omitted, the statistics card may not. There are various choices in the manual, but normally for beginners, the selection of ALL simplifies difficult choices. In the FREQUENCIES program, the statistics card with ALL will give the mean, standard error, median, mode, standard deviation, variance, kurtosis, skewness, range, maximum, and minimum. Any of these may be selected by number. For example, 1, 2, 3 would select only the mean, standard error, and median.

READ INPUT DATA

(Total = 3 cards) This card reads exactly as here and is followed immediately by the data deck.

DATA DECK (insert 450 cards)

PEARSON CORR
STATISTICS

Another task definition and another statistics card may be inserted before the end of the deck. In early runs, do not do this. Wait until you gain some experience.

END CARDS: FINISH

This card terminates the processing of the run input.

/* This card or a similar one usually accompanies the FINISH card at the end of the run.

(Total = 2 cards) Grand total of program cards = 34 cards (with 450 data cards)

NOTES: Notice that not all the cards listed here are necessarily used in the FREQUENCIES run. Some are shown to indicate places in the deck and their possible use at a later date with another program. Remember that whatever program you use, it must fit the assumptions of the level of statistical analysis that you use. Correlation uses continuous data, chi-square uses discrete data; therefore, when you use chi-square, make sure that your data are RECODE(d) if they are continuous-type data.

The FREQUENCIES deck is almost the same for all other runs. Very few cards change. The sequence remains fairly constant. The variables and the input format may change, but the rest of the deck is reasonably sequentially constant. There are programs that require extra cards, such as SUBFILE LIST, and there are some special features. With practice you will learn them. In most early runs you will do, only the task definition changes. With RECODE, you will learn to add a new value labels card. Usually, the smallest program deck is at least 15 cards (all required cards for a proper printout.)

USE FILE: Prepare a deck based on the entries here and write or type notes on each card as to its use. Staple the *right-hand* side. You will then have a ready file to check your own cards. Add to your file as you gain experience. Having a deck in your hands is better than having a textbook. Check the computer center for changes in format and programs. The SPSS manual will help you a lot as you progress.

SETTING UP THE PROGRAM

We have already selected the program FREQUENCIES as the one we will use for the initial exploration of the data deck. This program will tell us all the data in the various categories; it will give us absolute and relative data, percentages, means, standard deviation, and even a count of the cards in the deck, which is included as a variable. Because it is, the computer faithfully executes a mean and standard deviation of the number of cards, even though this information is useless. (The computer will often execute information that is not needed. Avoid wasting time examining garbage.)

Remember the restrictions on using the program format. Names are separated by commas or spaces, elements are separated by slashes (/). Never break an element on a card; for instance, in "AGE: (1) 18-28," the section "(1) 18-28" is a complete element and if broken will cause the computer to read wrongly. Names may not be broken into two pieces. If slashes are omitted, the computer cannot separate elements, and it will print garbage. When errors occur, the computer will detect most of them and notify you whether they occur in the control or specification field. Some errors are detailed by the computer; others are hard to find and need an expert. Many are careless typing errors, some are card-sequence errors, and occasionally the computer is in error—but rarely so.

Beware of typing a capital O for zero, or a small l for 1. Do not be afraid to ask for help. Be alert while you are typing your entries against entering some extreme score in a wrong category—for example, a 3 or 5 for *Sex*, where it should be either a 1 or 2. Spelling errors happen all the time; LABEL often appears as LABLE. Spaces are omitted in the rush, and some are put in where they are not needed, as in PAGE SIZE, which should read PAGESIZE. Don't be impatient with the machine. Learn to walk away and cool off. Examine and check your work carefully and often. Often a friend or an instructor will find the mistake you have repeatedly overlooked.

In the Table 8.1, *each line is a card, and each card is in sequence, and each card MUST be perfect.* Any deviations will abort the run or cause computer error. You must be precise. *Check the cards, check the sequence, check the sample size against the data deck, check the number of entries on each card, check your spelling.* It is simple if you follow the rules. Learning computer skills will save you endless hours of work and give you access to a whole new world of power and knowledge. Once you have learned to "drive" one computer, you will find the rest more or less the same.

THE PRINTOUT

Assuming that your cards were error-free and the turnaround time was ten minutes, your computer printout will probably be placed in a file box for you to pick up. It is usually placed in a box under your last digit in your access number (assuming ten pick-up boxes). You will identify it by the BSCLASS5 on the front sheet, or whatever you used in that space. Some use any five letters after BS–BSSTUDY5, BSPLANS5, and so on. If several of you are using the same BSCLASS, then the last number will separate you, and if two have the same last number, then the names inside will differentiate.

The first line printed is your job card, with your nine-letter ID and then a lot of printing that concerns the terminal, ending in the time used, usually in seconds. Next comes the program heading, STATISTICAL PACKAGE FOR THE SOCIAL SCIENCES (the second card in the deck); this is followed by a printout of all the program cards, with a table indicating the variable against the column on the data card. The number of variables is counted, and that is the number read. The labels and values are printed out. Then the task definition–in this case, FREQUENCIES–is printed with the STATISTICS underneath. As no file was set up, the FILE is called NONAME, and its creation date is recorded. What follows is a complete listing of all client numbers by code from 1 to 450, with one case for each number. If this is not correct, the run is in error. Ignore the statistics on this section. This use of case numbers as a variable easily identifies missing or duplicated cards, or one too many.

Tables in the Printout

The first table to appear is the one for *age*. This will be recorded as in *Table 8.2*. *Race* and *sex* are as in *Tables 8.3* and *8.4*. These tables are continued throughout the printout. It must be remembered that the statistics here are computed on the coded scores and thus have little real value; it is the absolute numbers and the percentages that have value, especially for discrete-type data. Check the categories for "wild" numbers such as 3 for *sex*.

Table 8.2. Frequency Data for Age

AGE CATEGORY LABEL	CODE	ABSOLUTE FREQ	RELATIVE FREQ (PCT)	ADJUSTED FREQ (PCT)	CUM FREQ (PCT)
18-28	1	219	48.7	48.7	48.7
29-39	2	102	22.7	22.7	71.4
40-50	3	73	16.2	16.2	87.6
OVER 50	4	56	12.4	12.4	100.0
	TOTAL	450	100.0	100.0	
VALID CASES	450	MISSING CASES	0		

Note: Statistics are omitted, as calculations are based on code scores 1-4. Note that the cumulative percentage gives a good idea where the mean age is–50% occurs at about 29-30 yrs.

Table 8.3. Frequency Data for Race

RACE [Under the same headings]					
WHITE	1	345	76.7	76.7	76.7
BLACK	2	91	20.2	20.2	96.9
OTHER	3	14	3.1	3.1	100.0
	TOTAL	450	100.0	100.0	

Table 8.4. Frequency Data for Sex

SEX					
MALE	1	234	52.0	52.0	52.0
FEMALE	2	216	48.0	48.0	100.0
	TOTAL	450	100.0	100.0	

Table 8.5. Frequency Data for Attitude Toward City Police

CITY ATT: ATTITUDE TOWARD CITY POLICE (N = 450)

CODE	A. FREQ	R. FREQ%	C. FREQ%
8	2	0.4	0.4
9	4	0.9	1.3
10	11	2.4	3.7
11	21	4.7	8.4
12	57	12.7	21.1
13	88	19.6	40.7
14	91	20.2	60.9
15	79	17.6	78.5
16	48	10.7	89.2
17	24	5.3	94.5
18	11	2.4	96.9
19	10	2.2	99.1
20	4	0.9	100.0
	450		

Mean = 14.05
Standard deviation = 2.062
Standard error = 0.097

The statistics have real value when we are dealing with continuous data or a numerical ranking of several values. The scale "CITYATT" prints out as in *Table 8.5* (scales abbreviated). Since the actual range was 6–24, the mean would be set at 15. Thus we could see that above a score of 15, less than 22 percent have unfavorable attitudes toward the city police. If we accept the mean at 14, then less than 40 percent have an unfavorable attitude. The frequency of the scores on this scale is well distributed, with little skewness (bias to right or left of the curve) or kurtosis (peaking or flattening of the curve). Notice that the absolute frequencies add up to 450 and the cumulative percentage adds up to 100 percent. The mean coincides with a 50 percent estimate. There were no scores at 6, 7, 21, 22, 23, 24 (or no extreme scores). The standard error indicates that we can be 95 percent confident that our mean falls within ± 0.2, a very close estimate (1.96 x 0.097).

This kind of frequency data gives the researcher an immediate idea of what is happening. It begins to give some variables importance and eliminate others. From the frequency data, we are now able to proceed to correlation data. If the tables are set down neatly, a great deal of time is saved in sorting out what is valuable and what is not.

Data Analysis Format

Over the years I have found that, unless the computer prints out a frequency program in book form, the best way to begin analysis is to sit down and tabulate the pertinent information on a single page, if possible. A great deal of the computer printing—at least 50 and often 90 percent—has no meaning and should be ignored, but much that is valuable is not seen until it is sorted out. The most important data are, of course, the variable name, the percentage in the appropriate category, and a listing of the absolute number at the side. If we need a confidence level for the percentage, it can be calculated from the table in Chapter 9. The standard error may be listed in a range from the lowest to the highest. All the other information may be disregarded for small discrete data, and carefully sorted if the data are continuous. The format should be set out clearly, simply, and without any notations. Its place in the final presentation is discussed later in this text.

Data analysis from the frequency printout is the single most important piece of information in the whole statistical level of analysis. It decides where you go, what you do, and how you do it. See *Tables 8.6* and *8.7*, taken from the computer printout of the FREQUENCIES program.

Note that Table 8.7 dichotomizes easily into *agree/disagree*. Approximately half the population surveyed agreed that the city police use modern procedures, respond quickly to calls, and have effective community relations, and that sexual matters should be of no concern of the police. A majority (63.6 percent) felt that the police should enforce the law for minor crimes; 80.5 percent that budget cutbacks had reduced police effectiveness. Overall, using these questions as a scale, 60.9 percent had an unfavorable attitude toward police policies and procedures.

These tables complete the data analysis and provide the key for further analysis. All the useful data, such as percentages, means, and standard deviations, have been culled from the printout. We now have a complete analysis of each variable (univariate analysis), or a one-way analysis, as it is called. We have a complete picture of the distribution characteristics of each variable.

Table 8.6. City Population Described from Sample (N = 450)

Variable	Category		Percentage
AGE:	18–28 yrs.		48.7
	29–39		22.7
	40–50		16.2
	Over 50		12.4
RACE:	White		76.7
	Black		20.2
	Other		3.1
SEX:	Male		52.0
	Female		48.0
RELIGION:	Catholic		53.8
	Protestant		25.1
	Jewish		3.8
	Other		17.3
POLITICAL PREFERENCE:	Republican		26.9
	Democrat		47.6
	Independent		25.6
FINANCIAL STATUS	$0–8,000		46.7
	$9,000–17,000		32.4
	$18,000–25,000		16.7
	$26,000+		4.2
POLICE COURTESY		Yes	76.4
		No	23.6
POLICE RESPONSE (Emergency)		Yes	65.6
		No	34.5
POLICE IMAGE (Neatness)		Yes	74.2
		No	25.8
POLICE PATROL (Adequate)		Yes	50.9
		No	49.1
POLICE CORRUPTION		Yes	54.2
		No	45.8
POLICE APPEARANCE APPROVAL (from above)			63.2

95% confidence interval = ± 4.5%
Standard error (varying) 0.02–0.05

Comments on Data Analysis

The format changes for every design, in that the names of the variables may be different and the frequencies are different. Generally, the design can remain the same, provided it uses the proper sequence of variables and goes through the variable

Table 8.7. Public Approval of Police Policy and Procedures (N = 450)

Variable	Percentages			
	Strongly agree	*Agree*	*Disagree*	*Strongly disagree*
Approval of modern methods and developments	2.0	48.4	40.0	9.6
Approval of police response to calls	3.3	49.1	40.7	6.9
Approval of police-community relations	1.3	48.7	40.4	9.6
Approval of police law enforcement	14.0	22.4	33.3	30.3
Budget approval and effectiveness	25.6	54.9	15.3	4.2
Approval of police views on morality	17.6	30.4	40.7	11.3

list with the printout as a backup. Its use is that it gives not only percentages but also sample size, enabling the reader to calculate absolute numbers. Given the absolute numbers, other calculations may be performed. Percentages without sample size really have very little meaning. Also, the reader will catch the direction of the percentages and where they add up to 100 percent; thus the necessary adjustments can be made.

FREQUENCIES, then, is a great exploratory device. The computer saves hours of endless calculations and sets up the tables very neatly. It is up to you to take what you need from the statistical smorgasbord. Data analysis of frequencies precedes the analysis of two variables, and of the effect of the independent variable upon the dependent. Before we look closer at association, it is wise to look at correlation. But first note that the frequency analysis gives you means to dichotomize continuous data, so that if you have to, you can recode the variable into high/low categories above and below the mean. You then turn continuous data into discrete data.

SOME ERRORS IN ENTERING DATA

When you are operating a keypunch, it is easy to become distracted and make mistakes. One of the most frequent but most difficult errors to find occurs when the key for numeric data is relaxed for a moment on entering and an ALPHA, or letter, creeps in. This completely aborts the computer calculations.

To find a data entry error:

1. Check your cards against your coding sheet or questionnaire.
2. Check the N OF CASES. *The number of data cards must equal your sample number.*

3. Check your cards for holes punched in the two unprinted spaces above the zeros. If there are any, there are errors in your *numeric* data. This area of the card is reserved for ALPHA, or letters. If you have such a card in your numeric data, it is wrong.
4. Check for two punches in the same column. If this occurs, the card is wrong. One punch per column indicates numeric data; double punches indicate ALPHA or signs. NEVER correct a card, ALWAYS use a new card.
5. Check for uneven size of punch holes. Large holes or misses are read wrongly, and the results will be in error. Don't improve on the keypunch by making your own adjustments with a knife or ballpoint pen. Use another card and another keypunch.
6. On a new keypunch, check the zero against the letter *o*, the numeric 1 against the capital letter *I*. Run a trial card, it is always worth it. Check the printout on the top of the card.
7. Some computers have a program to print your data deck–use it. It shows error faster than any other process.
8. If you have access to a verifier or reader, use it.

The error of one short in the number of cases shows up in the frequency printout as the cumulative total or absolute number of cases. For example, in a sample of 300, the frequency printout, the correlation matrix, and the marginal totals in chi-square would all show a consistent error of recording $N = 299$. But there is a more dangerous situation when a card is duplicated and there are 300 cards but one card has been counted twice. The error here shows up in the frequency printout; for example, if case 205 was duplicated, the printout would list:

202	1
203	1
204	1
205	2
207	1
208	1
etc.	

Note that 206 is missing; if it is included, we get 301 cards!

This is a very convenient check on large sample counts. The FREQUENCIES program on the SPSS system should always be used first to verify actual card data. Again, if a card is short, the printout will show an error, such as reading the last card–usually FINISH–and then:

ERROR IN CONTROL CARD	F
ERROR IN CONTROL CARD	I
ERROR IN CONTROL CARD	N

and so on, until the word FINISH appears. This indicates that the N count is at least one card short. If there are too many cards, the program cannot terminate properly or proceed to the next program. *It is wise to check that only one card exists for each number and that there is exactly the same number of cards as in the sample.*

Certain errors appear more than others. For instance, when using the job card, you must be certain that the digit after CLASS agrees with the last digit of your access number. In this example:

//BSCLASS5 JOB 333444555

they do not agree and the card is useless.

Also on the job card, make sure that you have enough time.

TIME=(0000,10)

is enough for most small jobs. If you are using a large number of cases with extensive analysis, expand your time. In 30 seconds, the computer will do a huge amount of work, so plan your work carefully. Do not go on fishing expeditions on the computer.

Make sure each data card has the same number of columns. You can check this by thumbing through the deck; odd ones will stand out. And watch spacing. //EXECSPSS is wrong; it should read // EXEC SPSS. Notice the spaces between // and EXEC, and between EXEC and SPSS. On the other hand, PAGESIZE is one word, so do not write PAGE SIZE.

Check your cards to see that you are entering your specifications *starting at column 16*, not at column 15 or 17. Be careful with your spelling—LABELS, please, not LABLES. Check your entries on your data cards. For example, if you are coding *sex* as 1 for male, 2 for female, do not punch a 0 or a 3, or a capital *I* for a 1.

Make sure your cards are in order. If they are not, the program will stop. Be careful when you add programs after your last data card. For example, if you add CROSSTABS and you have continuous data in the deck, your printout will give you enormous tables (depending on the range of data). It would be better to run your deck through with RECODE in the proper position before you decide to use nonparametric analysis with parametric data. Become familiar with SPSS, and use only the statistics and options that you need.

When using FORTRAN abbreviations, such as RELIG for *religion*, do not use the word *religion* again except in VAR LABELS where you explain RELIG. If you use RELIG in the variable list (or any other abbreviation, for that matter), you must use the same abbreviation in all other specification fields—RELIG BY EDUCAT, or RELIG (1) PROTESTANT (2) CATHOLIC, for example. Check your spelling on every card. Remember, if your specification field runs over onto another card, you need not reenter the control field. As in VARIABLE LIST, which may be quite long, just start your second card at column 16 and do not put a delimiter after your last entry.

For setting up your tables, the dependent variable is usually entered first in a list of variables, as in SCATTERGRAM, CROSSTABS, PEARSON CORR, NON-PAR CORR, REGRESSION, and so on.

If you observe the conventions carefully, you will enjoy a reasonable degree of success.

Common Computer Conventions

1. Proper access number with time available in account and agreement of the last access digit with the CLASS digit
2. Setting enough time on the job card (same for memory) for the project
3. Having N OF CASES the same as number of data-deck cards
4. Correct spacing with correct delimiters
5. Correct spelling as per FORTRAN conventions
6. Correct coding to comply with variable values
7. Correct order of all cards in the deck
8. Correct program for data (parametric or nonparametric)
9. Proper use of FORTRAN abbreviations in sequence
10. Proper entry of dependent variable (usually entered first)
11. Same number of columns used on each card in data deck
12. No bent or mutilated cards or double-punched entries

Not observing any one of these rules will stop the computer program or will cause the computer to print nonsense. In the case of item 1, it will not print at all; 2, it will stop in the middle of a printout; 3, it will print garbage; 4, 5, 6, or 7, it will stop the program; 8, it will give either massive printouts with no meaning or none at all; 9, it will produce strange results; 10, it will change the sequence of the variables; 11, it will completely foul up the data computations; 12, it will stop the program. Any of these results can be very frustrating.

You must take care in following the SPSS conventions and in checking your IBM deck. The precision in your research measurement must be more than matched by the precision in your technical ability.

KEEPING TRACK OF DATA

Each interview that is conducted should have a client number that is the only identification of that client. These become anonymous numbers in a file, but they are useful in keeping the number of samples in sequence. Moreover, if a sample is taken in several areas, the client number should also have a code identification for the area—such as 1 for city and 2 for suburbs; or 1 for Main Street Mall, 2 for West Plaza Mall, 3 for University Plaza Mall, and so on. This kind of area identification is useful if subfiles are used and if different areas are to be analyzed separately. Subfiles can also be computerized. This is a very good program for comparative surveys. It is important that each questionnaire is treated with care, is recorded and coded properly, and is not fabricated to suit the occasion. Each set of questionnaires should be counted carefully until sample size is reached.

On large surveys, taking several days or even weeks for interviews, care must be taken not to lose the data or leave them behind at the point of survey. It is very easy to become sidetracked in survey work and misplace data, in which case a day's work is wasted. It is a good idea to have a checklist for the end of each day. The checklist should indicate not only all the equipment you took out, but the number of questionnaires completed, where they are, and if they have been coded or entered on to FORTRAN coding sheets.

On large surveys, I keep a daily journal. At the end of the day, every item is entered—any event, conversation, difficulties, innovations, new ideas, or changes made. If I am working with a team, items to be discussed the next day are also entered. Accompanying the journal is a daily account of expenditures, totaled daily. If grant money or fellowship money is used, the record can speak for itself in terms of waste or accountability. Items include travel expenses, food, money paid to workers, money paid to clients, office supplies, equipment expenses, any sundries that may have been needed.

The journal and the daily account should be supplemented by pictures or photographs of people, places, events. A Polaroid or 35mm camera is excellent for recording events. Another useful item is the tape recorder. The pocket recorder, which can take a two-hour tape, is very useful for recording interviews and listening to them later to discover new information or better ways to conduct the interview. An interview should *never* be taped without the client's permission. Usually, respondents are willing to cooperate; children enjoy being taped, groups invariably give consent. The best recorder is one that does not have a conspicuous microphone and looks like a book on the table. My lead-in is, "This is a tape recorder, do you mind if I record this interview? All tapes are confidential, your identity will be protected."

Substantive Data

The short student survey does not need the implementation of other methods, since the time allotted in a semester or quarter session does not permit this. In a longer, more detailed venture—graduating year or graduate work—the survey ought to be backed up by field work, triangulation, use of nonreactive measures, and the credibility of field observations. Valuable data, often not part of the statistics but part of the substance of the research, may be lost otherwise. Very often, substance is developed that not only completely disproves what the researcher set out to do, but also completely disproves other studies made in the same area. Occasionally, accidental discovery occurs—perhaps when the alert researcher finds an "unexplainable" extreme in the data; or when, upon elaboration, a single item will not conform; or when there is a marked inconsistency in the frequency data. Such inconsistencies indicate the need for further research. Recording them in the presentation ensures that they are not lost.

At the front of all good research is the research *imagination*; at the back of all good research is the research *observation*.

SUMMARY

Writing a program for a simple run such as FREQUENCIES involves two main concepts: (1) knowledge of format limitations and rules, and (2) following those rules.

Computer programming is an exercise in precision. The card deck has five parts, each with several sections. There are the run cards, the data definition cards, the task definition cards, the data deck, and the end cards. We also have certain procedure cards running through the deck. Each has a certain strategic place, and certain sequences must be adhered to, such as always having a statistics card with a task definition card. In addition, there are word conventions and preparations that must be used in proper order. A name, a keyword, an element, or a delimiter must not be split. If more than one card is used to a complete statement, the control field is usually entered only on the first statement card.

The most important card is the variable list; this must agree with the ordering of the variables on the data cards. Upon this list is created the input format, which tells the computer exactly how to read the variables. Although variable labels and value labels are optional, they are of great use in the computer printout in setting up tables, so they must be accurate. Also, the data deck must be the same size as the number of cases in the sample.

The program writing is made easier by using a clear, simple instrument. Be careful when entering values, in case you have decided upon a certain method and have reversed some values. Making a scale out of a series of questions adds dimension to your project, but the scale must be consistent.

Keypunching the program requires a little more expertise. You must learn to use both alpha and numeric and also to be absolutely perfect in your coded entries. The program setup provides you with a guide. Use the SPSS manual if you run into difficulties. By all means, ask for help. Practice running programs, but *do not be too ambitious*. Go slowly and learn the ropes; there is a lot to learn, and one printout does not make you a computer expert. Avoid error by reading, checking, and rechecking your card deck. Make a practice deck to carry around with you, and make your notes on it.

When you finally get to the reader and wait for your printout, the work is only just begun. Now you must analyze your one-way frequency program data. Take only what you need and what is relevant from the computer printout. Enter it neatly on one-page tables and do not forget the sample size. You may make comments on the tables only concerning the data you have; you may not exercise judgment or personal opinion.

EXERCISES

1. How many cards would you use per case? Explain the entries for a single case, beginning with your ID number.

2. Explain the items on an IBM card and how they correspond with a FORTRAN coding sheet. Explain control and specification fields.
3. Suggest alternative coding and categories for the following: Education, Occupation, Marital Status, Sentencing Ranking, Firearms Possession, Death Penalty, Commission of a Crime. (Do not use *yes/no* responses.)
4. Invent some hypothetical responses for 20 clients to the police questionnaire in the chapter. Code the response, keypunch on IBM cards, use a group ID and a client number (01-20). Check your cards carefully for errors.
5. How would you keep track of survey data?
6. Discuss the advantages of the use of daily journals, diaries, tape recorders, and cameras on research survey projects.
7. What is substantive data? How does it differ from statistical data? What is qualitative data? quantitative data? What are the parts of an IBM deck?
8. Comment upon serendipity, innovation, imagination, observation, expectation, stereotypes, prejudice, bias, precision, representation.
9. What kinds of error can you accumulate in the research project? How would you control for some of them? What is the difference between sampling error and instrument error?
10. Design a project and list all the places where error can occur. List your controls at the appropriate places.
11. Why use numeric coding rather than alpha? How many "bits" of information can you punch on an IBM card? What is GIGO? What is the difference between an alpha punch and a numeric punch? How does the computer score? Why use 0-9 for coding?
12. What is marginal coding? multiple-response coding? direct entry? What are their advantages and disadvantages?
13. How would you locate a data entry error? Make some, and observe the results. Punch an *i* for a 1 or an *o* for a zero, and compare the cards. How would you detect one card short?
14. Will sample error be larger or smaller in cluster sampling? Why not take a simple random sample?
15. Construct the deck as required in the text.
16. Write the program you will use on the FORTRAN coding sheets. Enter the items square by square; watch the coding conventions.
17. If you are uncertain of your code, write it down on a code sheet or in a code book.
18. Assuming you have used real data and have entered your program successfully, write a data analysis as per the tables in the chapter. Your data should give you three neat tables to compare with the text.
19. How would you code the following individual case? Offender, aged 22, arrested 8 August, 1978, charged with armed robbery, entered guilty plea, sentenced to

five years, eight prior arrests, victim badly assaulted, amount involved $65, no fixed address, no occupation, grade 6 education, unmarried, Protestant, no relatives.

20. Design a code that will include:
    (a) Street and location of offense
    (b) Type of offense committed
    (c) Day and time of crime
    (d) Offender's age, race, sex, education, occupation, religion, marital status
    (e) Offender's residence
    (f) Victim's age, race, sex, education, occupation, religion, marital status
    (g) Victim's residence
    How could you use this information? Could you predict? prevent? protect?
21. How would you incorporate police strategy into the case above? How would you include cost?
22. List some items that cause fear (of crime) and try to design questions that will get effective answers. Watch out for leading questions, personal bias, and key words.
23. How would you analyze the effectiveness of police patrols—by the number of patrols? by the increase in the number of arrests? by the reduction in crime in an area? by police satisfaction with procedure? by the amount of money expended?
24. Design a list of categories for determining police promotion.
25. Design a study on automobile accidents and criminal negligence.

FOR FURTHER READING

Babbie, Earl R., *The Practice of Social Research*. Belmont, Calif: Wadsworth, 1975. See Chaps. 8, 13.

Bassler, R., and E. O. Joslin, *Applications of Computer Systems*. Arlington, Va: College Readings, 1974.

Coombs, C. H., *A Theory of Data*. New York: John Wiley, 1964.

Davis, Gordon B., *An Introduction to Electronic Computers*. New York: McGraw-Hill, 1965.

Forsythe, A. I., et al., *Computer Science: A First Course*. New York: John Wiley, 1970.

Galtung, J., *Theory and Methods of Social Research*. New York: Columbia University Press, 1967.

Gear, C. W., *Introduction to Computer Science*. Chicago: Science Research Associates, 1973.

Huck, A., *Reading Statistics and Research*. New York: Harper & Row, 1974.

Leedy, Paul, *Practical Research*. New York: Macmillan, 1974.

Lohnes, P., and W. Cooley, *Introduction to Statistical Procedures: With Computer Exercises.* New York: John Wiley, 1968.

Moser, C. A., and G. Kalton, *Survey Methods in Social Investigation.* New York: Basic Books, 1972.

Riess, A., et al., *Occupations and Social Status.* New York: Free Press, 1961.

Selltiz, Claire, et al., *Research Methods in Social Relations* (3rd ed.). New York: Holt, Rinehart & Winston, 1976. See Chap. 13, "Data Processing."

Sonquist, John A., and William C. Dunkelberg, *Survey and Opinion Research,* pp. 73–195, "Coding and Code Construction." Englewood Cliffs, N.J.: Prentice-Hall, 1977.

Sterling, T. D., and S. V. Pollack, *Introduction to Statistical Data Processing.* Englewood Cliffs, N.J.: Prentice-Hall, 1968.

Veldman, Donald J., *FORTRAN Programming for the Behavioral Sciences.* New York: Holt, Rinehart & Winston, 1967.

FURTHER READING FOR COMPUTER TECHNOLOGY

Anderson, Ronald E., "A Bibliography of Social Science Computing," *Computing Reviews,* July 1974, pp. 247–61.

Armor, D. J., and A. S. Couch, *The DATA-TEXT Primer.* New York: Free Press, 1972.

Bates, F., and M. L. Douglas, *Programming Language/One* (2nd ed.). Englewood Cliffs, N.J.: Prentice-Hall, 1970.

Borko, Harold, ed., *Computer Applications in the Behavioral Sciences.* Englewood Cliffs, N.J.: Prentice-Hall, 1962.

Brier, Alan, and Ian Robinson, *Computers and the Social Sciences.* New York: Columbia University Press, 1974.

Burroughs Corporation, *B2500 and B3500 Problem Oriented Language.* Generator (POLGEN) Reference Manual. Detroit, 1971.

Chapin, N., *Computers: A System Approach.* New York: Van Nostrand, 1971.

David, J. A., and J. H. Strernick, *The IMPRESS Primer.* Hanover, N.H.: Dartmouth College Press, 1971.

Janda, K., *Data Processing: Applications to Political Science.* Evanston, Ill.: Northwestern University Press, 1969.

Klecka, William R., et al., *SPSS Primer: Statistical Package for the Social Sciences.* New York: McGraw-Hill, 1975.

Kossack, C. F., and A. Henschke, *Introduction to Statistics and Computer Programming.* San Francisco: Holden-Day, 1975.

McCracken, D. A., *Guide to FORTRAN Programming.* New York: John Wiley, 1961.

Martin, J., and A. R. D. Norman, *The Computerized Society.* Englewood Cliffs, N.J.: Prentice-Hall, 1970.

Moore, Richard W., *Introduction to the Use of Computer Packages for Statistical Analyses.* Englewood Cliffs, N.J.: Prentice-Hall, 1978.

Nie, Norman H., et al., *Statistical Package for the Social Sciences* (2nd ed.). New York: McGraw-Hill, 1975.

Sharpe, W. F., *BASIC: An Introduction to Computer Programming Using the BASIC Language*. New York: Free Press, 1967.

STATJOB Series. Madison: Academic Computing Center, University of Wisconsin, 1976.

STATSYSTEM: Statistical Analysis System User's Guide. New York: General Electric Corp. Info. Services, 1971.

Taviss, I., ed., *The Computer Impact.* Englewood Cliffs, N.J.: Prentice-Hall, 1970.

9

Sampling Theory and Statistics

In this chapter, the underlying statistical theory is discussed, with emphasis on the normal curve and sampling theory. Probability is dealt with, but briefly, since the use of the theory occurs at the beginning of the research. Inferential and descriptive statistics are the basis for the survey research method. The method of logical reasoning is inductive, using inferential statistics and moving from data to the parent population. Probability statistics that move from the universe to the particular fact, or from the population to the sample (deductive logic) are rarely used. However, one cannot exist without the other, and each is equally important in its own way. In the survey research method, the emphasis is on inferential statistics.

Table 9.1 shows the statistics encountered in the research adventure. Most have Greek signs, and all are part of a statistical language. Formulas are given in the text as they occur and are summarized in Appendix 2 in a useful table. Most statistics can be set up on calculators or computers, but we must know how they work and what they do. Most formulas given here are those used on calculators and are usually more complex and reliable than older textbook formulas.

The substitution of numbers for formula involves a basic knowledge of algebra, common sense in the manipulation of arithmetic, and an awareness of formula transposition and transformation that will save time. Even using calculators, the time saved by a knowledge of formula can be worthwhile. A basic grasp of statistics

Table 9.1. Statistical Concepts and Symbols

Descriptive statistics describe population parameters (limits) and masses of data such as sample frequencies.

Inferential statistics are sample estimates used to make inferences about the parent population.

Descriptive parameters		Sample estimates
N (population)		n (sample size)
σ^2 (sigma squared)	Variation	σ^2 or s^2
σ (sigma)	Deviation (may be z score)	σ or s
μ (mu)	Mean	$\bar{x}$ (x-bar)
ρ (rho)	Correlation	r (PPM)
N (μ, σ)	Normal distribution	N ($\bar{x}$, s)
f	Frequency	f
σ_μ	Standard error of the mean	$s_{\bar{x}}$ (estimated)

Sample test statistics

Pearson product moment	$= r$	Degrees of freedom	= df
Student's T test	$= t$	Level of significance	$= \alpha$ (alpha)
Chi-square	$= \chi^2$	Contingency coefficient	$= C$
F ratio test	$= F$	Pearson's Phi	$= \phi$
Type 1 error	$= \alpha$ (alpha)	Gamma	$= \gamma$
Type 2 error	$= \beta$ (beta)	Reject the null hypothesis when . . .	= R:

Note: Frequencies are also expressed as relative and cumulative *percentages.* There are other specialized test statistics used in more complex statistical analysis, both parametric and nonparametric.

formula, changes in the identification of symbols, and knowledge of assumptions and limitations will help considerably in progress through various levels of statistical analysis. Most of the statistical signs are Greek letters. Perhaps the most used is the summation sign, Σ, or sigma, which means, "Add all the numbers in that column or category."

Raw score, so called because it is not a transformed score, is the original basic measurement or test score. It is usually designated as x if there is one variable. A second variable is designated as y, and a third as z. However, most of the calculations show x and y, or the use of two variables. The square-root sign is frequently used, as in $\sqrt{\Sigma x}$, the square root of all the summed values of x category. The mean of a category, or the average, is designated by a bar over that variable, as in $\bar{x}$, called x-bar. Capitals usually refer to the population, lowercase letters to the sample. Powers, or indices, such as x^2, mean that the value of x is squared or multiplied by itself. It is wise to keep track of all powers and roots right to the end of the equation. Remember to do all the work inside the brackets before you remove them, and watch exactly where the indices are in relation to the brackets, inside or outside.

HOW TO USE THIS CHAPTER

A great deal of statistical ground is covered in this chapter. Rather than spending a lot of time with statistical analysis, read the chapter through once carefully, and then take it a little at a time until you feel comfortable with a grasp of the basics. It is important to understand the following:

1. The relationship of the binomial probability distribution to proportions as they exist in the real world.
2. The theory of the normal curve and how it approximates both the probability distribution and the real world.
3. The difference between a sample with its single mean and many (theoretical) samples with their many means, and the *sampling distribution* of those means and how that distribution also approximates the normal curve.
4. The standard deviation of scores in a single sample, and the standard error (deviation) of the means of many samples; and how the standard error gives rise to confidence intervals and confidence levels.
5. How proportions under the normal curve can be converted to standard scores such as standard deviation, standard error, z scores, and confidence intervals, all of which measure the distance from the mean in terms of units of standard deviation. Moreover, the proportions under the normal curve can also be read as percentages and so used for confidence levels.
6. The regions of rejection for the null hypothesis, why certain levels of significance are set, and how these levels are used in decision making.
7. The fact that since most of the information calculated is taken from sample statistics used as estimates for population parameters, sample size is a very important factor in these calculations.
8. The importance of the central limit theorem—that it enables us to use the normal curve for a population of any shape.

Table 9.2. The Functions of Statistical Sample Estimates

Statistical purpose	Measure described	Function	Symbol
Sampling	Used for actual or absolute count and for calculation of degrees of freedom.	Sample size Unbiased estimate	n df $(n-1)$
Comparison	Use of data for determination of representation, and sample profile based on data for several variables. Used to examine sample data content.	Relative and cumulative frequencies and percentages	f %
Location	Describes central tendency. Mean is vital to calculations and is average score.	Mean Median Mode	$\overline{x}$ Md. Mo.

Table 9.2. The Functions of Statistical Sample Estimates (cont'd.)

Statistical purpose	Measure described	Function	Symbol
Dispersion	Used to find spread of scores in sample.	Range	$x_{max} - x_{min}$
	Variation of scores.	Variation	σ^2 or s
	Standardized variation from the mean.	Deviation	z σ or s
Association	Used to determine direction, strength, and order of variables.	Correlation (does not show order)	r PPM or Pearson r
	Bivariate analysis in contingency tables.	Chi-square	χ^2
Prediction	Used for trends, anticipated results, pattern outcomes.	Time series Regression Outcomes	Y $\hat{y}$ (y-hat) O
Ranking	Use of frequency data and weighting to make hierarchies. Also used to develop graphs, tables, and diagrams used for social index construction.	Frequencies and percentages are ordered, weighted, ranked.	f %
Decision	Statistical significance is the level of significance (confidence level) chosen to reject the null hypothesis. The confidence limits are the specified range of rejection set by the significance levels in comparison of tabled values. Tabled values are based upon normal curve distributions.	Confidence level Confidence limits Level of significance Table values	C.L. C.I. t, r, χ^2, F
Limitation	Use of estimation to show relationship of sample to parent population. Use of sampling error to calculate confidence limits. Limits are set by standard deviations. Limit is determined by level.	Sampling error	s_e $s_{\overline{x}}$ z_α
Elaboration	Comparison or analysis of means and variables is extended to determine causal order, causal effect, special relationships.	Multivariate analysis in contingency tables Multiple/partial regression	χ^2 r_{xyz}, F
	Comparison of differences.	T test Analysis of variance	t F

9. That even though the underlying statistical theory is the quantitative base of mathematical decision making, this should not be considered the only way to make decisions. We must think out the substance of statistics.

10. The necessity, in working with theoretical models and probabilities, to remain on guard for error.

Sample estimates, which we use to make inferences to the parent population, have statistical purposes based upon their functions, which are indicated in Table 9.2. These are ten ways to use sample statistics, either alone or in combination. Some data analysis is simple, some is complex. ***All statistical tests are based upon certain assumptions*** for the data (Table 9.3), so be sure that you conform to these requirements.

Table 9.3. Assumptions for Statistical Procedures

Theory	Item	Assumptions
Sampling	Sample	1. *Independent random sampling.* Each person has equal chance of selection. 2. *Homoscedasticity.* There must be equal variance, or equal variance is assumed. 3. *Normal distribution* of the characteristic in the population and sample.
The normal curve	Sample and population distribution	1. *Model of a theoretical probability outcome for an ideal population.* 2. The area under the curve is unity and is divided into *constant proportions.* 3. *The mean is zero, standard deviation is 1.*
Central limit theorem	Sampling Means Distribution	1. *Sample size* is large (30 or more). 2. Sample means are distributed in a *normal curve pattern.* 3. The sample mean as an *unbiased estimate* of the population mean is used to determine the interval in which the population mean will fall.
Sampling error	Type 1 Type 2	Rejection of true null hypothesis. Retention of false null hypothesis.
Statistical Test Correlation	Pearson r r	1. Random sample as above. 2. Continuous-interval-type data. 3. Variation on both variables is concomitant. 4. Data for both variables are linear.
Independence	Chi-square χ^2	1. Random sample as above, large sample. 2. Discrete data from two variables. 3. Approximates normal curve. 4. If expected values equal observed values, independence exists.
Analysis of variance	Anova F	1. Random samples as above, large size. 2. Two or more variables. 3. Equal means, equal variances. 4. Usually parametric, but may be used with non-parametric data with care.

VARIATION AND STANDARD DEVIATION

If we sum all the squares of all the scores on either side of the mean and divide that sum by the number of scores, we get an average squared distance from the mean. This is called *variation*. If we use $(n - 1)$, which is also the number of the degrees of freedom, as the denominator, we get an unbiased estimate of that average squared distance. We now have:

$$\text{Variation} = s^2 = \frac{\text{Sum of the squares}}{\text{Degrees of freedom}} = \frac{SS}{(n-1)} \text{ or } \frac{SS}{\text{df}}$$

There is a similarity between the mean, which is an average measure, and variation. Note that variation is the distance from the mean squared, or $(x - \bar{x})^2$; the mean is an average of all the scores, or $\bar{x} = \Sigma x/n$. These scores may have any value, and the variation may have very high values. However, the mean can be standardized, and in fact we can choose its value. If we can standardize variation in some way, there is no doubt we will have a very useful statistical measure. We have already obtained an unbiased estimate, and to produce an unbiased estimate of the average dispersion of scores about the mean, we simply find the square root of the variation. Mathematically, it can be shown in a very easy proof that:

$$\text{Variation} = s^2 = \frac{n\Sigma x^2 - (\Sigma x)^2}{n(n-1)}: \text{ Standard deviation} = \sqrt{s^2} = s$$

Standard deviation gives us a constant with which to determine proportions of scores between the mean and standard deviation, or between standard deviations; it is expressed in the same units as the original measure and is vital to inferential statements. Each unit contains the value of s; for instance, if in IQ, $s = 15$ or one standard deviation ($1s$ or 1σ), two standard deviations would equal 30, and so on. Left of the mean, units are negative; to the right, they are positive.

STANDARD SCORES

Data may be transformed. When the original score is used, it is called a *raw score*; when it is transformed, it takes the name of its new distribution. Some linear data are transformed into linear transformations such as percentiles. The object of transformation of scores is to give them more meaning in relation to one another. Another linear transformation is the creation of standard scores from data. *Transformed scores* that contain means and standard deviations are called *standard scores*. One of the most useful transformations in statistics is a score that will give a mean of 0 and a standard deviation of 1. For example, IQ tests are calculated on this basis.

If we take a raw score, subtract the mean, and divide it by the standard deviation; the new score will be a z score. To return to the IQ score, supposing that the score was 125, the test mean 100, and the standard deviation 15, then:

$$z = \frac{x - \bar{x}}{s} = \frac{125 - 100}{15} = \frac{25}{15} = 1.66$$

The z score states that the raw score is 1.66 standard deviations above the mean of 0. A z score may be negative as well as positive. Scores may be transformed into any desirable mean and standard deviation by $Z = M + Sz$, where the new score Z is obtained by setting the desired mean M, and adding it to the product of the old z score and the new required standard deviation:[1]

$$\begin{aligned} Z &= 100 \text{ (new mean)} + 15 \text{ (new s.d.)} \times 0.8 \text{ (}z\text{ score)} \\ &= 100 + 12 \\ &= 112 \end{aligned}$$

Standardized Scores and the Normal Curve

It can be shown mathematically that the mean of z scores is zero and that the variance is 1. If the variance is 1, then the square root of the variance, the deviation, is also 1. This is most useful, as the distribution of z scores also approximates the distribution of the normal curve. In this case, we have a unique measure to use with the standard normal distribution. The population mean will coincide with the z score mean, and we have $\bar{z} = \mu = 0$. We also have the standard score, z itself, which shows how far the score is from the mean in terms of units of standard deviations. If you remember, $z = x - \bar{x}/\sigma$, which means that as the standard deviation of z scores is unity, the standard deviation also coincides with the population standard deviation, or $s_z = \sigma = 1$, where s_z = the standard deviation of z scores and σ = the population standard deviation. This may be extended to a sampling distribution of z where $s_{\bar{z}} = s/\sqrt{n}$. It would appear logical that where the mean is 0 and the standard deviation is 1, the sampling distribution would equal the proportional distribution of the normal curve. The fact is that it does.

Certain z scores need to be remembered: As the normal curve is divided into constant proportion, the z scores are also constants; proportions can also be changed to percentages. Constants are:

$z = 1$ = 34.13% under the normal curve
$z = 1.645$ = 45% under the normal curve
$z = 1.96$ = 47.5% under the normal curve
$z = 2$ = 47.73% under the normal curve
$z = 2.58$ = 49.5% under the normal curve
$z = 3$ = 49.9% under the normal curve

[1] z scores are in units of standard deviation, the mean is zero, the sum of scores is zero, the distribution form is the same as the original data. Scores may be used to show (area) percentages under the normal curve.

Confidence intervals are simply intervals on either side of the mean, or *double the z score* by adding and subtracting the z score to the mean. Thus we would find that 90 percent of the means' scores would fall in an interval where $z = 1.645$ was added and subtracted to the mean (and we could be 90 percent confident that the population mean was in this interval). Now we can establish intervals and levels based upon z_c scores:

$$z_c = +z \text{ and } -z$$
$$z_c = z\ (+\overline{x}\ -) \text{ Curve interval}$$
$$z_c = z \text{ constant}$$

where

$z_c = 1$	68.26%	confidence interval
$z_c = 1.645$	90%	confidence interval
$z_c = 1.96$	95%	confidence interval
$z_c = 2$	95.46%	confidence interval
$z_c = 2.58$	99%	confidence interval
$z_c = 3$	99.7%	confidence interval

All that needs to be done is setting out the formula:

$$\text{C.I.} = \overline{x} \pm z s_e$$

$$\text{where } s_e = s_{\overline{x}} = \frac{s}{\sqrt{n}} \ : \pm z = z_c$$

Take a mean of 100 with a standard deviation of 15, sample $n = 100$; we have a confidence interval of 95 percent, as follows:

$$z = 1.96; \ z_c = \pm 1.96$$

$$100 \pm 1.96 \left(\frac{15}{\sqrt{100}}\right) = 100 \pm 1.96\ (1.5)$$
$$= 100 \pm 3$$
$$95\% \text{ C.I.} = \ 97\text{–}103$$

We can be 95 percent sure that the population mean falls in that interval. The z scores and the normal curve have provided us with a very convenient way to turn point estimates into intervals. All we have done with the z score is to apply it to the upper and lower limits of the parent mean (using the sample mean and the sample standard deviation as estimates). By applying the z score to both sides of the mean, we established an interval (and a confidence level) in which the parent mean must fall.

DEGREES OF FREEDOM

Degrees of freedom are the restrictions placed upon our calculations in order to produce unbiased estimates. Consider the numbers 5, 4, 6, 8; their sum is 23. If we hold any one number–say, 8–the other three numbers are *free to vary* until the total is again 23. The degrees of freedom here (hypothetically) equal $n - 1 = 3$. This is true of any number in the series given; it will always be $n - 1$ for the total to equal 23.

The same thing happens when we are dealing with means. If we have two means ($n = 2$), only one ($n - 1$) is free to vary, so there is one degree of freedom, df = 1. In different equations or different formulas, the number of degrees of freedom is indicated by the nature of the formula. The Pearson r df = $n - z$; in chi-square, it is the number of rows minus 1, times the number of columns minus 1, or $(r - 1)(c - 1)$ = df. The number of degrees of freedom determines the tabled size of the significance used. *Degrees of freedom, then, are the number of independent scores (or squares, or cells) in the total.*

These restrictions enable us to make unbiased estimates. *Each distribution of the test statistic varies with the number of the degrees of freedom, so that there are different intervals for rejection of the null.* For example, the mean of the χ^2 distribution (with one exception) equals the df, or $\chi^2_{\bar{x}}$ = df, and thus changes every time the df changes. And as you know, *each distribution of the sample statistic approximates the normal curve if the sample size is large*. Thus, there are different intervals with different means.

QUALITATIVE DATA

When handling discrete data, such as the data from nominal dichotomous variables, we may use only *frequencies* for computation. In *sex*, the number of males and the number of females can be counted. In *race*, the number of blacks and the number of whites may be counted. But in these variables, there is no frequency distribution unless the samples are increased. For example, in the variable *toss of a coin*, the dichotomous categories are *heads* and *tails*. A coin must fall into one or the other, and heads may occur as frequently as tails. Whenever we are using a variable that has this type of mutually exclusive and exhaustive characteristic, we may plot the frequency of the occurrence based upon the probability. The probability of heads or tails may be seen as $p = 0.5$ and $q = 1 - p = 0.5$. For each toss, we may plot all the heads. Normally, it takes about 1,000 tosses before there is an equal number of heads and tails. The nature of this distribution may be calculated, approximated, and subjected to statistical assumptions. A mean can be calculated, also standard deviation (all from qualitative data).

Such data are binomial (two choices); n is known, has a frequency (can be counted), has a probability (either/or), and has a distribution. In the graph or plot, the score is usually on the bottom, and the relative frequency is on the side (the vertical axis). The coordinates or axes (of graphs) are the vertical *ordinate* and the horizontal *abscissa*; x scores are usually on the abscissa and y scores on the ordinate.

BINOMIAL VARIABLES

Qualitative data become measurable when the frequency of the same characteristic, item, or event is observed more than once. If we were tossing a coin. The toss is the binomial variable, a dichotomous choice of heads or tails. Variables that exercise a binomial choice–such as heads or tails, true or false, male or female, belong or not belong, above or below, satisfied or not satisfied, or any other mutually exclusive categories where one *must* be in one or the other–lend themselves to a distribution known as the binomial probability distribution. *The BPD is a theoretical model.* Some believe it is fact, but it is not. The first rule is that every characteristic, trait, item, or event must fit into one of two classes. The second is that there is a definite probability of the event; that is, there is a probability, p, and a nonprobability, q, which add up to unity, or 1. In a true/false situation, the value of $p = 0.5$ and $q = 0.5$, or $q = 1 - p$. The BPD equation is given by:

$$P = \binom{n}{r} p^r q^{n-r}$$

where (in sampling with replacement)

$$\begin{aligned} n &= \text{size of sample of events, items, or characteristics} \\ r &= \text{number of events in the first category} = p^r \\ n - r &= \text{number of events in the second category} = q^{n-r} \\ p &= \text{probability of event in first category} \\ q &= \text{probability of event in second category} \end{aligned}$$

Small values of n have already been calculated in most probability tables. Suppose, for example, that we were investigating the chances of arresting a person in ten situations where the probability of arrest was *yes* if committed, *no* if not committed. The probability is $p = 0.5$, $q = 1 - p = 0.5$. The *possibility of arrest* is the variable from 0 to 10. The number of possible *combinations*

$$\binom{n}{r} \text{ may be calculated, where } \binom{n}{r} = \frac{n!}{r!\,(n-r)!}.$$

For Table 9.4 we have *assumed* ten criminal situations in which the probability of arrest exists if the crime is randomly committed; the probability of arrest is a simple *yes* if committed, *no* if not, or a 50 percent chance. The table shows that the chances of committing all ten offenses randomly and getting away are one in a

Table 9.4. Theoretical Random Shoplifting and Probability of Arrest

		Possibility of arrest in ten criminal situations		
r	$C\binom{n}{r}$	p^r	q^{n-r}	**Probability**
10	1	0.5^{10}	0.5^0	0.001 $n = 10$
9	10	0.5^9	0.5^1	0.01
8	45	0.5^8	0.5^2	0.044
7	120	0.5^7	0.5^3	0.12
6	210	0.5^6	0.5^4	0.2
5	252	0.5^5	0.5^5	0.25
4	210	0.5^4	0.5^6	0.2
3	120	0.5^3	0.5^7	0.12
2	45	0.5^2	0.5^8	0.044
1	10	0.5^1	0.5^9	0.01
0	1	0.5^0	0.5^{10}	0.001
	$N = 10$	$(p = 1 - q)$		Total $P = 1$
	$(0! = 1)$	$(p^0 = q^0 = 1)$	BPD $= (p + q)^n = \Sigma\binom{n}{r}p^r q^{n-r} = 1$	

Note: $\binom{10}{10} = \binom{10}{0}$; $\binom{10}{9} = \binom{10}{1}$; $\binom{10}{8} = \binom{10}{2}$; $\binom{10}{7} = \binom{10}{3}$; $\binom{10}{6} = \binom{10}{4}$; $= Rf = \% =$ Prob.

1,000. Assuming that the situation is that of a shoplifter committing random offenses, the chances of arrest for the first crime are very slim, approximately one in 100, but as the number of crimes increases, the possibility of arrest increases. Remember, the probability column is additive: For two crimes, the possibility is .055, or 55 chances out of 1,000; for five crimes, the chances of getting arrested

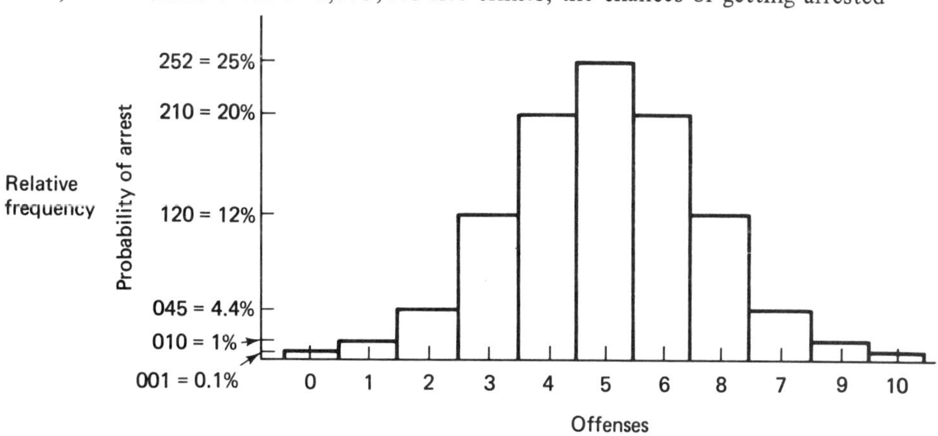

Distribution of chance of arrest against offenses

Fig. 9-1 Histogram for possibility of arrest for ten random offenses. (Note the continuity correction for discrete data; in plotting a cumulative ogive each data point is taken from the end of each interval.)

are 0.625, or 62.5 percent. Remember also that this is a theoretical model; one of the assumptions here is that the criminal gets caught after ten crimes!

The binomial probability distibution can be plotted as a frequency histogram or a bar graph showing how the probabilities occur. From the histogram, a curve may be approximated. This curve is known as the normal approximation of the binomial distribution. The accuracy of the curve depends upon:

1. Sample size—the larger the sample, the better the curve.
2. Probability value of p. If p equals or is close to 0.5, or if np or nq are equal to or greater than 5, the approximation is truer.
3. The mean equals np (sample size times probability).
4. For discrete data, use the Yates continuity correction.

From Figures 9-1 and 9-2, it can be seen that the BPD lends itself to approximation of the normal curve. If we increase the sample size, the approximation becomes very close indeed. We may also plot a cumulative percentage graph, called an ogive. The relative frequency may be expressed as a proportion, a percentage, or a probability. Note that the $Rf = \binom{n}{r}$ in this case.

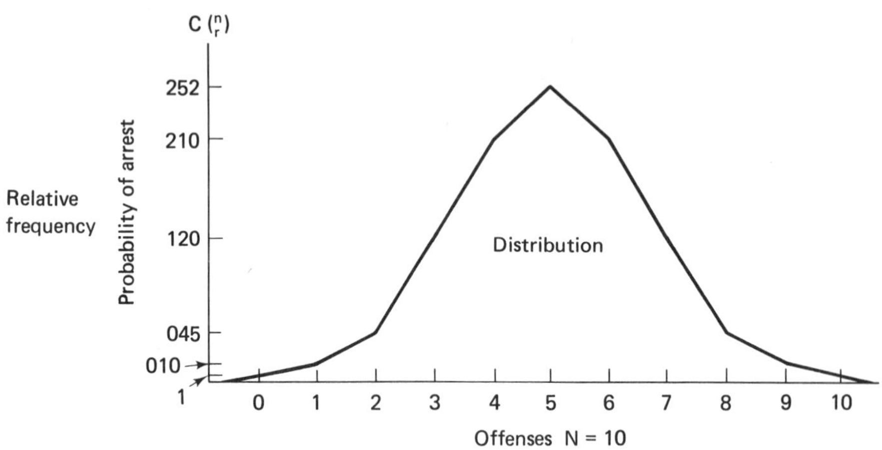

Fig. 9-2 Frequency polygon

RULES FOR BPD SAMPLING

1. The basic rule for all sampling is that samples drawn from a parent population provide estimates of the characteristic parameters that pertain to the total population. Randomization and representation ensure that traits, characteristics, items, or events in the parent population are in the sample.

2. Sample statistics must be distributed around a population mean in a known way. Sample means are distributed around the parent population mean according to

probability theory. (The mean $\bar{x} = np$; standard deviation $s = \sqrt{npq}$).[2]

3. This theory provides a formula to estimate how the sample means are distributed about the parent mean. The formula has three parts: (a) the parent population parameters (pq); (b) sample size $= n$; and (c) standard error $= s_e = \sqrt{pq/n}$. The parent mean may be estimated by sample size times probability, or np. (It is preferred to keep p close to 0.5.)

4. Larger samples yield smaller errors, and larger numbers of test items give a closer approximation to the normal curve.

5. All statements of accuracy concerning the sample inference must specify both a confidence level and a confidence interval. (C.L. = confidence level; C.I. = confidence interval.) Thus, the researcher reports that he is X percent confident that the population parameter falls between two specified values.

6. Because of the nature of the equation, if the sample size is quadrupled, the sample error is reduced by half, or:

$$\frac{1}{2} s_e = \sqrt{\frac{pq}{4n}}$$

This clearly demonstrates the reduction of error by increasing sample size. For example, error caused by a sample of 100 cases may be cut in half by using 400 cases.

7. Confidence intervals may be constructed very easily. Assume a sample of 100 cases ($n = 100$) and a probability of win or lose (0.5). The parent population parameter would be np, or 50 percent. The standard error based on the equation above would be 0.5, or 5 percent. Thus, one standard error would be 50 ± 5, or 45 to 55 percent. Or:

1σ = 45–55%	Approx. 68% interval
2σ = 40–60%	Approx. 95% interval
3σ = 35–65%	Approx. 99% interval

8. Confidence levels are the degree of confidence we have that the parent population parameter or mean falls between the interval values specified. In the foregoing intervals, given levels of confidence have already been calculated. Thus, we could say we are 95 percent confident that the population mean falls between 40 and 60 percent. *We cannot say that the result is 95 percent accurate or that 95 percent of the sample falls in the interval.*

[2] Thus, for larger samples when $n \geqslant 100$:

$$\sigma = s = \sqrt{npq} = \sqrt{\frac{n\Sigma x^2 - (\Sigma x)^2}{n(n-1)}}$$

which is another way of saying that the BPD approximates the normal curve and that frequency data fall into proportions.

9. The inteıval of 40-60 percent is called the range, and our confidence in that interval is called the confidence level. *The confidence interval is a function of the confidence level as well as a function of sample size*. Lower levels and larger sizes give smaller intervals.

10. The BPD is primarily used for proportions and percentages. If the sample size constitutes a large proportion of the parent population, this increases the accuracy. Ten percent is a very accurate sample size. Table 9.5 gives an indication of how percentage-point spread diminishes as sample size increases. Figures are given for 99, 95, and 68 percent confidence intervals.

Table 9.5. Interval Table

Sample size n	Add or subtract percentage to $\bar{x}$ %		
	99% (3σ)	*95% (2σ)*	*68% (1σ)*
50	18	14	7
100	13	10	5
200	9	7	3.5
300	7	6	3
400	6.5	5	2.5
500	6	4	2
600	5	4	2
700	5	4	2
800	4.5	3.5	2
900	4	3	1.5
1,000	4	3	1.5
1,500	3	2.5	1
2,000	3	2	1

To use the table, simply take the sample mean percentage and add or subtract the percentage points in the appropriate column. For example, in a sample of 400 inmates, if 48 percent voted to end a work stoppage, we could be 95 percent sure that the population mean was between 43 and 53 percent. In other words, we could be reasonably certain that over half were in favor—the point spread indicates that the true mean falls somewhere in that interval, and we are 95 percent sure that it does. This table can deal only with percentages and proportions, and is based upon a 50 percent probability—a 50-50 chance of falling into one or the other of two categories ($p = 0.5; q = 1 - p = 0.5$).

THE NORMAL CURVE

To a great extent, the size of the sample limits the error because of two main theorems, the law of large numbers and the central limit theorem.

The law of large numbers states that the greater the sample size, the greater the regression to the norm. That is, the more cases that are selected, the closer the results will be to average. Obviously, if we gather data from only a few people, the result will hardly be representative of the population. On the other hand, we must beware of numbers in themselves as proof of accuracy. *The sample, even if large, must be representative.* The law of numbers implies that by using a large sample, we should approximate a reasonable distribution of scores, since errors and extremes tend to cancel each other out.

The central limit theorem states that as the sample size increases (to infinity), the distribution of the sample means approximates the distribution of the normal curve. This means that the more samples we take, assuming that they are of adequate size, the more the distribution of the means of those samples begins to take on a bell-shaped curve. (This curve is sometimes known as the Gaussian curve, after its inventor, Carl Gauss. Gauss completed the work of Laplace and Demoivre,[3] but it was Quetelet and Galton who realized the application of the normal curve to research methods.)

The normal curve is easily the most significant statistical statement, since it represents the basis for most sampling theory. The BPD can be shown mathematically to approximate the normal curve if the sample is large enough and if the number of test items is large. Assuming that several hundred were sampled and that instead of ten choices of random crime, we had had 50, the frequency polygon plotted would appear as in Figure 9-3, and the normal curve would literally fit it.

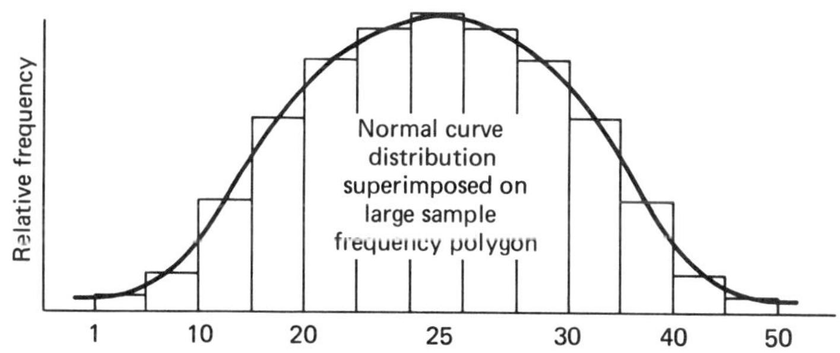

Fig. 9-3 Fitting normal curve to frequency polygon

Like the frequency polygon, the normal curve is a mathematical model based upon probability or chance. Many frequency distributions approximate the normal curve, and thus it becomes statistically invaluable. It should be noted that whenever one is using frequency polygons or the normal curve, both are:

Graphs of distributions (the normal curve is more complex)
Theoretical mathematical models
Models of probability outcomes
Models of the proportions between frequency and area

[3] Demoivre is credited with inventing the normal probability distribution in 1733, based upon his "curve of errors."

Properties of the Normal Curve

The plotting of the normal curve is made possible by the use of a formula that assumes an infinite number of normal or standard curves. It is the plot of frequency distributions whose outcomes depend upon chance. Although it is a mathematical and theoretical model, there is no doubt that statistics has profited greatly by its use. Its many disadvantages are offset by many superior advantages. It is based upon assumptions that the data used are continuous, interval, and may be plotted as $y = f(x)$, or values of variable y are a function of values of variable x. It is assumed also that characteristics are distributed normally throughout the population, that sample data are independently random sampled, that y values are positive for all values of variable x, that the population is infinite, that the total area under the curve is unity, that the curve never touches the x axis, and that it is bell-shaped, with a range of ±3 standard deviations.

The main advantage is that it is uniform; the mean, median, and mode coincide. It is a very close approximation to the real world;[4] characteristics used in research often occur in conformity to the normal-curve distribution. The area under the normal curve is unity; the mean divides it into two halves, and other *constant proportions* are easily ascertained, such as division into areas of standard deviation. If large samples are used, the normal curve may be used to describe distributions of scores (range), interpret dispersion by standard deviation (variability), and make statements of probability from confidence intervals and levels (decision making).

The normal curve assumes that means are sampled to infinity (from an infinite population). The sample means will spread (distribute) about the population mean in a known way, according to the central limit theorem. In practice, most estimations are made from one or two samples, using the theoretical assumptions of the normal curve. The normal curve gives a range of means with $\mu = X_{\bar{x}}$, based upon infinite samples; we never really know the population mean.

It may be seen from Figure 9-5 that each mean will finally fit into the normal curve in a known way, based upon the central limit theorem. If the sample size is large enough, the distribution pattern will approximate the normal curve. Now note that each sample has its own distribution or normal-curve shape. There are large families of normal curves, not just a standard of one. But the shape is nearly always the same, and the distribution follows a known pattern; the proportions remain the same. *In fact, proportions are really special cases of the means.* This may be seen by comparing formulas for the standard deviation and standard error of both the proportions and the means.

Another point to keep in mind is that there is no such thing as a normal population; it is a theoretical construct, but it is all we have and it is very useful. The whole theory of normal curves depends upon the probability that certain proportions exist in the population. So we may say:

[4] The area under the curve contains 100% of all cases.

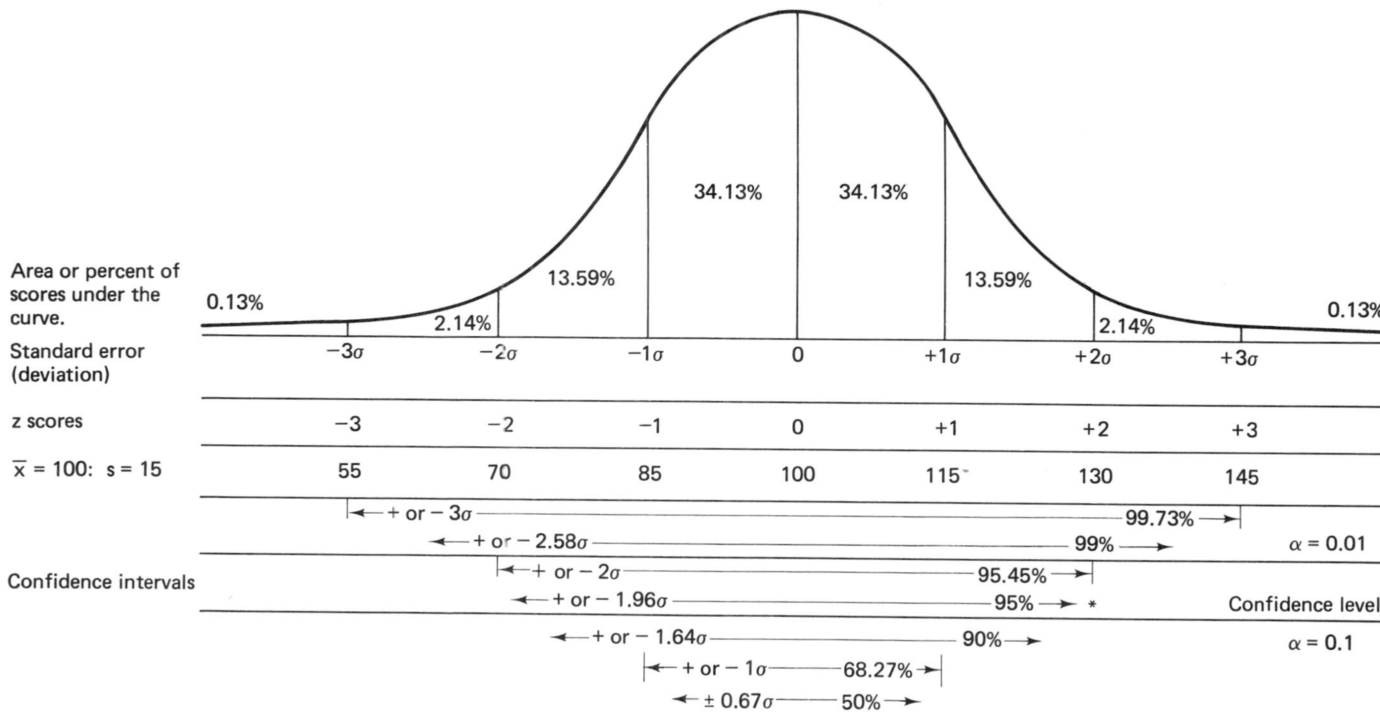

*The 95 percent C.L., or $\alpha = 0.05$, is the most used level in the social sciences

Fig. 9-4 Properties of the normal curve, based upon probability and proportionate distribution

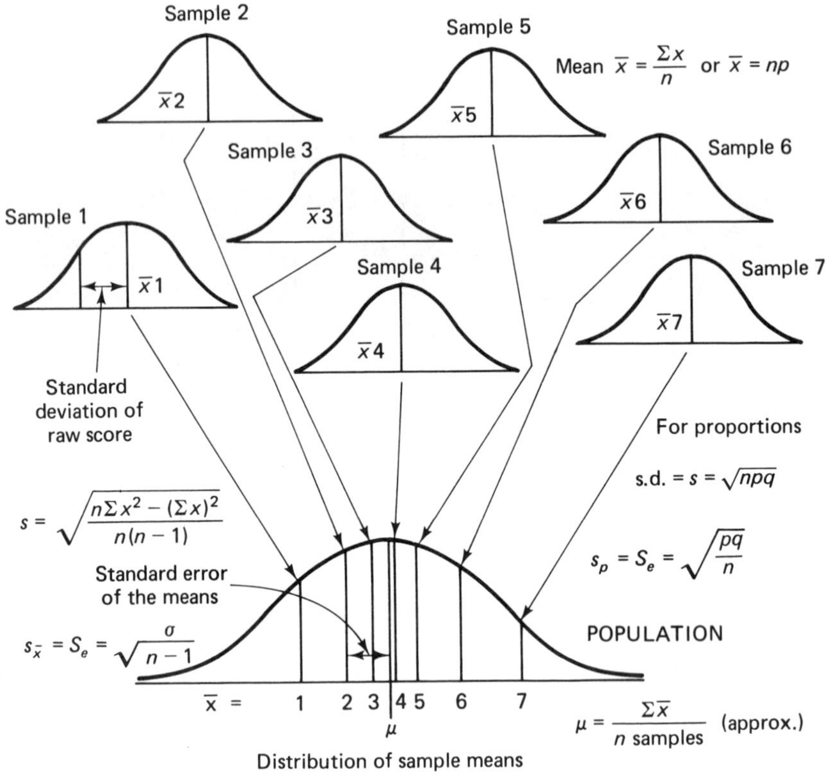

Fig. 9-5 Theoretical sampling distribution of means

1. There is no known measure of the normal population.
2. The population mean is unknown and may be *estimated*.
3. If the sample is large, its normal distribution may be *measured*.
4. From the sample statistic, the normal distribution of sampling means may be *calculated*.
5. *No matter what the form of the parent population*, sample sizes of 30 or more enable us to use the central limit theorem to test differences in the sample mean and the population mean based upon the normal curve.
6. The population mean is always fixed; it is the sample mean that varies. The standard error is the average square root of that variance.

STANDARD DEVIATION AND STANDARD ERROR

Occasionally there is confusion between the standard deviation and the standard error. The *standard deviation* refers to the sample and is the distribution of scores about the mean of the sample. The *standard error* refers to the means of several samples distributed about the population mean. It tells how close the sample mean is to the population mean. The smaller the error, the closer it is. If we have many samples, we also have many sample means. These may all be put in one category and have their own distribution. If they are, a mean of the means may be calculated, and also a standard deviation of those means about the calculated mean. The standard deviation of the several means really shows the error of those means in reference to the population mean, and that is really an "average error," or a *standard error* of the means. The mean of all the sample means should approximate the population mean.

Further, the standard deviation of each particular sample may also be put in one category, giving a distribution based on the standard deviations of the samples. We can do this with almost any group of sample statistics. Some interesting things happen when we group sample statistics into their own distributions. First of all, *when the sample size is equal to or greater than 30, the sampling distribution of the means approximates the normal curve*. This means that when sample size is less than 30 cases, the distribution of such a sample mean will *not* follow predictive patterns of the normal curve. The larger the sample size, the smaller the standard error.

Second, *when the sample size equals or is greater than 100 cases, the sampling distribution of the standard deviations approximates the normal curve.* The standard deviation of each sample is the "average" distance of each score from the mean, or the average error in that sample. If, then, we can make our sample size errors approximate the normal (score) distribution, we get closer to making our sample a model of the normal curve itself. We can approximate several (theoretical) samples, and in so doing increase our statistical validity.

In practice, most samples are single samples, occasionally two samples, and rarely three or more. Thus, we have to proceed on the data of a single sample most of the time. Therefore, it is important that we follow the rules above, never dropping below 30, and if possible keeping above 100 cases. Standard error, like standard deviation, is cut in half when the size is quadrupled (see rule 6 for BPD sampling). The difference is that *standard error* applies to the many scores of sample means, whereas the *standard deviation* applies to the raw scores of the single sample data. Unless there are many samples, standard deviation applies to reality and standard error is theoretical.

Standard deviation in a single sample for raw-score data is:

$$s = \sqrt{\frac{n\Sigma x^2 - (\Sigma x)^2}{n(n-1)}} = \sqrt{\frac{\Sigma fx^2}{n} - (\bar{x})}$$

or, for proportions:[5]

$$s = \sqrt{npq}$$

[5] $s = \sqrt{\bar{x^2} - (\bar{x})^2}$ or the s.d. = $\sqrt{\text{the mean of the squared raw scores minus the mean squared.}}$

Standard error for many sample means in a single category is:

$$s_{\bar{x}} = s_e = \frac{\sigma}{\sqrt{n}} \quad \text{or} \quad \sigma_{\bar{x}} = \frac{\sigma}{\sqrt{n-1}}$$

For proportions:

$$s_p = s_e = \sqrt{\frac{pq}{n}}$$

The mean of the sample:

$$\bar{x} = \frac{\Sigma x}{n} \quad \text{or} \quad \frac{\Sigma fx}{n}$$

The mean of the means of several samples:

$$\bar{X}_{\bar{x}} = \frac{\Sigma \bar{x}}{n \text{ samples}} = \mu \text{ (approximately)}$$

Although the standard deviation in a sample may be large, the standard error will be smaller, because we are using means (averages) instead of raw scores. Means used in standard error are approximations of the parent population mean, and the larger the number of cases in the sample, the closer the distribution will be to the normal curve (see the central limit theorem).

Use of the Standard Error

Let us assume that in a sample of 100, the age range was 18-65 years, the mean 40.4 years, standard deviation 11.2, and we wish to calculate the standard error. Assuming many samples were taken (which in fact they were not), the standard deviation may be used as an estimate in the formula:

$$s_e = \frac{\sigma}{\sqrt{n}}$$

Substituting ($s = \sigma$):

$$s_e = \frac{11.2}{\sqrt{100}}$$

or, for a better estimate (using $n - 1$):

$$= \frac{11.2}{\sqrt{100 - 1}}$$

$$= 1.12 \text{ years}$$

The standard error of several samples assumes that the distribution of the means about the population mean would be 1.12 years; in other words, the "average" spread of scores of means would be much smaller. In the parent population, we could expect the standard deviation to be much smaller; unlike in the sample, we would now find our 95 percent interval in the range 38.2-42.6 years.

What has happened is that we are assuming the age characteristics in our sample to be equally distributed in the parent population. If they are, then the population mean will fall in our confidence interval based upon our standard error. That is, we can be 95 percent certain that the *population mean* will fall in that specified interval. Remember, we are dealing with the means, not the raw scores, and the standard error is the deviation of the means, not the deviation of the raw scores. The sample still has its own mean and its own standard deviation; all we have done is to use those figures for estimating population parameters. The standard deviation of the sample still tells us the average age spread for that sample; the mean of that sample remains the same. We have used the sample size and the standard deviation as an estimate to calculate unknown population limits.

The standard error has a special use, as we have mentioned: It can give an estimation of the confidence interval and confidence limits. This is obtained by multiplying the interval that is set by the level required. Supposing we require a 95 percent level of confidence, or one chance in 20 that we are wrong, then we take that interval and multiply it by the standard error. The product is then added to and subtracted from the mean to give the interval and the level. For example:

$$\begin{aligned} \text{C.L.} &= 95\% = \pm 1.96\sigma = z_c \\ s_e &= 1.12 \text{ (from example)} \\ \text{C.I.} &= \bar{x} \pm 1.96(s_e) \\ &= 40.4 \pm (1.96 \times 1.12) \\ &= 40.4 \pm 2.2 \\ &= 38.2 - 42.6 \text{ yrs.} \end{aligned}$$

Thus, we are 95 percent confident that the population mean falls in that interval. *We never really know the population mean, but we can estimate where it will fall from the sample statistics.* We do know the sample mean, and if there are a large number of cases in the sample, then by the central limit theorem we can be sure that our estimate is very close to the population mean. *All statistical statements should contain both an interval and a level of confidence.*

If we choose to tighten the level of confidence to 99 percent, we would be wrong only one time in 100, but we would also widen the interval. For example:

$$\begin{aligned} \text{C.L.} &= 99\% \quad 99\% = 2.58\sigma \\ s_e &= 1.12 \\ \text{C.I.} &= 40.4 \pm (2.58 \times 1.12) \\ &= 40.4 \pm 2.9 \\ &= 37.5 - 43.3 \text{ (Compare to 95\% C.I.)} \end{aligned}$$

Thus, we could be 99 percent confident that our population mean falls in that interval, but the interval is now wider. The higher the level, the wider the band. Remember that this example is a large sample and is only used to illustrate the point.

The standard error, like the standard deviation, is a very important piece of information. It enables us to make decisions based upon intervals and levels of confidence. In actual testing, the confidence interval is constructed so that if the mean of the null hypothesis is outside the interval, the null hypothesis is rejected. In other words, the region of rejection is outside the region of retention, and the statistical significance is found in rejecting the null hypothesis, or by placing it in the region of rejection, which is determined by the confidence level, the level of significance, or alpha, α, being $1 - \text{C.L.}$ Thus, $\alpha = 0.05 = 1 - 0.95$ (the percentage is now expressed as a decimal). Note that the interval is also a function of sample size and that large samples reduce standard error. *Quadrupling the sample will halve the interval, at the same level of confidence.*[6]

POINTS AND BANDS

Sample statistics are merely points of reference. They enable us to get a foothold on the unknown. From those *point estimates*, we are able to construct *intervals*, or a range or band in which the unknown quantity (the population mean) may fall. From these bands, or ranges of estimates, or intervals, we can then establish areas on the normal curve that will be acceptable for either retaining or rejecting the hypothesis. These larger areas are confidence intervals and are usually the greater portion under the normal curve. The smaller areas, the regions of rejection, are on the ends. They are known as "tails." If our hypothesis falls in them, it is rejected.

Note that the population mean, even if it is unknown, is fixed; the interval may vary like the sample mean, but the population mean is set. The estimation of the population mean from an unbiased estimate determines its approximate location, but theoretically, the parent population mean is set right in the middle of the normal probability distribution or at the peak of the normal curve.

The regions of rejection are known as test regions for obvious reasons. The tests of the hypotheses are often referred to as one- or two-tail tests, from the way the test area is constructed at the end of the normal curve. One-tail refers to the single end of the curve used as a region of rejection for the null hypothesis. A two-tail test refers to the use of both ends of the curve.

There are restrictions on which test is used. Normally, an arbitrary level of 0.05 is set as the test level for rejection of the null hypothesis. This gives a 1-in-20 chance of error, of rejecting the null hypothesis when it is true. It may be seen in Figure 9-6 that the area of rejection for a positive one-tail test is actually 5 percent of the normal curve, or 0.05. Only the area in the single tail is used, and the z score

[6] Quadrupling the sample size also halves the standard deviation and the standard error.

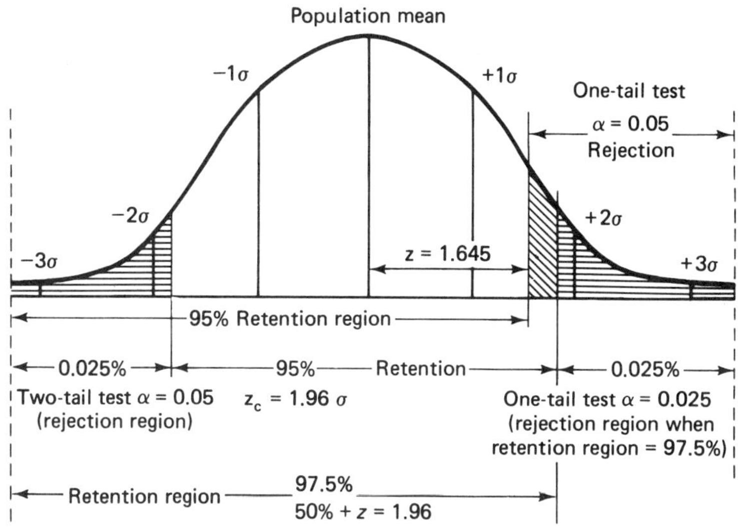

Fig. 9-6 Test areas under the normal curve

is 50 percent plus 1.645, or 95 percent. In a two-tail test, the 0.05 is split into two tails, one at each end of the curve, each containing 2.5 percent of the total area of rejection. Thus the two tails add up to 5 percent, leaving ± 1.96σ or 95 percent under the curve. Had a single-tail test been used (at either end), the region of rejection would have been 0.025 for a one-tail test. The *z* scores are the same as standard deviations in this case.

Note that the shaded areas represent the areas of test rejection. A one-tail test occurs at one end only, a two-tail test puts the region of retention in the middle. If the region of retention is moved to include either tail, a one-tail test results. For example, if the 95 percent two-tail area is expanded to become 97.5 percent, then a one-tail test of 0.025 results. Test areas are set depending upon the degree of error that is tolerated. It may be from 0.3 in an exploratory design to 0.001 in a very tight design. In the first case, we are willing to assume that we will be rejecting the null hypothesis when it is true (Type 1 error) 30 percent of the time; in the second case, we are only willing to assume error on a 1-in-1,000 situation. Do not forget that the tighter the level of significance, the easier it is to make a type 2 error (retaining the hypothesis when it is false). It is fairly easy to remember that when the two-tail test is 0.2, the one-tail level is 0.1, adding one tail using the same area of retention; or 0.1 at the two-tail level is 0.05 at the one-tail level, using a 90 percent retention or 95 percent area for each; or 0.05 for a two-tail test is 0.025 for a one-tail, using ± 1.96 for the two-tail and 50 percent *either* plus or minus 1.96 for the one-tail. (See Figure 9-6). Remember, a one-tail test may occur at either end of the curve, plus or minus, depending upon whichever is chosen. Most one-tail tests are positive. Tables 9.6 and 9.7 furnish additional explanations.

Table 9.6. Test Scores and Relative Areas of Rejection

Normal curve retention area	z_c score or s (σ) + and −	Area in test tail	*Alpha* or α Level of significance		Area in each test tail
			one-tail	*two-tail*	
90%	1.645	10%	0.1	0.05	5%
95%	1.96	5%	0.05	0.025	2.5%
97.5%	2.24	$2\frac{1}{2}$%	0.025	0.0125	1.25%
99%	2.58	1%	0.01	0.005	0.5%

Note: In a single tail, the area of rejection = 100% − (50% + z), $\alpha = 1 - (0.5 + z$ area). When calculating the interval, the formula C.I. = $\bar{x} \pm z_c (s_{\bar{x}})$ may be used; the z score is in fact the confidence level based upon the area or proportion under the normal curve. The test rejection area is 100% − z (in %), or 1 − C.L., and $1 - z_c = 1 -$ C.L. when reduced to proportions, or:

$$1 - \text{C.L.} = 1 - z_c = \alpha = \text{level of significance}$$

or the *statistical significance* of the rejection of the null hypothesis.

Table 9.7. Use of One-tail and Two-tail Tests

Hypothesis	Statistic	Choice of test
H_0 A = B	Correlation Positive or negative Positive and negative	One-tail (either end) Two-tail (both ends)
H_a $\bar{x} \neq \bar{y}$	Unless direction is specified	Two-tail test
H_a $P > Q$ or $P < Q$	Chi-square, positive only	One-tail test

The area of test rejection must be stated with the proper significance level and whether it is a one-tail or a two-tail test. Assuming that the test statistic follows the normal distribution, the level of significance usually sets the (interval) region of rejection.

SUMMARY

We have seen how sampling theory takes care of actually getting the sample from the parent population, and how randomization and representation are essential qualities of the sample. Probability theory adds another dimension to sampling and begins to provide a quantitative base upon which to make our decisions.

Probability deals with frequencies, proportions, and percentages. It is in fact the chance outcome of results. Although we know the expected direction of our research (determinism), we are certain of that outcome only in terms of probabilities. Fortunately, statistics has provided us with a normal distribution of outcomes. If in fact some of the characteristics we seek are normally distributed in the population, our sampling will (if the sample is large) fall into a definite pattern of probabilities. The proportions of these probabilities may be plotted on a curve, and the distribution of the normal curve approximates the binomial probability distribution.

Not only may we use a standard normal distribution and a standard normal curve, but we can also use standardized scores. These scores measure distance from the mean in terms of units of standard deviation; z scores have the very convenient mean of 0 and a standard deviation of 1, and they approximate the normal curve. Thus, we may construct confidence intervals and confidence levels based upon z scores.

The normal curve is based upon probability, but the central limit theorem permits us to use any population and still use the normal curve provided the sample size is large enough. The central limit theorem is based upon a theoretical distribution of sample means. The distance of the means from the population mean is called the standard error. As between standard error and standard deviation, the latter deals with raw scores in the sample, the former with the distribution of sample means. The normal curve also aids us in decision making by using the tails of the curve as areas of rejection of the null hypothesis. These areas may be set arbitrarily, but they are usually set at 0.05. This means that our chances of rejecting the null hypothesis if it is true are one in 20, and that if the null hypothesis falls in this area of 5 percent, we are 95 percent confident that the mean (parent mean, or H_a) falls in the retention area. C.I.s and C.L.s are necessary for any statistical statement. In the statement itself, we set a level of significance and a region of rejection. Usually, we use one-tail tests, since these are more powerful than two-tail tests, which set limits at both ends of the area of retention under the normal curve.

Statistical theory, probability theory in particular, underlies the normal curve. However, from this point on, we deal little with probability and more with inferential statistics. We are concerned with what to do with the sample statistic and how we can make inferences back to the parent population. There are many disadvantages to the theoretical model, but it does have considerable sophistication in that the normal curve approximates the parent population, and our estimates do have a logical and sequential development.

EXERCISES

1. Write out the symbols for population mean, sample mean, variation, standard deviation, standard error, level of significance, Type 1 error, Type 2 error, degrees of freedom, correlation, chi-square, sample size, null hypothesis.
2. Explain the following:

$$R: \chi^2 \geqslant 3.84, \quad df = 1, \quad \alpha = 0.05$$

3. Explain three measures of dispersion; of location; of association.
4. What is statistical significance?
5. Give three assumptions for sampling theory; for the normal curve; for the central limit theorem. Explain the central limit theorem.
6. What is a standard score? Give three examples and explain the use of each.
7. What are the qualities of z scores?

8. With a mean of 50 and a standard deviation of 10, contruct a confidence interval of 95 percent. What is the range? Make a statement concerning the population mean.
9. When does qualitative data become quantitative? Give an example.
10. Given the scores 8, 8, 8, 7, 7, 3, 5, 9, 9, 9, 4, 2, 2, 1, 6, 6, 6, 1, 3, 5, what is n? Calculate the variation; the mean; the standard deviation. *Use a calculator with squares and square roots.*
11. What has happened to the mode in exercise 10? the median?
12. Give z scores for ages 34, 41, 65. Use the formula.
13. Give two formulas for the mean; explain both, with examples. What sample size is necessary for the approximation of the normal curve?
14. Give a rule of thumb for standard deviation. What happens to standard deviation when you increase the sample size four times? Is this also true for standard error?
15. Toss a coin 100 times and count the numbers of heads. Plot a graph showing the frequency on the ordinate and the number of heads on the abscissa. Then do the tosses in batches of tens and plot each series of results for ten trials. The vertical scale should read 0–10–20–30 . . . 100. The horizontal scale should read from 1 to 10.
16. Describe p and q in terms of one chance in five, one in ten, and one in twenty.
17. On the basis of cumulative frequency probability, what is the chance of arrest after eight successful shoplifts? (Use Table 9.4.)
18. Larger samples mean smaller errors. Explain this and prove it.
19. All statistical statements must include at least two essentials. What are they?
20. (a) Given a sample size of 400, how many percentage points would you add or subtract to a given sample outcome to establish where the population mean would fall? ($p = 0.5$)

    (b) Out of 100 inmates, 40 feel they could escape; would you use a 99 percent or a 95 percent level of confidence for your interval? Explain why. And what would your conclusions be on a possible mass breakout?
21. Describe exactly the sampling distribution of the means. Give the formula. Why is it so important?
22. What is the usual risk we are prepared to take in testing a hypothesis? Could we be wrong?
23. There are two limits on sample error. What are they?
24. What is the underlying base of statistical sampling theory?
25. Describe some properties of the normal curve.
26. What is it that may be estimated? observed? calculated?
27. Describe differences between standard error and standard deviation. Give examples.
28. Explain two rules for sampling distributions.

29. The numbers of arrests for 11 people ($n = 11$) were 3, 4, 5, 6, 7, 7, 7, 8, 8, 8, 9. What are the mean, mode, median, standard deviation, standard error, and a 95 percent C.I.?
30. Quadruple the sample, to 44. What happens to the interval?
31. Using the standard deviation only, where would one arrest fall in your distribution? 15 arrests? How many standard deviations from the mean in the sample distribution?
32. When would you use a one-tail test? a two-tail test?
33. Outline the rules for hypothesis testing.
34. What are degrees of freedom? What do they do?
35. How would you rate a small statistical significance in a large sample as compared to a large statistical significance in a small sample? What is substantive significance?

For the following exercises, use a calculator that has squares and square roots or is programmed. If you can use a terminal, do so.

36. Find the mean, standard deviation, and a 95 percent interval for 5, 7, 9, 11, 15, 17, 23, 27, 34, 36, 38, 40, 45, 52, 55, 60, 70, 73, 80, 81, 86. Find the standard error and establish a 95 percent C.I.
37. You are looking through records of parole success, and you discover that after sentence, 80 percent return. How would you show this on a normal curve?
38. We have the following grouped data:

Cases	Number of convictions
5	12
6	10
4	14
2	8
10	4
12	2
11	1

Calculate:
(a) Mean for 50 cases, using $\bar{x} = \Sigma fx/n$
(b) Standard deviation for the frequency data
(c) Standard error
(d) 99 percent C.I.

39. Discuss: A man's chances on parole appear to be 80 percent in the first year, decreasing by 20 percent each year, so that the chance of making it in the fifth year is zero. What is the statistical significance? the substantive significance? Would you abolish parole on this argument?
40. On a firing range, your average score is 50 bull's-eyes out of 100 shots. Would you be prepared to wager that somewhere in the next 100 shots, you could make 65? 60?

FOR FURTHER READING

Anderson, T. R., and M. Zelditch, Jr., *A Basic Course in Statistics* (3rd ed.). New York: Holt, Rinehart & Winston, 1974.

Babbie, Earl R., *Survey Research Methods.* Belmont, Calif.: Wadsworth, 1973. See Chaps. 16, 17.

Blalock, Hubert M., Jr., *Social Statistics.* New York: McGraw-Hill, 1972.

Blank, S. S., *Descriptive Statistics.* New York: Appleton-Century-Crofts, 1968.

Bradley, Jack I., and James N. McClelland, *Basic Statistical Concepts.* Glenview, Ill.: Scott, Foresman, 1978.

Bruning, James L., and B. L. Kintz, *Computational Handbook of Statistics.* Glenview, Ill.: Scott, Foresman, 1977.

Dayton, C. M., and C. L. Stunkard, *Statistics for Problem Solving.* New York: McGraw-Hill, 1971.

Fisher, R., *The Design of Experiments* (6th ed.). New York: Hafner, 1951.

Forcese, Dennis, and Stephen Richer, *Social Research Methods.* Englewood Cliffs, N.J.: Prentice-Hall, 1977.

Freeman, Linton C., *Elementary Applied Statistics.* New York: John Wiley, 1965.

Glass, Gene V., and Julian C. Stanley, *Statistical Methods in Psychology and Education.* Englewood Cliffs, N.J.: Prentice-Hall, 1970.

Gordon, Marshall, and Norman Schaumberger, *A First Course in Statistics.* New York: Macmillan, 1978.

Hays, W. L., *Statistics for the Social Sciences* (2nd ed.). New York: Holt, Rinehart & Winston, 1973.

Horowitz, Leonard M., *Elements of Statistics for Psychology and Education.* New York: McGraw-Hill, 1974.

Johnson, Allan G., *Social Statistics without Tears.* New York: McGraw-Hill, 1977.

Johnson, M., and R. Liebert, *Elementary Statistics.* North Scituate, Mass.: Duxbury Press, 1973.

Keppel, G., *Designa and Analysis.* Englewood Cliffs, N.J.: Prentice-Hall, 1973.

Levin, Jack, *Elementary Statistics in Social Research.* New York: Harper & Row, 1973.

Mendenhall, W., and L. Ott, *Understanding Statistics.* North Scituate, Mass.: Duxbury Press, 1972.

——, and Richard F. Larson, *Statistics: A Tool for the Social Sciences.* North Scituate, Mass: Duxbury Press, 1974.

Pierce, Albert, *Fundamentals of Non-Parametric Statistics,* Belmont, Calif.: Dickerson, 1969.

Robbins, Herbert, and John Van Ryzin, *Introduction to Statistics.* Chicago: Science Research Associates, 1975.

Roscoe, John T., *Fundamental Research Statistics.* New York: Holt, Rinehart & Winston, 1969.

Runyon, R. P., and A. Haber, *Fundamentals of Behavioral Statistics.* Reading, Mass.: Addison-Wesley, 1972.

Schmidt, Marty J., *Understanding and Using Statistics: Basic Concepts.* Lexington, Mass.: Heath, 1975.

Senter, R. J., *Analysis of Data.* Glenview, Ill.: Scott, Foresman, 1969.

Siegal, Sidney, *Non-Parametric Statistics.* New York: McGraw-Hill, 1956.

Silverman, Eliot N., and Linda A. Brody, *Statistics: A Common Sense Approach.* Boston: Prindle, Webber and Schmidt, 1973.

Spiegal, Murray R., *Theory and Problems of Statistics.* New York: McGraw-Hill, 1961.

Tamur, Judith M., et al., *Statistics: A Guide to the Unknown.* San Francisco: Holden-Day, 1972.

Weinberg, George H., and John A. Schumaker, *Statistics: An Intuitive Approach* (3rd ed.). Monterey, Calif.: Brooks/Cole, 1974.

Williams, Bill, *A Sampler on Sampling.* New York: John Wiley, 1978.

10

Bivariate Analysis: Correlation, Regression, and Prediction

CORRELATION

The Value of Correlation between Two Variables

Correlation enables us to find the *strength of the relationship* from −1 through zero to +1—the closer to zero, the weaker the relationship; the closer to plus or minus 1, the stronger it is. Large samples do not affect the correlation, but *they do affect the level of significance*. Thus, a small correlation may be quite significant in a large sample. A large significance in a small sample may not have that much meaning, but it really depends on what you are talking about. A 0.6 correlation between drunk driving and accidents may be quite significant, but the same correlation between two police officers administering the same test would indicate something seriously wrong with the testing procedure. The two officers ought to correlate much higher in the same situation for the test to be worthwhile.

Correlation also helps us find the *direction of the relationship*. It is in fact a way to show how two variables vary together. Perfect correlation would indicate that all the raw scores of both variables graphed in a straight line. This situation rarely, if ever, arises in the social sciences. Some of the diagrams in this chapter show the types of correlation that one may expect. Again let me point out that the most serious mistake in correlation is assuming cause and effect. In this type of equation, one variable has as much importance as the other. Cause and effect may be indicated, but the correlation will not of itself establish it.

The Pearson Product Moment Correlation

The Pearson Product Moment, called the PPM or the Pearson r, shows the correlation or the covariance of two variables, assuming that they have normal distribution, are randomly sampled, and have linear distribution of data. It really measures the variation in one as the other changes—the concomitant variation. There are several

$$r = \frac{\text{Covariance of } x \cdot y}{(\text{Standard deviation } x)\ (\text{Standard deviation } y)}$$

$$r = \frac{n\Sigma xy - \Sigma x \Sigma y}{\sqrt{(n\Sigma x^2 - (\Sigma x)^2)\ (n\Sigma y^2 - (\Sigma y)^2)}} \quad \text{(Calculator formula)}$$

$$r = \frac{\Sigma xy}{n s_x s_y}$$

where x is the difference from $\overline{x}$
y is the difference from $\overline{y}$
n is the sample size
s_x is the standard deviation of x
s_y is the standard deviation of y

$$r = \frac{SPxy}{\sqrt{SSx \cdot SSy}} = \frac{\text{Covariance (Sum of the products)}}{\sqrt{\text{Sum of the squares}}}$$

x and y are differences from the mean on this side of the = sign

$$\left\{ \text{where } SP = \Sigma xy - \frac{(\Sigma x)\ (\Sigma y)}{n} \right\}$$

$$\left\{ \begin{array}{l} \text{and } SSx = \Sigma x^2 - \dfrac{(\Sigma x)^2}{n} \\ \text{and } SSy = \Sigma y^2 - \dfrac{(\Sigma y)^2}{n} \end{array} \right\}$$

x and y are raw scores on this side

Thus: $$r = \frac{\Sigma xy - \dfrac{(\Sigma x)\ (\Sigma y)}{n}}{\sqrt{(\Sigma x^2 - \dfrac{(\Sigma x)^2}{n})\ (\Sigma y^2 - \dfrac{(\Sigma y)^2}{n})}}$$

And multiplying by n:

$$r = \frac{n\Sigma xy - \Sigma x \Sigma y}{\sqrt{(n\Sigma x^2 - (\Sigma x)^2)\ (n\Sigma y^2 - (\Sigma y)^2)}}$$ or the calculator formula.

Fig. 10-1 The relationship of the PPM to average squared distance from the mean

ways of expressing this statistically (see Figure 10-1). The variables are of the interval type.[1]

Another Way of Looking at PPM

If you recall, the PPM was defined as:

$$r = \frac{\text{Covariance of } x \cdot y}{(\text{s.d. } x)\,(\text{s.d. } y)}$$

The deviation is the square root of the variation, which means that we could write the equation:

$$r^2 = \frac{(\text{Covariance } x \cdot y)^2}{(\text{Variance } x)\,(\text{Variance } y)}$$

$$r^2 = \frac{\dfrac{(\Sigma xy)^2}{n^2}}{\dfrac{\Sigma(x)^2 \cdot \Sigma(y)^2}{n^2}} = (\text{Dividing by } n^2)\ \frac{(\Sigma xy)^2}{\Sigma(x)^2 \cdot \Sigma(y)^2}$$

$$r = \sqrt{\frac{(\Sigma xy)^2}{(\Sigma x^2)\,(\Sigma y^2)}} = \frac{\Sigma xy}{\sqrt{(\Sigma x^2)\,(\Sigma y^2)}} = \frac{SPxy}{\sqrt{SSx \cdot SSy}}$$

All the equations above demonstrate proof of PPM, and $x = (x - \bar{x})$ and $y = (y - \bar{y})$ in the equations. From the last equation, using the sum of the products (*SP*), raw scores may be substituted as in Figure 10-1 to arrive at the calculator formula.

The value of r^2 is that it interprets the amount of total variation in the one variable that can be explained by the other. Thus, if $r = 0.5$, then $r^2 = 0.25$–and 0.25, or 25 percent, would be the total variation explained by another variable. We know that, by algebra:

$$\text{Total variation} = \text{Explained variation} + \text{Unexplained variation}$$

and that:

$$\frac{\text{Explained}}{\text{Total}} = \frac{\text{Total}}{\text{Total}} - \frac{\text{Unexplained}}{\text{Total}}\ (\div \text{ by Total})$$

$$\uparrow \qquad\qquad \uparrow \qquad\qquad \uparrow$$

$$= \quad r^2 \quad = 1 - (\text{Proportion of unexplained variation})$$

$$= \text{in this case, } 1 - 0.75$$

The square root of $1 - r^2$ times the s_y equals the standard error of the estimate, which is really the standard deviation of prediction scores based on regression

[1] For parametric analysis, at least one variable should have continuous-type data. It is preferable statistically that both variables have interval or ratio-type data.

equations derived from PPM correlation equations. In the standard error or the estimate, we are estimating the possible error in predicting scores, in that they are likely to fall within a given interval based upon the predicted score. For this equation, the standard deviation of y is found by using $n - 2$.

We have moved away from correlation in showing its relationship to regression. *Correlation shows us the strength of the relationship of two variables in the way they can be used to predict*. Regression actually shows us the predictive results. The better the correlation, the less error in prediction (the smaller the standard error of the estimate). The weaker the correlation, the harder it is to predict and find a best-fitting regression line and, consequently, the greater the error or the standard error of the estimate. The word *regression* simply means going, falling, or dropping back. In this case, there is a falling back to the mean to enable a straight line to be fitted. From this best-fitting line, scores may be predicted. Practically speaking, correlation, regression, and prediction are very closely related, and one leads to the other.

They also lead to partial and multiple correlation and to multiple regression. These higher and more sophisticated forms of statistical analysis all have their base in the simple building blocks of the mean, the variance, and the standard deviation. When you finally come to use them, the computers will relieve you of the mathematical strain, but make sure that you know what they do and their limitations.

A Visual Glimpse of Correlation

A positive correlation results when the values of variable x increase with or decrease with the values of variable y. As x goes up, y goes up, or as x goes down, y goes down. In the first diagram in Figure 10-2, as the number of arrests goes up, the number of convictions increases. In the next figure, for the negative correlation, as values of x increase, the values of y decrease, or vice versa. The graph shows that the more time spent in prison, the lower the chances of staying out. In these first two examples, there is an obvious line of best fit, a mean that runs clear through the scattergram or the plots of the x and y values. In a perfect (positive or negative) correlation, all the points fall on the line. The last figure shows no correlation between race and crimes committed. The lines (horizontal or vertical) may be drawn anywhere, and there is no correlation—no line of best fit, no mean, no regression line.

Correlation goes from −1 through zero to +1. The closer to plus or minus 1, the better the correlation, which means that the raw scores cluster about the line in a certain way. The closer to unity, the tighter the scores are to the mean or the line of best fit. We have seen how the sign, plus or minus, indicates *direction*, and we know that the correlation itself will indicate the strength of the association, in that 0.7 correlation appears stronger than 0.2. But we must beware of error. In Figure 10-3, the correlation is the same for both—approximately 0.8. The first diagram looks much more impressive, steeper, and more eyecatching than the sleepy partner

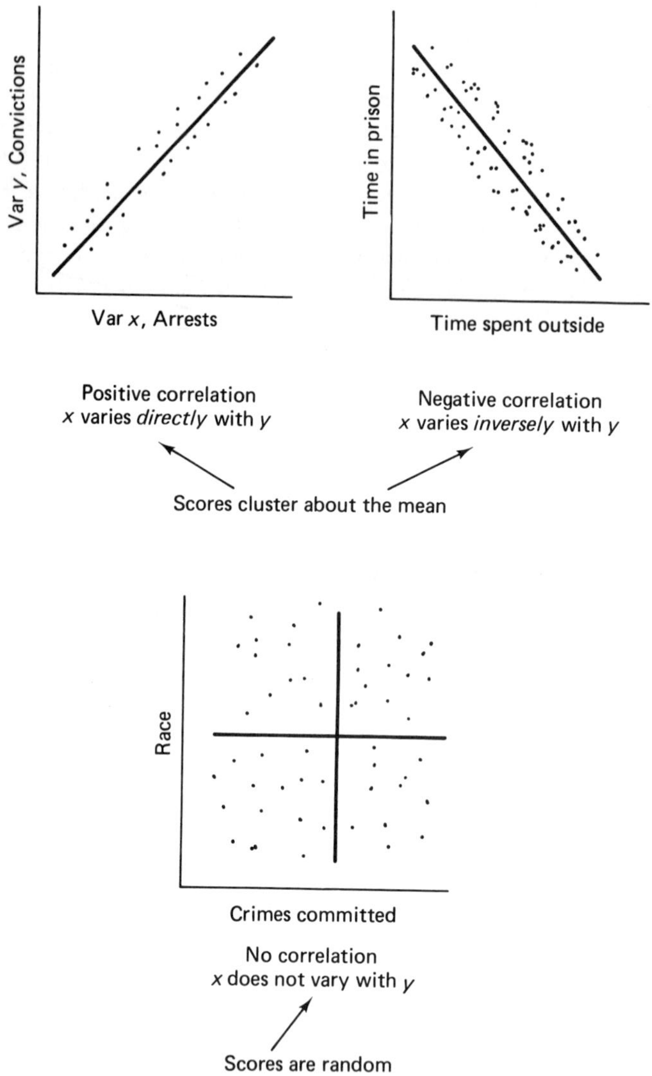

Fig. 10-2 Types of correlation—linear bivariate direction

on the right. Yet the raw scores *cluster about the mean equally* for both. Correlation, then, does *not* tell us about the impact of one variable upon another. It does not tell us the unit change in y caused by one unit of x. Correlation is limited to telling us only that one variable varies with another. Regression, on the other hand, can tell us how much impact one has upon the other by indicating causality and measuring the slope of the mean.

It is assumed that normally most correlations are linear, and that the data will fall

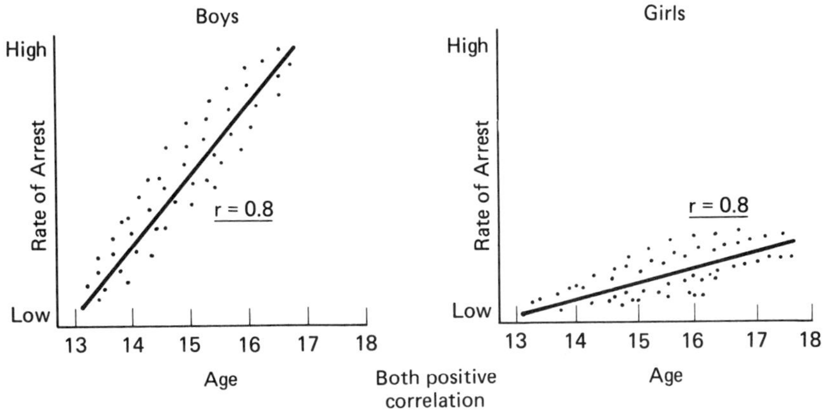

Fig. 10-3 Correlation (cluster) impact (slope)

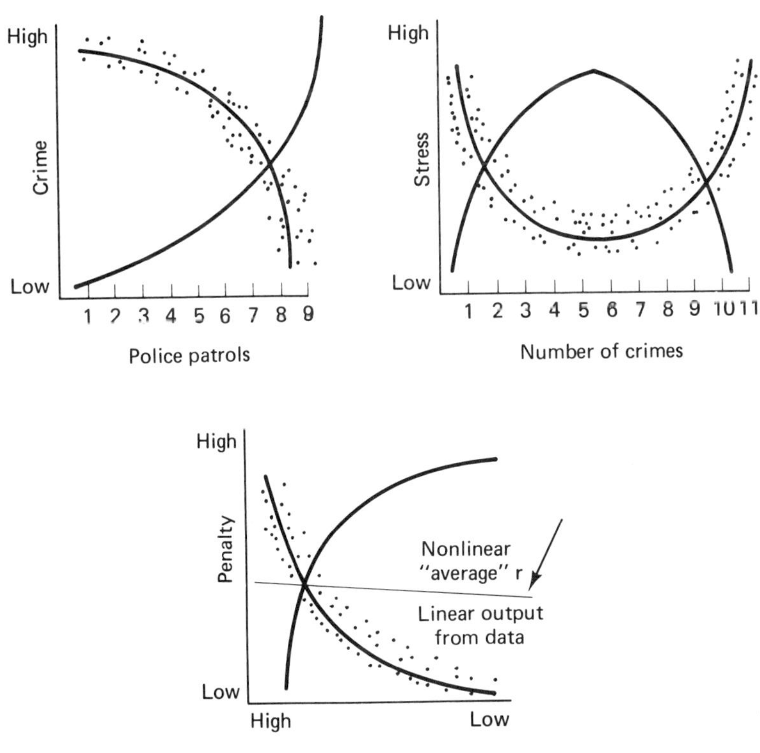

Fig. 10-4 Types of correlation curves

in a straight line. However, in some circumstances, the data will fall in a curvilinear plot, and then we must use a curvilinear formula for the correlation. It is best to use the program for producing the scattergram on the computer so that, when in doubt, you may detect curvilinear data. The computer will plot the data and they can be inspected visually for whatever shape the correlation takes.

In Figure 10-4 are several curves that may be encountered. The most formidable is the U-shaped curve. In this case, the graph shows that stress decreases for a few offenses but increases as the number and the fear of getting caught increase. The first shows how crime takes a sudden dip when patrols reach a certain point or number. The last shows that with a lessening of penalties, marijuana arrests decrease on a curve.

All these are hypothetical, but they do illustrate what you can look for on a scattergram. *Not all data are linear.* It is entirely possible to get a linear correlation for nonlinear data if you feed the wrong formula into the computer, as in the last graph.

When we deal with regression, we can begin to assume causal relationship; and certainly time order, dominance, and influence will help us decide the effect of the independent variable upon the dependent variable. Whereas in correlation, x and y are equal in terms of causality, in regression this is not so. The effect of x on y (the I.V. upon the D.V.) is clearly different when we measure the slope of the line. Figure 10-3 shows age as having much more effect on males than on females in similar samples drawn for reviewing arrest. We must beware of citing the same correlation coefficient when in fact there is quite a difference. A quick look at a scattergram will disclose the nature of the impact.

Although we will not use regression analysis in this text, there is no reason why the student should not go ahead and set up a program if he or she desires to use it. Simply, the slope of the regression line, which is computer-calculated, shows the unit change of y for the one unit of x. *The greater the effect of* x *for one unit, the steeper the line*. In regression we can use the value of x (I.V.) to predict the value of y (D.V.). *The whole function of correlation is to show the strength of the relationship so that we can predict accurately*. The *regression coefficient* is the slope showing the effect of x on y, or the effect of the independent variable upon the dependent variable. In other words, although correlation and regression are generated from similar statistics, correlation is either way (symmetrical) while regression is causal (asymmetrical).

Correlation and Significance

Although we cannot determine impact from correlation coefficients (r), we can determine *significance*. Significance is affected by sample size. The tabled value is read using $n - 2$ degrees of freedom. If the calculated value equals or exceeds the tabled value, a significant correlation exists. As the sample size increases, the tabled value becomes smaller. The corresponding values for $n - 2$ are slightly larger for a smaller alpha value; that is, α 0.005 values are larger than α 0.05 values. Say, for a sample of 102, tabled value for $n - 2$ or 100 at α 0.05 (one-tail) = 0.164; for α 0.005 (one-tail) = 0.254. But note that there is a "Catch 22." In the formula above, n is the number of paired scores, or the number of x, y scores. (This will become clearer when we construct a matrix for calculating the PPM.) In other words, for

Table 10.1. Pearson Correlation of Arrests by Convictions

R: $r \geqslant 0.55$, df = 8, α = 0.05*

N of Cases	No. of arrests (x variable)	No. of convictions (y variable)	x^2	y^2	Product xy
1	6	4	36	16	24
2	7	5	49	25	35
3	9	6	81	36	54
4	12	8	144	64	96
5	14	10	196	100	140
6	12	12	144	144	144
7	11	10	121	100	110
8	14	9	196	81	126
9	8	8	64	64	64
10	9	6	81	36	54
N= 10	$\Sigma x = 102$	$\Sigma y = 78$	$\Sigma x^2 = 1{,}112$	$\Sigma y^2 = 666$	$\Sigma xy = 847$

$(\Sigma x)^2 = 10{,}404$ $(\Sigma y)^2 = 6{,}084$

$(\Sigma x)(\Sigma y) = 7{,}956$

Calculator formula for PPM:

$$r = \frac{n\Sigma xy - (\Sigma x)(\Sigma y)}{\sqrt{[n\Sigma x^2 - (\Sigma x)^2]\,[n\Sigma y^2 - (\Sigma y)^2]}}$$

Substituting:

$$r = \frac{(10 \cdot 847) - 7{,}956}{\sqrt{[(10 \cdot 1{,}112) - 10{,}404]\,[(10 \cdot 666) - 6{,}084]}}$$

$$r = \frac{8{,}470 - 7{,}956}{\sqrt{(11{,}120 - 10{,}404)\,(6{,}660 - 6{,}084)}} = \frac{514}{\sqrt{716 \cdot 576}} = \frac{514}{\sqrt{412{,}416}}$$

$$r = \frac{514}{642.2} = 0.8 \quad \text{df} = N - 2 = 8 \quad \alpha = \text{Sig. at } 0.005$$

The correlation between arrests and convictions is (+).8, which means there is a strong relationship, and it would be possible to predict the number of convictions from the number of arrests. Reject the null hypothesis.

*Reject the H_0 when r is equal to or greater than 0.55, with 8 degrees of freedom at the α 0.05 level of significance.

102 cases of x raw scores and 102 y raw scores, we really only have 102 x, y scores for correlation: $n - 2 = 102 - 2 = 100$.

Remember that a large significance for a small sample of, say, 30 with a correlation of 0.5 at $\alpha = 0.01$ may look very impressive. However, the correlation of 0.3 for (the same variable) a sample of 100 at α 0.01 is much more impressive even if the correlation is smaller. It is a stronger association and will give us a better predictive measure for regression. In any case, significance levels are printed on the computer printouts. You may refer to the tables if there is doubt. Consider what is correlated and the effect of what you are saying about the relationship between two variables.

Using a Correlation Matrix

Pearson r is best understood when the equation is set down and a matrix is used to convert the scores to formulas used in the equation. Supposing, for example, we were curious about the relationship of arrests to convictions. We select a sample of 50 juveniles to test this relationship. We also investigate background data, and thus we have a problem in parametric and nonparametric relationships. First we will look at the PPM from the data of the 50 cases. The variable x is the number of arrests, and the variable y is the number of convictions. We ask, Is there a correlation between arrests and convictions? The null hypothesis is simply stated:

H_o: There is no relationship between the number of convictions and the number of arrests.

H_a: The number of convictions is related to the number of arrests.

Now, 50 cases are easy to enter on the IBM cards, and the computer will process the run within minutes. For this example we will take a hypothetical section of the sample, ten cases, to show how the process works and x, y variables are correlated. You must be clear in your mind of the difference between Σx^2, the *sum of the squares* of each x raw score, which comes at the bottom of the column for x^2, and $(\Sigma x)^2$, which is the *sum of the raw scores*—found at the bottom of the raw-score total—*squared.* Keep in mind that most of the work is done for you on a matrix; learn the method and what it does, so that when the computers and calculators do all the work, you know what is happening. *Note the arrows in the calculations.*

Comments on the PPM Matrix

In the matrix (Table 10.1), the variables are designated x and y. Each pair of variables is opposite its case number—for example, in case 1, $x = 6$ convictions and $y = 4$ arrests. The variable values are squared, $x^2 = 36$, $y^2 = 16$. These values are entered in the appropriate columns. The final column is the product of x and y, or xy

= 24. The columns are summed, to give Σx, Σy, Σx^2, Σy^2, and Σxy. While we are at it, we square Σx as $(\Sigma x)^2$ or $102^2 = 10{,}404$, and the same for Σy, $(\Sigma y)^2 = 78^2 = 6{,}084$. We also find the product of the sums of x and y, or $\Sigma x \Sigma y = 102 \times 78 = 7{,}956$. We note that N or $n = 10$. The rest is simple substitution, by following the arrows to the right places and remembering where n goes. All the work is done in the matrix, and the calculation is now one of arithmetic, provided that you *do not forget the square-root sign over the denominator*. Sometimes the correlation is negative, in which case the answer is given in a minus quantity.

A calculator will run through the equation quickly. Some terminals and some programmable calculators do all this automatically, along with many other features, including a scattergram, regression, slope, and intercept, and all the intervening steps with means and standard deviations. This is how correlation works; familiarize yourself with the formula. Note that if you have calculated standard deviations, you have done most of the work already. Check your work; it is easy to make mistakes in substitution. This useful formula is the basis for correlation, regression, and prediction.

Assumptions and Restrictions for Correlation

The example given in Table 10.1 shows exactly where everything goes, and statistically it all fits very nicely to give a PPM of 0.8—a very definite correlation between the two variables. We have assumed for the purposes of calculation that:

1. The data are linear, interval (or ratio) type.
2. There is equal variance of the characteristic in a normal distribution in the parent population.
3. The sample is both random and representative.

There are certain errors present that we should be aware of:

1. In this case, the sample size is too small. Samples of less than 30 are doubtful at best.
2. Any statement we make applies only to the sample; it is too small to make any inference to the parent population—we should have at least 100 cases, or a total population if this was an institution.
3. The correlation may not necessarily be strong. If the sample size was larger, it could disappear. Small samples with large significance often change when sample size is increased.
4. This is *not* a causal statement. It merely states that there is a relationship between arrests and convictions.

Even though we cannot make a causal statement, it does become clear that arrests come before convictions in a time-order sequence, and that arrests would be the I.V., with number of convictions the D.V. But we cannot state this from just correlation. We do have sufficient evidence to proceed to further statistical analysis to establish a causal chain. Our significance came from a table of PPM values for a one-tail test. The degrees of freedom were set at $N - 2$, where N was the number of paired variables (x and y)—in this case, df = 8 or 10 – 2. Tabled values were 0.55 at α 0.05, 0.7 at α 0.01, and 0.76 at α 0.005. Our hypothetical correlation was significant to the α 0.005 level.

Nonparametric Correlation

We have two ways to go for nonparametric ordinal-type data. One is Spearman rank correlation, or r_s, and the other is Kendall's tau, or τ. Both are for dealing with data that can be ranked or ordered. Let us assume that the scores on arrests and conviction can be ranked, for *Spearman's rho.*

Arrests: 6, 7, 8, 9, 9, 11, 12, 12, 14, 14
Convictions: 4, 5, 6, 6, 8, 8, 9, 10, 10, 12

We have ordered the data; now we rank the data, and if there are ties, we simply sum the *ranks* (not the scores) and divide the total evenly between the tied ranks:

Arrests	6	7	8	9	9	11	12	12	14	14
Rank: x	1	2	3	4.5	4.5	6	7.5	7.5	9.5	9.5
Convictions	4	5	6	6	8	8	9	10	10	12
Rank: y	1	2	3.5	3.5	5.5	5.5	7	8.5	8.5	10

We now set up a matrix: $N = 10$.

Arrests, x	Convictions, y	x rank	y rank	$(y - x)$ Difference, d	Squared Difference, d^2
6	4	1	1	0	0
7	5	2	2	0	0
8	6	3	3.5	0.5	0.25
9	6	4.5	3.5	−1	1
9	8	4.5	5.5	1	1
11	8	6	5.5	−0.5	0.25
12	9	7.5	7	−0.5	0.25
12	10	7.5	8.5	1	1
14	10	9.5	8.5	−1	1
14	12	9.5	10	0.5	0.25
					$\Sigma d^2 = 5$

Substituting:

$$r_s = 1 - \frac{6\Sigma d^2}{n(n^2 - 1)} = 1 - \frac{6(5)}{10(99)} = 1 - \frac{30}{990}$$

$$r_s = 1 - 0.03 = 0.97 \text{ (Sig. at 0.05)}$$

In effect, this is the Pearson correlation for the same data in ranks. If there are a large number of ties, the results will be questionable. The r_s improves with sample size, but the assumption is that data are continuously distributed and nonparametric. Pearson r is preferred for continuous data, and this example is given to show the relation of one to the other. Ordinarily, the computer will print out whichever you prefer. Again, beware of linear "averages" concealing curvilinear data. The advantage of the Spearman r_s is its ease of calculation; all you need are the ranks and the differences. The difference is y rank minus x rank, then the difference is squared and the squares are summed. Significance values are higher for Spearman, and you will note that the coefficient is somewhat higher. Note also that if the second part of the formula equals 1, there is no correlation, or $r_s = 1 - 1 = 0$. If the total equals 0 or 2, there will be perfect correlation, or $r_s = 1 - 0 = 1$, or $1 - 2 = -1$.

The correlation deals with the relationship between ranks, and is therefore somewhat ambiguous in terms of strength. All we can say is that there is a *strong tendency* for the number of arrests to increase with the number of convictions, or vice versa; in correlation you may say it either way, although it sounds better to say that there is a strong tendency for the number of convictions to increase with the number of arrests. Do be careful of what you are saying, and do not be misled by correlation into assuming cause and effect. Both Spearman's rho, or r_s, and Kendall's tau, or τ, are useful. Both have corrections for tied scores that involve lengthy formulas. Kendall's tau does give a better result for tied scores, and it does not depend upon normal distribution. Tau tends to be smaller than Pearson r.

Kendall's Tau

This correlation coefficient for nonparametric data consists of ordering or ranking one variable in its natural order, with the other variable also being ordered but being placed alongside the first variable in the ranks that coincide with the first. Thus, we have a situation wherein one variable is ranked in order, and the ranked scores of the other are then matched. Then a statistic S is taken based upon the number of ranks that are higher and lower than the score used. In practice it is not complicated, but its description is. With ties in scores, it is even more complex. Using the data from arrests and convictions, the Kendall's tau is 0.72, or much lower than the Pearson r or the Spearman rho.

Kendall's tau without ties is as follows:

$$\tau = \frac{2\Sigma S}{n(n-1)}$$

The correction for ties, as in the present case, is complex and involves further formulas. Spearman's rho is higher because of the square differences, Kendall's tau is lower because it treats each case separately. The statistic S is computed by taking the first rank on the first variable, then counting all the ranks above it on the second variable and all those below it on the second variable, and subtracting those below from those above. Then the next rank on the first variable is taken and compared to all the ranks above it on the second variable, and so on. Let us look at a simple tau without ranks, and see how it is computed, in Table 10.2.

Table 10.2. Ordering Data for Kendall's Tau (without ties)

Case number	A = arrests	C = convictions	A-rank	C-rank
1	6	4	1	1
2	7	5	2	2
3	9	6	3	3
4	10	8	4	5
5	16	11	10	8
6	15	12	9	9
7	11	10	5	7
8	14	9	8	6
9	12	7	6	4
10	13	13	7	10

Calculation data: $N = 10$

Case number	A-rank	C-rank	*S* statistic
1	1	1	$S = (9 - 0)$
2	2	2	$(8 - 0)$
3	3	3	$(7 - 0)$
4	4	5	$(5 - 1)$
7	5	7	$(3 - 2)$
9	6	4	$(4 - 0)$
10	7	10	$(0 - 3)$
8	8	6	$(2 - 0)$
6	9	9	$(0 - 1)$
5	10	8 ↓	
			$\Sigma S = 31$

$$\text{Tau} = \tau = \frac{2\Sigma S}{n(n-1)} = \frac{62}{90} = 0.69$$

Where $S = 5 - 1$, the fourth A-rank, this means that taking the fourth rank of arrests, and looking at C-rank (down) (convictions), there are five ranks in C-rank above rank 5 in C (7, 10, 6, 9, and 8) and one below (4). Thus we arrive at $5 - 1$, or a total of 4. This illustrates the *S* procedure by moving from one variable to the ranks in the other. This is the way the computer works. For tied ranks, there is a further adjustment. As stated, tau is better for many tied ranks than Spearman. Spearman is better for continuous data on an ordinal base without ties. One- or two-tail tests may be used. However, when direction is known, a one-tail test of significance is more appropriate.

Pearson's r, Spearman's r_s, and Kendall's τ all vary from -1 to $+1$. Tau is generally used when there are a large number of cases in a small number of categories (nonparametric); Spearman is used when the number of cases per category is smaller; and Pearson is used for continuous-interval (parametric) data regardless of sample size or category number.

Scattergrams

Scattergrams are best printed using linear-type interval or ratio data. If the data used are discrete, all the points plotted appear on the axis used. For example, with sex, if 1 designates male and 2 designates female, the horizontal axis would simply be limited to two values, 1 and 2. All the values of race would be limited to 1 for white and 2 for black. In this type of printout, where *Race* was the vertical axis, (y) and *Sex* was the horizontal axis (x), all one would see would be values of x and y printed on the edges or the corners of the graph. Why not do this one to see how it comes out? It really has no meaning. On the other hand, continuous data such as age, arrests, and convictions will plot out very clearly and give valid data. *Therefore, scattergrams should be limited to situations in which both variables have continuous-type data.*

The card may be placed after VALUE LABELS and should read:

```
                16
SCATTERGRAM     AGE WITH ARRESTS, CONVICT/ARRESTS WITH CONVICT
STATISTICS      ALL
READ INPUT DATA
```

Three graphs will be printed: age with arrests, age with convictions, and arrests with convictions. Notice that the key word WITH produces a graph for every variable, and that the / delimiter separates the next graph of arrests with conviction. Once the output is obtained, it is a good practice to estimate the line of best fit and actually draw it in on the printout. This is a check on the linearity of the data. It can then be compared with the calculated regression line that can be drawn from the intercept and slope. The computer will also print the value for r, r^2, significance, and standard error of the estimate, as well as means, deviations, and covariance.

After the last data card, number 50, you may insert another program. In fact, you may insert any number of programs if they are in order and if they are logical. You may insert:

```
                16
PEARSON CORR    AGE TO CONVICT
STATISTICS      ALL
```

and:

```
NONPAR CORR        AGE TO CONVICT
OPTIONS            6
[No STATISTICS card used]
```

In this case, three further runs of Pearson, Spearman, and Kendall will be generated so that you may compare the results.

Of course, as you get proficient, you will be able to select just the data you need, such as:

```
                   16
PEARSON CORR       ARRESTS WITH CONVICT
STATISTICS         ALL
```

From your own expertise, you will be able to avoid fishing expeditions and get right to the point of what it is that you need. You will also be able to specify the statistics and options you need. Once you acquire a familiarity with the SPSS program, you will learn the various conventions and what you can and cannot do. If you wish, on this program, you may start with:

```
                   16
FREQUENCIES        GENERAL=ALL
STATISTICS         ALL
```

and then insert all three programs at the end, just in front of the FINISH card. A complete deck setup is shown in Table 10.3 so that you can check your own. The output is fairly large. Use only the data that are useful, study what the computer does, and compare the various results by sorting them out and writing them down on separate sheets.

Be sure to increase your time for this run. Write up the data analysis just for practice and see exactly what you have in terms of the 50 juvenile cases that have been selected. Note the way the computer gives you a correlation matrix, a table of all the correlation values. Examine the scattergrams and decide if the data can be expressed as linear and if indeed the assumptions for correlation apply. If you are using the FREQUENCIES run, here is a chance for you to use an OPTIONS card if the programs are in your computer center. The task definition cards are:

```
                   16
FREQUENCIES        GENERAL=ALL
OPTIONS            3, 6, 8, 9
STATISTICS         ALL
```

This OPTIONS output, under the SPSS format, will produce:

Option 3—Output is printed on an $8\frac{1}{2}'' \times 11''$ page (notebook size).
Option 6—Output bigger than one page will be condensed.
Option 8—Output will print a histogram for each variable.
Option 9—Output will print a reference dictionary of tables.

Table 10.3. Data Information for Deck for Four Programs Run

Client number	Age	Race	Sex	Religion	Number of arrests	Number of convictions
1	14	Black	Male	Protestant	20	9
2	15	White	Female	Jewish	10	8
3	16	White	Female	Catholic	14	6
4	17	White	Male	Protestant	12	6
5	18	White	Female	Catholic	10	6
6	15	White	Male	Jewish	08	4
7	16	Black	Female	Protestant	16	8
8	17	White	Female	Protestant	06	2
9	14	Black	Male	Catholic	04	2
10	15	White	Male	Catholic	08	2
11	16	Black	Female	Protestant	12	6
12	14	White	Male	Catholic	04	2
13	15	White	Female	Jewish	28	9
14	16	White	Male	Protestant	24	9
15	17	White	Female	Catholic	08	8
16	18	White	Male	Protestant	22	8
17	14	Black	Male	Jewish	08	4
18	15	White	Female	Catholic	08	4
19	16	White	Male	Catholic	36	9
20	17	White	Female	Protestant	20	5
21	18	White	Male	Protestant	08	6
22	16	Black	Male	Catholic	08	7
23	17	Black	Male	Jewish	10	8
24	14	White	Male	Protestant	10	9
25	13	Black	Female	Catholic	10	8
26	15	Black	Female	Protestant	11	7
27	16	White	Male	Catholic	07	6
28	17	Black	Male	Protestant	05	5
29	18	Black	Male	Protestant	08	4
30	13	White	Male	Protestant	07	3
31	14	Black	Male	Protestant	05	1
32	15	Black	Male	Protestant	10	1
33	16	White	Male	Protestant	15	9
34	17	White	Male	Protestant	14	7
35	18	White	Female	Protestant	12	6
36	17	Black	Female	Protestant	12	6
37	16	Black	Male	Catholic	06	3
38	15	Black	Male	Catholic	06	3
39	14	White	Female	Protestant	02	1
40	13	White	Male	Protestant	03	1
41	14	Black	Female	Catholic	02	1
42	18	Black	Male	Catholic	03	1
43	17	White	Male	Protestant	05	2
44	16	White	Male	Protestant	04	2
45	15	White	Male	Protestant	04	2
46	14	Black	Male	Protestant	08	4
47	13	Black	Male	Protestant	14	6
48	14	Black	Male	Protestant	10	5
49	18	Black	Female	Catholic	18	7
50	16	Black	Male	Catholic	20	8

Note once again that in this program, *no* STATISTICS card is used with NONPAR CORR; only the OPTIONS card is used to generate Kendall's tau as well as Spearman's rho. OPTIONS cards are seldom used, but they are extremely useful when used properly.

These programs are designed to get the student familiar with the computer. It is difficult and demanding work, and it *must* be precise. With time and practice comes mastery.

The coding for the data of Table 10.3 is as follows: The first entry on the data card is the numeric ID (the last three digits of the Social Security number are good for this), then the client number, then the client's age. *Race* is coded 1 for white, 2 for black; *sex* is coded 1 for male, 2 for female; *religion* is coded 1 for Protestant, 2 for Catholic, 3 for Jewish. Then the number of arrests is entered, then the number of convictions. Two columns are used for client number, age, and number of arrests; all the rest are single columns. Thus, client number 1 is entered as 01; three arrests as 03. The first data card should look like Figure 10-5.

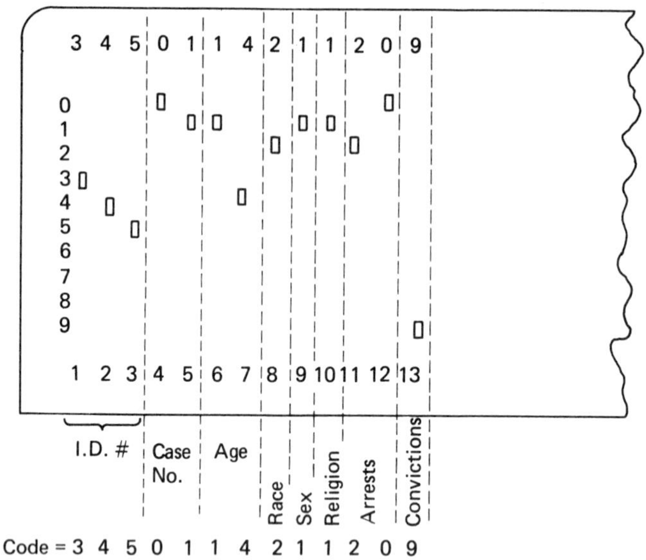

Fig. 10-5 IBM data deck card

The printed top line on the IBM card corresponds with the coded data from the FORTRAN coding sheet, or whatever writeout was used. The dotted lines indicate where the variables are situated on the IBM card, the order in which they are entered, and the number of columns per variable. The last entry is made in column 13, as it is for every card in the data deck. If entries stop at column 12 or go on to column 14, there is error and the card must be redone.

Check all 50 data cards carefully. Make sure there are exactly 50, not 49 or 51. Make sure that every card is in perfect shape—no bent, spindled, or mutilated cards. Check the punch holes to see there are no uneven punches. Check the top of your card; if any entries occur above the numeric section—that is, above the line of zeros—you have entered an alpha character instead of a numeric.

The card deck shown in Table 10.4 will run the four programs. In some computers, the job cards and end cards may be different, so check your computer center for details. You cannot have access to the computer without either a proper job card or an access number. Notice the adherence to SPSS conventions. The last digit after CLASS (or whatever word you use) must agree with the last digit of the access number. Your personal ID is always a nine-letter alpha, usually your name. PAGESIZE is *one* word. The INPUT FORMAT skips your own numeric ID on the data cards and reads the CLIENT as a variable. This enables you to check on your number of cases to see if you have 50 clients with different case cards. The first task definition is FREQUENCIES, with the options already explained. At the end

Table 10.4. Checking the Deck for the Computer Run

```
//BSCLASS5 JOB '33344455', 'ANONYMOUS', REGION=320K, TIME=(0000,10)
// EXEC SPSS
               16
PAGESIZE       80
RUN NAME       FREQUENCIES SCATTERGRAM CORRELATION
FILE NAME      FOUR PROGRAMS
VARIABLE LIST  CLIENT, AGE, RACE, SEX, RELIG, ARRESTS, CONVICT
INPUT MEDIUM   CARD
N OF CASES     50
INPUT FORMAT   FIXED(3X, 2F2.0, 3F1.0, F2.0, F1.0)
VAR LABELS     RELIG RELIGION/ARRESTS NUMBER OF ARRESTS/
               CONVICT NUMBER OF CONVICTIONS       [2nd card]
VALUE LABELS   RACE (1)WHITE (2)BLACK/SEX (1)MALE (2)FEMALE/
               RELIG (1)PROTESTANT (2)CATHOLIC (3)JEW      [2nd card]
FREQUENCIES    GENERAL=ALL
OPTIONS        3,6,8,9
STATISTICS     ALL
READ INPUT DATA
[Insert data deck of 50 data cards here.]
SCATTERGRAM    AGE WITH ARRESTS, CONVICT/ARRESTS WITH CONVICT
STATISTICS     ALL
PEARSON CORR   AGE TO CONVICT
STATISTICS     ALL
NONPAR CORR    AGE TO CONVICT
OPTIONS        6
FINISH
/*
[Total of 22 control cards; 25 in control deck]
```

Note: Use only one IBM card per line. All data cards have 13 columns.

of the data deck we have inserted a program for SCATTERGRAM, using the continuous data for age, arrests, and convictions. Then we have requested a Pearson correlation matrix to show correlation of all the variables, and we have set a program for Spearman's nonparametric correlation and have included Kendall's tau (OPTION 6). There is no statistic card for NONPAR CORR.

From the output you may compare the results. Notice that Spearman's rho (r_s) is higher than Pearson r, and that Kendall's tau is lower than Pearson r. Check your significance levels and decide whether you will retain or reject your null hypothesis. There appears to be a strong correlation of arrests with conviction ($r = 0.73$, $\alpha = 0.001$) and age with conviction ($r = 0.23$, $\alpha = 0.053$), a weaker correlation of age with arrests ($r = 0.2$, $\alpha = 0.08$), and a weaker one still with sex with arrests ($r_s = 0.2$, $\alpha = 0.076$). Compare the parametric and nonparametric results.

Comments on the Correlation Output

Upon your completing the run, the statistics will show a square correlation matrix for the Pearson r. Half of this is redundant—you will notice that a diagonal line can join all the $r = 1.00$s through the matrix—but it is convenient. The Spearman and Kendall are set out in pairs of variables. Note that the significance level for alpha is printed with each correlation, as well as the sample size of $n = 50$. Look carefully through the data and note all that specify a level of 0.05, or nearly that. There are only a few that rate any attention; the rest indicate that the chances of the result are too high to establish any causal effect. For example, RACE with RELIGION is $S = 0.4$; this means that we have a 40 percent chance of being wrong, or that the relationship could have occurred accidentally. The level is too high, and we retain the H_0 that there is no relationship between race and religion, which is fairly meaningless anyway. However, on the correlation between arrests and convictions, the $r = 0.73$ and $\alpha = 0.001$, we have a strong relationship with a high degree of confidence that we are right, or one in 1,000 that we are wrong. Thus, we reject the H_0 because there is a relationship between arrests and convictions. There is a statistical difference and a statistical significance, a *statistical difference* between the tabled value and the calculated value, and a *statistical significance* in the level of rejection of the H_0 at 0.001. Thus, we can reject the H_0 with confidence. The sample size is acceptable. Notice the difference in r and r_s in SEX with ARRESTS. This will be explored later in chi-square.

A GLIMPSE AT REGRESSION

Although we will not use regression analysis in this text, it is nice to know that we already have access to it in the information that is printed in the SCATTERGRAM subprogram. It is assumed that the entry of the variables is such that x variable (independent, or I.V.) will be placed at the bottom, across the page on the horizontal axis. The y variable, or dependent, will be printed on the vertical axis. This can be done by using the concepts of time-order, dominance, and influence in entering the variables for the program. The y variable should be entered first, then the independent or x variable. In this case, to obtain a regression analysis and assuming that in fact there is a causal relationship between age and convictions or between convictions and arrests, the card would read:

```
                      16
SCATTERGRAM           ARRESTS, CONVICT WITH AGE/CONVICT WITH
                         ARRESTS
STATISTICS            ALL
```

In this case, the x variable would appear on the horizontal axis, and the regression slope would be calculated for the change in y caused by one unit of x. You may run this card if you wish. The given slope and intercept may then be used as follows. The regression equation is:

$$\hat{Y} = a + bx$$

where $\hat{Y}$ is the predicted score derived from a, the intercept, plus b, the slope, times the raw score for x. There are formulas for obtaining both a and b based upon the Pearson r. For the slope:

$$b = \frac{n\Sigma xy - \Sigma x \Sigma y}{n\Sigma x^2 - (\Sigma x)^2}$$

For the intercept:

$$a = \bar{y} - b\bar{x} \quad \text{or} \quad \frac{\Sigma y - b\Sigma x}{n}$$

It is easy to recognize the formula from the Pearson r equation. However, all this is done for you on the printout. You are given a and b; now it is easy to predict a given value of y for a value of x. Note, however, that predicting x on y is not the same as predicting y on x. There may be some similarities at the lower end of the scale, but there are greater differences as the scores go higher. Also, when there is (very rarely) perfect correlation, you can predict x on y or y on x without a difference.

If you have run the new scattergram, you will find that the slope is 0.287 and the intercept is 2. On your old scattergram, the slope was $b = 1.8$ with the intercept $a = 1.14$ for arrests with convictions. Now we have CONVICT set up as the D.V. with ARRESTS as the I.V., and $b = 0.287$ and the intercept $a = 2$. Using the equation $\hat{Y} = a + bx$ and substituting, we can ask ourselves, What is the best estimate of the number of convictions (y variable) for 20 arrests (x variable)?

$$\hat{Y} = 2.00 + (0.287 \times 20) = 8 \text{ (to the nearest whole number)}$$

We have estimated a value of y from x. This is simple regression. We have also assumed that arrests come before convictions, and thus arrests are the x variable, the independent variable that causes change in the number of convictions, the y variable. We have advanced from correlation, where we cannot assume cause and effect, to regression, where we use one variable to predict values on another. In this case, we must assume some order to affirm the logic of our prediction.

If you check your frequency data, you will find that the mean for arrests is 10.7 and the mean for convictions is 2.7; by substituting in the formula $a = \bar{y} - b\bar{x}$, you will find that $a = 2$ when $b = 0.287$. You may also calculate b if you wish from the data given, using arrests as x and convictions as y.

Regression, then, is easy when computers and calculators do the work for you. You should understand what you are doing and work a few simple problems manually. Draw the lines of "best fit" on your scattergrams, and ask yourself which is predicting what on the other–are you using x on y or y on x? If you keep x or the I.V. on the bottom, horizontal axis, you should not have too much trouble.

Ask yourself the logic of your calculations: Are you doing things in a logical order? Is what you are saying making sense? Are you sure about what is influencing what and what changes are occurring? The whole object of research is prediction, and there are precious few continuous data in the social sciences that we can use for prediction. Most of our data are qualitative, and we convert them to quantitative data. But when you can use parametric analysis, use it carefully and precisely. Remember that the standard error of the estimate is also printed to help you know the extent of error in your predictions. The amount of standard error of the estimate (in this case, 1.8) tells you that 68 percent of your predictions will score within plus or minus 1.8, or that 95 percent will score within plus or minus 3.5 of the predicted score. All the hard work of calculation is done by the computer.

CORRELATION, REGRESSION, AND PREDICTION

The regression equation, or establishing the best fitting line to plots of scores, is based upon the Pearson Product Moment. The line of best fit, as it is called, is an attempt to establish a mean for scores using continuous data. It can also be used for prediction. We can take the best r scores from a correlation matrix and enter them into a regression equation. From the results we can determine the variables with the greatest effect or influence upon the dependent variable. Correlation is the base upon which regression is built. In the correlation equation, the variables are assumed to be of equal value and importance; they show a relationship but to all intents and purposes are independent. *There is no independent variable exerting an influence on a dependent variable because there is no dependent variable in the equation.* In the regression equation, this is not so. The difference, even though we are using similar equations, is shown in Table 10.5.

Correlation helps us sift the relationships so that the more important ones may be used for regression or further analysis. Although we are able to focus on what is significant, we should be careful that we do not miss any unusual effects and that

Table 10.5. Differences for Correlation and Regression Analysis

	Correlation	Item	Regression
1	PPM only	Based upon PPM and predictive equation	Yes
2	No	Shows causal order—effect of I.V. on D.V.	Yes
3	Yes	Gives strength and direction of relationship	Yes
4	Yes	Gives significance of relationship	Yes
5	No	Shows impact by unit change in slope	Yes
6	No	Used to predict outcomes	Yes
7	Yes	Ranked to show importance for prediction	Yes
8	No	Ranked to show causal influence	Yes
9	No	Used to estimate error in prediction	Yes
10	No	Used for decision making	Yes

we are operating within the assumptions on which our data are based. In each case, correlation and regression, we assumed continuous linear data. There are other equations for curvilinear data.

Much as we desire to predict outcomes—and this is the ultimate aim of science—we need to exercise caution in using statistical tools! For example, if we are using linear data, there is no guarantee that our section of the linear graph is not part of a curvilinear outcome. Such an outcome could change our prediction.

In Figure 10-6, prediction 1 is based upon an assumption that past data and future data will be linear. It is also based upon statistical averages and an assumption that we have measured correctly all the necessary factors in the equation. Prediction 2 differs from 1 in that, as a possible actual outcome, it cannot be predicted from the equation used for prediction 1. Similarly, prediction 3 as a possible outcome is obscured from the researcher because of incomplete data.

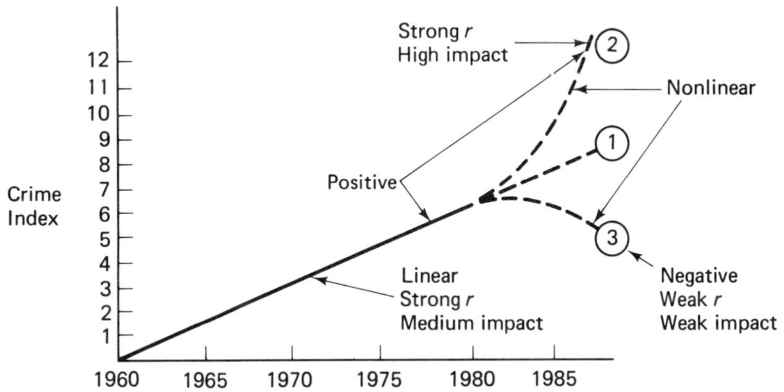

Fig. 10-6 Possible predictive outcomes

Assumptions for Prediction

In using our topic for research and in using the results of that research for prediction, we are basing our prediction upon three assumptions:

1. That it is based upon the prior fact of the existence of quantitative variables A and B.
2. That there has been scientific research using statistical methods to show correlation and causal relationship between A and B.
3. That statistical analysis and trend indicates that in the near future, A will cause B, or that B will occur because of A.[2]

In this way, our predictions are firmly anchored in present research, past facts, and statistical probability. If we deal solely with qualitative concepts and *a priori* assumptions, our predictions begin to resemble horoscopes. *Most decision making depends upon the three assumptions outlined.*

Notice that the assumptions do not depend upon faith, common sense, or traditional authority. Our prediction or decision making attempts to remove error and provide verification and scientific objectivity. Decision making is a form of prediction, in that the decision deals with a future event or the application of the prediction. Prediction is the foretelling of events, and decision making is the controlling of events. *The importance of prediction is that it gives us knowledge of the relationship of the variables we are investigating. If we know that the event may be predicted, then we have alternative choices and may make a decision to affect the outcome of our prediction.*

Predictions can be based upon accumulated facts. In the physical sciences, such predictions are common; for example, we know when the gas tank on a car will be empty, how much electrical energy an appliance will consume, what will happen when we fire a loaded gun, and so on. But even in the physical sciences, doubt arises when uncertain variables are used, such as in attempting to predict when we will use up all the world's resources.[3]

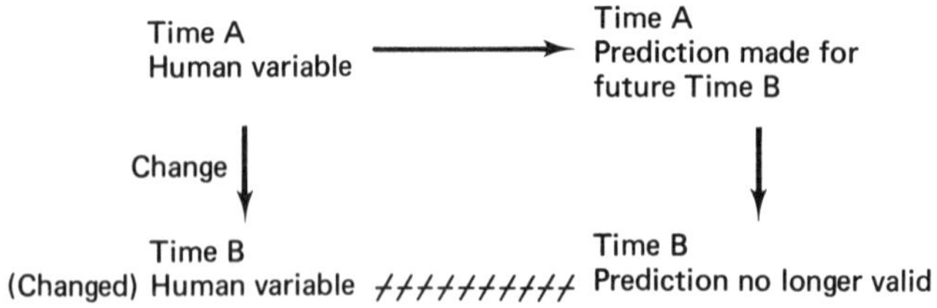

Fig. 10-7 Prediction and time change

[2] The regression line will be extended (in theory) to show the effect of the independent variable A on dependent variable B at some future time.

[3] Donella H. Meadows et al., *Limits to Growth* (New York: Universe Books, 1972).

Prediction is even more difficult when dealing with human variations. Change occurs so often and sometimes so rapidly that variables on which the prediction was based now no longer resemble the originals. In Figure 10-7, the longer the time between A and B, the greater the chance of error. Because time increases the chance of change, predictions should at best be short-term.

Prediction implies a prior established law constructed on firmly established facts. We have few facts in criminology, and even fewer laws. We do have accelerated social change[4] and a great deal of human variation in both the research area and the researcher.

Prediction as a Link between Research and Decision

As Figure 10-8 shows, the prediction—knowing that some event will occur—gives us seven ways in which to make a decision, from a decision to let the event occur again to a decision to prevent it totally by eliminating variable *A*, variable *B*, or both. We

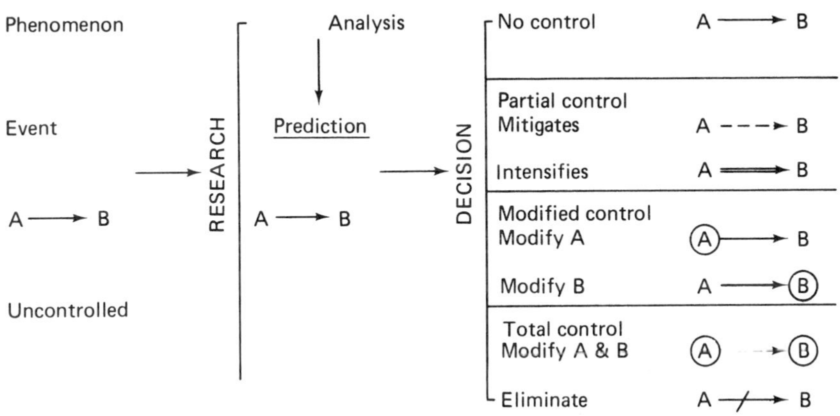

Fig. 10-8 The seven possible decisions

may intensify or mitigate the effects of *A* upon *B*, as in partial control, or we may modify *A* or *B* or both. Mitigation or intensification of the effect of *A* upon *B* may be achieved by inserting another variable between them to act as a catalyst (intensify) or as a screen (mitigate).

A favorite item in criminology has been the problem of recidivism. Men who serve time tend to return to serve more time.

Felons in prison → Paroled felons who return to prison
(Variable A) (Variable B)

It is easy to predict the return rate from conviction figures and incarceration figures. Prevention is not so easy. The decision process here is to intervene between

[4] Alvin Toffler, *Future Shock* (New York: Random House, 1970).

A and *B* in order to at least lower the rate of return. One way to do this may be to release inmates who show good adjustment to prison programs.

Several scales for predicting parole success have been devised. The prominent ones are by Ohlin in Illinois.[5] Fox in Michigan,[6] and Warren in California.[7] Fox's scale was based upon the inmate's adjustment to prison programs and prison life, which, it was felt, would prepare the inmate to stay outside the prison. Fox included eleven factors: work reports, cell-block officer reports, chaplain's report, school officer's report, discipline reports, visits, letters, finances, type of misconduct if any, and work and school records of stability. Each of these items was weighted, the total score indicating future success on parole.

Fox has not only modified variable *A* by including programs for adjustment, but also mitigated the effect of variable *A* upon *B* by inserting a screening process (parole-success prediction). According to our model, we now have modified control supplemented by partial control in the hopes of eliminating variable *B* and thus giving total control. Although *B* was not eliminated, considerable progress was made.

The prediction process was linked to the decision-making process and implemented with a fair degree of success. It must be remembered that if there is a great deal of time between decision and implementation, the variables change and the decision will become ineffective, no longer applying to the circumstances upon which it was based.

CAUSALITY

In the section on regression, we began to examine the meaning of causal effects. Cause precedes effect in time, and thus, in the time order of the variables, the independent variable precedes the dependent. It is also the variable least likely to change and most likely to influence or cause change in the other. Variables in the causal chain must also be quantitatively or empirically related before we can measure the effects of one upon the other, and a relationship must exist that cannot be explained away by something else having caused the effect. There must be a logical sequence of events and phenomena that reveals differences due to causal networks.

Correlation is not a criterion for cause and effect, although it can indicate relationship. In other words, we must be able to bypass obvious causal relationships to get at solutions to problems. Criminal intent appears to be a necessary cause of crime, but why is it that most people do not commit crimes? Rehabilitation pro-

[5] Lloyd E. Ohlin, *Selection for a Parole* (New York: Russell Sage Foundation, 1951).

[6] Vernon B. Fox, *Introduction to Criminology* (Englewood Cliffs, N.J.: Prentice-Hall, 1976), pp. 357–58.

[7] Marguerite Q. Warren, "Classification of Offenders as an Aid to Efficient Management and Effective Treatment," *Journal of Criminal Law, Criminology and Police Science*, 62, no. 2 (June 1971), 250.

grams are necessary and supplemental to the prison philosophy of corrections, yet no one has determined why most fail and few succeed. Certainly, we will not abandon them because of failure. We need to understand the reason for failure rather than take a step backward into the past of regressive sanctions. If we use logic to sort out the variables in the causal chain, we can then make decisions on the relationships that we discover.

Working with the computer, with its enormous speed, accuracy, and efficiency, can be an exciting and fascinating experience; but it can easily distract you from what you are setting out to do. It is entirely possible to devote too much time to printouts and not enough to just thinking about what is happening. Calculators and computers can only solve computations; only human imagination can locate or solve societal problems. After 20 years of computer game playing, 85 percent of all our research is still ineffective, primarily because of dependence on the computer instead of the human mind. The electronic brain is an aid to the human brain, not a replacement of it. Our machine technology has advanced far beyond our present cultural limits, and there is a great need to pause, reflect, and attempt to understand not only causes but the consequences of our actions. Research in the social sciences is a survival science. It depends upon researchers, not printouts.

SUMMARY

We have developed a program that we can use to examine data collected from survey research. First we can analyze the one-way frequency data and see exactly what we have in terms of statistical description. Then we can look at the graphs of the linear data (interval or ratio type), and we can set up correlation matrices. In order to confirm our reasoning, we can analyze the data in terms of a parametric and nonparametric correlation. The correlations, although they do not tell us cause and effect, do indicate if there are relationships that are worth further investigation, and do help us to predict phenomena. Thus, we go from frequency data to correlation data to higher levels of analysis such as chi-square and regression. Regression will enable us to predict the values of one variable, the dependent, based upon the values of the other, independent variable.

All the major work of calculation is performed by electronic brains, but we must know how the calculations are performed in order to understand the computer output. The correlation program will give us direction of relationship, positive or negative, strength of the relationship, and its level of significance. We must decipher the numbers into meaning and determine substantive significance from statistical significance. The strength of the relationship will indicate whether the variables can be used for prediction. Prediction, which is based upon the regression equation, is very similar to correlation, but should not be confused with it. Prediction implies causality; correlation does not.

One of the assumptions for correlation is that the data must be linear. The SCATTERGRAM program will plot the data to enable you to determine if correlation is feasible. In the scattergram correlation tells you how the scores cluster round the mean, but it does not tell you the impact of those scores (slope). Not all data are linear, and there are special equations to deal with curvilinear data.

Using a PPM matrix will help you get some idea of where the data go and how they are used. You should know this to check machine calculations. A calculator will help you with the harder, longer numbers.

Nonparametric data may be converted to quantitative, ordinal-type data, and we may use Spearman *r* and Kendall's tau. There are computer programs to handle these calculations. If you use them, make sure your data fit the assumptions for these programs.

When preparing your IBM deck for a combination of programs, make sure your cards are in order, are properly punched, and have the exact number of cases specified.

The printout on these four programs—FREQUENCIES, SCATTERGRAM, correlation, and nonparametric correlation, is fairly extensive. Examine it carefully; take out the tables you need and compare them. See if you can understand the regression prediction.

Frequencies and correlation enable us to look at variables and relationships. From this point, we may examine causality, the effect of the independent variable on the dependent variable.

EXERCISES

1. What is the "central theme of research"?
2. If one variable increases as the other decreases, they are said to vary__________, and the direction is ____________________. If they increase together or decrease together in value, they vary____________________, and the direction is ____________________.
3. Correlation does not indicate ____________________, but it does show the strength of the relationship so that the variables can be used for ______________.
4. What are the assumptions for correlation?
5. Distinguish between parametric correlation and nonparametric correlation. Name the methods and identify the symbols.
6. What type of data do you use with nonparametric correlation?
7. What are the disadvantages of nonparametric correlation?
8. Explain the PPM, write the equation, name the parts of the equation, and state how it is based on the concept of variance.
9. What is the effect of the size of the sample on correlation?

10. What is r^2 ? Show how it is derived, and explain the equation.
11. What is regression? How is it similar to correlation?
12. Draw a graph showing a positive correlation between alcoholism and accidents, a negative correlation between number of police per sector and crime reduction, and no correlation between race and crime.
13. Comment upon correlation and impact of one variable upon another. Graph a high negative impact and a low positive correlation with a low impact.
14. What is the difference between linear and nonlinear data?
15. Is significance of, say, 0.7 in a sample of 35 as important as a correlation of 0.25 in a sample of 250 (same variable) at 0.05?
16. Write the PPM (algebraic) and show how the parts fit into a matrix. How would you decide on the number of degrees of freedom?
17. Why use a scattergram? How would you use the program? What information is available on the printout? What precautions should you use?
18. From the text, run the program on juvenile arrests and convictions. Write a data analysis, $n = 50$. When you set the program up for the run (four programs), be precise.
19. Why put ARRESTS first in the third scattergram? Is this the dependent variable? independent variable? What are the criteria for making the decision? How would you enter the program for regression? Why?
20. What is meant by "ranking correlations"?
21. Which comes first, cause or effect? What is a causal chain? What are obvious solutions? Name some.
22. Comment on the advantages and disadvantages of correlation.
23. Using the data given below, compute the PPM, Spearman's rho, and, if you can, Kendall's tau. Compare the results. Use a 0.05 level of significance.

Number of drinks, avg. per year	300	350	400	450	500	550	600	650	700	750	800	850
Number of accidents per year	0	1	1	2	2	2	3	3	4	5	6	7

(a) Calculate manually, using matrices and a calculator.
(b) Program and compare your results.

24. When 30 officers took an examination for police promotion, 25 scored better than 90%. Correlation with five previous years averaged 0.2. What would be your conclusions? What if the correlation was 0.9? Is the sample of 30 large enough for your conclusions to be valid? What would you propose, and why? Could your findings be admissible?
25. Is there a relationship between homicide and aggravated assault? Compare the figures for the last twelve years, round them off if they are large, and compute. Does this kind of correlation prove anything?
26. From the data in exercise 23, predict the number of accidents for a driver who consumes an average of 1,000 drinks per year—a modest three per day (hypoth-

etical data). How many accidents would you predict for a four-a-day driver?

27. In studying the use of weapons in homicide, what would you look for?
28. Comment upon correlation, prediction, impact, slope, predictive outcomes, trends, longitudinal studies, expenditure.
29. What is meant by "looking beyond the obvious"?
30. Complete the following matrix:

Month	Number of burglaries x	Number of B&Es solved y	x^2	y^2	xy
Jan.	42	21	1764	441	882
Feb.	36	15			
Mar.	74	50			
Apr.	38	20			
May	56	46			
June	84	41			
July	74	40			
Aug.	88	36			
Sept.	75	56			
Oct.	66	40			
Nov.	48	44			
Dec.	44	34			

N = 12 for the twelve months in the year under analysis. Find the range, standard deviation of x, y, the means, PPM r, r^2. Comment on the best month, the worst month, the mode, the median. After doing the PPM, rank the data and perform Spearman's rho. If you can do it, try Kendall's tau. After you have done all this by manual calculation, set up a program for the computer. If you use SCATTERGRAM, predict the following year of solved crimes based upon a 10% increase in burglaries–i.e., Jan. = 46, Feb. = 40, Mar. = 81, and so on. For your SCATTERGRAM, use B&Es solved as the y variable. Thus, if your variable name was SOLVED, your card would read:

```
                    16
SCATTERGRAM         SOLVED WITH BURGLARY
```

You will need a calculator to aid you in the calculation. If you use a programmable calculator, try running this with the squares and square roots before you use an x_i, y_i program. Follow the format laid down in this chapter. Write up the data analysis, comment on the correlation and, if you do the regression, comment on that.

FOR FURTHER READING

Babbie, Earl R., *Survey Research Methods*. Belmont, Calif.: Wadsworth, 1973.

Bailey, Daniel E., *Probability and Statistics*. New York: John Wiley, 1971.

Blalock, Hubert M., Jr., *Social Statistics* (2nd ed.). New York: McGraw-Hill, 1972.

Ezekial, Mordecai, and Karl A. Fox, *Correlation and Regression Analysis* (3rd ed.). New York: John Wiley, 1959.

Johnson, Allan G., *Social Statistics without Tears*. New York: McGraw-Hill, 1977.

Kerlinger, Fred N., *Foundations of Behavioral Research* (2nd ed.). Chaps. 35, 36. New York: Holt, Rinehart & Winston, 1973.

——, **and E. Pedhazur,** *Multiple Regression in Behavioral Research*. New York: Holt, Rinehart & Winston, 1973.

Levin, Jack, *Elementary Statistics in Social Research*. New York: Harper & Row, 1973.

Nie, Norman H., et al., *SPSS Manual* (2nd ed.). New York: McGraw-Hill, 1975. Attach *Computer Update* for 1977.

Runyon, R. P., and A. Haber, *Fundamentals of Behavioral Statistics,* Reading, Mass.: Addison-Wesley, 1972.

Schutte, Jerald G., *Everything You Always Wanted to Know about Elementary Statistics*. Englewood Cliffs, N.J.: Prentice-Hall, 1977.

11

Chi-Square, Association, and the Causal Chain

Chi-square is easily one of the most useful statistical levels of analysis that we have for the social sciences. It handles nonparametric data, it can use parametric data that have been converted to discrete, and it will give an indication of causal effect. It does not explain causality, but it does indicate the nature and extent of the effect of one variable upon another. Most of our data are qualitative, and quite a lot of them are dichotomous. Thus, chi-square will aid us in the causal interpretation of those data.

There is one serious flaw in chi-square analysis. If the sample is increased, sooner or later a point is reached where the null hypothesis can be rejected. Of course, this assumes that there was some weak relationship in the first place. This will become more obvious as we begin to look at chi-square tables.

The chi-square analysis is based upon the assumption that the null hypothesis will be retained if the expected scores equal the observed scores. Should this happen, independence is assumed between the variables and the null is retained, as there is no relationship. In effect, we assume that we are dealing with two separate populations with separate means. The difference between the means has its own distribution and its own normal curve—in this case, the chi-square curve. We also assume that the two populations are identical, with equal means and equal variances; if there is a difference, then there is a relationship and the expected scores do not equal the observed scores.

The expected scores are calculated from the formula:

$$(\text{Row} \times \text{Column}) \div \text{Number in the sample}$$

Let us look at some expected scores:

H_0: There is no relationship between religious beliefs and the number of crimes committed.

Religion = I.V.; Crimes = D.V.

$$R: \chi^2 \geqslant 3.84, \ \alpha = 0.05, \ df = 1$$

In the sample in Table 11.1, N = 200, or 100 Catholics and 100 Protestants. The number of crimes was dichotomized down the mean, so that those above 5 were

Table 11.1. Relationship of Religion to Crime (1)

		Religion		
		Catholic	*Protestant*	
Crime	*High*	A 20	B 20	40 (Row total = R = 40)
	Low	C 80	D 80	160 (Row total = R = 160)
		100 (Column total = C = 100)	100 (C = 100)	200 (Total number of cases = N = 200)

high, and those below 5 were low. If we use the formula for the expected scores as above, and remember that these scores are observed or actual data scores, then we may compare the observed to the expected:

$$E = \frac{R \times C}{N}$$

$$E \text{ Cell A} = \frac{40 \times 100}{200} = 20$$

A simple calculation indicates that the expected scores for this hypothesis would actually equal the data we have already observed. Further, a look at the cross-products of the cells would indicate that they are equal too. You may also note that once you have obtained the score for cell A, it is a matter of simple arithmetic to get the rest (B = Row total – A; C = Column total – A; D = Row total – C). A quick check on the totals of the expected scores shows that they must conform to the observed totals in the margins.

The concept of the margin is extremely important. The totals in the margins, or *marginals*, as they are called, are even more important when we use percentages to standardize the scores for comparison. At the present time, we have observed that our calculated expected scores have indeed equaled the observed data. Thus, without any further calculations, we know from the theory that there is no relationship and independence exists in and between the two variables of religion and crimes. Apparently, by retaining the null hypothesis, we are saying that it really makes no difference what one's religious beliefs are as far as committing crimes is concerned. I would point out that in this case, no matter how much the sample was increased, the results would not change. There is no relationship, independence and spuriousness are assured, there is no effect of religion on crime, and one is quite coincidental or accidental to the other.

In a case like this, where the expected scores equal the observed, where the cross-products of A × D equal (or almost equal) B × C, there is no further need for calculation. The null hypothesis should be retained with the usual reservations. But, you may ask, what if the expected scores do not equal the observed data scores? Supposing that if we sampled Kali worshippers and Quakers, we found some other result, that religious beliefs did influence criminal intent, even though we still use the same null hypothesis. We would expect the results to be different, and it would be strange if they were not:

H_o: There is no relationship between religious beliefs and criminal acts.

$$R: \chi^2 \geqslant 3.84, \quad \alpha = 0.05, df = 1$$

Again in Table 11.2, N = 200, and we have been most fortunate in locating 100 members of the secret Kali cult, whose way to Nirvana depends upon the amount

Table 11.2. Relationship of Religion to Crime (2)

		Religion		
		Quaker	*Kali*	
Crime	*High*	A 20	B 95	115
	Low	C 80	D 5	85
		100	100	200

of blood they can spill. Unfortunately, five of them were novices who had not as yet spilt one drop. The expected scores may be calculated by the same formula:

$$E \text{ Cell A} = \frac{\overset{R}{115} \times \overset{C}{100}}{\underset{N}{200}} = 57 \text{ (to nearest whole number)}$$

The same numbers apply to cell B, but in order for the numbers to equal the total (115), Cell B = 58. We may now obtain cell C (100 – 57) = 43, and cell D (100 –58) = 42. Notice that C + D (expected values) = 85 Row total.

Table 11.3. Relationship of Religion to Crime (3)–Observed and Expected Scores

		Religion				
		Quaker		*Kali*		
		Observed	Expected	Observed	Expected	
Crime	*High*	20	57	95	58	115
	Low	80	43	5	42	85
		100	100	100	100	200

Now we may compare the expected values with the observed values. Looking at the *contingency table*, or 2 x 2, as this is called, we can see (Table 11.3) that there is a difference.

FORMULAS FOR CHI-SQUARE

This comparison in the table brings us to the formula for computing chi-square. There are three formulas, all easily calculated on a hand calculator with bracketing convention. The first is:

$$\chi^2 = \Sigma \frac{(O - E)^2}{E}$$

which leads to:

$$\chi^2 = \Sigma \frac{O^2}{E} - N$$

or, chi-square equals the sum of all the scores where O = the observed data score, E = the calculated expected score.

If we set this down in matrix form (Table 11.4), the whole problem becomes

Table 11.4. A Matrix for Calculating Chi-square

	Observed	**Expected**	$O - E$	$(O - E)^2$	$\frac{(O - E)^2}{E}$
Cell A	20	57	−37	1,369	24
Cell B	95	58	+37	1,369	23.6
Cell C	80	43	+37	1,369	31.8
Cell D	5	42	−37	1,369	32.6
Totals, Σ	200	200	0	Reject H_O $\chi^2 = 112$ $= \Sigma \frac{(O - E)^2}{E}$	

simplified. Note that the total observed equal the total expected scores, and that the total of $O - E$ always equals zero. The squaring of $O - E$ provides the numerator for division by the expected scores. The sum of the final column, $\Sigma (O - E)^2/E$, is equal to chi square (χ^2).

The second formula may be set down in matrix form also.[1] In this case, the chi-square value of 112 is far greater than the tabled value of 3.84 for an alpha level of significance at 0.05 and one degree of freedom. Degrees of freedom for chi-square are calculated by the formula df = (Rows − 1) (Columns − 1). Thus, in a 2 × 2 table, df = (2 − 1) (2 − 1) = 1; in a larger table—say, a 3 × 4—df = (3 − 1) (4 − 1) = 6. The level of significance may be set where appropriate, usually at 0.05.

Alternate Methods of Checking Calculations

An alternate method of using chi-square may be used for 2 × 2 tables. The cells are lettered ABCD for reference, and we may thus view the contingency table as in Figure 11-1. The formula then becomes:

$$\chi^2 = \frac{n\,[(\mathrm{AD} - \mathrm{BC}) - n/2]^2}{(\mathrm{A} + \mathrm{B})\,(\mathrm{C} + \mathrm{D})\,(\mathrm{A} + \mathrm{C})\,(\mathrm{B} + \mathrm{D})} \qquad \text{(Yates Correction for } 2 \times 2 \text{ table)}$$

Using our data from religion and crime in Figure 11-2 and substituting:

$$\chi^2 = \frac{200\,[(100 - 7600) - 100]^2}{115 \times 85 \times 100 \times 100} = 112$$

In calculating the result of the cross products, AD − BC, it really does not matter which number comes first. The larger of the two may be put first to simplify the outcome; in this case, 7,400 to be squared and multiplied by 200. The chi-square result is as before; all we have done is use a different method. Notice that chi-square values are always positive.

A	B	A+B	
C	D	C+D	
A+C	C+D	*N*	(*N* = Sample size)

Fig. 11-1 The Chi-square 2 × 2 contingency table

This method may be used directly on a calculator, and the only caution is to watch the brackets and the squaring of the results. All the necessary figures are already available in the marginals, with the exception of the cross-products.

[1] In the second formula, do not forget to subtract N from the sum of O^2/E. This formula is somewhat faster and only needs O, E, with O^2 and O^2/E in the matrix with totals.

ASSUMPTIONS FOR CHI-SQUARE

The direction of the relationship with qualitative or discrete data is not exactly the same as with continuous data. Your reading of direction depends upon what you are talking about. Therefore, if a statistic is used that indicates direction for discrete data, be very careful how you interpret. Often the interpretation can be changed by varying the labels on the cells, such as placing High and Low in reverse order, or by placing Kali before Quaker in the headings. *Chi-square indicates the significance of the relationship between the two variables used* (row and column). We may use discrete or higher-order data. However, for nonparametric data, the chi-square statistical test is probably the most important, and the most used.

Ordinarily, the assumptions for chi-square are these:

1. Two variables are used with nonparametric, discrete-type, usually dichotomous nominal data. (Higher-order data may be used.)
2. The samples are random, the characteristics are evenly distributed in the parent population with equal variances, and representation reflects stratification.
3. The null hypothesis is a statement of no relationship between the variables. If there is no relationship, independence exists and there is no association or connection between the variables.
4. The null hypothesis is rejected if the calculated value equals or is greater than the tabled value.
5. The χ^2 statistic is an approximation of the multinomial probability distribution.
6. Causality is indicated but is not explained.
7. Proportions developed from frequency data used (only frequency data are used) may be converted to percentages and compared.
8. The statistic is always positive; however, direction *may* be indicated by cross-products of the cells.

RESTRICTIONS FOR CHI-SQUARE

There are certain restrictions on the use of the chi-square statistic, in addition to those that have been indicated.

1. The sample size should be large because of the nature of the approximation to the multinomial probability distribution; at least 80% of the cells should be above 5. Less than 5 items per cell tends to cause error.
2. The sum of the expected frequencies must equal the sum of the observed frequencies. This must be true for totals in rows and columns. Also, row and column totals for both expected and observed frequencies must equal sample size, or N.
3. The degrees of freedom[2] are determined by the number of rows minus 1, times the number of columns minus 1, or df = $(R - 1)(C - 1)$.

[2] The value of chi-square also increases with table size, which governs the number of degrees of freedom. The same relationship requires a higher chi-square in a larger table.

4. In a 2 × 2 bivariate contingency table, the Yates Correction or continuity correction should be used. If *N* is less than 20, use Fisher's Exact Probability Test.
5. A one-tail test is appropriate for the chi-square statistic.
6. Smaller cell categories should be collapsed to give better cell readings above 5, as indicated in item 1.
7. In order to avoid extensive tabulation and small cell frequencies, continuous data or extensive ordinal data should be divided by means or levels into discrete nominal data. Tables larger than 5 × 5 (df = 16) begin to get unwieldy and lose meaning.
8. If the calculated value of χ^2 is equal to or greater than the tabled value for the appropriate level of significance and degrees of freedom, the null hypothesis is rejected. However, closeness to the tabled value may also indicate that further research is needed by increasing the sample size.
9. Frequencies in the tables may be presented as proportions or percentages. If they are, the totals must indicate the direction of the percentage.
10. Once percentages have been made, comparisons are made in the opposite direction. If the percentages are across, then comparisons are made down; if percentages are down, the comparisons are made across. In any case, the proper comparison is made by comparing percentage values of the dependent variable in or across subgroups of the independent variable.[3] Item 10 will be explained at length in the reading of tables.

STRENGTH OF ASSOCIATION FOR 2 × 2 TABLES

It has been mentioned already that the cross-products give us an idea of association. A very popular measure for 2 × 2 tables is Yule's *Q*, which uses this concept:

$$Q = \frac{(a \cdot d) - (b \cdot c)}{(a \cdot d) + (b \cdot c)} \quad \text{from} \quad \begin{array}{|c|c|} \hline a & b \\ \hline c & d \\ \hline \end{array} \quad a \cdot d = a \times b$$

Q scores from −1 to +1, and the closer to unity, the stronger the association, or the weaker the independence between the variables. *Q* is easily calculated and gives a very good estimate of strength; however, it can be used only with 2 × 2 tables. Pearson phi coefficient is also good for 2 × 2 tables:

$$\text{Phi} = \phi = \frac{(a \cdot d) - (b \cdot c)}{\sqrt{(a + b)(c + d)(a + c)(b + d)}}$$

The denominator is the square root of the product of the marginals. Phi squared explains the proportion of variation in the dependent variable explained by the

[3] Compared percentages that are equal or within 5 points indicate zero or insignificant relationship, or independence of variables.

independent variable (much like eta squared). *Q* scores are usually larger than phi scores; phi is usually more accurate.

Notice that the greater the difference between the cross-products–the greater the strength of the association–the larger the *Q* or phi coefficient. This also shows in proportions and in percentages. In fact, percentages also indicate the internal strength of the association. The contingency coefficient, *C*, may be used on larger tables; and for ordinal data, gamma is used. Keep in mind what type of data you are using and the size of your tables. Significance is only half the battle; knowing the strength of the relationship is the other half. Watch out for empty cells in your tables and in your calculations.

SAMPLE SIZE AND CHI-SQUARE

Let us assume that we are testing the null hypothesis that there is no difference between education levels in attitude toward the death penalty (reinstatement). We create a sample of 200. We then find the results as in Table 11.5.

$$\text{R: } \chi^2 \geqslant 3.84, \alpha = 0.05, \text{df} = 1$$

and the $\chi^2 = 3.38$, or below the tabled level of 3.84. It would appear that we would retain the null hypothesis, or at least fail to reject, since we could not reject the null in all honesty. Further testing would be indicated. However, when we consider

Table 11.5. Relationship of Education and Favoring the Death Penalty

		Education level		
		High School	*College*	
Favor death penalty	*Yes*	57	43	100
	No	43	57	100
		100	100	200

doubling the sample size to 400 and assume that the same numbers fall in the same categories–that is, 114 in cell A, 86 in cell B, 114 in cell C, and 86 in cell D–we find that something happens to the chi-square value. It now becomes 7.29, or twice the original value.

In these calculations, the continuity correction, or Yates Correction, has been used for tables where df = 1. This correction ($n/2$) is used in the second formula shown. When using the other formulas without the correction, the result is a little higher at 3.92, but the effect of doubling is much clearer, and a 400 sample size gives a χ^2 of 7.84. *If cell proportions remain the same, chi-square varies directly with sample size*; double the sample and you double chi-square.

Significance of the Test Statistic

You will have noticed that rejection of the null hypothesis depends upon whether the calculated value of chi-square equals or exceeds the tabled value. The tabled value depends upon the level of significance selected and the degrees of freedom. A very simple table, Table 11.6, will indicate this.

Table 11.6. Simple χ^2 Value Table

Degrees of Freedom	One-Tail Test, Level of Significance		
df = (*r* – 1) (*c* – 1)	0.1	0.05	0.01
1	2.71	3.84	6.63
2	4.61	5.99	9.21
3	6.25	7.81	11.3
4	7.78	9.49	13.3
5	9.24	11.1	15.1
6	10.6	12.6	16.8

The significance of increasing the sample was seen in the previous example. Small samples produce distortions; much more valid results are obtained with large samples that are representative as well as random. If the internal percentages indicate that further research is warranted, sample size should be increased, since further research may indicate that the original sample was not representative.

Care must be taken not to manipulate the sample size merely to obtain significance. Table size will also cause the statistic to vary. For example, collapsing a 3 x 4 (df = 6) to a 2 x 2 (df = 1) reduces χ^2 from 12.6 ($\alpha = 0.05$) to 3.84 ($\alpha = 0.05$) for the same relationship. The chi-square statistic will vary with (is a function of) sample size and degrees of freedom (table size); and it will change with the level of significance that is chosen.

Comments on Chi-Square Statistics

The chi-square statistic will give the significance of the relationship, the strength of the relationship, and on occasion the direction of the relationship. The partial relationships of each subcategory of the variables (or the contingency relationships) may be fully described in the bivariate table. In the table on gun control, support and nonsupport by each sex, and the statistical significance of the relationship in the rejection of the H_o, the direction indicates that as more females say yes, more males say no, and vice versa. The cross-products of the cells (AD – BC) indicate a strong relationship, and on the other hand, the cross-products of race and crime show equality and a chi-square of zero. It is worth looking at the cross-products to

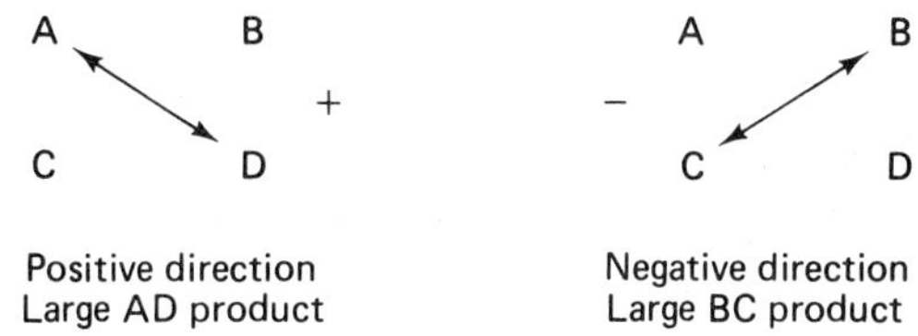

Fig. 11-2 Direction in contingency tables

gain information on strength and direction of association. A large AD product could indicate a strong positive association, and a large BC could indicate a strong negative association. Be cautious in your interpretation. The look at cross-products is more for a visual estimate than a final decision. You should be cautious about deciding direction from the sign, but generally, it is as in Figure 11-2. Small cross-products, near-equal products, or empty cells usually indicate insignificant or no relationship at all, as do compared percentages that are within 5 percent of each other. Large differences in compared percentages give indication of strength of internal association, but not necessarily a significant chi-square statistic.

RULES FOR THE CONSTRUCTION OF TABLES

Because chi-square contains so much vital statistical information, tables should meet certain standards:

1. Tables should have a proper heading.
2. The categories and content of the variable should be clearly presented. The independent variable and its categories are quite distinct from the dependent variable and its categories.
3. Usually the independent variable is on top and the dependent variable at the side. *The I.V. is always percentaged when known. Compare the D.V. percentages across the I.V. subgroups.*
4. The table should be drawn neatly and the labels appropriately set at proper intervals, indicating exactly what data are in what cell.
5. If percentages are used, they must be clearly explained by the base upon which they are computed; for example, in cell A, "80% (45)." The marginals must indicate the direction of the totaling, and all totals must meet the *N* requirement. For instance:

   64% = 192 (percentages are computed on marginal totals.)
   36% = 108
   ______
   100 (Percentage down [I.V.])
   (300) (Actual number is bracketed.)

6. In agreement with rule 2, all categories must be clearly explained in the text. This also means that any answers, omissions, or other data should be indicated in the text if they apply to the table under consideration.

7. The statistical statement of the null hypothesis is set at the foot of the table; e.g., R: $\chi^2 \geqslant 3.84, \alpha = 0.05$, df = 1.
8. The results and conclusion of the statistical analysis are set down showing the retention or rejection of the H_o.
9. The substance of the table is presented in the text. Comparisons of the I.V. subgroups in terms of the D.V. values must be entered. *All statements must be from the tables.*
10. Neatly enter any relevant computer data such as gamma, phi, etc.
11. In your text, comment factually upon statistical significance and substantive significance.

The writing of chi-square tables is an exercise in neatness, logic, and parsimony. All the data should be there to enable a reader to grasp fully what has been attempted in the research. In the sample table, you will see how many statements may be made.

SAMPLE TABLE FOR CHI-SQUARE

Gun Control—Support by Sex (N = 1,000)

		Sex		
		Male	*Female*	
Support	*Yes*	40 (200)	80 (400)	60 (600)
	No	60 (300)	20 (100)	40 (400)
		100 (500)	100 (500)	100 (1,000)

R: $\chi^2 \geqslant 3.84, \alpha = 0.05$, df = 1.
$\chi^2 = 165$ Reject the H_o.

Statements on the bivariate 2 × 2 contingency table above:

1. 200 males supported gun control (Cell A)
2. 300 males did not support gun control (Cell C)
3. 400 females supported gun control (Cell B)
4. 100 females did not support gun control (Cell D)
5. 200 males and 400 females support gun control (Cells A and B)
6. 300 males and 100 females do not support gun control (Cells C and D)
7. The sample contains 500 males and 500 females. Sample = 1,000.
8. 600 support gun control, 400 do not.

Statements 1–4 are made from the cells; statements 5 and 6 are made inside the table; statements 7 and 8 are made from the marginals. Statements 9 and 10 are comparative:

9. More males do not support gun control. (300:200)
10. More females do support gun control. (400:100)

Summary by *percentage comparison* (the D.V. compared across the I.V.):

11. Twice as many females as males favor gun control (80% to 40%).
12. Males are three times as likely not to support gun control as females (60% to 20%).
13. Generally, people (male *and* female) do favor gun control 60% to 40%, the female vote weighing heavily in the total.

Statements 11 and 12 are made from internal comparison across the independent variable. Statement 13 is made from the marginal percentage. The I.V. column is percentaged, whenever it is known. The D.V. is compared across the I.V.

14. The null hypothesis, there is no difference between sex and attitudes toward gun control, is rejected at the 0.05 level of significance with one degree of freedom, as the calculated value of 165 exceeds the tabled value of 3.84.

Table 11.7. Relationship of Race to Crime

		Race		
		Black	*White*	
Crime	*Low* 0–5	33 (47)	33 (20)	33 (67)
	High 6–10	67 (94)	67 (40)	67 (134)
		100 (141)	100 (60)	100 (201)

If we examine Table 11.7 which shows the relationship of race to crime, the chi-square table indicates a sample size of $N = 201$. In spite of the figures that show that blacks have over twice as many in the high crime range of 6–10 crimes per person, or 94 to 40 in absolute numbers, the comparison of percentages reveals no relationship, as they are the same.[4] Blacks equal whites in both high crime and low crime; 67 percent for each in the high crime range and 33 percent for each in the low crime range. The marginals support these data. Numerically, it would appear that twice as many blacks as whites are involved in high crime, but 141 blacks and 60 whites were sampled, and the chi-square statistic shows that in fact crime occurs equally in terms of race, and the null hypothesis is retained.

The Collapsing of Cells with Small Frequencies

Large chi-square tables often run into the problem of insufficient items or frequency data to fill the number of cells used. At least 80 percent of the cells must be above 5. *When the observed score–the cell total–is zero, there is no relationship existent for*

[4] If compared percentages are the same or within five points of each other, the relationship is zero or insignificant.

that cell, but the calculation will give a reading to be included in the total for chi-square.

The 4 x 4 table in Table 11.8 was based on a sample of 100, responding to, "The police in this community are doing a good job." The null hypothesis was that there was no difference in racial attitudes to police performance. The sample was composed of 26 black males, 22 black females, 22 white males, and 30 white females,

Table 11.8. Relationship of Race to Police Performance

	Race				
	Black		*White*		
Police Performance	Male	Female	Male	Female	
Strongly disagree	0	8	0	15	23
Disagree	12	8	0	5	25
Agree	0	0	12	10	22
Strongly agree	14	6	10	0	30
	26	22	22	30	100

which would indicate reasonable sampling. But here, it seems that a sample of 100 was simply not sufficient to generate a proper bivariate analysis, since six cells are empty, one is 5, one 6, and two are 8; in other words, 37 percent are empty and 62 percent are under 10.

From this table, we would reject the null hypothesis if we failed to examine the printout of the actual tabled values for each cell.

$$R: \chi^2 \geqslant 16.9, \alpha = 0.05, df = 9$$

$\chi^2 = 75.8$ *Reject the H_o* (based on calculations).

But see what happens when, using the same hypothesis, we collapse the cells. We will dichotomize by race, ignoring sex, and put "strongly agree" with "agree" and "strongly disagree" with "disagree"; the results are as in Table 11.9. Observe that all cells are valid.

From Table 11.9.:

$$R: \chi^2 \geqslant 3.84, \alpha = 0.05, df = 1$$

$\chi^2 = 3.19$ *Fail to reject the H_o.*

Table 11.9. Collapsing of Cells from Table 11.8

		Race		
		Black	*White*	
Police Performance	*Low*	28	20	48
	High	20	32	52
		48	52	100

The collapsing of the cells reveals that there is no difference between racial attitudes and police performance. We are too close to retain the null, but we cannot reject it. The internal percentages show that whites rate police performance higher than blacks do, by 62 to 42 percent, and further research is indicated.

There is another way of collapsing these cells by looking at sexual differences (male and female response) as distinct from racial response, as in Table 11.10.

Table 11.10. Police Performance by Sex

		Sex		
		Male	*Female*	
Police Performance	*Low*	12	36	48
	High	36	16	52
		48	52	100

Here, the null hypothesis is, "There is no difference in sexual attitudes toward police performance." We have collected all the male scores, black and white, for "strongly disagree" and "disagree" (Low) and for "strongly agree" and "agree" (High), and done the same for female responses. The computed value shows:

$$\text{R: } \chi^2 \geqslant 3.84, \alpha = 0.05, \text{ df} = 1$$

$$\chi^2 = 17.8 \qquad \textit{Reject the } H_o.$$

Men rate the police higher than women do by more than 2 to 1, or 75 to 30 percent. A relationship has been observed that was not in the original hypothesis.

Empty cells warn us that the chi-square statistic is distorted and is wrong. Reading the chi-square calculated value can be exciting—there seems to be such a strong relationship—but the simple fact is that *there may not be any association at all.* Collapsing the cells can be profitable in avoiding error and in detecting other relationships that may exist. The computer will print the error without ever letting you know. You must check the cells yourself.

Warnings on Computer Printouts

Computers are not magic; they do not necessarily give you what you expect. They are not Delphic oracles, Roman sybils, or science-fiction creations that talk back. They do only the work you give them, but they do it faithfully, speedily, and accurately according to your specifications. However, in the social sciences, because we deal with many variables and are constantly on guard for error, our greatest asset, the computer, is also our greatest liability. We must not accept calculations without examination of the printouts to see what has been done.

Remember, *all our calculations are based upon theoretical mathematical or statistical models.* Those models are often inaccurate, but if you feed data into the computer, it will execute the program you desire—in this case, cross-tabulations for chi-square computation—and the results can be ridiculous if certain format restrictions are not obeyed. A large sample does not necessarily mean that you may have an unlimited number of cells in your cross-tabs, or a 10 × 10 with only 100 cases in your sample.

A simple arithmetic calculation will determine the practicality of your table size. *Assume a minimum of ten cases per cell*, and add ten for every four cells; or alternatively, count 50 for every four cells. A 2 × 2 should be 50 cases; a 4 × 4 should be (16 × 10) + 40 = 200; a 5 × 5 is a minimum of N = 300. You cannot obtain valid results from empty cells, small cells, or small samples using discrete data.

We have seen how the computer will give a high chi-square value for empty cells, and from that value a wrong decision may be made. *The usefulness of the cross-tabulation printout is brought out when you look at the count in the cells for any relationships you may have assumed or have missed.* The computer will do its work. If you recall, the same thing happens in correlation, where the computer will average scores regardless of how they fall in the scattergram. Thus, a correlation may indicate a completely false picture of a linear result from nonlinear data; so it is advisable to inspect the scattergram to determine computer credibility.

These are simple computer programs. As programs become more complex, error may be cumulative, in which case the entire printout may be numerical garbage. For example, a matrix of correlations that has been computed on assumed linear data will be useless for any further work, but all too often such matrices have been used as a base for complex analysis. *The danger is in failing to examine the printout, accepting it as gospel truth.*

I find it expedient to have in my mind an estimate of what *should* happen. I also check computer calculations on a hand calculator. Estimates eliminate wild calculations and also alert you to error. Computers are assets, but they do *your* work. *You have the ultimate responsibility, and all error is your own.* Computers calculate; only you can reason.

CROSS-TABULATIONS

The SPSS program has an excellent program called CROSSTABS. There are various ways of setting this task definition into action. The program will print the tables for chi-square bivariate contingency analysis; it calculates chi-square values; it gives the level of significance, degrees of freedom, Cramer's V, the contingency coefficient, lambda, Kendall's tau b and c, gamma, Somer's D, and eta. It also gives Pearson r. Of all of these statistics, chi-square, C, and gamma are the most used.[5] For getting the most out of the program, the data must be input properly. Discrete data in limited categories work fine. Continuous data should be dichotomized along the mean or along appropriate divisions of rank order (high, medium, low). The sub-

[5] C is used for nominal data, gamma for ordinal data to determine strength of the association.

program used for this is RECODE, which puts data in the divisions you set. Let us assume that we will use CROSSTABS for the data used on arrests and convictions ($N = 50$) in the preceding chapter.

First of all, we need to look at the *FREQUENCIES* printout to decide where to make our divisions of the continuous data used in the categories ARRESTS and CONVICT. Second, we note that the mean for ARRESTS is 10.7. We decide that 11 is the mean. Looking at the cumulative frequency, we note that 66 percent were 11 or under and 34 percent were above 11—converting to numbers, 33 and 17 respectively. Third, we may now decide to make 1, or Low, stand for 2 through 11, and 2, or High, stand for 12 through 36. We have dichotomized along the mean.

Fourth, now that we have set limits for recording continuous data to discrete data, we may write a RECODE card and also a new VALUE LABELS card to correspond with the new entry. We repeat these steps for CONVICT, noticing that the mean is 5, and that 24 are 5 or under, and 26 are over 5. Therefore, 1 through 5 = 1 (Low), and 6 through 9 = 2 (High). These values may be entered on the RECODE and VALUE LABELS cards. Fifth, we are in a position to construct our own chi-square, Table 11.11.

Table 11.11. Convictions by Arrests

		Arrests		
		Low	*High*	
Convict	*Low*			24
	High			26
		33	17	50

R: $\chi^2 \geqslant 3.84, \alpha = .05, \text{df} = 1$

This process is useful for small amounts of data, such as $N = 50$. Notice that the smallest expected score will fall in cell B ($17 \times 24/50 = 8$). This means that the lowest number of scores is of those in the range of *over twelve* arrests with *under five* convictions, and all we need do is quickly check the 50 cases for these. We are lucky; there is just one, and that is all we need. From that single case we can calculate the entire chi-square table: Cell A = 23, cell C = 10, cell D = 16. Using the Yates Correction formula, $\chi^2 = 15.8$. We reject the null hypothesis before the computer even sees the data. (This takes about five minutes with a good calculator; actual calculations take only seconds.)

Percentages

In this case, we solved a most interesting problem very quickly by being alert to what can be done before the data need to be entered. However, with large samples, the procedure is the same, and we shall complete the rest of the exercise on the computer—which shows how you can work with the computer instead of letting the computer do it all. You must be alert for shortcuts and time-saving procedures, and often human intervention is faster and more accurate.

The computer will also print out the percentages within the cells for comparison both ways (be careful to note where the totals are summed). Usually, the very top row of numbers in the cell is the actual cell frequency; the second row is the percentage that is totaled across and must be compared down; the third row is the percentage that is totaled down and compared across;[6] the last or fourth row is the percentage of the sample size. Thus, if the fourth row was 10, you would know that this was 10 percent of the sample size, and if $N = 50$, the cell size would be 5, and 5 would be on the first row of the cell numbers. Therefore, looking in a cell where $N = 50$:

8 Actual frequency
45.6 Percentage totaled across, to 100%
11.1 Percentage totaled down; compare across
16.0 Percentage of sample size ($N = 50$), agrees with row 1.

Percentages are easily calculated:

$$\% = \frac{\text{Actual number}}{\text{Appropriate total}} \times 100$$

Percentage for row 4:

$$\frac{\text{Row 1}}{N} \times 100 = \frac{8}{50} \times 100 = 16\%$$

Examine the internal percentages carefully and compare in the proper direction, *across categories of the I. V.*

SETTING UP THE COMPUTER IBM DECK

Check back to your practice deck. You will notice that RECODE goes immediately after the INPUT FORMAT card. For this run, the cards should read:

```
         16
RECODE   ARRESTS (2 THRU 11=1) (12 THRU 36=2)/
         CONVICT (1 THRU 5=1) (6 THRU 9=2)
```

This may all be entered on one card. A new VALUE LABELS card is needed:

```
                     16
VALUE LABELS         ARRESTS, CONVICT (1)LOW (2)HIGH
```

[6] Row 3 is the most important if the table is set up with the I.V. at the top.

This card may go in front of the other VALUE LABELS cards. We now have two new cards converting continuous data into discrete data and avoiding literally scores of empty cells. If we try to spread 50 cases over a table 19 x 9 (171 cells), we can see immediately that not 20 percent but 80 percent will be empty. For a square this big, we really need a sample of at least 2,000 cases. And even then, the printout is unwieldy and becomes somewhat redundant.

The actual task definition is set up:

```
                16
CROSSTABS       TABLES=CONVICT BY AGE TO ARRESTS/
                ARRESTS BY AGE TO RELIG
STATISTICS      ALL
```

This may also be entered on one card. Note the use of keyword conventions such as THRU on RECODE and BY on CROSSTABS. The STATISTICS card must follow the task definition card. Another convention, as in SCATTERGRAM and REGRESSION, is that the y variable, the dependent variable, is entered first and is on the side, and the x or independent variable is then entered and is printed across. Thus, CONVICT will be on the side and AGE TO ARRESTS on top going across. See Table 11.13. The actual deck is set up in Table 11.12.

You have now had access to the computer for several programs: FREQUENCIES, SCATTERGRAM, PEARSON CORR, NONPAR CORR, RECODE, and CROSS-

Table 11.12. Deck for CROSSTABS Run

```
                    16
//BSCLASS5                    (JOB CARD)        [as before]
// EXEC SPSS                  (PROGRAM CARD)
PAGESIZE            80
RUN NAME            CROSSTABS
FILE NAME           RECODE
VARIABLE LIST       CLIENT, . . .               [as before]
INPUT MEDIUM        CARD
N OF CASES          50
INPUT FORMAT        FIXED (3X, 2F2.0, 3F1.0, F2.0, F1.0)
RECODE              ARRESTS (2 THRU 11=1) (12 THRU 36=2)/CONVICT . . . etc.
VAR LABELS          RELIG RELIGION [as before]
VALUE LABELS        RACE (1)WHITE (2)BLACK [as before]
                    ARRESTS, CONVICT (1)LOW (2)HIGH
CROSSTABS           TABLES=CONVICT BY AGE TO ARRESTS/ARRESTS BY . . .
STATISTICS          ALL
READ INPUT DATA

Data deck of 50 cards

FINISH
/*
```

Notice that this deck is abbreviated; the actual cards have already been written in the text—for example, RECODE and CROSSTABS. This run is quick, and ten seconds (0000,10) is ample. The several tables that are output can be examined carefully.

TABS. These are all basic subprograms and do a vast amount of work for you. Learn them well. Most research analysis begins this way, by way of exploration and looking at what is actually there. Develop several basic decks and keep check on changes made at the computer center. Be very careful with conventions and format. Watch your spelling, entries, and spaces on your program cards. Read the SPSS manual and get familiar with the nature of programming in the social sciences. Always keep in mind the assumptions under which your data are restricted.

STATEMENTS FROM THE PRINTOUT FOR CHI-SQUARE

Table 11.13. The Relationship of Juvenile Arrests to Convictions

		Arrests: *Low*	Arrests: *High*	
Convictions	*Low*	23 70%	1 6%	24 48%
	High	10 30%	16 94%	26 52%
		33 100%	17 100%	50 = 100%

$$R: \chi^2 \geqslant 3.84, \ \alpha = 0.05, \ df = 1$$

Computed $\chi^2 = 15.8$ *Reject the* H_o.

Inside the table:

1. Twenty-three juveniles with a low number of arrests also have a low rate of conviction. Only one has a low number of convictions with a high number of arrests.
2. Sixteen juveniles with a high arrest rate also have a high number of convictions. Ten with a low arrest rate have a high number of convictions.

Outside the table, in the marginals:

1. In this sample of 50, there were 33 juveniles with low arrests, 17 with high arrests; 24 with low convictions and 26 with high convictions.
2. Of the 50, 52% had a high number of convictions.

By percentage comparison across the independent variable:

1. In respect to a low number of convictions, those with a low number of arrests are twelve times more likely to appear in this category (70% to 6%). (Caution: Cell B has only one case.)
2. In the category of a high number of convictions, those with a high arrest rate are three times more likely to appear (94% to 30%).

3. We reject the H_0. There *is* a relationship between the number of arrests and the number of convictions. It would appear that those with few arrests have few convictions and those with many arrests have a high rate of conviction.

The Use of Accessory Data Included in the Tables

Several different statistics are given along with the chi-square statistic, most of which are not used in the early forms of analysis. Because sample size is usually above 25, Fisher's Exact Probability Test is seldom used, but it does appear when the sample size is small. It is fairly simple to use but is complex to describe and needs special tables.

Table 11.14. Chi-Square Statistics

Chi-square χ^2	Used for determination of association of nominal-level or higher-order variables. Will give strength, significance, and direction. Comparisons may be made inside the cells of the frequency table.
Cramer's V *V*	A coefficient based upon chi-square to measure relationship; the closer to 1, the more perfect the relationship.
Contingency coefficient $C = \sqrt{\dfrac{\chi^2}{N + \chi^2}}$	A correlation coefficient for use with nominal data for tables larger than 2 × 2. Phi may be used for 2 × 2 tables. The size of *C* is 0.7 for a 2 × 2, 0.8 for a 3 × 3, 0.87 for a 4 × 4. It requires large *N*.
Lambda λ (asymmetric and symmetric)	Measures association; is used for proportional reduction of error in nominal-level variables and is based on the prediction of categories of one variable when the other is known.
Uncertainty coefficient (asymmetric and symmetric)	Asymmetric is where the row variable is the D.V.; symmetric is where either may be the D.V.
Kendall's tau *b, c* τ_b τ_c	Equals phi in a 2 × 2 and is used for nominal data.
Gamma γ	A correlation for grouped data. Used with ordinal scale variables. Gives the strength of internal association. Used on 2 × 3 or larger.
Somer's D *D* (asymmetric and symmetric)	Used on ordinal data.
Eta	Used for interval or ratio dependent variable with a nominal-type independent variable. Measures dissimilarity of means.
Eta^2	Correlation ratio, or the proportion of variance in the D.V. explained by the I.V.
Pearson *r*	Correlation coefficient based upon PPM. (Used with caution on qualitative data.)
Pearson phi, ϕ	Measure of association, useful for 2 × 2.

These statistics are listed in Table 11.14. Most are not applicable to the 2 x 2 table, and the one that is—*C*, the contingency coefficient—is limited to a maximum reading of 0.707 for a 2 x 2. Usually, the closer the statistics are to 1, the stronger the association. Gamma is usually a little lower, eta a little higher. The most important reading is the chi-square statistic with its significance level. Should there be a curious disagreement in the statistics, look into the cells to see what is happening.

Again, the statistics on the bottom of the contingency table are not nearly as important as the relationships in the cells themselves that are indicated by percentages. If you have set your table up properly, with the I.V. on the top, you may compare percentages of the D.V. across the I.V. in the third row. This row is totaled down to 100 percent, and compared across. *The partial relationships in the tables are really the basis for the final decision; they indicate the substance of what the research is about.*

USING A CALCULATOR FOR CHI-SQUARE

When collapsing a large number of cells, or even doing a simple problem, it is often faster to use a calculator. Here is an example solved by using a calculator with memory and parentheses:

		Crimes		
		Low	*High*	
Number of accidents	*Low*	20	10	30
	High	6	16	22
		26	26	52

$n = 52$

Formula:

$$\chi^2 = \frac{n((AD - BC) - n/2)^2}{(A + B)(C + D)(A + C)(B + D)}$$

This may be keyed into the calculator:

(,20,x ,16,),–,(,10,x ,6,),=,–,(,52,÷,2,),=,x^2 ,x ,52,=,÷,26,÷,26,÷,30,÷,22,=[6.38]

Or: bracket, 20, multiply, 16, bracket, minus, bracket, 10, multiply, 6, bracket, equals, minus, bracket, 52, divide, 2, bracket, equals, square, multiply, 52, equals, divide, 26, divide, 26, divide, 30, divide, 22, equals (answer, 6.38).

This may be speeded up by entering totals rather than multiply/divide by easy numbers: 320, minus, 60, minus, 26, equals, square (times itself), multiply, 52, equals, divide, 26, divide, 26, divide, 30, divide, 22, equals (6.38).

Some calculators use a function key for squaring, some do not. Assuming your calculator does not use a function key, the steps are as in Table 11.15.

Once you are familiar with the calculation, you will speed up and enter certain obvious figures without going through each calculation. This process is detailed because it may set the stage for a program. You would have to enter labels or names for each part, but once this is done, all you would have to do is run the data in—the cell frequencies and the marginals; all the rest would be done for you, as the calculator would have "learned" your operating procedure or program. In fact, even the marginals could be omitted on a program; you could designate A + B, and so on. All you would need then are the totals for A, B, C, and D.

There is nothing complex about programming. It is the way in which you detail the steps of your calculation. These 32 steps will take you through any large

Table 11.15.

Step	Press key	Display shows
1	((open bracket)	0
2	20 (cell A)	20
3	× (times)	20
4	16 (cell D)	16
5	) (close bracket)	320
6	– (minus)	320
7	(	320
8	10 (cell B)	10
9	× (times)	10
10	6 (cell C)	6
11	)	60
12	= (equals)	260
13	– (minus)	260
14	(	260
15	52 (*n*)	52
16	÷ (divide)	52
17	2	2
18	)	26
19	= (equals)	234
20	x^2 (square)	54756
21	× (times)	54756
22	52 (*n*)	52
23	=	2847312
24	÷ (divide)	2847312
25	26 (marginals, A + C)	26
26	÷	109512
27	26 (B + D)	26
28	÷	4212
29	30 (A + B)	30
30	÷	140.4
31	22 (C + D)	22
32	÷ or =	6.38

(Answer) = χ^2

number for a 2 x 2 table without any calculation. The calculator does all the work for you. This calculation is much faster than punching cards or even using the terminal; it takes very little time, less than a minute. The same is true for correlation. Once you have worked out the steps, you can perform even the most difficult calculations very rapidly.

SUMMARY

In this chapter, we have looked at the usefulness of the chi-square statistic, its advantages when set out in contingency tables, so that we may compare the partial relationships of the variables. But this is only a beginning. Cross-tabulation is invaluable in sorting out causal relationships by controlling for variables in the causal chain. We move from bivariate analysis to multivariate analysis by extending the bivariate analysis that we use in chi-square to a *series* of bivariate analyses. We shall see this in effect in another chapter.

Chi-square is a building block of great importance in the research method. With the advent of the computer and the calculator, we can now complete complex analysis in a fraction of the time it used to take. But we must beware of meeting the restrictions placed upon us by statistical limitations. *We cannot take any form of statistical analysis for granted.*

Chi-square will give us the strength of the association, the causal relationship, the significance, and the direction, and it will even indicate unsuspected relationships. The clue to success is in the neatness of preparation of the tables and the clarity of presentation of the data. You should be able to *see* what is there. The more you use chi-square and the more you calculate different tables yourself, the more you will understand its versatility. Wherever possible, convert to nonparametric, discrete-type nominal-level data, and keep your tables within proportional size. Beware of empty cells.

There are three ways to calculate the chi-square statistic. In addition, the internal cell frequencies may be converted to percentages, thus giving standardized scores for comparison. The dependent variable is compared across categories of the percentaged independent variable, showing internal relationships. Totals in the margins are known as marginals; they are useful for the calculation of percentages. Cross-multiplication of cells will indicate if a relationship exists; if the products are equal or close to equal, the variables are independent and no relationship exists.

Although we may use continuous data, it is preferable to use discrete data, since numerous cells may result in faulty calculations. If the cells contain less than five cases, they should be collapsed. Small contingency tables give a rapid estimation of whether or not a relationship exists.

Large samples are preferred, but size should not be deliberately increased to give a desired result. Small samples or cell frequencies of 0 to 4 can produce distortion.

Tables should be constructed so that the I.V. is on top and the D.V. at the side.

The tables should show clearly what is being done. Statements from the tables are a summary of the percentages and comparison of those percentages.

Although direction may be taken from chi-square tables, care should be used in its interpretation. The chi-square statistic is a valuable tool. If you keep to the assumptions and restrictions for its use, it will prove an asset to your work in survey research.

EXERCISES

1. What are the assumptions for chi-square? the restrictions?
2. How would you define expected values? How would you calculate them? How many do you need to compute?
3. Three formulas are given for chi-square; write them. Indicate the Yates correction for continuity.
4. What are marginals? Can you make statements from the marginals?
5. Explain R: $\chi^2 \geqslant 3.84$, $\alpha = 0.05$, df = 1. Include as much information as you can. When would you reject or retain the H_o?
6. If you see that the result is different from your original hypothesis, would you change your hypothesis?
7. Assuming that proportions in the cells remain the same, what happens when you double the sample? triple the sample?
8. In a 4 × 4 table, you have five empty cells. What would you do? Explain why.
9. What are the rules for table writing?
10. Create a table based upon sex and criminal intent (Low, High). Now make 14 statements about that table.
11. What does "significance, strength, and direction of the relationship" mean? Indicate direction in a diagram. What caution should you exercise?
12. What happens when the computer prints out continuous data in a cross-tabulation on, say, a 10 × 10 table with $N = 100$?
13. Give a rule of thumb for cell size and sample size. Comment on table size.
14. Write computer RECODE and CROSSTABS cards for the data on arrests and convictions in the preceding chapter. Put the I.V. on top.
15. Complete the run and make at least ten statements on each cross-tab. Decide whether to reject or retain the H_o.
16. Why do you compare across the I.V. categories?
17. What is the contingency coefficient? gamma? eta^2? r?
18. Why is chi-square so important in social research?
19. What is a partial relationship? Give an example.

20. Significance is only part of the explanation; explain how you find the strength of the association.
21. Compute the marginals, percentages, and chi-square, given the following data:

		Sex	
		Male	*Female*
Crime	*Low*	45	80
	High	90	30

Make statements from the table; formulate an H_o and decide upon your findings.

22. For the table above, calculate the Yules *Q* and the Pearson phi, and compare.
23. You are given the following data:

		Drugs			
		1	*2*	*3*	*4*
Accidents	*1*	8	6	0	10
	2	0	3	3	6
	3	0	10	4	0
	4	6	0	5	4

$N = 65$

What would you do? Why? Finish the calculations.

24. Given cell A = 12, cell B = 48, cell C = 28, and cell D = 112, calculate the expected frequencies, percentages, and chi-square. What are the cross-tabulations?
25. Double the scores in exercise 24. What happens to χ^2? Now double the scores in exercise 21; what happens here?

FOR FURTHER READING

Blalock, Hubert M., *An Introduction to Social Research.* Englewood Cliffs, N.J.: Prentice-Hall, 1970.

——, *Social Statistics* (2nd ed.). New York: McGraw-Hill, 1972.

——, **and A. E. Blalock,** eds., *Methodology in Social Research.* New York: McGraw-Hill, 1968.

Bradley, James V., *Distribution-Free Statistical Tests.* Englewood Cliffs, N.J.: Prentice-Hall, 1968.

Bruning, James L., and B. L. Kintz, *Computational Handbook of Statistics* (2nd ed.). Glenview, Ill.: Scott, Foresman, 1977.

Cooley, W. W., and P. R. Lohnes, *Multivariate Data Analysis.* New York: John Wiley, 1971.

Coombs, C. H., *A Theory of Data.* New York: John Wiley, 1964.

Davis, J. A., *Elementary Survey Analysis.* Englewood Cliffs, N.J.: Prentice-Hall, 1971.

Diesing, P., *Patterns of Discovery in the Social Sciences.* Chicago: Aldine, 1971.

Downie, N. M., and R. W. Heath, *Basic Statistical Methods.* New York: Harper & Row, 1965.

Edwards, Allen, *Statistical Methods.* New York: Holt, Rinehart & Winston, 1967.

Galtung, J., *Theory and Methods of Social Research.* London: Allen & Unwin, 1967.

Hays, W. L., *Statistics for the Social Sciences* (2nd ed.). New York: Holt, Rinehart & Winston, 1973.

Horowitz, Leonard M., *Elements of Statistics for Psychology and Education.* New York: McGraw-Hill, 1974.

Keppel, G., *Design and Analysis: A Researcher's Handbook.* Englewood Cliffs, N.J.: Prentice-Hall, 1973.

Moser, C. A., and G. Kalton, *Survey Methods in Social Investigation* (2nd ed.). New York: Basic Books, 1972.

Robbins, H., and J. Van Ryzin, *Introduction to Statistics.* Chicago: Science Research Associates, 1975.

Rosenberg, Morris, *The Logic of Survey Analysis.* New York: Basic Books, 1968.

Siegal, Sidney, *Nonparametric Statistics for the Behavioral Sciences.* New York: McGraw-Hill, 1956.

Silverman, E. N., and L. A. Brody, *Statistics: A Common Sense Approach.* Boston: Prindle, Webber and Schmidt, 1973.

Stouffer, Samuel A., *Social Research to Test Ideas.* New York: Free Press, 1962.

Winer, B. J., *Statistical Principles in Experimental Design* (2nd ed.). New York: McGraw-Hill, 1971.

12

Using Two or More Samples in Theory and Practice

In the chapter on sampling, the phrase was used, "sampling to infinity." Of course, this is impossible to do; it is a theoretical construct designed to prove a mathematical point. In practice, we seldom use more than one sample, because of the restrictions of time and money. For the purposes of proving our results, we *assume* two samples or two populations. This assumption is vital to our statistical estimates.

But if we can take more than one sample, we are approximating our construct and moving closer to the truth. If we can triangulate and get three samples or more, and if they are large samples, we are rapidly reducing sample error and establishing our findings within a very narrow range (beyond 0.05). Depending upon the type of design, the data we use, and the level of our statistical analysis, we are extending our research beyond the superficial and into logical, pragmatic findings.

Moreover, by the use of multiple variables in multiple samples, the independent variables may be used as test or control variables to further ascertain the proof of what we are seeking. Similarity and dissimilarity of effects on the dependent variable in similar samples by the independent variable adds, or subtracts from, validity.

RELATIONSHIPS AND ASSOCIATIONS

After frequency data analysis, we looked at correlation and the possible relationships that could exist in our collected data. We then sorted out the variables that had possible association, possible cause-and-effect relationships, and tested them using a chi-square analysis. All the time we were doing this, we followed certain statistical assumptions concerning linear data and parametric or nonparametric data, and assumptions from sampling theory.

The real problem in analysis is not only in finding differences, statistical and substantive, but in detecting the causal links, rejecting spurious variables, and detecting trends and predictive consequences. If, after noting the links of cause and effect, we can say that if this variable is used then this result will follow, then we have indicated a possible solution to a problem. We can do this several ways using parametric and nonparametric data. In effect, we create a test situation, rather than a pure-chance investigation. We may examine the effects on a control group and an independent group; develop a pretest, posttest situation; use matched samples; use independent samples; compare samples from different populations; we may even use one sample for testing and assume two populations. This last point will become clearer as we go along.

THE DIFFERENCES OF MEANS

When we compare two samples, or the means of those samples, we are in effect looking at what happens in a before-and-after situation, a comparative situation, or a controlled situation where we are manipulating the independent variable. In all cases, we are looking at the effects on the dependent or criterion variable that are caused by the independent variable. We use certain assumptions, such as random sampling, normal distribution, equal variances, that the means of the two populations are equal; that when we are using parametric data, the dependent variable is at least of the interval type; that the data are linear. Nonparametric data may not require the assumption of normal distribution or be so strict on the matter of equal variances, but the equality of means of the two populations is assumed.

Again, the central limit theorem ensures the normality of distribution for large samples. Small samples always run the risk of error from lack of randomization, representation, and homoscedasticity (homogeneity of variance). The T-test* is a powerful, efficient test for parametric data, and the Mann Whitney U-test is most satisfactory for ordinal-type data. The chi-square test is really a special case of the T-test for nominal-type data. As stated before, the chi-square test may be used with discrete or continuous data. We know that the chi-square statistic is based upon the difference between the observed and the expected scores and that this statistic of differences has its own normal distribution. The same is true for differences between sample means.

Assumptions for Differences of the Means

Just as means have their own normal curve in the same way that raw scores have their curve, so too calculated statistics based upon differences of means also have

*Note: t is used interchangeably with T as the t statistic is computer printed as T.

their own distributions, which approximate the normal curve as sample size increases. Thus, the chi-square statistic has its curve, the T statistic has its curve, and any differences that we observe in the calculation of differences between population means may be compared with the distribution of the test statistic.

When we compare two samples, or categories of variables, we assume that the means of the two populations are equal. Let us look at a previous situation where we examined support for gun control in male and female populations.[1] In this case, the populations were equal—500 in each. However, this equality is not essential; it does make for better comparison, better statistics, but it is not as important as equal means in the two populations. Another point worth remembering is that whereas chi-square deals with average squared variances, owing to the nature of frequency data, continuous data such as are used in the t statistic more nearly approximate the binomial probability distribution. However, in large samples, both statistics share the advantages of the central limit theorem.

If we assume that there are two hypothetical populations, one male and one female, our hypothesis (H_o) would be that if $\mu_1 = \mu_2$, then we retain the null hypothesis, and if $\mu_1 \neq \mu_2$, then we reject the null. In the first case, if the means are equal or nearly equal, then independence applies and there is really no effect on the dependent variable by the independent variable—in this case, sex has no effect upon attitude toward gun control. Our research hypothesis (H_a) says this is not so, sex does affect one's attitude toward gun control. Thus, we have created two hypothetical populations; within those populations, we have assumed equal means, equal variances, and normal distribution. This may be seen in Figure 12-1.[2]

In this diagram, both sample means, $\bar{x}_1$ and $\bar{x}_2$, coincide with μ_1 and μ_2, and $\mu_1 = \mu_2$. The two means are equal, and independence is shown in both; males and

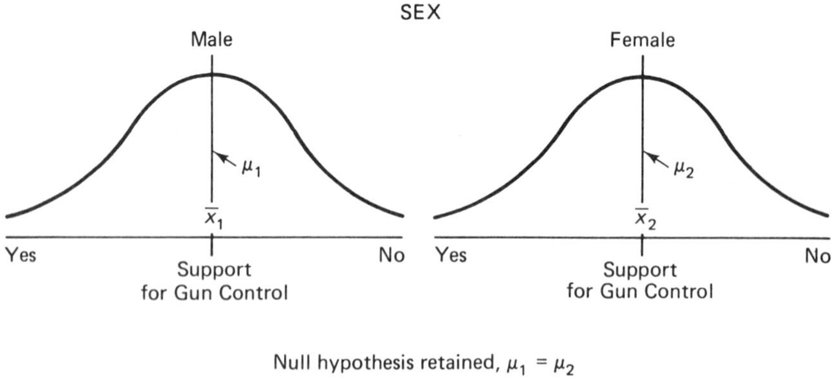

Fig. 12-1 Independent hypothetical populations

[1] See "Sample Table for Chi-Square," in Chapter 11.

[2] In the chi-square statistic, there is a sampling distribution of differences of the means for every cell in the number of the degrees of freedom. We have a difference between the observed mean (from actual data) and the hypothetical expected mean for every cell. These differences form the chi-square distribution, based upon the correct degrees of freedom.

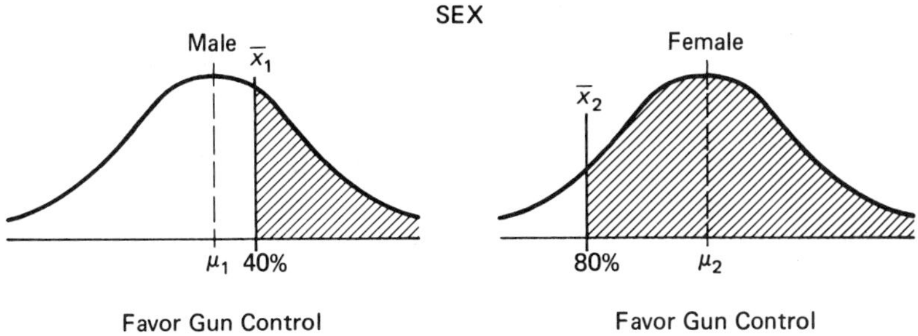

(In the hypothetical populations, $\mu_1 = \mu_2$.)

Fig. 12-2 Differences in means in two hypothetical populations

females are equally concerned about gun control, and there is no difference, no effect upon the dependent variable by the independent.

The actual results were different: Data indicated that 40 percent of the males and 80 percent of the females supported gun control. Thus, when we look at the means of our two hypothetical populations, we see something like Figure 12-2. The means differ from the assumed population means and they differ from each other.

We can see this better if we actually superimpose the two distributions. In the case where we retain the null, they fit perfectly and there is no difference: $\bar{x}_1 = \bar{x}_2$; $\mu_1 = \mu_2$. In this case, they fit perfectly, but the sample means are in quite different places. It would appear that women favor gun control twice as much as men do. Sex has a definite effect upon one's attitude toward gun control, and we would reject the null because $\bar{x}_1 \neq \bar{x}_2$. The means are not equal. *This difference of the means ($\bar{x}_1 - \mu_1$; $\bar{x}_2 - \mu_2$) may be computed as a single statistic, and from infinite differences a distribution can be plotted that assumes the shape of the normal curve.*[3] We may then compare our calculated statistic to the tabled values developed

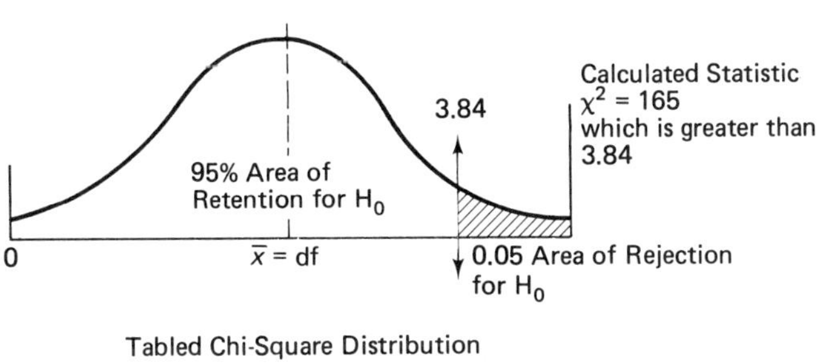

Fig. 12-3 Chi-square distribution of differences of means

While small values χ^2 do not resemble the normal distribution curve, larger values do.

[3] The chi-square distribution is $\chi^2 = (\Sigma \frac{X - \mu}{\sigma})^2 = \Sigma z^2$.

in the curve. Normally when we know the direction of our result, positive or negative, we use a one-tail test. If we use = or ≠, then we use a two-tail test. In this case, using chi-square, we use a one-tail test.

In comparing our test statistic to the tabled values, it would appear as in Figure 12-3. The calculated χ^2 is in fact the difference of the means $(\overline{x}, \mu)$, and when compared to the tabled distribution of the differences of the means, it falls in the area of rejection. The whole idea of testing differences depends upon the construction of statistical models and hypothetical models. We depend upon probabilities to arrive somewhere near the truth. It is worth noting that the family of curves for both chi-square and T-test are based upon the number of degrees of freedom. The area of rejection is based upon the level of significance chosen.

In summary: The differences of the means, based upon establishing two hypothetical populations, may be calculated as a single statistic. This statistic may be compared to a tabled value based upon a distribution of infinite differences. It should be noted that the two hypothetical populations are taken from the parent population.

Parametric and Nonparametric Data and Prediction

No matter what method of testing we use, or what data, the ultimate outcome of our testing should be prediction. With parametric data, we can not only set up a test situation, but also proceed from correlation to regression and thus prediction. Nonparametric data from test situations provide us with excellent results in terms of causal effects and correlations, but little to go on in terms of prediction; we can obtain that information only from examination of the partial relationships in the contingency table. In any test situation, especially one involving a treatment or test effect of the independent upon the dependent (criterion) variable, we need to ask and answer the following:

1. What effect did the treatment have on the experimental group?
2. Was it significantly different from the control group (or other sample)?
3. Can it be verified (replicated)?
4. Are the outcomes predictable?

If the situation is one of pretest, posttest, or two treatments at different intervals, we still need to know if the outcomes yield predictable results. Two-sample testing is somewhat limited, but it does provide an excellent setting for testing and calculating the effects of the test or treatment used. An examination of the statistics will indicate relationships, associations, and consequences. We then exercise cautious logic in making our predictions—*if* we have observed trends.

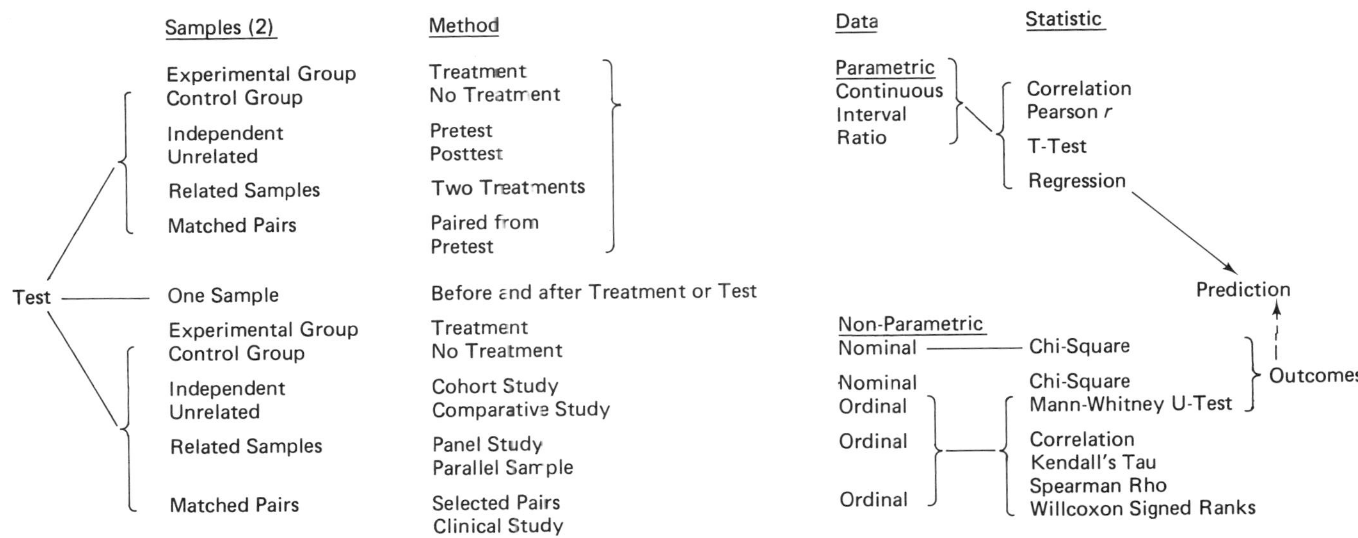

Fig. 12-4 Relationship of test procedures to prediction (two samples)

For the T-test, the dependent variable at least must be interval; for Chi-square and other non-parametric tests, continuous data may be dichotomized or ranked. If correlation exists, then it is a short step to detect causal association. From association we can then indicate trend, outcome, and prediction.

The T-Test

This single statistic is in fact a *sampling distribution of the differences of the means.* If there are no differences, there is in fact one population for both samples; if there is a difference, we establish two populations and measure that difference. However, *in reality* there is only one population from which the sample or samples have been drawn. Theory has enabled us to construct a statistic for measuring differences—a theoretical population for each category of the variable, or for each variable itself. From such theoretical reasoning it is easy to see that if there is a difference between the means, then the greater that difference, the more significant the impact of the independent variable upon the dependent variable.

So far we have talked about the difference of means from nonparametric data, the kind we are most likely to use. On occasion, we do use special situations where we can control the independent variable and use two groups. One of them is given a treatment or special test and is called the *experimental group*. The other is not given any special test or treatment and basically remains the same; this is called the *control group*. What we want to see is the effect of the treatment—if it works and if it causes any significant difference between the experimental group and the control group. Sometimes we match pairs from the pretest group; sometimes the samples are related, as in a panel study; sometimes they are independent samples and not related. In all cases, we test for differences between the groups. When we use scales or tests that give us interval-type data, we may use the T-test, an effective test that is great for exact measurement of differences when using only two samples. It has various applications. A sample of 100 is adequate; a sample of less than 30 is poor for a research situation, however the advantage of the t-test is that it is used for small samples, less than 30, and that it gives an approximation to the normal curve.

The formula for independent samples is:

$$t = \frac{\bar{x} - \bar{y}}{s_{e\bar{x} - \bar{y}}}$$

which is another way of saying that t equals the differences of the means divided by the standard error of those differences. Thus, we must first estimate the standard error of the means. The standard error may be calculated as the standard deviation divided by the square root of the sample size, or:

$$S_e = \frac{\sigma}{\sqrt{n}} = \sqrt{\frac{\sigma^2}{n}}$$

In this case, we are interested in the difference of the means of samples x and y, which may be calculated:

$$\sqrt{\frac{s^2 + s^2}{n_x + n_y}} = s_{e\bar{x}-\bar{y}}$$

where

$$s^2 = \frac{(n_x - 1)s_x{}^2 + (n_y - 1)s_y{}^2}{n_x + n_y - 2}$$

$$= \text{Pooled variance}$$

where

x = one sample
y = the other sample
n_x = one sample size
n_y = 2nd sample size

If the sample sizes are equal, a lot of time in calculation is saved, but this is not necessary for the test. The t statistic may be calculated:

$$t = \frac{\bar{x} - \bar{y}}{\sqrt{\frac{s^2}{n_x} + \frac{s^2}{n_y}}}$$

Example of the T-Test for Independent Samples

The algebra of this calculation is not difficult. The two standard errors or differences from the population mean are added to give the standard error of the difference. If the samples are equal or nearly equal and fairly large, the assumptions of normal distribution and equal variance are not so important. Let us look at a practical application of the T-test for two independent samples.

We have randomly selected two samples of inmates to check the reduction of stress as measured by blood pressure. One group is given exercise and favorable treatment, the other is simply continued on the same day-to-day schedule. The reduction of blood pressure in the first group would indicate a reduction of stress owing to favorable treatment. We take for this example ten in each group.

$$H_o = \mu_x = \mu_y; \; H_a = \mu_x \neq \mu_y$$
$$n_x = n_y = 10$$
$$df = n_x + n_y - 2 = 18$$

At the 0.05 level, one-tail test, df = 18, R: $t \geqslant 1.734$. The x group, like the y group, is measured, and the drop in blood pressure is recorded by a point scale:

x scores = 10, 10, 8, 8, 7, 6, 5, 4, 3, 2
y scores = 4, 4, 3, 3, 0, 0, 0, –2, –2, –4 (minus means rise in pressure)

$n_x = 10$, mean of x or $\overline{x} = 6.3$; variance, or $\sigma^2 = s^2 = 7.7$
$n_y = 10$, mean of y or $\overline{y} = 0.6$; variance, or $\sigma^2 = s^2 = 7.8$
Using formula: Difference of means = Computed $s^2 = 7.75$

Substituting in t formula: $t = \dfrac{5.7}{1.245} = 4.58$ (greater than tabled value)

Reject H_o. There is a significant difference in group x, showing a reduction in stress from favorable treatment.

The T-Test for Related Samples

Assume that in order to test the effects of legal background on criminal sentencing, we select inmates who had committed the same or similar crimes but had appeared in different courts for sentencing. It would be easy to ascertain the legal background of the judges, and they could be divided into two groups, those with expertise in criminal law and those who specialized in other matters. Assume also that we find ten pairs of inmates; ten is a very convenient number, although in practice, 30 or more pairs would be practical and give good results.

H_o = Group 1 (judges with criminal expertise) sentences = Group 2 sentences
H_a = Group 1 sentences $\neq$ Group 2 sentences
Two-tail test at $\alpha = 0.05$, df = 9, R: $t \leqslant -2.26$, $t \geqslant +2.26$

At first glance (Table 12.1), it looks as though the judges with noncriminal expertise are more lenient. Nevertheless, we shall use a formula for related samples for the t statistic.

For related samples:

Table 12.1.

Inmates matched for offenses	Criminal judges	Non-criminal judges	Difference	D^2
1	10 yrs.	5 yrs.	5	25
2	5	10	−5	25
3	5	1	4	16
4	10	10	0	0
5	7	5	2	4
6	7	5	2	4
7	5	3	2	4
8	6	2	4	16
9	2	1	1	1
10	10	5	5	25
$N = 10$	$\Sigma x = 67$ $\overline{x} = 6.7$ yrs.	$\Sigma y = 47$ $\overline{y} = 4.7$ yrs.	$\Sigma D = 20$	$\Sigma D^2 = 120$

$$t = \frac{\Sigma D}{\sqrt{\dfrac{n\Sigma D^2 - (\Sigma D)}{n-1}}}$$

From the matrix for the differences, we may substitute and find that:

$$t = \frac{20}{\sqrt{\dfrac{1200 - 400}{9}}} = \frac{20}{9.43} = 2.12$$

We are testing the difference between the two groups and are not sure which is best, so we use a two-tail test. With df = 9, at a level of $\alpha = 0.05$, we reject the H_0 when our calculated t is equal to or less than -2.26, or equal to or greater than $+2.26$ (R: $t \leqslant -2.26$, $t \geqslant +2.26$). In this case we *retain the H_o*, as our calculated value of 2.12 is within the area of retention. (Notice that we would reject the null if we had used a one-tail test, or a 0.1 level for a two-tail test.) The nature of rejection or retention depends upon the hypothesis statement (whether it is a one-tail or a two-tail test), and upon the level of significance chosen, together with the degrees of freedom. Do not forget that when using related samples or matched pairs, n equals the number of matched pairs.

Whereas we have found that there is no difference in sentencing based upon background in criminal law, the results do indicate further testing and most certainly a larger sample. The T-test is a powerful statistic, extremely useful in test situations. Notice that in the t statistic for related samples, we are using the standard error of the differences of the means where the means themselves are calculated from differences between sample scores.

All that is needed are the scores from two samples, or the results of two tests on the same sample. An interesting point is raised in the example given for the judges and their sentences. If we dichotomize the sentences along the means into high and low using the means of 6.7 and 4.7, we may construct a contingency table as in Figure 12-5. From cross-multiplication, cell A times cell D equals cell B times cell C. From the partials and the marginals, $\chi^2 = 0$. There is no relationship between a

		Judges' Background: Criminal Law	Judges' Background: Non-Criminal Law	
Sentences	Low	A 5	B 5	10
	High	C 5	D 5	10
		10	10	20

Fig. 12-5 Judges by sentences

judge's background and his or her sentences. We retain the H_o ($\alpha = 0.05$, df = 1, R: $\chi^2 \geqslant 3.84$).

This would appear to be the end of the matter, but there is still a nagging doubt and a suspicion that maybe judges who are not versed in criminal law will be easier. Looking at the table for the two samples of matched inmates, we can see that in seven cases out of ten, easier sentences were handed down by the non-criminal-law judges, on one occasion the same sentence was used, and only on two occasions did the judges exceed the sentences of criminal-law judges. Thus, one would appear to have a 70 percent chance of getting a better deal if one were faced with the prospect of imprisonment. In this case, the research hypothesis would have to be changed to reflect the theory that non-criminal-law judges are more lenient, indicating a one-tail test, in which case we would indeed reject the null and indicate which group was more lenient (we would be testing *more or less* rather than *not equal*). Thus, whereas there is no difference in *giving* the sentences based upon background, there is a difference based on *receiving* the sentence. The substance indicates it is more blessed to receive than give, if you have the right judge.

Small samples tend to play tricks, and this is a good example. Rather than philosophizing over the merits of the analysis, it is much better to obtain a larger sample and then test.

1. *Look at the means*—compare them.
2. *Look at the data* for each sample and its *distribution*.
3. *Compare the differences* and reflect on them; why do they occur the way they do?
4. *Examine the statistics* and return to the data; do they hold up? All statistics are based upon theoretical models.
5. *Would you be willing to stand alone on the logic of your conclusions?*

T-Tests and SPSS

The task definition or procedure card for T-test is quite simple. For tests between groups, the groups must first be defined, then the variables that are to be examined. A deck set up for the data on the number of arrests and the number of convictions may be as follows:

```
                    16
T-TEST              GROUPS=RACE/VARIABLES=ARRESTS, CONVICT/
                    PAIRS=AGE, ARRESTS, CONVICT
READ INPUT DATA
```

Notice that there is no statistics card. The groups specified are black and white. The computer printout will show that in terms of arrests or convictions, there is no significant finding. Blacks and whites are treated as independent samples. Under PAIRS, each pair is compared, and we find that we have significant findings for age/arrest, age/convictions, and arrests/convictions, age/convictions giving a *t* value of

26.7. Also, the mean, standard deviation, standard error, difference of the means, s.d. of difference, s.e. of difference, correlation, probability (two-tail), degrees of freedom, and two-tail probability for *t* value are printed in the table across the page.

This program is fast and compact, and it gives a great deal of information in a very readable form. The computer is able to separate the single sample of 50 cases into two independent samples, or even to pair cases from independent samples to create the assumption necessary for T-test operation.

Summary of T-Test Assumptions

The T-test is a very good test to use when we can manipulate or control in an experimental setting. The dependent variable at least should be interval-type data. Small samples may be used and a sample of 30 is adequate; nevertheless larger samples are preferred. The test may be one-tail to the right if the hypothesis calls for *greater than*, or to the left if the hypothesis calls for *less than*. A two-tail test is used in situations where we have no certainty of the outcome, as in *equal to or not equal to*. Although we assume a normal distribution and equal variances, if the sample size is large enough, these assumptions are not nearly as important as *the assumption of equal means in our two (hypothetical) populations.*

We increase precision by using related samples, and we assume that the differences are normally distributed in the parent population.

In effect, when we use the T-test, we are testing the difference of means of two populations, using the same criterion (dependent variable) for both samples; or, if using one sample, for both tests. We still obtain the greatest measure of accuracy when using randomization and representation. Provided these things are present, the *t* statistic assumes its own normal curve, and we may compare our calculated value with the tabled value. Our calculated value should exceed the tabled value for us to reject the null hypothesis. With T-tests, we are examining differences of effects or between effects. Sometimes we use a "treatment," which is a way of differentiating the groups.

Looking Beyond the Means

In the T-test, we see the difference of the effects of controlling certain variables. For example, if we were to test the effect of TV programs on two groups, we could expose one group to TV and the other to none. We might decide that the criterion variable was involvement in violence. If the experimental group (the one watching TV) tested higher in crimes or acts of violence, we would be cautious but probably correct in concluding that the TV programs had caused, or had an effect on, the audience behavior patterns.

This idea of controlling is important, in that we had assumed that there was no difference in the two groups until we introduced the effects of TV programs. Now, had we received the two groups *after* the experiment and discovered that one was different—that is, had a higher record of violence—then our job would have been to detect *why* one group was different from the other. Eventually, after eliminating various factors in the causes of violence, we would have narrowed the selection down to the fact that one group had experienced TV programs and the other had not.

This takes time, and the use of control variables indicates what is not there rather than cause and effect. We are able to detect spurious or extraneous relationships very quickly, but detecting causal order involves a more detailed examination of the control results. When we look past the two-variable relationship to a third or fourth variable, we are actually elaborating on the relationships.

ANALYSIS OF VARIANCE

When we use the T-test, we assume that we are using only two samples, or that we are using two random samples or two matched or paired samples. In either case, we have an independent variable and a criterion or dependent variable. We also assume that we are using normally distributed and homoscedastic populations with equal means.

These four assumptions are also used when we use more than two samples. Comparing the means for more than two samples involves a special technique in statistics, known as *analysis of variance*. We analyze the variation between the means of the samples in one equation. If there is no variance, then we meet the requirements of the null hypothesis; if there is a significant difference between the means, then we reject the null. Variance estimates are obtained by dividing the *sum of the squares* by the degrees of freedom. We have two types of sums of squares: the *sum of the squares between* the sample variables, which is divided by $k - 1$, or the number of samples minus 1; and the *sum of the squares within* each sample, which is divided by $n - k$, or the number of cases in the total sample minus the number of samples. These two calculations give us *mean squares between*, MS_b, and *mean squares within*, MS_w. If we divide the former by the latter, MS_b/MS_w, we get a ratio known as the F ratio. If the F ratio exceeds the tabled value, we reject the null. The F ratio is tabled under two sets of degrees of freedom, the $n - k$ being at the side and $k - 1$ at the top of the table. The F reading occurs where they intersect.

Simple Analysis of Variance

Analysis of variance is best explained by an example. Assume that we use three samples drawn from the court cases in three cities, New York, Chicago, and San Francisco. For calculation convenience, we will use ten cases in each sample. The score given for each case is the number of months served in county jail divided by the number of offenses committed. The null hypothesis will state that there is no

Table 12.2.

Case item	New York		Chicago		San Francisco	
	Ratio	*Square*	*Ratio*	*Square*	*Ratio*	*Square*
1	10	100	8	64	9	81
2	10	100	8	64	6	36
3	9	81	7	49	5	25
4	9	81	6	36	5	25
5	8	64	6	36	4	16
6	8	64	5	25	3	9
7	7	49	4	16	3	9
8	6	36	3	9	2	4
9	6	36	3	9	2	4
10	5	25	2	4	2	4
$N = 10 \times 3 = 30$	78	636	52	312	41	213

Note: The ratio is the x column and is squared in the adjacent column.

difference in the means of the three cities—that no matter where you commit an offense, the time served will be the same. The alternate says that there is a difference in the means, and it does make a difference where you commit an offense. The data are shown in Table 12.2.

The null hypothesis may be stated:

$$H_o: \mu_1 = \mu_2 = \mu_3$$

The alternate:

$$H_a: \mu_1 \neq \mu_2 \neq \mu_3$$

Sample 1, $N = 10$; Sample 2, $N = 10$; Sample 3, $N = 10$
From the F table: R: $F \geqslant 3.35$, when df $= 2, 27, \alpha - 0.05$

We have all the data necessary for the calculation. For analysis of variance, we need three main calculations, from which all the others are derived:

1. The sum of the squares for every case: $636 + 312 + 213 =$ 1,161
2. The sum of the squares for sum of the raw scores in each sample, divided by the number of cases in each sample:

$$\frac{(78)^2}{10} + \frac{(52)^2}{10} + \frac{(41)^2}{10} = \qquad 1{,}047$$

3. The sum of all the raw scores, squared and divided by the total number of cases ($N = 30$):

$$\frac{(78 + 52 + 41)^2}{10 + 10 + 10} = \frac{(171)^2}{30} = \qquad 975$$

We now have all the data we need for the rest of the calculations:

4. The sum of the squares between may be calculated by number 2 minus number 3:

$$SS_b = 1{,}047 - 975 = \qquad 72$$

5. The sum of the squares within is number 1 minus number 2:

$$SS_w = 1{,}161 - 1{,}047 = \qquad 114$$

6. The sum of the squares total may be derived two ways, by adding 4 and 5 or by subtracting 3 from 1:

$$SS_t = 72 + 114 = 1{,}161 - 975 = \qquad 186$$

7. The mean square between is obtained by dividing the SS_b by $k - 1$ (number of groups or samples minus 1):

$$MS_b = \frac{SS_b}{k-1} = \frac{72}{2} = \qquad 36$$

8. The mean square within is obtained by dividing the SS_w by the number of cases minus the number of samples:

$$MS_w = \frac{SS_w}{n-k} = \frac{114}{27} = \qquad 4.2$$

9. The F ratio is derived by dividing number 7 by number 8:

$$MS_b/MS_w = \frac{36}{4.2} = \qquad 8.6$$

10. Compare to the tabled reading for F at df = 2, 27, $\alpha = 0.05$ = 3.35

Calculated F is greater than tabled F. Reject the null hypothesis.

[Note that in the F table, $n_1 = k - 1$ and is at the top (in this case, =2), and $n_2 = n - k$ (=27) and is read down the side. The F value is at the intersection.]

The results from analysis of variance may be summarized very neatly, as in Table 12.3. We can see at a glance the degrees of freedom, the sum of squares, mean squares, and the F ratio. We reject the null. If we look at the original scores for the three cities, we can see that the means are:

New York = $\bar{x}$ = 7.8; Chicago = $\bar{x}$ = 5.2; San Francisco = $\bar{x}$ = 4.1

Table 12.3. Summary of Analysis of Variance

Variation	DF	Sum of squares	Mean squares
Between samples	2 $(k-1)$	72 (SS_b)	36 (MS_b)
Within samples	27 $(n-k)$	114 (SS_w)	4.2 (MS_w)
Total	29 $(n-1)$	186 (SS_t)	$F = 8.6$

There is a difference in the means; from the illustrative data, it would apparently be better to serve time for a misdemeanor in San Francisco.

This simple analysis of variance is the basic pattern for many advanced designs. It is a powerful test, used often in a situation comparing different populations where the same criterion or dependent variable is used. Notice that the total variation, the sum of the squares, is broken down into its components so that the mean variation caused by the independent variable (MS_b) is divided by the mean sampling error (MS_w). If these two are the same, then there is approximation to unity or independence or no difference between the means. The analysis of variance, as its name implies, examines the variation in the dependent variable caused by variation in the independent variable—which is the whole point of research.

Analysis of Variance on the Computer

ANOVA, or analysis of variance, is entered on the computer by specifying the dependent variable first, then using the BY convention, listing the independent variables with maximum and minimum values. The RECODE system may be used to convert data to smaller numbers. In the present problem, the task specification card would read:

```
                  16
ANOVA             AVMONSER BY NEWYORK(5,10) CHICAGO(2,8) SANFRAN(2,9)
OPTIONS           3
STATISTICS        1
```

(AVMONSER means average months served.)

A simple analysis of variance is also printed out on the subprogram BREAKDOWN in summary form. I prefer the BREAKDOWN program for a simple analysis of variance. The task cards are:

```
                  16
BREAKDOWN         TABLES=AVMONSER BY NEWYORK,CHICAGO,SANFRAN
STATISTICS        ALL
```

The STATISTICS card ensures a simple analysis of variance, a test of linearity, Pearson r (goodness of fit), and r^2. If the data are somewhat limited, the entire problem may be computed on a calculator or terminal much faster. The ten-step procedure given is very rapid, and only three major calculations are required. You must know the degrees of freedom for each calculation, and you must remember the sequence of the operation. Keep in mind that you can use too many cells and that you may need to RECODE, depending on the capacity of the program. The dependent variable must be interval- or ratio-type measurement.

ELABORATION USING CONTINUOUS DATA

One way of handling three or more variables of mixed type, quantitative and qualitative, using continuous and discrete data, is to make all the variables nominal or ordinal. We then use Q, chi-square, Mann-Whitney U-test, and other nonparametric statistics. On the other hand, we can "convert" our nominal and ordinal data into limited continuous data and use them with our interval- and ratio-type variables. In this way we may use parametric-type analysis—namely, multiple regression. Simple regression is a zero-order relationship between only two variables; usually, both are continuous as in Pearson correlation, or one is continuous as in the T-test. (Correlation is *not* regression, but may permit regression analysis.) Multiple regression is another form of multivariate analysis, except that the data used are parametric. As in nonparametric analysis, chi-square in particular, we may use several independent variables to explain what is happening to the dependent variable (a multifactor approach); from our tests and controls, we can determine hierarchies of variable impact on the dependent variable. We can make tables of variables that have the greatest effect on the dependent variable. In addition, with regression, we can predict what will happen to the dependent variable. If you recall, simple regression is another name for the best-fitting slope between plotted variable data (x and y). When several variables are used, the slopes may be standardized and, once standardized, may be compared.

Multiple regression analysis is too complex to delve into in this text, but it is available on an SPSS program, and it is one our best forms of statistical analysis. The beta (B) standardized slopes, or beta weights, as they are called, are also known as standardized regression coefficients and path coefficients. They are all printed for you on the SPSS program. The unstandardized slopes are known as partial slopes, β slopes (using a lowercase beta), and b weights. The beta weights, or B weights, can be compared and set out in hierarchies.

Warning: When using such sophisticated data, everything looks two-dimensional on the printout and it all looks the same. It is not. You must keep your mind on what you are using. *You must think in terms of the variables rather than the numbers. You are not just comparing one statistic with another; you are comparing the effects of one variable upon another.* The variables are very dissimilar, not even remotely resembling each other (age, race, religion, education, location, crime, and so on), and to compare them requires a great deal of logical thought. The fact that the computer makes them "standardized" in no way relieves you of the responsibility of logical analysis.

Remember, too, that even sophisticated multiple regression analysis has disadvantages as well as advantages. Large samples tend to produce very small correlations, or small partial slopes, but this does not mean they are not significant. You must use your judgment.

THE FUNCTIONS OF STATISTICAL SAMPLE ESTIMATES

Sample estimates are used to make inferences from the sample to the parent population. As I have emphasized, random samples, or those samples containing representation and randomization, are the best. The sample estimates give us frequency data from which we may estimate the frequency or percentage of the characteristic in the parent population. They give us data on which we may compare one variable to another. We may even use the data to determine association, correlation, and causal effect. The data may be set within prescribed limits for the basis of retention or rejection of the null hypothesis. The mean of the sample may be used as an approximation to the population mean, the standard deviation of the sample may be used as a population estimate. The distribution of various samples may be used as a basis for determination of the population distribution.

In theory, we would like to sample parent populations to infinity, and take an infinite number of samples with replacement. This is impossible. In practice, we seldom take more than one sample. (If we are diligent and have time and money, we take two or more.) This means that all our statistical estimates are going to be based upon the information given in the one sample. If that sample is wrong, then all the calculations are wrong—*and there is always a 0.05 chance, or 1 in 20, that this is the case.*

That is why it is important to use more than one sample. Moreover, the sample should be of a reasonable size, definitely larger than 30 cases and preferably closer to 100 or more. The sample data are the base for statistical calculations that involve estimations of parent population parameters. Sampling theory is based upon frequency distributions and the fact that such distributions approximate the normal curve. Any two samples will differ with respect to their means. It is this difference in means that is important. Just as scores within a sample have a distribution, a mean, and a standard deviation, so too the separate means or differences of means have their own distribution, mean, and standard deviation. Theoretically, many samples have many means—say, $\bar{x}_1, \bar{x}_2, \bar{x}_3, \bar{x}_4, \bar{x}_5, \bar{x}_6, \bar{x}_7$ to $\bar{x}_n$. These means or differences may be aggregated or summed and then divided by the number of the means or differences to produce an average:

$$\text{Mean of means} = \bar{X}_{\bar{x}} = \frac{\Sigma\bar{x}\ (1 \text{ to end})}{n \text{ of means}} = \text{Approx. } \mu \text{ (pop. mean)}$$

They may also be used to calculate a standard deviation, known as the *standard error* of the means. This distribution of means about the population parameter or population mean is the basis of the normal curve. *The "average" distance of the means from the population mean is the standard error*, written as s_e or $s_{\bar{x}}$ and known as the standard error of the means. Because the population mean is unknown, the sample standard deviation is used in the estimation of the standard error, along with the unbiased estimate of the sample mean.

The Problem of Sample Size

Occasionally, the question arises of what the actual sample size should be,[4] or how many cases should be included in a sample taken from a parent population. To my

[4] Sample size should also consider the variables in the study.

mind, this is academic as long as there is some randomization and emphasis on representation. However, knowing that sample sizes are best at over 100, with a maximum of 1,500 (assuming randomization and representation), it is sometimes worthwhile to estimate what size may be minimum for a result. We can set the assumed result within a confidence interval, and we can even assume an outcome, such as win or lose, success or failure, or any outcome that permits a *pq* relationship of probability. The mechanics of the equation are as follows:

1. Assume the limits of success, say, of a vote in a large city of 400,000. The voting population would probably be 100,000. A 2,000 majority would represent a 52%/48% win. However, in terms of proportion, the 2,000 votes would be 0.02 of the 100,000. *Thus we have established a limit of success (or failure), which can be used as a constant, or* c.
2. The probability of a win is 0.5. The closer we are to $p = 0.5$ = Probability, the better the distribution.
3. We can establish a confidence interval of 90%, 95%, or 99%, depending upon how close we wish our estimate to be, or $z\ \alpha$.
4. With all this, we know that the standard deviation (σ) and sample size determine the interval. Using an idea called bound limits or set limits, we can find an estimated sample size (n).
5. The formula is

$$\frac{p\,(z\ \alpha)}{c} = \sqrt{n}.$$

Suppose $p = 0.5$ (win or lose), $z_c = 95\%$ or $\pm\ 1.96$, and $c = 0.02$ (2,000 votes). Substituting:

$$\frac{0.5\ (1.96)}{0.02} = \sqrt{n};\ 49 = \sqrt{n};\ 2{,}401 = n$$

Estimated sample size = 2,400.

The formula given is derived from:

$$n = \frac{(z\ \alpha\sqrt{pq})^2}{c^2}$$

where

$$\begin{aligned} z\ \alpha &= \text{the } 95\%\ \text{C.I. of} \pm 1.96\ \sigma \\ &= z_c \end{aligned}$$

Of course, the $z\ \alpha$ may well be 90 or 99 percent, in which case the range on either side of the mean (the limits) is set by the appropriate measure of z deviations. p is set as close to 0.5 as possible. I find the shortened formula in number 5 above faster on a calculator.

Using a standard deviation instead of a proportion poses a slightly different problem. First, it is necessary to estimate a standard deviation of a small sample (not less than 30) and then use this estimate for the equation:

$$n = \frac{(z\,\alpha \cdot \sigma)^2}{c^2} = \frac{(1.96 \times 0.5)^2}{(0.02)^2} = 2{,}401$$

For example, if we assume our standard deviation is 0.5 (a reasonable estimate for a large sample), then our n, or sample size, is still 2,400. Also assuming that we do not know the probability of the outcome, we can still estimate sample size by:

$$n = \frac{1}{4}\,\frac{z\,\alpha^2}{c^2} \quad \text{or} \quad \frac{z\,\alpha}{c} = \sqrt{4n} = 2{,}401$$

Remember that $z\,\alpha$ = C.I. = z_c. For a rapid calculation, a 95 percent interval may be estimated using $z_c = 2$, and n will equal 2,500.

In this calculation of a voting population of 100,000, the city may be divided into five areas (multistage) of 20,000; the vote margin of 2,000 then becomes $c = 0.1$, and the sample size in each precinct becomes 100 (rounded off).

As noted before, this method of sample-size determination is more academic than practical and serves only to be used as an estimate. A multistage approach would arrive at the same results.

In the use of two or more samples, the problem of size is dependent upon four factors:

1. *The research design and statistics used*. For example, in a two-group situation using a T-test, it is easy to handle small samples, provided of course that we meet the assumptions for randomization and representation. If we are using a chi-square design, we need to keep our sample large enough to avoid empty cells in our tables. We need to know the number of categories, number of cells, and anticipated minimum sample size. A sample of 100 would be useless for a 4 × 4 table but would be ample for a 2 × 2. In other words, we need to know if our sample will be adequate for the statistics we will be using.

2. *The resources available*. It takes time and money to obtain good samples. Large samples require staff and supervisors. If you are overambitious, you may not meet your sample requirements; conversely, too small a sample will produce distortion in your results. Choosing the right sample size is often a matter of experience, practicality, and availability.

3. *Trial and error*. Because there is no simple answer to the problem of sample size, it sometimes becomes a matter of trial and error, particularly when the results are close to tabled values and a slight increase could change the results one way or the other. Although our objective is to reject the null hypothesis, we should not deliberately manipulate sample size in order to obtain statistical significance. Nevertheless, experimentation with sample size is in order if the research is to be objective and scientific.

4. *Accuracy desired*. If we are using our sample to predict, we need to be reasonably accurate. Remember, if you quadruple your sample size, you reduce the standard error by half; in other words, there is less error and more accuracy (or tends to be) in increasing the sample size. Again, if there is little variance of the desired characteristic in the population, a small sample will do. On the other hand,

a large range in the variable will require an appropriate-size sample to meet the large number of categories. Remember that large numbers will not necessarily ensure accurate results.

Size of the sample in itself is no criterion for accuracy; it must be compared to the size of the parent population. A sample of 1,000 in a city of 50,000 can be just as accurate as a similar-size sample in a city of 500,000.

SUMMARY

One of the problems in survey research is the use of multiple variables and of multiple samples containing multiple variables. We are always examining our data for the explanation of the effect the independent variable is causing on the dependent variable. When we deal with more than one sample, we compare the means of those samples. Each sample has its own assumed, hypothetical base. We assume that the populations are equal, that the means are equal, and that variances and distribution are equal. If there are differences, this will show in the means. The differences of the means may be reduced to a single statistic, which has its own distribution and, like most others, conforms to the central limit theorem and approximates the normal curve. This is true for parametric and nonparametric data. There are special tests for each category. For two samples, where the data are interval or ratio, we may use the T-test. We may also use matched pairs. Of course, our data are based upon random/representative selection.

If there are more than two samples, we may use analysis of variance. If there are more than two samples and multiple variables, we may use multiple regression analysis. The T-test enables us to set up experimental and control groups. The experimental group receives the treatment, the control group does not.

We must beware of two things when using complex analysis:

1. Small samples give strange results, especially if they contain extremes.
2. Statistics need to be examined in terms of what you are actually testing. Do not use statistics to "cook the books."

A good example of this was of the judges and their sentences—it depended where you were sitting. You must look at the means, compare the differences, consider the outcomes. Getting results from the computer is only part of the analysis; the serious part is what you do with the findings and how you present your conclusions.

Using more than two samples involves comparing more than two means. This presents a special problem in statistics, known as a *problem of comparison*. However, a simple analysis of variance enables us to decide if differences do exist. Analysis of variance also introduces the reader to the basic block of many complex designs. It is really not so complex if one follows the prescribed sequence. What you do with the results is what really counts. Again, you can perform the calculations on the computer, calculator, or terminal, and the results are very impressive. Knowing what you are doing is even more impressive.

You have also been introduced to simple regression, which is the basis for multiple regression. Regression printouts are large when you use multiple variables. Familiarize yourself on a small scale before you take a jump into deep water.

EXERCISES

1. There are three things associated with the "real problem in analysis." What are they? Analysis also deals with two other problems; what are they?
2. Three situations occur, or can occur, in comparing means. Name the situations.
3. What are the four assumptions for comparing means?
4. Write a hypothesis for the T-test. What size sample would you use? Explain your reasons. What type of data?
5. When would you use a one-tail test? a two-tail test?
6. Explain the concept of hypothetical samples used for hypothesis testing.
7. What are the criteria for a test situation?
8. Draw up a table showing the assumptions and restrictions for using the T-test.
9. Double all the scores on blood pressure and stress and calculate the new t score.
10. Dichotomize the scores (doubled scores) along the mean and organize into a 2×2 table (High, Low; x and y). Calculate the chi-square, compare to your T-test score. Are the results the same?
11. Write a task definition card using the T-test; recode and use the chi-square.
12. Write a design for testing the relationship between watching violence on TV and committing crimes of violence. Use a two-sample approach.
13. What are the assumptions for using more than three samples? When would you use ANOVA? When would you use elaboration?
14. Explain how analysis of variance deals with variation from the independent variable and sampling error.
15. Write a hypothesis for ANOVA on release success from three prisons.
16. How do you calculate the degrees of freedom for ANOVA?
17. Resolve, using ANOVA and a calculator:

New York		Chicago		San Francisco	
x	x^2	x	x^2	x	x^2
11		11		11	
10		9		7	
9		8		5	
8		7		3	
7		6		3	
7		5		2	
6		4		2	
5		3			
4					

Notice that the column numbers are unequal: For N.Y., $n = 9$; Chicago, $n = 8$; San Francisco, $n = 7$; total, $N = 24$. Square your scores, follow the ten steps for simple analysis of variance. The tabled value for F at 0.05 = 3.47. Decide upon the retention or rejection of the hypothesis, $H_o = \mu_1 = \mu_2 = \mu_3$.

18. Put your results in a summary table. How do you calculate the F ratio?
19. Write an ANOVA program for your problem.
20. What is multiple regression? What is simple regression analysis?
21. What are restrictions on the regression analysis?
22. What does a correlation coefficient measure as compared to a regression slope?
23. What is one way of finding out if your data are linear or curvilinear?
24. Why should we use multiple regression or analysis of variance?
25. No matter how simple or how complex the statistics become, there are two limitations you should observe. What are they? Explain.
26. A group of ten inmates volunteered for a behavior modification experiment designed to improve learning. They were tested before and after the "learning situation." Increase in scores indicates improvement; the hypothesis is that the BM improves learning. Significance level is set at 0.05 for rejection of the H_o.

Subject	Before BM	After BM
1	18	23
2	25	25
3	19	28
4	26	32
5	27	22
6	16	15
7	29	35
8	22	18
9	31	32
10	24	26

For the table above: $H_a: \mu_2 > \mu_1$; $H_o: \mu_1 = \mu_2$; $n = 10$, df = 9.

27. Two groups of policemen are tested by a psychologist for stress reaction. Test the hypothesis that officers are better able to handle stress than patrolmen. $N = 20$; df = 18.

Scores

Officers	*Patrolmen*
36	36
33	30
35	33
30	35
38	30
33	38
30	36
28	31
36	28
31	33

A third group was tested, female clerical, with scores reading 37, 37, 30, 35, 34, 36, 33, 39, 33, 36. Run a T-test on the first H_o, $\mu_1 = \mu_2$. Run an analysis of variance on the H_o, $\mu_1 = \mu_2 = \mu_3$. What are your conclusions on the T-test? What are your results on the analysis of variance?

28. Two guns are tested on a firing range by the same marksman; 50 shots are fired, using the weapons randomly. The scores are:

Gun 1	Gun 2	Score
20 Shots	25	5 Bull's-eye
10	15	4
20	10	3

which is better at 0.01?

FOR FURTHER READING

Best, John W., *Research in Education* (3rd ed.). Chaps. 7, 8. Englewood Cliffs, N.J.: Prentice-Hall, 1977.

Blalock, Hubert M., Jr., *Social Statistics* (2nd ed.). Part 4. New York: McGraw-Hill, 1972.

Book, Stephen A., *Statistics: Basic Techniques for Solving Applied Problems,* Chaps. 9–11. New York: McGraw-Hill, 1977.

Byrkit, Donald R., *Elements of Statistics* (2nd ed.). Chaps. 11–13. New York: D. Van Nostrand, 1972.

Dyckman, T. R. and L. J. Thomas, *Fundamental Statistics for Business and Economics*, Chaps. 14, 15, 18. Englewood Cliffs, N.J.: Prentice-Hall, 1977.

Edwards, Allan L., *Experimental Design in Psychological Research.* New York: Holt, Rinehart & Winston, 1972.

Ellis, Richard B., *Statistical Inference-Basic Concepts*, Chaps. 11–15. Englewood Cliffs, N.J.: Prentice-Hall, 1975.

Franklin, B., and H. Osborne, *Research Methods: Issues and Insights.* Belmont, Calif.: Wadsworth, 1971.

Hardwick, Curtis D., and L. F. Petrinovich, *Understanding Research in the Social Sciences.* Philadelphia: Saunders, 1975.

Keppel, G., *Design and Analysis: A Researcher's Handbook.* Englewood Cliffs, N.J.: Prentice-Hall, 1973.

Kish, Leslie, *Survey Sampling.* New York: John Wiley, 1965.

Lazarsfeld, P., and M. Rosenberg, *The Language of Social Research* (rev. ed.), New York: Free Press, 1971.

Marateck, Samuel L., *Introduction to Probability and Statistics* (A Harper and Row Media Program) Modules 7–10. New York: Harper & Row, Pub., 1977.

Mason, E. J., and W. J. Bramble, *Understanding and Conducting Research.* New York: McGraw-Hill, 1978.

Neale, J. M., and R. M. Liebert, *Science and Behaviour: An Introduction to Methods of Research.* Englewood Cliffs, N.J.: Prentice-Hall, 1973.

Netter, Gwynn, *Explaining Crime* (2nd ed.). New York: McGraw-Hill, 1978.

Rosenberg, Morris, *The Logic of Survey Analysis*. New York: Basic Books, 1968.

Susser, Mervyn, *Causal Thinking in the Health Sciences*. New York: Oxford University Press, 1973.

Zeisal, Hans, *Say it With Figures* (5th ed., rev.). New York: Harper & Row, Pub., 1968.

13

Using More than Two Variables for Analysis

Up to this point, we have been discussing two-variable relationships, even though several of our research designs called for more than two variables. We have assumed that most of our association could be explained in terms of two-variable tables. But that is not exactly true. The best research depends upon looking deeper into the design and using control or test variables. That is, we examine the relationship in terms of a third or even a fourth variable. In the examples that follow, you will see how the entire research picture changes when we use test variables. In one instance, we have to completely reverse ourselves on the original hypothesis; in the other, we have to reconsider the nature of the model and restate our conclusions. Both examples clearly indicate the importance of research in depth. We are forced to rethink our conclusions by using logic in our analysis of what at first looked entirely plausible.

Using more than two variables requires that you use sophisticated techniques; that you use more care in selection of your sample, the sample size, and analysis of your computer printouts; and most of all, that you use care in the selection of your test variable. If you remember that all sophisticated analysis is based on the building block of two-variable relationships, you should not have too much trouble. You are now ready to enter the world of multivariate analysis.

MULTIVARIATE ANALYSIS–ELABORATION

No matter how complex the arrangement of variables in a design, it will always break down to a two-variable relationship, or a series of two-variable relationships.

Even when we establish hierarchies in multiple regression, we are still looking at the effect of one upon another. This is an advantage in some ways, but it is a disadvantage in others, because it limits the nature of the design.

In practice, not only are our variables quantitative and qualitative, but the data themselves vary from simple nominal to complex ratio. Thus we find ourselves looking at relationships between variables of contrasting data types—say, nominal to interval, ordinal to interval, ordinal to ratio, nominal to ratio, and so on. And when we reduce our data to discrete data, we run the danger of losing sophistication in the statistical analysis. We must always be on guard for error and be alert to consequences in the use and manipulation of data.

Because much of our data are discrete (nominal) or can be reduced to nominal-type data, chi-square is an extremely useful tool for testing two-variable relationships. Thus, when there is a series of indicated or alleged relationships, a series of chi-square tests will help sort out the nature of those relationships. For example, in our problem on juvenile arrests and convictions, we need to know the effect of age. Does age affect the strong relationship of arrests to convictions? We need to be certain that the association is meaningful, we need to know and understand the causal relationship, and, even if we are satisfied, we need to know if it exists among other groups.

Without any controlling variables, the two-variable relationship is a zero-order relationship. With one controlling variable, it is a first-order relationship; with two variables controlled, a second-order relationship, and so on.

We begin the elaboration of the relationship seen in a two-variable table by asking, Is there more than a statistical relationship? Are the results valid, factual, and substantive? By using a third variable to control, we can answer some of these questions. In our example, we have seen a strong causal effect, in that we can predict the number of convictions from the number of arrests. The question now is, How does this stand up when we break it down for age? sex? religion? If it is valid, it will stand up and be as strong in any of those categories. If it is not, then the moment we control for any of those variables, the relationship between arrests and convictions will get smaller or disappear entirely.

When we control, we take all the categories in that particular group—say, sex—and separate them into component parts of male and female; then we test the relationship between arrests and convictions in each of those categories. We are in effect controlling for sex and testing the same criterion in two different (hypothetical) populations. We can do this for as many control variables as we wish. *We never control the criterion or dependent variable.*

Using the Elaboration Model

There are certain restrictions on the use of the elaboration model that need to be restated. (Credit must be given to Paul Lazarsfeld, who did most of the pioneer groundwork in development of this model, and to Morris Rosenberg for his contribution.) The basic rules are these:

1. To use the model, we need to be certain that the relationship is both statistical and substantive.
2. Even if the relationship exists, we need to know if it exists among or is affected by other variables.
3. If indeed a causal relationship is detected, we need to understand the effect of the independent variable(s) on the dependent variable(s).
4. To set up controls, there must be a relationship between all the variables.
5. If the data indicate relationship, then regardless of statistical information, we need to examine the results for validity and replication.
6. We may progress from zero-order relationships (using only two variables) to first-order relationships (using one control variable) to second- and third-order relationships. In effect, we may begin to establish a hierarchy of variable effects.

The elaboration model is the cornerstone of scientific research. It forces the researcher to reexamine his conclusions and to include other factors in the causal chain. Moreover, the nature of this type of research alerts the researcher to possible effects that are concealed or distorted by other variables in the research model. Fallacies that have been overlooked in zero-order relationships become clear in elaboration procedures. If the relationship is destroyed by elaboration, then the causal model is in error and the nature of the original design indicates spuriousness.

STATISTICAL RULES FOR ELABORATION

1. There must be a minimum of three variables in the model, with one variable being the control or test variable.
2. The dependent variable is never used as a control variable.
3. Contingency tables for elaboration should be kept as small as possible, preferably 2 × 2, unless the nature of the design permits a greater number.
4. If a larger number of cells are used, the sample size should be large enough to ensure a cell number of at least five, or preferably a minimum of ten. Thus, a minimum sample size for all practical purposes in a three-variable relationship, using eight cells (two 2 × 2 bivariate contingency tables) should be at least 100.
5. Not only should the χ^2 relationships be examined, but partial relationships within the cells (percentages) should also be examined.
6. Products of cross-multiplication of the cells (A × D and B × C) will indicate spuriousness if they are equal or near equal.
7. The effect of the control variable should be noted:
   (a) Is the relationship maintained?
   (b) Does it strengthen or diminish?
   (c) Are the effects equal?
   (d) Does the relationship disappear?
   (e) What is the effect upon the causal statement (hypothesis)?

The control variable virtually sets up two standardized tables, so that if the relationship is correct, the control variable should make no difference in the interpretation. This is best seen in the examples that follow. The control variable is a device by which we are able to determine if our findings are consistent and if they hold up under scrutiny. We use the third or control variable to establish or correct the relationship we first observed in the effect of the independent upon the dependent variable. The control variable may be independent, intervening, antecedent, conditional, component, conjoint, or even extraneous–it may never be dependent.

Using a First-Order Model

A recent newspaper article reported a study by a religious group purporting to have found that listening to rock music was a major cause of pregnancy in teenagers. In other words, girls who listened to rock 'n' roll with their boyfriends were suddenly subject to overpowering influences. Statistics were actually cited to "prove" this. A single cross-sectional study had been taken, showing that 72 percent of unwed mothers listened to rock 'n' roll music. The result was a great public burning of rock 'n' roll records, with a corresponding religious revival–and, of course, absolutely no change in the number of unwed mothers.

The study was extended to include married mothers and their preferences in music. We now had wed and unwed mothers, rock 'n' roll music, and other choices (classical, pop, and so on)–sufficient data for a simple bivariate contingency table based upon a sample of 400.[1] The first table is shown in Figure 13-1; from it, we reject the null hypothesis, that choice of music does not affect motherhood, and accept the alternate hypothesis, that rock 'n' roll music influences unwed motherhood.

There must be a relationship shown between all the variables, and under this consideration, we now look at the relationship for age (dichotomizing age as under

	Wed	Unwed	
Other Music	A 100	B 60	160
Rock 'n' Roll	C 80	D 160	240
	180	220	400

$\chi^2 = 31.8$, df = 1, $\alpha = 0.05$

Fig. 13-1 Musical preference by motherhood

[1] Illustrative data.

20 and over 20). In fact, we look at the relationship of age to musical preference and also to motherhood. Age has been chosen as the test variable because *age is common* to both wed and unwed groups and is excellent as a test variable for the following reasons:

1. If preference for rock music does in fact influence girls' unwed motherhood, it should show equally in age groups; i.e., those over 20 and those under 20 should be equally influenced by the sounds of rock.
2. Because age is a commonality and, in this case, there is a small spread of years (16–25), the percent of unwed mothers ought to show consistently in categories of the independent variables, motherhood being the dependent variable.
3. The use of age as a test or control variable actually produces two standardized tables—bivariate contingency tables—in which we can compare the effect of the independent variable (musical preference) upon the dependent variable (motherhood).
4. Based upon our observation of relationships shown in the comparison of the tables, we can "regroup" all the variables preceding the dependent variable. In other words, we may modify the model *after* stating conclusions based upon the elaboration.
5. Modification of the model may show that:
   (a) The relationship is spurious (no further model needed).
   (b) The model order of variables is wrong (order needs changing).
   (c) Distortion or suppression of effects has occurred and the hypothesis needs to be restated (new research is indicated).
6. In line with number 5 above, the acceptance of a false hypothesis, based upon statistical significance, has been explained in the elaboration of the relationships. (This point is explained later in the text.)

In Figure 13-2, we begin already to detect a visual difference in the strength of the chi-square. This value is very significant. The internal percentages, based upon

	Age: Over 20 yrs.	Age: Under 20 yrs.	
Other Music	A_y 120/75%	B_y 40/17%	160
Rock 'n' Roll	C_y 40/25%	D_y 200/83%	240
	160/100%	240/100%	400

$\chi^2 = 133.69$, df = 1, $\alpha = 0.05$

Fig. 13-2 Musical preference by age

comparing musical preference in age-group categories, also indicate a forthcoming change.[2]

Now see Figure 13-3. Again the χ^2 value is very significant, and the internal percentages, compared *across*, reveal the significance of using age as a test variable. Using age as a test variable or a control variable simply means that we are separating the two groups, over 20 years and under 20 years, into separate tables and observing the effects of musical preference on motherhood in these two categories.

	Age: Over 20 yrs.	Age: Under 20 yrs.	
Wed Mothers	A_x 120/75%	B_x 60/25%	180
Unwed Mothers	C_x 40/25%	D_x 180/75%	220
	160/100%	240/100%	400

$\chi^2 = 94.96$, df = 1, $\alpha = 0.05$

Fig. 13-3 Motherhood by age

First-Order Elaboration

From the basic zero-order or two-variable model, elaboration occurs when a third variable is introduced as a test or control variable. This relationship is as in Figure 13-4 and is called a first-order relationship or elaboration of the zero order. It is based upon the elaboration paradigm (reasoning) as set forth by Paul Lazarsfeld.

In this first-order elaboration, we see that for each table for age, the chi-square is zero. Thus we can safely assume that the relationship between rock 'n' roll and motherhood is spurious, is somewhat accidental, and is a fortuitous circumstance. There really is no relationship between rock music and pregnancy; but notice how the initial assumption was borne out by statistical significance until we looked deeper into the relationship.

Deriving the Figures from the Tables

It has been briefly mentioned that all the figures necessary may be derived from the tables—that is, from the three zero-order tables. Looking at the first-order

[2] Note how A_y, B_y, A_x, B_x appear in the table when we *control* for age; note also how $A_1 + A_2$ (Figure 13-4) equals A (Figure 13-1).

	Over 20 yrs.			Under 20 yrs.		
	Motherhood			Motherhood		
Musical Preference	Wed	Unwed	Total	Wed	Unwed	Total
Other Music	A_1 90/75%	30/25%	A_y 120/100%	A_2 10/25%	30/75%	B_y 40/100%
Rock 'n' Roll	C_1 30/75%	10/25%	C_y 40/100%	C_2 50/25%	150/75%	D_y 200/100%
	A_x 120	C_x 40	160	B_x 60	D_x 180	240

$N = 400$

$\chi^2 = 0$ (Over 20 yrs.) $\chi^2 = 0$ (Under 20 yrs.)

df = 1, $\alpha = 0.05$

Fig. 13-4 Musical preference by motherhood, controlling for age

Note: Compare percentages *down*. Note that all figures are derived from zero-order tables. You may also control for ***musical preference*** to prove the point.

table where we control for *age*, we note that the bottom line (horizontal marginals) comes from the table "Motherhood by Age." The numbers 120 and 40 are taken from cells A_x and C_x (over 20) and the numbers 60 and 180 are taken from cells B_x and D_x in the same table. We thus complete the bottom line of our first-order table and have *motherhood by age* in categories over 20 and under 20.

Next, we take the vertical marginals from the first-order table and note that they are derived from the zero-order table "Musical Preference by Age." The numbers 120 and 40 come from cells A_y and C_y; the numbers 40 and 200 from cells B_y and. D_y. Note that the totals for each side of the first-order table are 160, the number of girls over 20, and 240, the number of girls under 20 ($N = 400$). All that is left is to complete the internal cells on the first-order table.

Note that the cells, both cells A in the first-order table, when summed, equal the one cell A in the zero-order table "Musical Preference by Motherhood." Similarly, both cells B in the first-order table sum to equal cell B in the same zero-order table. The same is true for C and D ($A_1 + A_2 = A$, and so on). All the totals must balance. This takes a little time to manipulate arithmetically. It is wise to start with the smallest cell first, keeping your eye on the name of the cells, since the names should agree.

The original church-based hypothesis that rock 'n' roll music caused pregnancy was based upon the model:

Rock 'n' Roll Music ⟶ Unwed Motherhood
(Independent Variable) (Dependent Variable)

And unfortunately, it *appeared* to be statistically founded. However, when we look at the proof, we find that it does not stand up under proper scientific scrutiny. When we introduce age as a test variable, the model becomes:

(Age⟶) Rock 'n' Roll Music⟶ Unwed Motherhood
(Control Variable)

And we notice from the results that we must now change the model to:

(I.V.) Age ⟶ Motherhood (D.V.)
Rock 'n' Roll (Spurious)
(Musical Preference)

The curved arrow signifies that the relationship is spurious and that musical preference has nothing to do with motherhood and is only incidental to age. Logically, we know that younger people prefer rock 'n' roll, and that younger people do tend to ignore social conformity in becoming parents before meeting social requirements. Therefore, by using common sense, we defeat ignorance even when it is cloaked in so-called statistical proof. What is more, we defeat it by using statistics in conjunction with proper methodology.

Types of Variable Relationships That Occur in Elaboration

The clue that age was so important showed up in the bivariate table of age by motherhood. Logic then indicated that controlling for age would reveal the true nature of the effect of musical preference, and of course it did. Musical preference had no effect upon motherhood in spite of the initial observations.

Often the control reveals more subtle differences. The test variable may indicate that it is intervening or antecedent, besides being extraneous or spurious. It may also mitigate or intensify relationships, or even reverse them. And on occasion, when the relationship is reduced to zero, the common sense of the operation may indicate that the variable is intervening rather than spurious. In the example given, *time order* indicated that age could not be an intervening variable[3] in musical preference and motherhood; thus, a new model had to be established, and we had proof of the spuriousness of the variable *musical preferences*. The criteria for independent variables, such as time order, dominance (least likely to change), and influence, still remain.

EFFECTS OF CONTROL VARIABLES AND MODEL ORDER

The relationship between the independent variable and the dependent variable *will disappear* under these conditions:

1. The model A ⟶ B (A causes or influences B) becomes A ⟶ C ⟶ B when the *control variable* by logical inference actually *intervenes* between the two variables, using the criteria of time order, dominance, and influence.
2. When the control variable does not logically intervene (and a three-way relationship persists), the original relationship A ⟶ B ceases to exist and is spurious, and the relationship now changes to

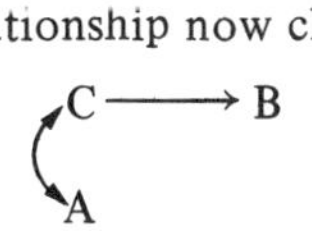

with variable A now being extraneous or spurious.

3. If the relationship is A ⟶ C ⟶ B and variable A is *antecedent to C*, which is the independent variable, then if C is controlled or becomes the test variable, the *relationship between A and dependent variable B will disappear*. Again, the logic of the association or relationship must be thought out. Remember that in this elaboration, the independent variable becomes the control variable.

The relationship between the independent variable and the dependent variable *will weaken* or lessen in these circumstances:

[3] Neither could it be an antecedent variable, as you will discover if you control for music.

1. If the control variable is *intervening* and the variable does not explain all the relationship, as in A ⟶ C ⟶ B, and C is the intervening variable. Then if the relationship is weakened and does not disappear altogether, the model should be refined to:

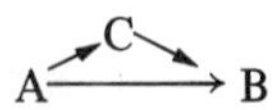

   since some effects of A are direct and some are through C.
2. Again, if the relationship *does not disappear*, then the model may well be A ⟶ C ⟶ B; and in this case, where *A is the control variable*, C is also the independent, and *if A is truly antecedent*, the relationship of the *independent variable C to dependent variable B should remain unchanged* in terms of internal percentages, although the chi-square value may lessen because of sample and cell size.

Variables used in control may intensify, mitigate, suppress, distort—even reverse the effects of the independent variable on the dependent variable:

1. In the model A ⟶ C ⟶ B, where A is antecedent, control of A may cause unknown or unanticipated results to occur in the tables. This can be especially true for geographical location, race, sex, and religion.
2. In the case where C is intervening, occasionally the intervening variable causes intensification and/or mitigation of effect.

In any elaboration, the results must be carefully thought out, models adjusted, and controls varied to prove or disprove the objective. We are out to affirm the null hypothesis, not the research or alternate hypothesis, and as Blalock says so well, "We must bend over backwards to prove ourselves wrong."

There are certain differences worth noting:

1. A variable is *extraneous* if it is prior to the independent and dependent variables; it is *antecedent* if it is directly causal to the independent variable, which in turn causes the dependent variable. An *extraneous* variable is never causal.
2. An *intervening variable* actually intervenes or *comes between* the independent variable and the dependent variable; it is part of the causal chain and is indeed an essential causal link under certain circumstances. It is differentiated from antecedent or independent variables by time order. *Extraneous* variables are never part of the time-order sequence. *Antecedent* variables come *before* the independent variable.
3. *Component* variables may appear anywhere in the causal model. They may be a breakdown of the antecedent variable, parts of the independent variable, parts of the intervening variable, or even parts of the dependent variable. Certainly, when parts of the antecedent or intervening (or independent), they may be used as control variables.
4. Occasionally relationships arise that are described as *conjoint*, when two or more variables exert influence on another, or as conditional, when a certain effect is conditional upon the presence of contrasting results. In a conditional relationship, we wish to understand why contrasting results have occurred—we want to know the *conditions* under which the contrasts (or differences in effect of the I.V. upon the D.V.) happened.

AN EXTENSION OF HYPOTHESIS CONCLUSIONS

Before, it was stated that when we accept or reject the null hypothesis, we have four choices (top of Figure 13-5). When using control variables in elaboration, we consider an extension of choices. As you see in the bottom section of Figure 13-5,

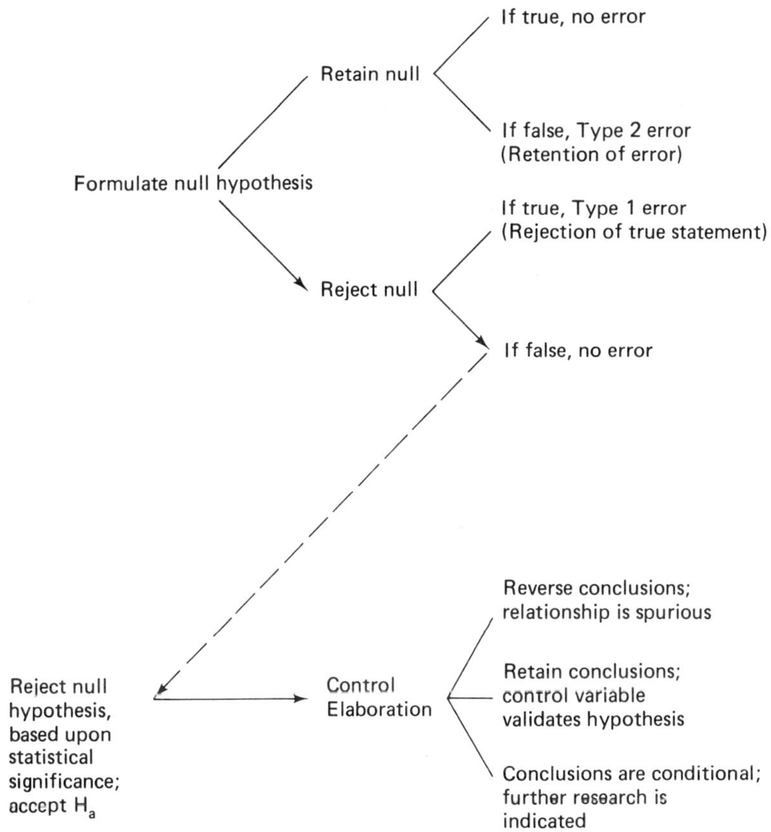

Fig. 13-5 Re-evaluation of hypothesis conclusions when using elaboration

only one condition is acceptable to the acceptance of the research hypothesis, that of validation of the hypothesis by the control variable. Thus, even when the initial relationship appears to be statistically sound and the research hypothesis appears correct, further investigation by the researcher may reveal that the relationship is spurious and the conclusions have to be restated in terms of what has been found in the elaboration process. In other words, what at first looks highly plausible may be merely scientific nonsense—a serious matter indeed.

Elaboration is highly complex, and even advanced researchers have a difficult time threading their way through the maze of intricacies in setting up a control model. Nevertheless, beginners ought to try, even if they only see pet projects go down the drain when they choose the correct control variable. Perhaps the hardest part of elaboration is that it attacks the ego rather than the theory, demolishing what seemed so magnificent. It removes myth, destroys superstition, and confirms the unacceptable. It promotes a rethinking of the conclusions made concerning the hypothesis. Thus, given proper uses, it is a most valuable asset in survey research.

ANOTHER LOOK AT ELABORATION

It has been commonly assumed that race is causal to crime—that blacks are more prone to crime than whites. By the use of adjusted data to illustrate a research point, the first gathering of facts supports that hypothesis.

H_0: There is no difference between races in the number of crimes committed.

		Race: *Black*	Race: *White*	
Crime	*Low*	A 40/44%	B 80/73%	120
Crime	*High*	C 50/56%	D 30/27%	80
		90/100%	110/100%	200

(Table value = 3.84)

$\chi^2 = 15.3$, df = 1, $\alpha = 0.05$ Reject the H_0.

Fig. 13-6 Crimes by race

Illustrative data. Note that cells have been lettered to correspond with cells in final first-order table.

From Figure 13-6, we can see that blacks have twice as high a crime rate as whites, or 56%:27%. It appears that race does influence crime. Now we also know that across the variable of race, both blacks and whites receive some sort of education. If we introduce education as a control variable, we may see the effect of that variable. First we must establish a relationship between education and crime, and also education and race. There must be a three-way relationship before we can control.

From Figure 13-7, we see that there are almost four times as many blacks in the low education group as whites, 66%:18%.) White are much better educated, 82%:34% (compare across).

		Race: *Black*	Race: *White*	
Education	*Low*	A_x 60/66%	B_x 20/18%	80
	High	C_x 30/34%	D_x 90/82%	120
		90/100%	110/100%	200

$\chi^2 = 46.5$, df = 1, $\alpha = 0.05$ Reject H_0.

Fig. 13-7 Education by race

		Education: *Low*	Education: *High*	
Crime	*Low*	A_y 20/25%	B_y 100/83%	120
	High	C_y 60/75%	D_y 20/17%	80
		80	120	200

$\chi^2 = 65.6$, df = 1, $\alpha = 0.05$ Reject H_0.

Fig. 13-8 Education by crime

Figure 13-8 shows that education definitely has an effect on crime; those in high crime have lower education, 75%:17%, whereas those in low crime have higher education, 83%:25%.

Already we begin to see that our first observation was not the final result. The strongest association appears to be between education and crime, with race and education running second. If we could line up the associations at this point, our model would suggest:

$$\text{Race} \longrightarrow \text{Education} \longrightarrow \text{Crime}$$

We need to control for education at this point (Figure 13-9) and see what happens.

	Education						
	Low			*High*			
	Race			Race			
Crime	Black	White		Black	White		
Low	A_1 15/25%	B_1 5/25%	A_y 20	A_2 25/83%	B_2 75/83%	B_y 100	
High	45/75%	15/75%	C_y 60	5/17%	15/17%	D_y 20	
	A_x 60/100%	B_x 20/100%	80	C_x 30/100%	D_x 90/100%	120	$N = 200$

$\chi^2 = 0$ $df = 1, \alpha = 0.05$ $\chi^2 = 0$

Retain H_0.

Fig. 13-9 Race by crime, controlling for education—first order

Note: Code in cells shows derivation of totals.

We observe that controlling for education totally explains the variable *race*. There is no difference in the rates for crime between blacks and whites. This is quite the reverse of our original findings in a zero-order relationship between race and crime. But unlike the case of association seen in musical preference and motherhood, there still remains the high association of race to education. At this point, we may assume that the most important variable is *education*. Thus, in a revised model we can state:

$$\text{Education} \longrightarrow \text{Crime}$$

–that is, education does have a distinct causal effect on crime. Also unlike the previous association, there is a definite time order. Musical preference could not possibly come before age in variable order; but in this sequence, race definitely comes before education in time order. You have to be born into a certain race before you are educated. Now the question is, Is race an independent or an antecedent variable? Is education independent or intervening? In either case, in a control variable we will get the results shown in Table 13.1. *When education is controlled,*

Table 13.1. Determination of Causal Order

	Control variable ↓	
1. Race antecedent	Education *Independent*	Crime dependent
2. Race independent	Education *Intervening*	Crime dependent

the relationship between race and crime disappears. The matter is resolved by looking at the χ^2 strengths and the time order in the causal chain. Race does influence education, and education does influence crime. The χ^2 readings lead us to accept 1 in Table 13-1, that race is antecedent to the independent variable of education. If we control for race (Figure 13-10), the relationship (χ^2) between education and crime lessens, *but it does remain the same.*[4] That is, the internal percentages in the table remain the same as in the original relationship. There is *no change in the relationship between education and crime* when we control for race. We now know logically that race *cannot* be independent or intervening, because the relationship between race and crime disappears when we control for education, so race must be *antecedent*, and we can conclude that education is indeed an independent variable because of time order, influence, and dominance.

Race influences education, and we know from other studies that education influences occupation and that occupation influences income. It would be fair to conclude that blacks are involved in crime only to the extent that their education is

[4] χ^2 lessens as sample size is reduced, but the percentages should *remain the same internally*.

		Race						
		Black Education			White Education			
		Low	High		Low	High		
Crime	Low	15/25%	25/83%	40	5/25%	75/83%	80	
	High	45/75%	5/17%	50	15/75%	15/17%	30	
		60/100%	30/100%	90	20/100%	90/100%	110	$N = 200$

df = 1, $\alpha = 0.05$

$\chi^2 = 25.2$ $\chi^2 = 25.2$

Fig. 13-10 Crime by education, controlling for race

limited by various social causes. All things being equal, race itself has no bearing on crime rates. The fact that χ^2 has lessened is because, all things being equal (cell size and percentages), the new chi-square will approximate a proportional reduction. The original relationship was $\chi^2 = 65.6$ with a sample of 200; in the sample above of average 100, we could expect a chi-square of half as much, or near 33. Actually, the cell sizes have changed even though the percentages have not; more important, the relationship *remains the same in terms of percentages.*

Our model is now completely changed. Race is no longer the independent variable. The model now becomes:

Race ⟶	Education ⟶	Crime
(Antecedent)	(Independent)	(Dependent)

Race influences education and education influences crime. Race, however, precedes education in time order and really has little effect upon crime except through education. From the original table of "Race by Crime," we could be led to a misleading conclusion because we had not looked into the matter of using a control variable. The moment we picked the right one, the entire picture changed. Moreover, it stood up when we challenged our own proof by controlling for our original "independent" variable (*race*).

This example shows how one must think through the results and not merely assign names for variables. Each variable in a model has logical, substantive, and statistical restrictions on where it goes and what it should be called. If it does not meet the criteria, then it should be challenged and changed.

Notice the nature of the logic:

1. A test or control variable is selected.
2. Relationships are established between all three variables.
3. Internal percentages and χ^2 strengths are noted.
4. A new model is proposed or the old one confirmed.
5. Under control, relationships are checked to see if they vanish, weaken, are lessened or intensified, or reverse.
6. Based on the results, a new model is compared to the one based on zero-order relationships.
7. Variables are reordered or renamed.
8. Other variables, such as the original "independent" variables, are controlled.
9. The results are checked and compared to the results obtained when using the first control variable.
10. The logic is now confirmed and is used to formulate a new model based upon logic, substance, and statistical findings.

Remember that even when statistical restrictions appear to be well founded, the last decision is one of logic, of determining the logical sequence of events and the logical substance and order of what you are doing. Numbers are not everything; they are merely an aid in your own final decision-making process. After the computer has yielded pages of printout and of neat tables for you to tear off and compare, the bottom line is still your own responsibility.

The key to elaboration is to select your control variable carefully. *Select the one that will give you the most impact.* It is usually the one right under your nose, one that is common to both variables in your original table. It may well be already on your instrument and punched into your data cards, just waiting for the right command. And after you have used it, control again to check your own conclusions.

USING THE COMPUTER FOR CONTROL VARIABLES

The computer will not only do all the work for you in elaboration, but print the tables for you to compare. (Cut the tables out and compare them neatly, instead of folding and unfolding reams of computer sheets.) One word of caution: *Do not run out of cases.* Use a sample large enough for the expected number of cells in your control tables. A normal 2 x 2, two times in a simple control, uses eight cells. A sample of 100 should be a minimum requirement if you are going to control. If you use a 3 x 2, your control table will use twelve cells. Remember to increase your sample accordingly.

The actual task specification card should read (using our example on race and crime):

```
               16
CROSSTABS      TABLES=CRIME BY RACE BY EDUCATION
```

This is followed by

```
STATISTICS     ALL
```

These cards are used assuming that you have used the RECODE convention and dichotomized your data on crime and education into high/low categories. Race is already limited to two categories. The second BY convention after RACE on the CROSSTABS card ensures that CRIME BY RACE is examined in each category of EDUCATION (High/Low). The data and tables will be printed out with the dependent variable CRIME at the side so that you may compare percentages across. Race will be on top, and each table will be printed in each category of the controlling variable. If you had used the data from juvenile arrests and convictions, you would notice immediately that the sample ($N = 50$) is too small.

The tables can be printed using:

```
               16
CROSSTABS      TABLES=CONVICT BY ARRESTS BY AGE TO RELIG
```

However, you will notice that in the first controlling variable of age, there are six categories–13, 14, 15, 16, 17, and 18 years. This means 6 x 4 or 24 cells, with only 50 cases. You will have to use Fisher's Exact Probability Test, and this is difficult if you don't know how. Even on *race*, the eight cells required are too many for the sample size, and you would have to use Fisher's Exact Probability Test again. The moment cell size falls below five cases, our calculations are suspect. With several cells below five, the calculations are very "iffy" indeed.

If you follow these rules, you should save time and frustration:

1. Write your task specification card with the dependent variable up front.
2. Calculate your sample size before you attempt to control. If your sample is less than 100, your results will be dubious. (A rule of thumb requires $N = 100$ for eight cells.)
3. Remember to recode and dichotomize your continuous data. You may dichotomize your cases along the mean into HIGH (above the mean) and LOW (below the mean).
4. Make sure all your program cards are in the right order.
5. You may control for more than one variable if you use the right word conventions.
6. When you get your printout, cut the tables out and compare.

Procedure for Using Computer Printouts for Analysis

Modern computers give the researcher access to masses of information, especially when using multiple variables. When a terminal, a programmable calculator, or a major computer is used, a printout is usually desired as a record of programmed calculations. Because the computer is so fast, one tends to use it to the maximum and, consequently, reams of computations are generated. Normally in social science research, the FREQUENCIES program is run first to ascertain the distribution of scores, percentages, means, standard deviation, standard error, range, and variance. From this information the researcher can determine the importance of selected variables.

However, one must not be misled by frequency data. What may appear significant in the distribution may well appear the opposite when used in bivariate or multivariate analysis. In the project on juvenile escape, data indicated that 64.7 percent of youths under detention felt that recreation was adequate; later analysis showed that, to the contrary, lack of recreation was a major factor in attempted escapes from the institution.

Note that frequency percentages will also correspond to marginal percentages in chi-square contingency tables. If you know the formula, the standard deviations and the variance can be used in correlation calculations. In either case, data used from frequency output should meet the assumptions of the statistics used.

FINDING RELATIONSHIPS

The type of variable used will give discrete or continuous data, depending upon its category. If possible, a dependent variable should give continuous data. Let us assume that we have 26 variables in our research investigation, not an unusual number. Assume that they are variables A to Z, with X, Y, and Z being dependent, X and Y being continuous, and Z being discrete (nominal). Variables A through W are independent, A through J are continuous, and K through W are discrete (nominal and ordinal). Because variables A through G are interval-type variables, we decide to proceed from frequency data to correlation. Remember that we can use non-parametric correlation for variables H through W (variables H, I, and J ranked ordinal). We now have:

Independent variables		**Dependent variables**	
A through G	Interval	X, Y	Interval
H, I, J	Ranked ordinal	Z	Nominal
K through W	Nominal and ordinal		

Correlation will give us relationship, strength of the association, and direction. *It will not indicate causality, even though we have set the variables in a proposed causal order for our own convenience.*

There is no point in correlating with all the variables at one time, since certain correlations will be duplicated when using nonparametric analysis. We may correlate with variable Z, even though the results are limited, and we may use nonparametric correlation (Spearman's rho and Kendall's tau) wherever appropriate.

Care must be taken in using correlation. Assume that from initial analysis of available data, we decide to use variables A through G to correlate with X, Y, and Z. Assume the data fall as in Table 13.2. (We may take the data from computer matrix printouts from PEARSON CORR.) These correlations are all zero-order noncausal relationships.

From this table we can select the best and order them as in Table 13.3. Notice that in rank-ordering correlations, assuming the sample size is constant, as the correlation coefficient decreases, the level of significance increases numerically. The strongest coefficients have the best significance—for example, A with X. The rank ordering here has established the ten best correlations, *not* the ten best causal relationships.

Table 13.2. Assumed Correlation Coefficients

Variables	Value	Variables	Value	Variables	Value
A with X	+0.55	A with Y	+0.43	A with Z	+0.51
B with X	−0.32	B with Y	−0.30	B with Z	−0.25
C with X	−0.21	C with Y	−0.21	C with Z	−0.15
D with X	+0.33	D with Y	+0.32	D with Z	+0.42
E with X	−0.39	E with Y	−0.21	E with Z	−0.19
F with X	+0.24	F with Y	−0.38	F with Z	−0.13
G with X	+0.11	G with Y	+0.09	G with Z	+0.12

Table 13.3. Rank-Order Summary of Correlations

Variables	Value	Signif.	Rank
A with X	+0.55	0.000	1
A with Z	+0.51	0.001	2
A with Y	+0.43	0.005	3
D with Z	+0.42	0.010	4
E with X	−0.39	0.015	5
F with Y	−0.38	0.025	6
D with X	+0.33	0.030	7
D with Y	+0.32	0.035	8
B with X	−0.32	0.040	9
B with Y	−0.30	0.050	10

All three dependent variables are represented. From examination of our hypothetical data, we now proceed to determine how we will establish causality by use of either regression or chi-square. For purposes of this text, we will select the variables for chi-square. If we had gone to regression, we have already selected the ten best, and it would be merely a matter of writing the correct program for the computer to determine the effects of the independent variables upon X, Y, and Z as dependent variables.

For chi-square, we may include all the other variables (H through W) if we wish. From the frequency data, we can dichotomize the scores along the means for each variable with continuous data. We may score the divisions High and Low, or we may decide upon four categories and use numbers such as 1-20, 21-30, 31-40, 41-50, or whatever the recoding calls for. Usually, five divisions is maximum, since the number of cells in a chi-square is determined by sample size (see Chapter 12). We even decide upon High, Medium, Low. The dependent variables must also be recoded, dichotomized along the means, or divided at appropriate intervals. Variable Z will remain as is, being nominal.

Summarizing Tables

Let us return to the hypothetical analysis of our variables, which have now been checked from the printouts on cross-tabulations. We observe the results in Table 13.3. The variables chosen are the ten best selected from the rank-ordering of the correlation matrix. We can now summarize the chi-square table as in Table 13.4. The remainder are insignificant and need no further attention.

At this point, we have established a hierarchy of causal relationships. We have determined the factors that are exerting the most influence upon the dependent

Table 13.4. Assumed Chi-Square Results

Variables	Chi-square value	Signif.	df.
A with X	7.89	0.005	1
A with Z	6.62	0.010	1
A with Y	3.89	0.050	1
D with Z	14.6	0.001	3
E with X	10.7	0.004	2
F with Y	18.4	0.000	2
D with X	2.5	0.6	3
D with Y	3.9	0.35	3
B with X	11.4	0.040	4
B with Y	1.8	0.8	4

variable. We can see that independent variable A exerts influence on X, Y, and Z. F has a strong causal influence on Y, as does D upon Z. Variables E, B, and A all affect X.

First-Order Testing of Zero-Order Relationships

Now that we have established a causal hierarchy, the next test is to take the top-ranked variables and use them in an elaboration with a common variable. Again, this is just a matter of writing the correct program for the computer. Assuming that we use variables 27, 28, 29, 30, 31, and 32 for control in elaboration, the results are as in Table 13.5.

Table 13.5. Summary of Chi-Square Values

Variables	Values	Signif.	Rank
F with Y	18.4	0.000	1
D with Z	14.6	0.001	2
E with X	10.7	0.004	3
A with X	7.89	0.005	4
A with Z	6.62	0.010	5
B with X	11.4	0.040	6
A with Y	3.89	0.050	7

From our hypothetical elaboration, we now see that only variable A stands up as an independent variable and exerts causal effect upon dependent variables X, Y, and Z. Other relationships that appeared in zero-order computations failed to hold up under first-order tests. The list of "independent" variables has been drastically cut down by logical analysis. The chances are that if we used regression analysis and established a hierarchy of beta weights, the parametric tests would confirm the

Table 13.6. Ranking Causal Variables

Results of Elaboration		Rank
F with Y	Spurious	
D with Z	Antecedent	
E with X	Intervening	
A with X	Independent and correct	1
A with Z	Independent and correct	2
B with X	Extraneous	
A with Y	Independent and correct	3

nonparametric tests. We would probably find all remaining variables insignificant.

This sequential development of computer tables and summary of those tables aids in selection of the best variables for testing. For an actual example of this program in use, see the study, "Casino Gambling" in the Appendix.

ANALYSIS USING SPSS

The logical sequence of analytical operations using the SPSS program in the social sciences is this:

1. Use FREQUENCIES to examine distributions and percentages. This program also enables you to build a profile. If there is any doubt as to linearity of the data, use SCATTERGRAM.

2. Select your variables for correlation. Use PEARSON CORR or NONPAR CORR to obtain matrices of correlation coefficients. From the matrices, develop hierarchies of correlation strengths and significance. In this rank-ordering of variable zero-order relationships, as r goes down (decreases), the significance value or level goes up or becomes less significant, provided the sample size is constant.

3. Although correlation does not explain causality or even indicate it, we set our variables in model order of proposed causality for our own convenience. From the summary of correlations, we are now in a position to examine causal relationships. We may now use REGRESSION if our data fit the assumptions for the equation, or more probably, CROSSTABS for chi-square analysis. If we use CROSSTABS, we may need to RECODE the data and possibly dichotomize along the means that we have obtained in FREQUENCIES. Care must be taken in using contingency tables, in that our sample size must be large enough for the number of cells (categories).

4. If we have used more than one sample, we may use BREAKDOWN or ANOVA, for a one-way simple analysis of variance, or T-TEST. The data must fit the assumptions of these programs.

5. From regression analysis, we can develop a rank-ordering of beta weights indicating importance in causal association and the effect of the independent

variables upon the dependent variables. From ANOVA, we may determine interaction and compare the means in order of effect. CROSSTABS will help us to sort out the significant values of χ^2 from the nonsignificant; from the significant values, we can summarize in a rank-order table.

6. The advantage of zero-order cross-tabulations is that we now observe *apparent* causality in our proposed model, if it exists at all. From the summary table, we can select the most dominant associations, and, by controlling for a common variable, we can examine first-order relationships.

7. The analysis of first-order relationships by elaboration will also be subject to summary and ranking; it is at this point that final conclusions may be made with a reasonable degree of certainty. First-order analysis is an extension of zero-order analysis, and CROSSTABS is used with control conventions.

8. The final analysis and explanations are the responsibility of the researcher; the computer is only a tool that performs calculations. It is up to the researcher to make sense from the data and to identify causality (if it exists) from the variables used.

9. The concept of summarizing and ranking is to gradually reduce the number of variables involved in the calculations. Even in multiple regression, having too many variables poduces complex and sometimes unwieldy results. It is advisable to deal with the strongest and best relationships. In real life, the correlations are often small, the χ^2 values may be "iffy," and only careful logical analysis will reveal causal associations. Often what appears statistically significant turns out to be spurious, or not related in the way we anticipated.

10. Consider carefully the theoretical limitations on statistical assumptions. We are manipulating variables mathematically in the computer, and then using those calculations to make inferences concerning human behavior. It is logical that the limitations imposed on the data exist after the calculations are made. Therefore, we must use statistics with the awareness that even though numbers create an impression of precision, the real precision is in the use of logic by the human mind. The charisma of numbers is no substitute for simply thinking things through.

The more variables you use in your calculations, the greater the size of the computer printouts and, consequently, the more time you will spend reading and deciphering. The objective is to use the computer to save time. The use of hand calculators (preferably preprogrammed or programmable) will assist you in checking the computer and will save you time on smaller calculations.

SUMMARY

This chapter has discussed the elaboration paradigm, the idea of using more than two variables to understand the complex nature of research. Chi-square uses qualitative data, which is the type we are most likely to use in social research. The careful selection of the test or control variable means that we are to prove or disprove the conclusions as well as the hypothesis. What we may have at first accepted may well be spurious. This means we may have to restate the conclusions based upon the two-variable tables.

We also see the importance of looking at the partial relationships within the tables, the percentages, and the strength of the association. The introduction of a third or test variable may completely change the results. Sample size is important; in the elaboration process, we must not run out of cases for the cells.

The test variable will give us two tables, both virtually standardized tables based upon categories of the test variable. Within those tables we see new relationships that establish, remove, or reverse the original relationships.

Elaboration is a method to discredit superstition and myth. It is a remarkable device to prove the hypothesis if it is indeed sound. Elaboration also establishes variable order in the model. There is really no element of chance or arbitrary naming of variable order; there are definite statistical restrictions, and they become clear in the elaboration process.

The variables may be antecedent, independent, intervening, or spurious. Under elaboration, there is no chance of not knowing where they fit. The rules are specific as to why relationships vanish, diminish, reverse, or emerge. Again, the statistics and the numbers involved in elaboration are impressive and may be significant, but unless they are logical and substantive, they should be treated carefully. The importance of elaboration is that it extends the theory of hypothesis rejection. What appears as statistically (and logically) true at first glance may not be so when it is tested under more exacting conditions. It is a device that compels us to rethink our conclusions.

The computer will do all the numerical work, but it will not do all the mental work involved in careful analysis of the tables. It is best to cut the tables out and compare them, category by category. If the results are not conclusive, then further research may be indicated. Comparison may indicate an entirely new finding for the alert researcher. Be alert for conditional relationships, distortion, or intensification of findings. Such results may indicate the need for a new approach.

Elaboration is the most important tool we have in the research field. It enables us to move into the field of multifactor and multivariate analysis. It widens the research spectrum, deepens our knowledge of variable relationships. And although it may damage our ego by destroying our brainchildren, it also prevents us from making fools of ourselves.

EXERCISES

1. What is a zero-order relationship? a first-order relationship? a zero finding in a relationship? a significant finding?
2. Why should we use first-order relationships?

3. Cite some of the basic rules for elaboration. What is elaboration? What is a control variable?
4. What happens when the relationship vanishes when using a test variable? How would you check the meaning of the two possible answers?
5. What are the statistical restrictions for elaboration?
6. What is meant by, "The control variable sets up two standardized tables"?
7. Explain *bivariate contingency tables; marginals; partials; spuriousness; intervening; antecedent.*
8. There must be a relationship between ______________ the variables (two of, three of, all, some of, none of). Why is this necessary?
9. Is it possible to detect the acceptance of a false hypothesis? How would you do this when it appears to be statistically sound?
10. How would you detect a spurious relationship? an intervening relationship? an antecedent relationship?
11. How would you use percentages to confirm your findings? Give an example and explain.
12. What are the criteria for determining variable order in the model? Suppose there is a strong relationship but no real time order; what kind of a relationship is this?
13. Draw a model where C is the independent variable and describe the results (when C is controlled) between A and dependent variable B. What is variable A?
14. Explain *extraneous; component variable; conjoint influence; mitigating effect; positive direction; conditional effect.*
15. Describe what can happen when the H_o is rejected in a zero-order relationship and there is apparently no error.
16. Explain why sample size is so important. As a first-order exercise, complete the problem on "Motherhood by Musical Preference," and control for musical preference. You have all the figures you need in the tables.
17. Write the formulas for the T-test; chi-square; simple regression. Comment on the meaning of the terms.
18. What is the difference between statistical inference and statistical significance? between internal validity and construct validity? between control variable and control group? between partial correlation and partial regression?
19. If you wanted to test the data on a body-type theory (zero-order), how would you select a variable for control, and how would you go about testing the design? Use the variables in H_a: Body type influences crime.
20. Write up an SPSS task card for testing your own program.
21. Given the following data, complete the first-order analysis, write the hypothesis and the statistical hypothesis (R: etc.), and complete the findings.

	Age: Under 35	Age: Over 35	
Rehab +	40	55	95
Rehab −	50	45	95
	90	100	190

	Age: Under 35	Age: Over 35	
Health +	30	80	110
Health −	60	20	80
	90	100	190

	Health: +	Health: −	
Rehab +	70	25	95
Rehab −	40	55	95
	110	80	190

+ = Good; – = Poor

Compose a model and, based upon first-order relationships, order the variables with their proper names. Give all chi-square scores, including percentages. Always compare the D.V. across the categories of the I.V. The H_0 is that health does not affect rehabilitation. Use age as your test variable. Rehab + indicates a good risk, – means a poor risk. Notice that *age* to *rehab* is valid at $\alpha = 0.2$ (a weak relationship). Compare carefully the percentages *and* the χ^2 in your first-order table. Remember, *all the scores in your first-order table are derived from the tables given.*

FOR FURTHER READING

Bisco, R. L., ed., *Data Bases, Computers, and the Social Sciences.* New York: John Wiley, 1970.

Bock, R. D., *Multivariate Statistical Method in Behavioral Research.* New York: McGraw-Hill, 1974.

Clark, Robert S., *Fundamentals of Criminal Justice Research.* Lexington, Mass.: Heath, 1977.

Cooley, W., and P. Lohnes, *Multivariate Data Analysis.* New York: John Wiley, 1971.

Denzin, N. K., *Sociological Methods.* Chicago: Aldine, 1970.

Frankel, M. R., *Inference from Survey Samples.* Ann Arbor: Institute for Social Research, University of Michigan, 1971.

Franklin, B., and H. Osborne, *Research Methods: Issues and Insights.* Belmont, Calif.: Wadsworth, 1971.

Freund, J. E., *Modern Elementary Statistics.* Englewood Cliffs, N.J.: Prentice-Hall, 1973.

Guilford, J. P., and B. Fruchter, *Fundamental Statistics in Psychology and Education.* New York: McGraw-Hill, 1973.

Haddon, William, *Accident Research.* New York: Harper & Row, Pub., 1964.

Iskrant, A. P., and P. V. Joliet, *Accidents and Homicide.* Cambridge, Mass.: Harvard University Press, 1968.

Johnson, Allan G., *Social Statistics without Tears,* Chaps. 6, 7. New York: McGraw-Hill, 1977.

Johnston, Norman, L. Savitz, and M. Wolfgang, *The Sociology of Punishment and Correction* (2nd ed.). New York: John Wiley, 1970. See Sections I and II.

Kerlinger, Fred N., *Foundations of Behavioral Research* (2nd ed.). New York: Holt, Rinehart & Winston, 1973.

Kish, Leslie, *Survey Sampling.* New York: John Wiley, 1965.

Lazarsfeld, Paul F., and Morris Rosenberg, *The Language of Social Research* (rev. ed.). New York: Free Press, 1971.

Mason, E. J., and W. J. Bramble, *Understanding and Conducting Research.* New York: McGraw-Hill, 1978.

Netter, Gwynn, *Explaining Crime* (2nd ed.). New York: McGraw-Hill, 1978.

Nie, Norman H., et al., *SPSS, Statistical Package for the Social Sciences,* Chaps. 16–20. New York: McGraw-Hill, 1975.

Selltiz, Claire, et al., *Research Methods in Social Relations* (3rd ed.). Holt, Rinehart & Winston, 1976. Chap. 14.

Viano, Emilio, ed., *Criminal Justice Research.* Lexington, Mass.: Heath, 1975.

14

Fallacy, Ethics, and Error

KINDS OF ERROR

It would appear that, based on the concept of Man ⟶ Design ⟶ Computer, there are three kinds of error: error in reasoning, error in the design, and computer error.

Fallacy is the error in reasoning that invites wrong conclusions and ends in misleading statements. It appears in many forms, as we shall see.

Error in the research design, which stems from improper or incorrect procedure in the examination of a problem, has been discussed. It occurs in the statement of the hypothesis, the operationalization of the variables, sampling procedure, and statistical analysis. We are able to control for error in the design and make adjustment accordingly.

Computer error is error in the machine and in its operation. Whereas fallacy is personal and design error is operational, computer error is technical. Technical error also appears in the operation of terminals, calculators, and other hardware. Design error that occurs in software—written programs—becomes technical error when fed into computers.

All research is a science of the control of error. The more we know about error—where it occurs, what it is, what the consequences are—the better able we are to deal with it. We need to be alert for error and, if possible, able to control it.

A major fallacy in research is the assumption that there is one best method. From the previous chapters, survey research might be assumed to be the best. This is not so. Although it is one of the best, it becomes better when used in conjunction with other methods. We do not yet have the sophistication to depend upon any single method. Despite the preeminence of survey research in the social sciences, efforts toward the quantification of human behavior, there are other methods to be discovered. However, we may say it is the best we have *at this time*.

Survey research does enable us to quantify and control in our examination of data and to proceed in a logical sequence. In addition, it can be used to tax and stretch the research imagination. Imagination is really the foundation for all research.[1] Its only boundary is fallacy, which distinguishes reasoned imagination from deception. If we are aware of fallacy, we will not deceive others or ourselves.

FALLACIES IN RESEARCH

If we were to control only for sample error, data error, and computer error, we would be missing a main point. All research is conducted by human beings, and all human beings make mistakes–sometimes small ones, occasionally enormous ones. The biggest mistakes are those that creep in when we are least aware, the mistakes of faulty reasoning. *Fallacies are not only mistakes in reasoning, they are deceptive errors*. Unless we are alert to them, they become part of the research and thus ruin a worthwhile project.

There are several major fallacies to be aware of. We have already mentioned some. They have no particular hierarchy; any one is destructive, and some are more destructive than others, but any combination will ensure misleading results by inviting wrong conclusions.

Ecological Fallacy

When the sample inference is generalized to other populations, the inference is wrong. Suppose we examined a downtown ghetto area and found that blacks commit more crimes than whites. It would be fallacious to assume that this was true for other populations. In this particular instance, it might be shown that blacks outnumbered whites, or that other factors generated high-crime areas–that race was merely accidental to the study. The immediate inference, taken from a sample and generalized to other communities, is dangerous and prejudicial, and will generate racial hostility.

Anytime an inference from a sample is applied to or generalized to a population

[1] Hans Zetterberg, *On Theory and Verification in Sociology* (Totowa, N.J.: Bedminster, 1966), p. 22. While "propositions are the central elements of theory," imagination is the central element of proposition.

other than the one from which it was taken (the parent population), ecological fallacy results. For instance, a sample of a residential district that contained mostly millionaires might contribute views on unemployment that would hardly be compatible with the rest of the population. A famous example is the poll mentioned earlier, when 2 million voters were sampled and the result generalized to the general voting population of the United States. The sample contained a distinct economic bias, excluding poor people, who turned out in large numbers on election day and completely upset the predictions of the *Literary Digest*. Fortunately, the ecological fallacy of generalizing a sample inference to other populations did not affect the outcome, although that might have been the intent.

It would be quite appropriate to use a specialized sample for specific inquiry, especially if a unique parent population was being examined. However, to use such a sample and then generalize to other populations results in error.[2] If we sample the National Rifle Association on attitudes toward firearms, it would be wrong to apply that inference to any other population other than the N.R.A. Similarly, if we sampled the KKK or a group of black prison inmates on prejudice, the inferences could apply only to those specialized groups and not to any other population.

One such ecological fallacy was witnessed in western New York, where the ethnic candidate had his pollster survey by phone a list of similar ethnic followers. The result showed that he would win the election by 9 to 1 over his opponent. The actual outcome was as predicted by proper sampling, and he lost.

Sampling fallacy occurs when extremes of the general population are accepted as being representative of the whole. *Ecological fallacy* occurs when inferences from those extreme samples are generalized to populations other than the ones from which they were taken.

Consider the advertising for a drug that says three out of five doctors recommend it. We are obviously meant to feel that most doctors advise us to use this product. But even though we know that the sample size is expressed as a ratio (unless only five doctors were surveyed), we do not know the actual sample size or what doctors were sampled. They could have been Ph.D.'s or doctors of divinity; or if they were all medical doctors, they could range from pediatricians to coroners—or even veterinarians. The point is that we are not told sample size or sample composition. It may have been an extreme, unrepresentative sample of small size, and to generalize the inference of such a sample—or, for that matter, any sample of doctors—to the consuming public is a fallacy. To compound the issue, the ad tells us that the doctors were tested on a drug, not on a name brand, and the inference from the drug is carried over to the name brand, which is not what the doctors, whoever they were, recommended at all.[3]

A similar situation can occur when we deal with offenders. If we apply our

[2] It is also an error to generalize when a large percentage of scores are missing, "don't knows," and independent. In 1970, four out of five opinion polls predicted election results wrongly in Great Britain, owing to large numbers of undecided votes.

[3] To see what doctors do prescribe, read Martin Gross, *The Doctors* (New York: Dell Pub. Co., Inc., 1966).

conclusions from hard-core criminals to all other criminals, including first offenders, we are in danger of assuming that the criminal population is "all the same." We know that this is not so. On the other hand, in order to secure appropriations for building programs, expansion of correctional forces, rehabilitative services, and the like, figures may be used that include all different kinds. For example, to say that a bigger and better prison is needed to accommodate more and more offenders becomes an ecological fallacy when, in basing the need on the violent offenders, all others are classified the same way. An analysis may show that only 20 percent of the inmate population needs additional security, whereas another 40 percent could safely be placed on parole or probation much more cheaply, and the remainder need no extra correctional facilities.

The Fallacy of Size

It is assumed that sample size will prevent a Type 2 error (retention of a false hypothesis stating that there is no relationship, when in fact there is), and that large numbers will diminish the standard error (increasing the sample fourfold cuts the standard error in half). We have seen how the large sample used in the ***Literary Digest*** poll failed to achieve the desired results. Size in itself is no guarantee of success.[4] Size cannot ensure representation, nor will it eliminate the possibility of a Type 1 *or* Type 2 error. If you recall, the more we move to avoid a Type 2 error by increasing size, the closer we move to a Type 1 error. Large samples create problems in the gathering of data, coding of data, and statistical analysis. Massive samples tend toward redundancy. If we desire huge numbers, we may as well take a census and embrace all the errors that go with census taking.

We also know that increasing size for qualitative data will give results in chi-square analysis that will make a weak relationship appear to be strong. Increasing the sample size (assuming the cell size remains nearly constant) in chi-square increases the chi-square statistic proportionately. Thus, in a 2 × 2 contingency table, a weak relationship of $\chi^2 = 3.38$ will suddenly become $\chi^2 = 7.29$, a strong relationship, when the sample size is doubled from 200 to 400 (see Figure 11-5, in Chapter 11). We must be extremely cautious in using size to determine results.

Size also affects correlation.[5] The larger the samples being correlated, the smaller the correlation tends to become. Thus, a small sample may give a clear indication of correlation, but in substance, that large correlation in a small sample may not be as important as the small correlation in the larger sample. Increasing the sample may diminish the correlation even more. Logically, we can proceed to infinity. The larger the sample, the narrower the dispersion of scores. We may increase the sample, and, assuming the scores remain fairly constant, the correlation will also

[4] Hubert M. Blalock, Jr., "Non-sampling Errors and Sample Size." *Social Statistics*, 2nd ed. (New York: McGraw-Hill, 1972), pp. 529–30.

[5] The significance of the PPM is a function of the sample size, or the r decreases as n increases for a similar α. Homogeneity also decreases r.

remain fairly constant. But in actual practice, as we increase the sample size, we decrease the standard error and thereby tend to increase accuracy. However, in increasing sample size, we tend to reach a point where scores bunch up and where a sample of over 1,500 has little more accuracy than one far smaller.

Large numbers and large sample sizes are no substitute for precision of measurement and accuracy in research procedure. Size eventually reaches a point of diminishing returns; you begin to lose efficiency, increase costs, lose control of masses of data, and waste time sorting the whole thing out.

We can handle small universes such as a large precinct, a prison population, limited regions, but to research a large population requires an appropriate sample with representation and backing up by other methods. The belief that size means success is fallacious. At the opposite end, too small a sample will mean bias. Reread the chapter on sampling theory to arrive at the proper size.

The fallacy of size incorporates *the fallacy of increasing the number of variables* Statistical problems associated with a large number of independent variables include heteroscedisticity, autocorrelation, and multicollinearity. A large number of variables, it is assumed, can explain effects better than a small number can. We know that many causal effects are part of a causal chain, or become the sum total of many other variable effects, or may be influenced by effects or variables not precisely identified. The fallacy here is assuming that by including everything in a variable catchall, we can locate the causal effects. The statistical results are time-consuming "fishing expeditions" that often result in an undesirable "catch of errors."[6]

A large number of variables is not necessary when a model is well thought out. It is true that the computer can now handle vast quantities of data, and that from those data we may determine variable effects, but the danger is in obscuring the main effects in a morass of numbers. If a model is clearly in our minds and we are proceeding along a predetermined theoretical path, the number of variables we use is secondary to the investigation. Of prime concern is the causal relationship we are researching. We are out to discover facts, not to see how many variables we can put in the equation at one time, or how large a sample we can use. Obviously, we do not go to the other extreme and use very small samples or a very limited number of variables that will result in bias. We need to decide on exactly the right formula to use, one that is practical, precise, and appropriate to the research objective.

The Particularistic or Reduction Fallacy

The opposite of the fallacy of size is at the other end of the spectrum, committed by the overparsimonious researcher who makes a god of economy. The error of particularism occurs when a complex problem is reduced to a single factor. Here,

[6] H. C. Selvin and A. Stuart, "Data Dredging Procedures in Survey Analysis," *American Statistician*, 20, 3 (1966), 20–23. See comments on "snooping," "fishing," and "hunting."

we have a reduction of the complex to the simple without sufficient logical or theoretical determination. Most social problems, unlike some mechanical problems, cannot be set right by a single minor adjustment. Social research presents problems that reach across time, geography, culture, and institutions.

Most of our early social research developed on single cross-sectional surveys taken in one place at one time, often producing only a single inference. These became known as one-shot, one-place, one-time surveys. From simple models, simple inferences were advanced. Contemporary research is multifactor, multidimensional, triangulated, and statistically sophisticated.[7] Even then, the results of modern research are recognized as only approximations based upon probabilities. Except as an exercise, there is no room for the single-factor, one-time, one-place survey. This type of study may be used by the media or for entertainment, but academically such use is license for the manipulation of knowledge. Academic professionalism demands accuracy, not fallacy. We cannot posit simple answers to complex problems.

The Fallacy of Absolutism, or the "Iron-Law Syndrome"

Proposing simple answers for complex problems brings forth another fallacy—the fallacy of absolutism. Usually, it arises from trying to find a law to explain problems when statistical or scientific evidence is lacking.[8] Some "iron laws" are amusing—such as Murphy's Law, which maintains that anything that can go wrong will, and at the worst possible time; or Parkinson's Law, which states that office work expands so as to fill the time available for its completion; or the Peter Principle, that people get promoted to the level of their incompetence.

Some are not so amusing. Malthus proposed an iron law of population growth—that because population increases by geometric proportion while land productivity increases by only arithmetic proportion, sooner or later we will run out of land and living substance (food). This iron law prevailed for years, but neither proportion holds true statistically.

Michels's Iron Law of Oligarchy states that leaders will say anything to get in power, and once in, will do everything to consolidate that power.[9] Although we do have some evidence on which to base such an opinion, there is precious little statistical proof. At best, such cynicism belongs to losers and frustrated office seekers. A corollary to this law is the so-called Two Laws of Politics: The first law

[7] A. H. Barton and Paul Lazarsfeld, "Qualitative Support of Theory," in *Issues in Participant Observation*, George McCall and J. L. Simmons, eds. (Reading, Mass.: Addison-Wesley, 1969), pp. 239–45.

[8] The flat-earth theory held the physical sciences back for centuries. It was compounded by an earth-centered-universe theory and a glass-spheres theory, both equally fallacious, but maintained by severe punishment for disbelief, or "heresy."

[9] Robert Michels, *Political Parties* (New York: Dover, 1959).

states that the aim of the politician is to get elected, the second law that all other laws pertain to the first law.

It would appear that iron laws or absolute laws may be politically motivated to suit certain circumstances. In criminology, we have the various contentions that rehabilitation does not work: "You must do the time for the crime;" "Once an addict, always an addict;" "Criminals are sick people;" and so on. We even have a "rotten-apple theory" for corruption in police departments.[10] Often such statements are a step away from absolutism.

In the physical sciences, absolutes are measures of probability, they are not finite. Absolute zeros, absolute melting points, absolute measurement are known to change with circumstances. In the social sciences, we do not deal with inert matter, but with people who have minds of their own. Thus, absolutes are impossible, and it is a fallacy to assume finality to any discovery concerning human behavior.

Underlying the idea of absolutes in the social sciences is the problem of definition of terms. Exact definition of terms applicable to human behavior appears to be transitory and varies from culture to culture. Thus, we have a vertical fluctuation through time and a horizontal instability through culture. This means that data collected on the basis of definitions used in the research have, at best, limited application.[11] This concept means that there can be no final definitions and therefore no final decisions. Whatever the conclusions may be, they are subject to change. In addition, research conclusions should be open to challenge and innovation.

The worst absolute of all is, "We have always done it this way," or, "This is the established method." Research should not be limited or restricted to any one method. Although we do need the limits of rationality, common sense, and the scientific method, we must never limit the research imagination. More than ever, we need new methodology to cope with the ever-expanding field of discovery. If we do not challenge the implied absolutism of present methodology, we encourage compartmentalism and eventually become a hybrid discipline.

The Fallacy of Self-Preservation

The fallacies of size and absolutism appear to be linked with the desire for infallibility, immortality, and indestructibility. Unfortunately, all three are impossible; human beings are fallible, mortal, and destructible.

In addition, the modern system of university endeavor that encourages research creates a pressure to generate status and prestige. Some people, acting under this pressure to attract huge grants through prestigious publications and significant research, resort to complex techniques and elaborate mechanisms supporting and

[10] Rodney Stark, *Police Riots* (Belmont, Calif.: Wadsworth, 1972), pp. 9–11.

[11] Arthur J. Bachrach, "The Problem of Definition." *Psychological Research*, 2nd ed. (New York: Random House, 1965), Chap. 4.

maintaining the status quo.[12] Some professors use students' work, some fabricate research findings, others use the cloak of university prestige. Some would rather die than watch a life's work evaporate under scrutiny. Such people are motivated by the desire for self-preservation, self-interest, and self-indulgence, rather than by the true academic virtues of self-assurance, self-denial, and self-discipline.

Sooner or later, someone somewhere will discover. penetrate, and expose the fabrication. In the physical sciences, it is a matter of history that Galileo's "heresy" eventually triumphed over religious fallacies. Even today, a person may suffer for opposing traditional views with an idea that will someday prove correct. In the social sciences, it is unlikely that we will be burned at the stake for statistical heresy, but it is likely that we will be subject to peer pressure to protect, conform, and preserve.

A common error in the presentation of statistical findings is to *rely on the numerical impact of statistics and ignore the theoretical limitations under which we operate*. Figures are more precise than words, and they give the "feeling of science."[13] Statistics, however precise, and especially those used in the behavioral sciences, are based upon probabilities, averages (means), and theoretical dispersions. The logic of survey research is in the mind of the researcher, not in the electronic computer. Statistics, computers, and calculators are tools, not brains.

It is error to manipulate findings to satisfy a pet theory, or to supplement a status position. It may be easy to do and tempting, but the results are unethical and damaging. If the researcher keeps the research objective clearly in mind and is aware of the theoretical restraints and assumptions, control for error will eliminate some imperfections. Control exercised by the researcher on logical reason, or self-control, is just as important as control in design or technological computation.

Statistical Fallacy

Statistical significance is the level at which we reject the null hypothesis. This level is arbitrary and is set at the amount of risk we wish to take. Varying the level of significance can change the statistical outcome, implying that the relationship has occurred by cause and effect, and some chance. We can never eliminate all the probability of chance, and even the slightest error in the statistical calculations increases that probability. But suppose the wrong statistical calculation was used; then the entire result would be fallacious—indeed, the chances of its being correct would be remote. This can happen when linear calculations are used for curvilinear data, or U-shaped data; or when the assumptions for a particular statistical method

[12] Earl R. Babbie, "The Debunking of Science," *Survey Research Methods* (Belmont, Calif.: Wadsworth, 1973), pp. 7–8.

[13] Paul F. Lazarsfeld, Foreword, in Hans Zeisal, *Say It with Figures*, 5th ed. (New York: Harper & Row Pub., 1968), p. xvi: 'What is needed. . .is an intelligent grasp of what figures stand for and what they can be used to express."

are not met. The wrong conclusion could be made even if the right calculation was used with the wrong significance level.

Again, most of our statistical calculations are based upon sample size. We have discussed error that can arise when the sample size is too small or is unrepresentative. We are also aware of small correlation in large samples and large chi-square statistics in huge samples, and the respective errors of those calculations.

In addition, statistical error appears to be an accompanying hazard of qualitative data. Nonparametric data are not nearly as precise as parametric data. Moreover, whatever the statistical significance may be, the importance is in the substantive significance, which, even though based upon statistics, is nonstatistical.

Correlation Fallacy

Because correlation is so important and is used so often, there is a tendency to give it qualities it does not possess. *It can never be used for causal explanation*; the fallacy occurs when it is. At best, correlation can only show the relationship between two variables and indicate whether or not they may be used for regression (prediction) equations. Correlation is a measure of association wherein one variable is equal to and as important as the other. It will give a strength to the association known as the correlation coefficient, or *r*, and it will even indicate direction and, if required, a significance level for the association.

If, for example, a high correlation was shown between divorced parents and juvenile delinquents, and this was reported as stating that divorce causes juvenile delinquency, a major fallacy has occurred. All that can be reported is a strong association between divorced parents and juvenile delinquency, nothing more; the statistical statement from the correlation might say, for instance:

> A high correlation of 0.6 at the 0.001 level of significance, showing a positive correlation between divorced parents and juvenile delinquency.

There is absolutely no cause and effect expressed in the correlation equation. If one does not know this, or is unaware of the theoretical limits of correlation, then the fallacy will occur over and over.

To prove this point, a study showed (purposely) that the incidence of office workers leaving employment was correlated to the incidence of V.D. in the community. The relationship was spurious, of course, and any inferences either way were entirely fallacious. Correlation fallacy involves the recognition of spurious relationships, symmetrical relationships, and fortuitous circumstances.

Correlation may occur because one variable causes another–X may cause Y, or Y may cause X–or because of a third variable, not identified. Correlation may be seen to occur by chance, by reciprocal interaction, or by coincidence. But no matter how correlation occurs, it may never be used for causal explanation. This would be a post hoc or correlation fallacy. Remember that whenever you use correlation, you must conform to the statistical assumptions for the equation, whether it be parametric or nonparametric.

Correlation, in fact, may be used to avoid fallacy. Because of its sophistication in using continuous data, it can unlock the door for further statistical analysis such as regression and prediction. Correlation, while showing a relationship, does so on the assumption that the variables are equal in importance. The change to regression formula moves from relationship and equal variable value to causal effect and the influence of the independent variable upon the dependent variable while still using the same variables. The use of the regression equation implies the use of causal criteria for determination of variable order. Not only are we seeking prediction, but in order to do so, we must use the criteria of time order, dominance, and influence to determine variable sequence in the regression equation. Even though the regression equation is similar to and based upon the Pearson Product Moment, to proceed with regression we must order the variables, whereas in the PPM, we need not do so.

Correlation is sometimes deceptive, in that what appears before us may seem already ordered. Consider the relationship of violent behavior and watching TV programs, long a hotly debated issue.[14] Morally, out of indignation or intuition, we may assume that violence is a product or cause of watching violent TV programs. Our studies may well indicate a correlation of, say, 0.7, and from this strong correlation coefficient we assume a causal relationship. Such a relationship is entirely without proof, and indeed may be spurious. We may *assume* (1) that watching TV causes violence; or (2) that violent people enjoy watching violent TV; or (3) that TV is a cathartic for violence, that without it there might be more violence in society. But these assumptions are strictly conjectural, hypothetical, and philosophical—meaningless when we consider correlation. All that we can truly say is that there is a high correlation between watching TV programs and violence, and that because of the strong relationship, the variables may be used in a regression equation.

From that point on, the researcher has to decide which comes first in time order, which is most dominant and least likely to change, and which is most likely to influence the other. The answer to the question of time order—for the present generation who are raised on TV—is a matter of "the chicken or the egg;" the question of dominance implies that the dependent variable is more likely to change than the independent, and once more we are in a dilemma as to which will change most, the person or the program; as to influence, we assume TV influences the person, but since influence implies control, the assumed "influence" of TV may well be confused with other, not so obvious, extraneous variables, such as parental conflict, poverty status, racial bigotry, and the like. Setting up a model on this

[14] S. Feshbach and R. D. Singer, *Television and Aggression* (San Francisco: Jossey-Bass, 1970); and UNESCO Reports and Papers on Mass Communications, no. 43, *The Effects of Television on Children and Adolescents.*

question of TV viewing and violence almost implies finding a predetermined scapegoat simply because of a high correlation.

This example shows that moving to regression from correlation is not without problems. It must be thought through, and care must be given to construction of the model. It is important to remember that *causality implies prediction, and prediction implies causality*. If we presume to predict violence on the basis of TV viewing, we are taking a calculated risk that the presumption will be in error if it is based solely on the results of correlation. We need to supplement our statistical proof by substantive proof. Some measures and observations may be such that we "feel them in our bones," knowing them instinctively to be right; but we are not in the business of *a priori* postulation. We are seriously engaged in scientific investigation, and we decry soothsaying, superstition, and prejudicial opinion. If we still feel we are on the right track but cannot prove it, we had best look around for better methods. Obviously, quantifying human behavior is not going to be easy.

Remember, once again, that *we are not out to prove anything; we are out to discover facts*. Although correlation is an invitation to go forward with research findings, it is also an entrapment for error and an invitation to exercise the research imagination. Correlation opens a Pandora's box of statistical good and evil. It is by being aware of the consequences of what you are doing that you decide which way to go. Do not enter into a *predictive fallacy* unless you are sure of the direction of causality.

The Fallacy of Visual Impact

Graphs are often used to express statistical findings. They may be presented in any number of ways. Some are presented to show facts; others to make a point or to cover up statistical shortcomings. The latter are usually complete with misleading averages and dubious percentages. Perhaps the worst offenders are the pictographs giving comparisons of size, showing ratios expressed in pies, the shapes of people, buildings, piles of cash, or insets on a line graph showing expressions of satisfaction.[15]

The graph, because of its "scientific" impact on the layperson, expresses far more precision than words. Therefore, graphs should be used with caution to avoid errors in either their presentation or their reception. If a graph is used, it should state clearly all the pertinent information and be presented as fairly as possible to avoid manipulating the reader.

Expressions such as those used in the media are not a part of true research presentation. Examples of poor graphs can be found in magazines and journals and on TV. They misrepresent and distort issues for the purpose of profit and vested interest, adding up to nothing more illuminating than a statistical sales pitch.

[15] A problem arises in translating a two-dimensional graph to a three-dimensional picture, or adding dimensions of time and feelings to a simple graph. Illustrations tend to draw attention away from the issues and toward preset conclusions.

The Christmas Tree Fallacy

No matter how you paint a rotten egg, it is still a rotten egg, or so goes an old Asian proverb. The truth is that no matter how well you bind your presentation, how fine the quality of the bond paper or parchment you use, if it is a poor research job, no amount of beauty will cover up that fact. There are already too many "snow jobs" filling library shelves—prestigious studies, but some of them impossible to read and some too heavy to hold. Some sway you with eloquence, some intimidate you with jargon, some overwhelm you with tables and diagrams, and some seduce you with prejudice. They are "Christmas trees" that have long since lost their tinsel and gloss. They were dressed up to impress the reader for the occasion, and some did. But their factual content, their readability, their social content were lost in a sacrifice of ethics to ambition. The last thing you do in a research project is present your report. It is a part of you. It is your mark of quality. Don't make it a Christmas tree, or a rotten egg.

Many fallacies have been presented here.[16] They are traps that are easily fallen into. They are errors. Research is a science in the control of error. It begins with concept error, goes to hypothesis error, accumulates sample error and data error, and finally ends in presentation error. In a way, it is like walking a tightrope; you need only one false step to fall.

THE ETHICS OF RESEARCH

As scientists, we have three obligations we must consider: to the discipline, to peers, and to the client.

In our obligation to the discipline, we are under an unwritten law to discover facts, to report them truthfully, and to share our findings with the academic community. Regardless of whether we work in pure or applied science, we are dedicated to improving the quality of life and ought not permit the introduction of research that will materially harm fellow humans. We should challenge other research and expect to be challenged.

A researcher respects other researchers, past and present, but that respect is for integrity and does not extend to protecting fallacy. It is an occupational hazard that one's work will be scrutinized, analyzed, and criticized. One's own research methods should be able to withstand ethical examination. In exploring the frontiers of knowledge, the researcher will not ride roughshod over colleagues, associates, students, or clients. To gain respect, treat others with respect.

[16] Not all the possible fallacies have been presented; you will meet others, and you may read about others in the bibliography.

Ethics toward the Respondent

In inquiring into people's lives, as we often do in survey research, we need to consider the rights of the client, whether paid or voluntary. Money may be used to compensate for time or as an incentive to respond, but never as a bribe or coercion, or in any way to distort the outcome of the inquiry. The following are other points regarding the rights of the respondent and the obligations of the researcher:

1. *Guaranteed anonymity* should be available if the client so desires. Each person has a right to be protected from intrusion or invasion of privacy. Often in surveys, information is disclosed that is of a very personal nature; the client has a *right of confidentiality* and anonymity if it is requested. In any case, such information is privileged and ought not to be disclosed to anyone else. In the course of an interview, much that is said is not used in the survey, and the client has the *right to expect protection from harm caused by any information disclosure*. Confidentiality protects what is said, anonymity protects who said it.

2. *The full nature and intent of the inquiry should be disclosed* to the client. The client has the *right to know* what is going on and how it will affect him. If there are to be exceptions to this ethic—as, for example, in research on lying and cheating—the investigator is under obligation to reveal his intent at the end of the experiment but is still under obligation to protect his client from harm. The right to know involves the *right to be protected from injury*. Unless the client specifically volunteers for an experiment involving risk (and is not under duress), the research should not damage the client either physically or psychologically.

3. *All responses should be voluntary*. Respondents should volunteer their services and never be coerced, threatened, abused, or intimidated. Neither will the researcher use deception to obtain incriminating data, nor expose the client to criminality, immorality, or perversion "in the name of science." Nothing is to be gained by unethical conduct or tainted research. *The client has the right to be free from deception and misconduct.*

4. The client has the *right to expect truthful and accurate reporting of the facts*, even if the results are contrary to the research expectations. Hiding the discovery of new facts will destroy good research.

5. While aware of possible bias and prejudice in the client, the researcher will be *impartial and objective*, recognizing that his or her own convictions may lead to bias.

Effects that Cause Fallacy

Protection of the client occasionally leads to undesired results. For example, informing the client of the nature of the research may cause the client to try harder or to try to conform to the anticipated outcome. This effect is known as the *Hawthorne effect*, from the Western Electric plant near Chicago where early experiments were undertaken.[17] Apparently, the workers there thought the experiments were testing their ability to increase production under any circumstances, such as increasing or decreasing the lighting; so production rose regardless of test conditions. *Knowledge of the nature of the experiment resulted in clients' influencing the outcome.*

This also happens in medical experiments when placebos are given. Although they are supposed to have no effect, it is estimated that 25 percent of those given them will claim improvement.[18] Unusual weight loss or apparent increase in mental or physical performance may well be due to prior knowledge of the experiment by the client, who felt that it would be nice to be on the "winning side."

Influence may also be exerted by the researcher, where the researcher knows the prior record of the client and *knowledge of the client influences the researcher* in scoring the outcomes. Such an effect is called *contamination*, because it literally contaminates the data.

Having little or no knowledge of the issues involved may induce the client to score on the basis of a favorable or unfavorable personality—that is, of whether the client likes or dislikes the person or institution in question. For example, if one liked a certain police department, one might be tempted to score it high regardless of the issues involved or their importance. Similarly, one would be somewhat cautious in revealing one's sexual habits to the same police department. This rating, *based upon impressions* or emotions, is called the *halo effect.*[19]

These effects may be summarized:

1. Client has knowledge of the issue but not of the researcher; Hawthorne effect may result.
2. Client has little knowledge of the issue but has impression or knowledge of the researcher; halo effect may result.
3. Researcher has knowledge of the issue and the client; contamination effect may result.
4. Researcher has knowledge of the issue and no knowledge or impressions of the client; correct, no effects anticipated.

The first three situations could result in fallacy and should be considered carefully when such conditions may be present. In the fourth, it is assumed that the researcher will proceed correctly without either deception or manipulation. Failure to do so will result not so much in fallacy as in something bordering on fraud.

[17] George C. Homans, on the "Bank Wiring Room" *The Human Group* (New York: Harcourt Brace Jovanovich, Inc., 1950).

[18] E. M. Jellinek, "Clinical Tests on Comparative Effectiveness of Analgesic Drugs," *Biometric Bulletin of A.S.A.*, 2 (October 1946), 87–91.

[19] Fred N. Kerlinger, *Foundations of Behavioral Research*, 2nd ed. (New York: Holt, Rinehart & Winston, 1973), pp. 548–49.

PROJECT ERROR

The research project may be broken down for the purposes of control into two main sections, the *design* and its *analysis*. Design may incorporate the *generation of ideas* and data; analysis is the *generation of findings* or conclusions.

Under the heading of ideas is the topic itself, the hypothesis, and the selection of the variables necessary to complete the research design. The generation of data is made by operationalization and sampling, which includes the description and explanation of the variables, instrument construction, specification of sampling procedure, actual sampling technique, and the scoring of data.

The generation of findings includes two parts: technical or computer processing, and interpretation or appraisal of the findings and the summary of them, including evaluation.

From this breakdown of the research project, we can identify several more points at which we can exercise control. A total of eleven points may be enumerated:

1a. Control in topic selection
1b. Control in making the hypothesis statement
1c. Control in variable definition, description, and explanation
2. Control in the selection of the sampling methodology
3. Control over question design and instrument construction
4. Control of the client interview or method used
5. Control over scoring and coding of data
6. Control of the use of statistical analysis
7a. Control of the logical analysis of findings
7b. Control over presentation of findings
7c. Control of evaluation

These points, keyed as above, are amplified in the text and table following.

Control of Error in the Research Design

From the moment we decide upon a *topic*, we must beware of error, such as the selection of a nonmeasurable metaphysical project containing conceptual fallacy. We must avoid projects that lack imagination and fail to motivate or stimulate interest. We need to be able to state the research *hypothesis* clearly and posit it in testable form. The *variables* should be clearly identified, defined, and explained.

The *sampling method* chosen should be one that fits the research objectives and will give a reasonably accurate picture of the parent population. The *instrument*, refined by pretest, should be able to generate the data needed for the research. At the key point in the research, the actual *interview* will generate the data necessary. Control over error at this point is essential.

Thus we have established the first four control points in the survey research method:

1. Control at topic selection, hypothesis statement, and variable definition and explanation–preliminary operationalization
2. Control for sample selection, method, and procedure
3. Control of the questionnaire–construction, pretest, redesign
4. Control of the interview–interviewers, ethics, and data

Control at points 2, 3, and 4 is of the operationalization of the project, the final testing of the instrument by interview upon a sample.

Error in Analysis

At points 5 and 6, control is exercised over numerical entry. Errors enter into coding by the failure to check entries, the duplication of entries, or the losing of entries. It is very easy to make mistakes at this point, especially if a complex coding system is used. The computer printouts need to be checked carefully, and calculations should be spot-checked. The final writing will depend upon the work performed on the statistical analysis.

The conclusions, presentation, and evaluation are the final written end of the project. These in fact summarize your research design and complete your research methodology.

Fallacy and the Research Project

The four primary control sections for error, with a total of eleven points where we can intercede to prevent or reduce error, are illustrated in Figure 14-1 and amplified in Table 14.1. As you can see, fallacy may creep in at any point in the project's design or analysis. The selection of the *topic* may be fallacious if the reasoning is faulty, and this will accumulate in the *hypothesis statement* at points 1a and 1b. At 1c, the fallacy may occur in the *number of variables* selected or the ambiguous *definition* of those variables. The model may also be a *single-factor model*, reducing the problem to particularistic fallacy. The *sample size* at point 2 may be too small or too large, inviting a fallacy of size. At point 3, the fallacy is one of construction of *leading or misleading questions*. During the interview at point 4, we must avoid the effects of *contamination, manipulation, halo effect*, and (Hawthorne) client *anticipation of outcomes*. Coding of data may lead to *numerical fallacy* in entering devious scores, wrong entries, and wrong codes. At point 6, *statistical fallacy* occurs with the wrong level of analysis, the use of false assumptions, and wrong levels of significance with the right level of statistical analysis.

It is in final logical analysis (7a) that most fallacies occur: *ecological fallacy*,

Table 14.1. Identification and Control of Error in the Research Project

Control	Research process	Type of error	Control
1.(a)	Selection of topic	Meta- or paraphysical conceptual error	Use observable phenomena.
		Lacks imagination Lacks interest	Research topic should solve problem.
(b)	Hypothesis statement	Not testable States opinion Ambiguous	State precise research hypothesis and testable null.
(c)	Variable selection	Cannot be identified	Description
		Cannot be tested	Definition
		Cannot be used in model	Explanation
2.	Sampling method	Vagueness, population not known	Specify population.
		Limited by time/ location	
		Type 2 error	Increase sample size.
		Poor sample–extremes Overspecialized	Use more than one sampling method.
		Lacks representation	Use random selection.
		Lacks homogeneity	Stratify.
		Lacks proportion	Multistage cluster.
		Lacks variable needs	Triangulate.
3.	Construction of instrument	Ambiguity/translation	Avoid jargon.
		Question error/ response set	Avoid leading questions.
		Needs redesign	Pretest/back-translate
		Too complex	Keep to the point.
		Poor scales	Use good design.
4.	Interview of client	Halo effect/ Hawthorne effect	Be impartial, impersonal.
		Bias/prejudice	Check sample/questions.
		Curbsiding	Check data.
		Manipulation/ contamination	Check worker.
		No protection for client	Check ethics.
5.	Coding of data	Complex codes	Use simple code.
		Wrong code/sample error	Check coding sheet.
		Printout error	Check IBM cards.
6.	Statistical analysis	Type 1 error	Tighten level of significance.
		Wrong level of analysis	Keep to statistical assumptions.
		Wrong calculations	Check for curvilinear data.
		Curvilinear data	
		Computer error	Check calculations.

Table 14.1. (cont'd.)

Control	Research process	Type of error	Control
7.(a)	Conclusions and interpretation of results	Wrong interpretation*	Check for Type 1 and Type 2 errors.
		Incorrect use of C.I. and C.L.	Check tables and calculated figures.
		Poor internal controls	Check statistical against substantive significance.
		Wrong causal statement	Elaborate.
		Incorrect use of correlation	Determine time order, dominance, and influence.
		Conclusions based upon single method	Examine frequencies, correlations, and chi-squares.
(b)	Presentation	Ambiguity	Be clear, concise, and precise.
		Confusion	Avoid redundancy, irrelevancy, useless data and tables, meaningless findings.
		No real substance	Report all major findings accurately.
(c)	Evaluation	No suggested improvement	Be critical of self and work.
		Low efficiency, output does not justify input	Evaluate project for future improvement in methodology.
			Further research should be indicated.

*Check data based upon assumptions of normal curve, confidence levels and confidence limits.

correlation or *post hoc fallacy, absolutism*, and *self-preservation*. At 7b, we must beware of *visual impact, Christmas tree*, and "snow." Evaluation (7c) should be free of fallacy, but here the most dangerous fallacy is that of faulty or *deceptive reasoning*, inviting wrong conclusions—the fallacy of fallacy itself.

Technical Error

Precision in measurement *must* become a habit for the researcher. If there is substance to the "transfer-of-training theory," wherein skills learned in one area carry over to another, then the precision practiced in measurement should carry over to computer skills. *Precision in computer operations is absolutely essential.* If there is a fallacy in computer operations, it is the belief that one can get by with less than perfect precision—the fallacy of presumption. Every word, every detail, every entry must be precisely as defined in the computer language that is being used. It is my experience that SPSS programs[20] are used more widely than any others in the social

[20] Norman H. Nie, C. Hadlai Hull, Jean G. Jenkins, Karin Steinbrenner, and Dale H. Brent, *Statistical Package for the Social Sciences*, 2nd ed. (New York: McGraw-Hill, 1975).

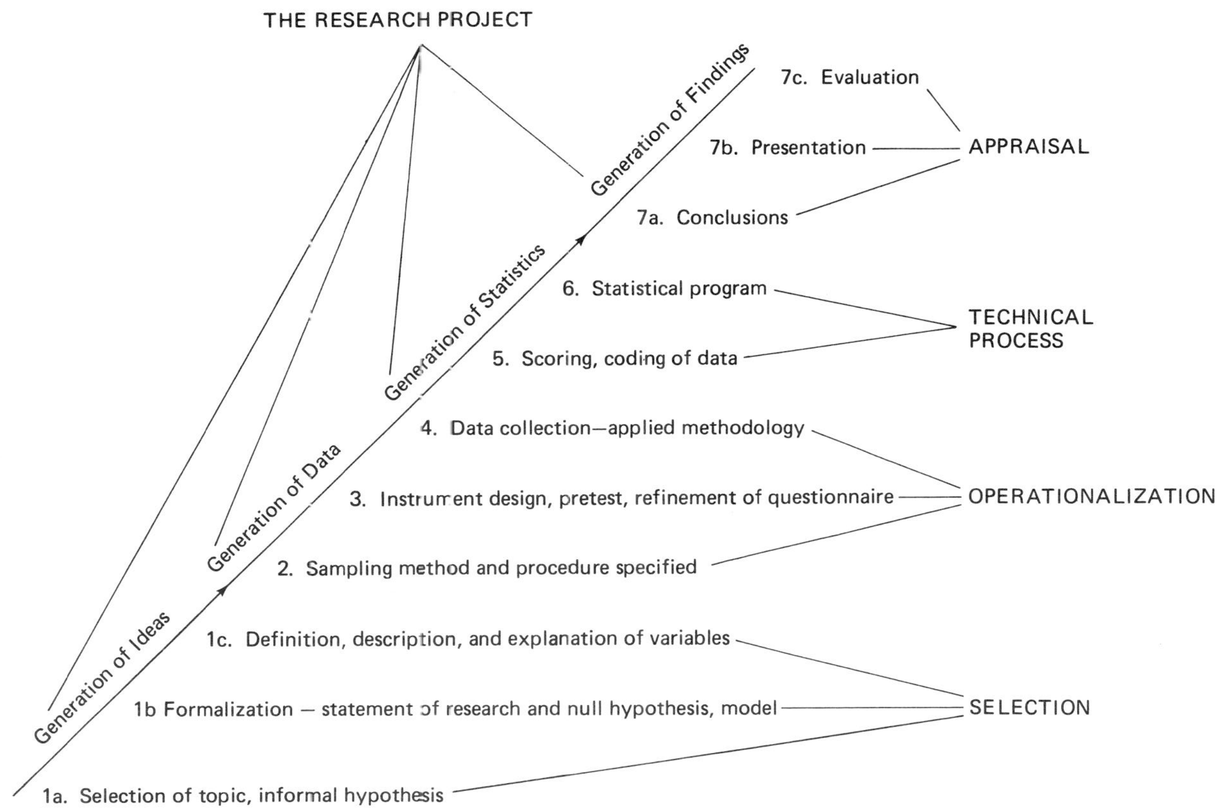

Fig. 14-1 Points of control in research design and analysis of the research project

sciences. SPSS requires *exact* conformity to computer language conventions. There is no room for error of any kind.

You will learn what the errors are by experience based upon past mistakes. Each time you use the computer, you will learn something new, and with the present rate of technical expansion, you will also learn new computer methodology. No matter how often you use the computer, always check your own data, then check the computer printouts. Do not accept anything that appears devoid of error; verify and check calculations by other methods.

Technical error can ruin a good project, but it is one error that you can spot and remedy. It may take time, especially if the error is in your data deck, but consider the time it would take if there were no computers.

SUMMARY

Fallacy occurs wherever there is faulty reasoning. It is an invitation to make the wrong conclusions. It abounds where there is bias, prejudice, and value judgment. Although life is made up of day-to-day value judgments and snap decisions based upon common sense, science demands more, in that our conclusions must be based upon reasonable facts that can be verified in some way. The more methods used for verification, the greater the validity.

The fallacies that have been presented in the text and related to points of control in the research project are these:

1. Fallacy of selection of metaphysical topic
2. Fallacy of false hypothesis statement (untestable or self-fulfilling)
3. Fallacy of number of variables
4. Fallacy of ambiguous definition of variables
5. Particularistic fallacy of single-factor model–reduction fallacy
6. Fallacy of leading or misleading questions
7. Hawthorne effect
8. Halo effect
9. Contamination
10. Manipulation
11. Numerical fallacy–wrong entries and wrong coding
12. Statistical fallacy–wrong statistical level of analysis
13. Fallacy of size–too big or too small
14. Fallacy of sampling extremes
15. Ecological fallacy
16. Correlation or post hoc fallacy
17. Hypothesis fallacy–Type 1 or Type 2 error (1st and 2nd order)
18. Predictive fallacy
19. Fallacy of absolutism

20. Self-preservation fallacy
21. Fallacy of visual impact
22. Christmas-tree fallacy
23. Evaluation fallacy
24. Computer fallacy

There is no particular hierarchy of fallacy; its destructiveness depends on where it occurs. Most fallacy occurs during the final logical analysis—the interpretation of results, the making of inferences, the analysis of one's own work. Often we invite fallacy by simply not being rigorous enough in criticism of our work.

Fallacy also involves self-interest and ethics. The more we protect self-interest, the less we are concerned with ethics, especially ethics concerning others.

Because of the deceptive nature of fallacy, it is hard to detect. A knowledge of fallacy enables us to be alert for it and control for it. We need to be particularly aware of ecological fallacy, or generalizing sample inferences to other than parent populations. Size, large or small, can also generate fallacy. Be on your guard for single-factor explanations and absolutes, and for post hoc and statistical fallacies. Avoid "dressing up" your final report with long words and visual impact. If your project is worthwhile, it will speak for itself. Quantity is no substitute for quality.

The research project has eleven points where you can exercise control on the outcome by reducing or eliminating error. Control of quantitative error is relatively simple; control of qualitative error is not so easy. Control points 4, 5, 6, and 7a are quantitative; some others, such as points 2, 3, and 7b, are both qualitative and semiquantitative.

Technical error occurs in the use of the computer. Nowhere in the research project is precision demanded more. The user must be absolutely precise, exact to the *n*th degree; otherwise, the machine will yield garbage or will not function at all.

The way to control error and fallacy is to be constantly alert for them and to check them as they occur. There is no cookbook method; you learn by doing.

EXERCISES

1. What are the three basic types of error?
2. Is survey research *the* best method? Give your reasons.
3. Explain ecological fallacy and give an example.
4. What is the fallacy of size? How does it affect outcomes with correlation? chi-square? What are the disadvantages of size? What is the correct size?
5. What is wrong with "hunting and fishing" expeditions? Can they be useful?
6. Explain the reduction fallacy and give an example.
7. Cite an "iron law" that you have heard of. Why is it untrue? What fallacy is involved here?

8. How can peer pressure affect your findings? If you were asked to review the research of your best friend and you found it in error, how would you handle this? Would you make a trade in case he reviews yours?
9. Self-preservation involves ethics. Explain how. Comment on any recent cases you know of. Anthropological research contains some famous bogus discoveries. See if you can locate one.
10. What are the rights of the client in research? the rights and obligations of the researcher?
11. Being ethical may involve other fallacies; explain how this can happen. What are three types of fallacy that can occur in the researcher–client relationship?
12. Comment on how statistical fallacy may occur. Can we eliminate the probability of chance effects? What can we do about chance?
13. What is another name for correlation fallacy? Explain how it can occur and why certain interpretations are fallacious.
14. How can correlation fallacy be extended into regression?
15. What are the fallacies of visual impact? Describe how TV commercials use "statistics" to increase sales.
16 What is the "Christmas tree" fallacy?
17. The research project may be broken down into several sections for the purposes of control; what are they? What points of control come under the heading of "generations of data"? Are these qualitative or quantitative?
18. How would you control for error in selection of the research design?
19. What can cause error in the presentation of findings?
20. What is the fallacy of presumption with computers?
21. Name some of the more common errors in computer operation.
22. Where do the worst errors usually occur? Give examples.
23. Define *fallacy, hierarchy, ethics, value judgment, ambiguity, post hoc, "snow job," manipulation.*
24. Comment on the use of value judgments, common sense, the scientific method. How can fallacy enter into any of these?
25. Of the fallacies given in the text, ask yourself if any can occur in your own research project.

FOR FURTHER READING

Adler, Irving, *Probability and Statistics for Everyman: How to Understand and Use the Laws of Chance*. New York: John Day, 1963.

Blackwell, David, *Basic Statistics*. New York: McGraw-Hill, 1969.

Campbell, Stephen K., *Flaws and Fallacies in Statistical Thinking*. Englewood Cliffs, N.J.: Prentice-Hall, 1974.

D'Arcy, J. A., *Chance and Choice: Practical Probability and Statistics*. London: Thames and Hudson, 1968.

Epstein, Richard A., *The Theory of Gambling and Statistical Logic*. New York: Academic Press, 1967.

Hadley, George, *Introduction to Business Statistics*. San Francisco: Holden-Day, 1968.

Hopkins, Harry, *The Numbers Game*. London: Secker & Warburg, 1973.

Huff, Darrell, *How to Lie with Statistics*. New York: W.W. Norton & Co., Inc., 1954.

Moroney, M. J., *Facts from Figures*. London: Penguin Books, 1951.

Oliver, Francis R., *What Do Statistics Show?* London: Hodder, 1964.

Reichard, Robert S., *The Numbers Game: Uses and Abuses of Managerial Statistics*. New York: McGraw-Hill, 1972.

Reichmann, William, *Use and Abuse of Statistics*. New York: Oxford Press, 1962.

Snedecor, George W., *Everyday Statistics: Facts and Fallacies*. Dubuque, Iowa: Wm.C. Brown, 1950.

Sorokin, Pitirim A., *Fads and Foibles in Modern Sociology and Related Sciences*. Chicago: Henry Regnery, 1956.

Spurr, William A., and Charles P. Bonini, *Statistical Analysis for Business Decisions*. Homewood, Ill.: Richard D. Irwin, 1967.

Stouffer, Samuel, *Social Research to Test Ideas*. New York: Free Press, 1962.

Szasz, Thomas S., *The Manufacture of Madness*. New York: Harper & Row, Pub., 1970.

Vesselo, Isaac R., *How to Read Statistics*. London: Harrap, 1962.

Wallis, W. Allen, and Harry V. Roberts, *The Nature of Statistics*. New York: Collier Books, 1962.

15

Computers and Research Logic

PROGRAMS AND LANGUAGES

In the last ten years, there has been a tremendous impact on the sciences by the newer computers. It is now possible to have a computer in your own home at a modest price.[1] Your home computer will have more power than the first, massive computers that were used for the Los Alamos project, but it will be a fraction of their size. Not only can you write your own programs; you can also enter into other systems, use stored data from other computers, have access to libraries of programs, and share with other researchers. No longer need you travel to the computer center; you can use terminals placed at strategic places. And if you are completely sophisticated, you can carry a terminal in your briefcase. And preprogrammed calculators, complete with clock and alarm, have been reduced to the size of a credit card.

Just as there are many makes of computers and calculators, many programming languages compete for your attention, but six seem to have survived better than the others. They are FORTRAN, widely used, COBOL, commercially used; ALGOL,

[1] A complete minicomputer with printer and an exceptional capacity of 64K RAM (Random Access Memory), complete with terminal, interface, and video screen, was selling recently for $4,500 and as production increases will probably be even cheaper. Video Brain, Radio Shack, and Apple II have developed sophisticated minicomputers for home use.

algorithmic language; APL; PL/1; and BASIC, which is very popular because it is relatively easy. Undoubtedly, newer languages will appear in the very near future, especially as computer speeds increase.

The four most used programs using cards and batch systems are SPSS, Statistical Package for the Social Sciences; SAS, the Statistical Analysis System; BMD, the Biomedical Computer Program; and OSIRIS, a statistical package for social-science data developed by the Institute of Social Research at the University of Michigan and the Interuniversity Consortium for Political Research. OSIRIS may be used by SPSS users with an OSIRIS-SPSS interface—a connection between input and output at your end and the OSIRIS "brain" (or CPU, central processing unit) at their end.

Basically, all computers have five main parts: a central processing unit (CPU), a memory, an interface, and an input-output device, all operated by the fifth part, the program.

There are two kinds of computers, analog and digital. Analog measures in terms of distance, like a slide rule, a timer, a thermostat, a lens focus on a camera, or a tuning dial. Digital computers, the ones we use, count numbers, just like digital watches, microwave ovens, TV channel settings, car mileage indicators, and telephone dials. Digital computers can only add. They add (positive or negative) in terms of binary numbers. Letters are converted into numbers in the CPU. Our decimal system is coded into binary numbers (BCD). Binary numbers are converted to octal or hexadecimal bases (8 or 16, respectively) for easier operation. However, the computer is controlled by Boolean algebra, or switching algebra, since only two numbers are involved in this type of math, 1 and 0. This type of binary logic can be interpreted as *on or off* and can be translated in terms of electronic circuits.

Even the most complex computers are controlled by a network of very simple basic units. It is the speed of the computer that is overwhelming. Recent advances in technology, notably the use of the transistor and the microprocessor, have revolutionized computers. The "brain" of the computer, which used to be the largest part, is now one of the smallest. Microprocessors with memories are really minicomputers; smaller than a thumbnail, they hold thousands of bits of memory.

Because of the compactness of new computers, you can now carry one in a briefcase and connect acoustically to other major computers, or you can have a terminal in your own home. Using BASIC, you can write your own programs, as BASIC is a higher-level computer programming language—probably the most popular computer language of over 100 that have been written. It is easy to learn and apply and is limited only by storage capacity in the memory bank. For example, 4K BASIC refers to 4,000 memory bytes, and 8K means 8,000 memory bytes.

Card and batch systems mentioned in this book will continue for some time, but they will probably be replaced eventually by magnetic tape, magnetic cards (very small), electrosensitive paper, disks, or magnetic bubbles (minute). The technology is developing extremely rapidly, with major changes every five years or less.

In terms of criminology and criminal justice, we have only just begun to explore the possibilities of computers.

Table 15.1. Tabulated History of the Computer

Inventor	Device	Time	Uses
Early man	Counting sticks, shells	5000 B.C.	Counting animals, crops, seasons
Chinese	Abacus	3000 B.C.	Trade, construction
Egyptians	Triangulation	3000 B.C.	Astronomy, irrigation
Western man	Mathematics, clocks, printing	to 15th century A.D.	Exploration, industry
Blaise Pascal	Counting machine	1642	Addition and subtraction
Gottfried Leibniz	Counting machine	1671	Multiplication and division
Michael Faraday	Electricity	1831	Electromagnetic theory
Charles Babbage	Analytical engine	1834	Digital computer
George Boole	Boolean algebra	1847	Binary logic and truth tables
George Hollerith	Punched cards	1890	U.S. census
Konrad Zuse	Electronic computer	1936	Civil engineering
Claude Shannon	Logic statements	1938	Applied Boolean theory to circuitry
Howard Aiken and IBM	Mark 1	1944	Electromechanical computer
Eckert and Mauchly	ENIAC	1946 Generation 0	Electronic digital computer
M. V. Wilkes	EDSAC	1947	As above for military
John von Neumann	EDVAC	1947	Atomic energy
	UNIVAC 1; IBM 701, 704, 709	1951–58 Generation 1	Commercial vacuum-tube type, rockets
	PHILCO 2000: IBM 7090, 7030,	1959–69 Generation 2	Commercial solid state
	UNIVAC LARC; CDC 6600		Super units, plastics/lasers
	IBM 360s: BURROUGHS 6500	1970 Generation 3	Solid state IC (small) communication
	ILLIAC IV: AADC (Navy)	1975 Generation 4	Solid state IC (medium) networks
			Space travel/satellites

LIMITS OF THE COMPUTER

On the time line of man, computers occupy a minimal space (see Table 15.1). But their significance is such that they will probably have more effect on civilization than the invention of the steam and internal combustion engines; they have begun what is in effect a second Industrial Revolution. In 1971, this electronic revolution arrived almost unannounced, with the introduction of the microprocessor, the "brain" of the computer. Merely connect the microprocessor to a memory, a monitor, and a keyboard, and you have a powerful minicomputer.

Terminals currently in use give access to large numbers of libraries. APL has a library list over 50 pages long, with programs from Genetics (13) to Information Retrieval (653). Terminals can also use data stored in major computer memory banks. Most libraries in the United States are now beginning to computerize their book references for access and retrieval.

Even though the computer is limited by power supply, mechanical construction, memory banks, and program capacity, it opens for us a new world of electronic instrument sophistication that gives us access to vast capabilities for processing data. With these new research tools, we are able to process complex statistical equations involving many variables, as well as to eliminate many variables that have no significant effect.

The use of computers is giving us a much more detailed grasp of social phenomena, and as time progresses, we may be able to measure human behavior in much the same way as height and weight. At present, most of our measurement is in terms of probability. Certainly with imagination and creative effort, we will succeed in advancing our discipline.

Computers have progressed rapidly over the last few years. From unwieldy banks of machines, they are now extremely compact. Many hand-held programmable calculators can outperform the old wall-to-wall computers.[2] Minicomputers have tremendous potential, and the new computers have unbelievable capacity, with the ability to print "mile-long" programs.[3] It would appear that the technology has progressed past the theoretical capacity, but we need that technological capacity to develop new theory, since the new computers will not only process mass memory banks, but they will control, command, and forecast according to the data and program input.

However, in spite of the enormous capacity of the computer, it is no match for its human counterpart. It will do only what you tell it to do, and it cannot think or analyze. The numbers supplied by computers are only calculations; you must supply the sense and the logic for the analysis. You must beware of computer error and check computer results. Do not depend upon the computer to "think" for you. It is only an aid to decision making, not a substitute.

[2] Programmable calculators can store data on magnetic tape, can print in alpha and numeric, and have interchangeable libraries.

[3] The remarkable 32-bit VAX-11/780, by Digital Education Computer Systems, Maynard, Mass., 1978.

Terminals are very easy to use, and even easier if you can type. The terminal keyboard is slightly different from the normal typewriter; it has special keys added and special entries on most keys. There are two basic kinds of terminals, those with TV screens (cathode-ray tubes, or CRTs) and those with printers (and screens). Both have their special applications. You can also enter several types of language on the terminal: APL, Applied Programming Language, the one used most; CRJE (pronounced "creejee"), Computer Remote Job Entry, which has a computer-like function; OCLC, which is used by library staffs; BASIC; and as time goes on, there will be others.

To improve your terminal skills, get to a terminal and study it carefully. Sit at the keyboard and look at the new keys. Understand what they are and how to use them. On some keyboards, you have to press two keys simultaneously. Some have extra keys to the left for getting on-line. Learn how to use the shift key for left and right brackets, and the caret (^), which is useful when you change a line. Learn the shortcuts from an experienced operator. Read the APL manual.

When you are about to use a program, *type* the commands on a 5 x 8 card and have the card with you so that you may follow the instructions without wasting time. By running several programs and playing a few games, you will quickly become familiar with the terminals. As your skill grows, learn the limits of the machine—how much it can take on a line, how much it can do on a program, how much it can save, and for how long.

Save good programs for later reference. Usually, APL programs are shorter than computer printouts. If you use a terminal with TV, learn how to command a printout.

APL is easy to use. First, you must have an access number or account number to get you into the APL library. If you have a printer, make sure the paper is in the machine. Next, turn the terminal on. Getting on-line usually requires a set coded sequence with a special combination of keys. The instructions are generally posted on the terminal or on the wall. Some terminals require that you dial in and wait for a special tone on your phone, then you cradle it and when a green light flashes on your keyboard, you are on-line; other terminals require that you enter by code on the keyboard. Once on-line, you enter your account number, usually by holding down the shift key and entering a right bracket and your number—for instance,)33344455—then pressing the carriage return.

When you are familiar with the APL programs, you may wish to advance to CRJE. This program is much more complex and actually simulates the computer, except that instead of using cards, you may enter your data directly into the memory banks. You may also type in your programs in the same order as in SPSS. You may manipulate your program, retype your data, correct errors, and get printouts much faster than using the computer with IBM cards. You may also enter your program on a library file and save it, enabling you to recall it at any time and have all the data at your fingertips ready for operation. There is nothing remarkable about any of the terminal programs. They do exactly what you want them to do, and they make all the mistakes you enter into the program.

You may even learn how to enter your own program. Programming is merely the coding of a sequence of steps used in solving a problem. You "teach" the terminal to follow you and memorize your input. Although terminals can be fun (as you will find out when you send messages, print pinups, or play 21), remember that they were designed to solve informational problems. Do not waste terminal time. Turn the terminal off when you are finished.

Different terminals have different commands for getting on-line and for commanding programs. There is a trend toward standardizing basic programs, in order to eliminate keypunching and speed up operation. However, you may find the terminals are "plugged" and you will have to wait in line until they are clear. Usually, a notice is posted telling you whether the system is UP (ready) or DOWN (not in operation).

Once you are on-line, terminals give you instant feedback. Learn how to use terminals, and practice until you feel at home with them. The program language is constantly being modified, and more and more programs are being added. Although different programs are not identical, many have similar characteristics.

APL Statistics Programs

Although each system has its various commands for access to different libraries, most systems will direct your next step. After you type in your access number, the machine will wait for your next command, which you should have ready on a card, taken from instructions on APL. For measures of central tendency, the command might be:

```
)PCOPY 2 INTROSTATV2 CTDGROUP
```

or perhaps:

```
)LOAD 2 INTROSTATV2 CTDGROUP
```

After you press the carriage return, the terminal will print back to you various data on the program and then wait for you to enter the next command. You may then type STAT and press the carriage return, and immediately the terminal will ask you to type in your list of data. You type in your numbers and press the carriage return. Within seconds, the terminal will print out your statistics for the data you have just entered, then wait for your next command. You may then type FDIST, which will give you a frequency distribution[4] depending upon the interval you set. Once again,

[4] Also a frequency histogram.

you must enter your data (unless you use a VECTOR, which will simply repeat your data). At the end, the terminal will wait for you to enter a new program or log off. *You must press the carriage return after each of your commands*, and you should know ahead of time what you are going to type in, since time costs money on terminals.

After getting the printout for FDIST, you can now type in:

)PCOPY 2 INTROSTATV2 CGROUP

CGROUP gives you correlation, CTDGROUP gives you central tendency; the initials before the GROUP give you the key to the program. Again after carriage return, the terminal will record the data and the program, advise you of current status, and wait for your next command. In this case, you will type:

PEARSON

The terminal will request two sets of data and tell you to type them in, one line at a time. After you complete your data and return the carriage, the printer takes over and computes Pearson *r* and a scattergram. Logging off is usually:

)OFF

and press the return. Wait and switch off. If you wish to use chi-square, the commands are:

)PCOPY 2 INTROSTATV2 CSGROUP

The program CHISQ2 will request only the observed data, and will also give you a table.

As you become familiar with APL, you will learn more about programs that are available. You may also learn ANOVA and various other statistical programs. There are also several game programs in the game libraries, ranging from CHESS to STAR-WARS, which will help you learn the terminal as it plays against you.

For small problems and small amounts of data, the terminal is very fast—so fast that it may be somewhat frightening. Yet if you remember that you are in control— just like driving a car—you will learn how to operate the terminal easily and comfortably.

CALCULATORS AND SOFTWARE

Calculators have become a part of daily life. They come in all shapes and sizes, and they do almost everything, including serving dinner and answering the phone. You find them on microwave ovens, wristwatches, wallets, clocks, telephones, radios, TVs, time switches, desk secretaries, and burglar alarms.

For survey research, they come in a number of sizes and shapes, from simple calculators with a few functions and a few keys to complex programmable calculators that record data on magnetic tape and use software modules. The programmable calculators are really minicomputers, or hand-held computers. They can actually outperform the early computers and have greater-capacity memory banks. And they write in both alpha and numeric. Printouts from calculators are neat, are easy to store, and give a permanent record of the program used.

For research, the calculator requires at least a square-root key, a square key, and one memory bank. This will get you through most calculation and will save you looking at tables. For more advanced work, you need a preprogrammed calculator. These vary all the way from five to 110 functions. Their advantage is in having many programs built in, so all you do is enter data and press the right keys. The disadvantage is that these are limited programs. Programs are called "software"; the actual instruments are called "hardware."

Many of the lengthy tables that most statistical textbooks provide in their appendixes have been rendered obsolete by computers and calculators. We rarely use tables anymore, since the tabled values or levels of significance are printed on the computer printouts, and may also be had from calculators using software modules with built-in programs. Computers and calculators generate random numbers; they give all the logarithms, squares, and square roots; they carry curve-fitting programs; and they calculate various levels faster than you can look them up. Once key figures are memorized or carried on a card, the research investigator knows where the value falls and can estimate other values.

Of course, certain tables are not yet in computers or programmable calculators; but these are rarely used. It is wise to select a statistical text that is pertinent to your own field, one that you like, and one that carries the tables you may need. Several are listed in this text. *The important point is to know how statistics work.* The actual calculations and the tedious work are now done by the machine, but *you must know what you are using and what you are doing and what is happening.* Practice a few easy examples to get the feel, then let the electronic brains do the hard ones and see if you can follow the sequences. Do not try to grasp all the statistics at one time; you will understand them much better once you see them in operation.

In fact, entering correlation is easy. Some calculators merely require that you enter the x number, then enter x_n or x_i, then the y number, then press y_n or y_i; at the end of the series, you press F (function), and you may then press r for correlation, SLOPE for slope, and INTCP for intercept. That is all there is to it. The results depend upon your accuracy and keeping your calculator in good shape. There is really no limit to what modern calculators can do. They eliminate card punching and travelling to and from computers and terminals, they keep better records, and they are instant. It is very much like having a computer in your hand.

"Software" originally referred to written programs, but now a new dimension has been added. Software programs are literally written or programmed into small, solid-state modules—tiny chips holding a whole library that is available to you whenever you need it. All you need do is insert the right module and you are ready. Newer calculators also record your data or programs on magnetic cards, which may be stored and then read when you insert them in the calculator. Printers can be attached to calculators so that permanent records may be made—of alpha messages as well as numeric data. Calculator records are neater, smaller, and easier to read than the bulky computer printouts. The calculator is opening up a whole new world of sophisticated statistical research capability.

THE USE OF COMPUTERS BY LAW-ENFORCEMENT AGENCIES

The speed of the computer has been a major factor in the detection of crime, especially vehicle crime. Highway patrol officers may now obtain, over their own computer, information on the registration of a vehicle they are following. At communications centers, police now have immediate access to prior arrest and conviction records by contacting the central computing unit. They are able to monitor and record all patrol personnel and dispatch them as needed to a crime or an accident. They can send fingerprints in by computer to be checked, and get back a detailed resumé of the suspect if it is on file.

The FBI computerizes all Uniform Crime Reports for analysis and uses the computer for special projects in the war against crime.

Central files are maintained by state and federal agencies to assist in the identification of criminals and their activities. Many computer networks are cross-linked.

Computers are used in crime labs, ballistics, production of composite pictures, information retrieval, dispersion of personnel, control of jails and prisons, and special security, as well as the normal administration and functioning of departments such as payroll and budget.

Operational Uses of Computers

Because of the enormous amounts of data accumulated in the apprehension and processing of offenders, computers are, by necessity, used extensively by criminal justice agencies. Their use has been expedited by various federal and state mandates to upgrade the effectiveness of police operations.

On the federal level, the FBI began operation of the National Crime Information Center (NCIC) in January 1967. The NCIC serves as a national crime index and as an aid in operations against increasing criminal mobility; it serves all 50 states, plus Washington, D.C., and Ottawa. It is basically an inventory and retrieval system, which now contains several million records. It stores data on stolen property, vehicles, and wanted persons, and data entered by participating agencies. It also stores computerized criminal histories of offenders for use by courts, police, and other criminal justice agencies, and it contains a fingerprint program and the Uniform Crime Reports (UCRs).

Under funding made available to the state agencies in 1968 by the Omnibus Crime Control and Safe Streets Acts (PL 90-351), and under direction of the Law Enforcement Assistance Administration (LEAA) that was established by that act, various Criminal Justice Information Systems (CJIS) were set up in the requesting states. The coordinating national agency, NCJIS, also set up a Grants Management Information Systems program (GMIS) with four operating subsystems—planning, application, financial, and audit. In addition, NCJIS developed a National Criminal Justice Statistics Data Base program (NCJSDB); a National Prison Statistics program carries all statistics on federal prisoners; and Comprehensive Data Systems programs (CDS) under LEAA direction are used to develop data collections in each state. The sheer volume of the data is such that 90 percent or more would be unused if it were not for the use of high-speed computers.

In 1969, Project SEARCH was designed, and in 1970 it was demonstrated to show the usefulness of interstate exchange of offender files. LEAA and SEARCH are also developing a criminalistics information system, a prisoner accounting system, a state court information system, and an organized-crime intelligence system. Recent computer research has been in satellite communications, holographic fingerprint comparison, standardized crime-scene reports, and state-level I.D. Although these lie in the area of applied statistics, several states are now developing statistical analysis units for use in understanding and preventing crime.

Two other subsystems deserve special mention because of their application to state and local agencies. They are the Offender Based Tracking System (OBT), sometimes called Offender Based Transaction Systems, and the Law Enforcement Teletype System (LETS).

Criminal Justice Information Systems (CJIS)

Briefly, the purpose of the CJIS is to provide operational support to increase effectiveness. It is an interrelated network of data gathering, filing, coding, communications, and computers. It normally operates on four levels: national, state, county, and local. The basic data, derived from the local agencies, are merely indexed, filed, and inventoried at the higher levels. It is interesting to note that many major techniques in computer processing are being developed at the agency level. Figure 15-1 will provide a good idea of the extent of the CJIS.

The CJIS is the major system, having many subsystems within it. (The CJIS is itself a subsystem of the National Criminal Justice Information System.) In essence, the large computer with extended capacity stores the data from smaller units and makes its programs and memory available to authorized users. Each of the 50 states

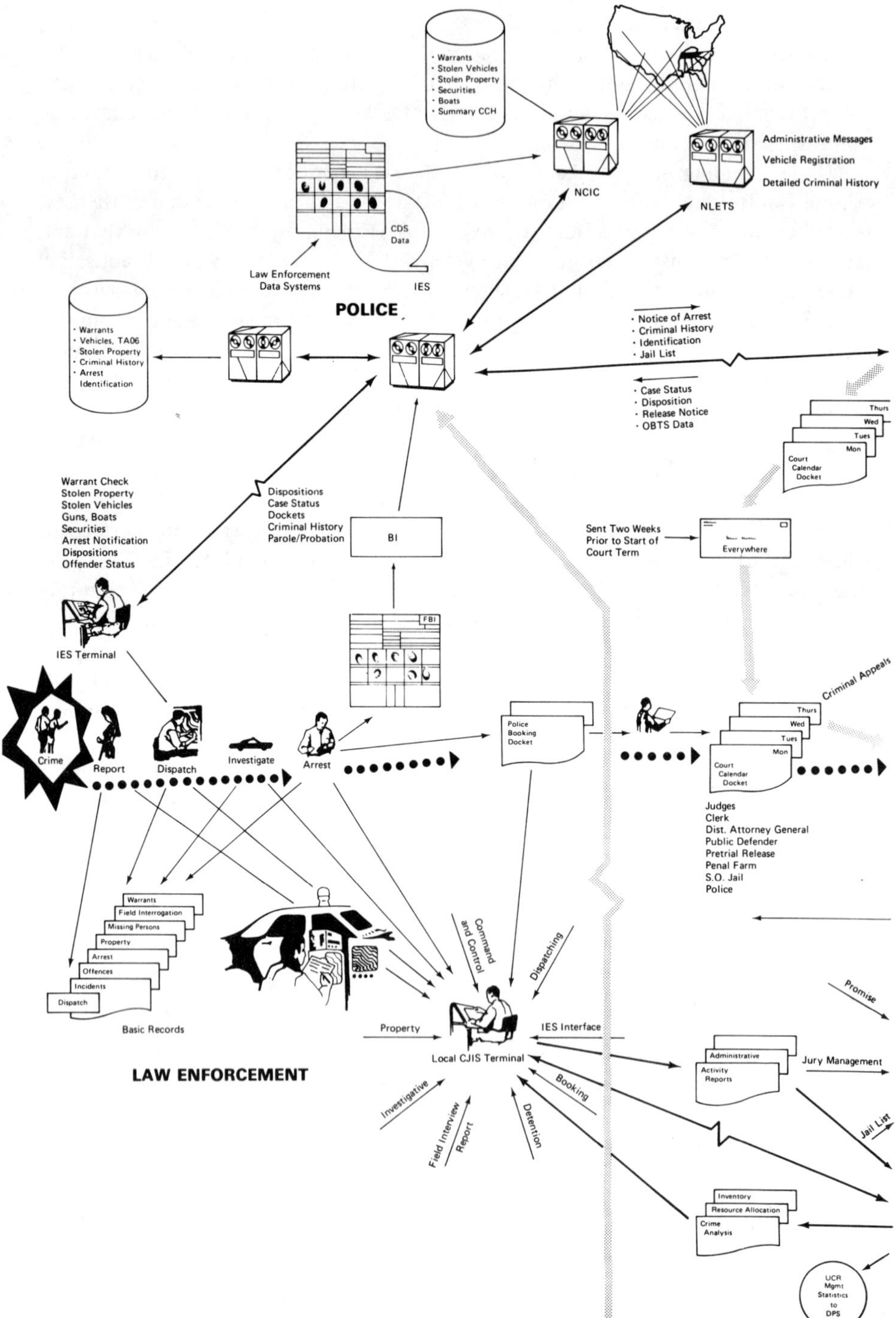

Fig. 15-1 Criminal Justice Information System

Reproduced by courtesy of the LEAA and Tennessee Law Enforcement Planning Commission.

CRIMINAL JUSTICE INFORMATION SYSTEM

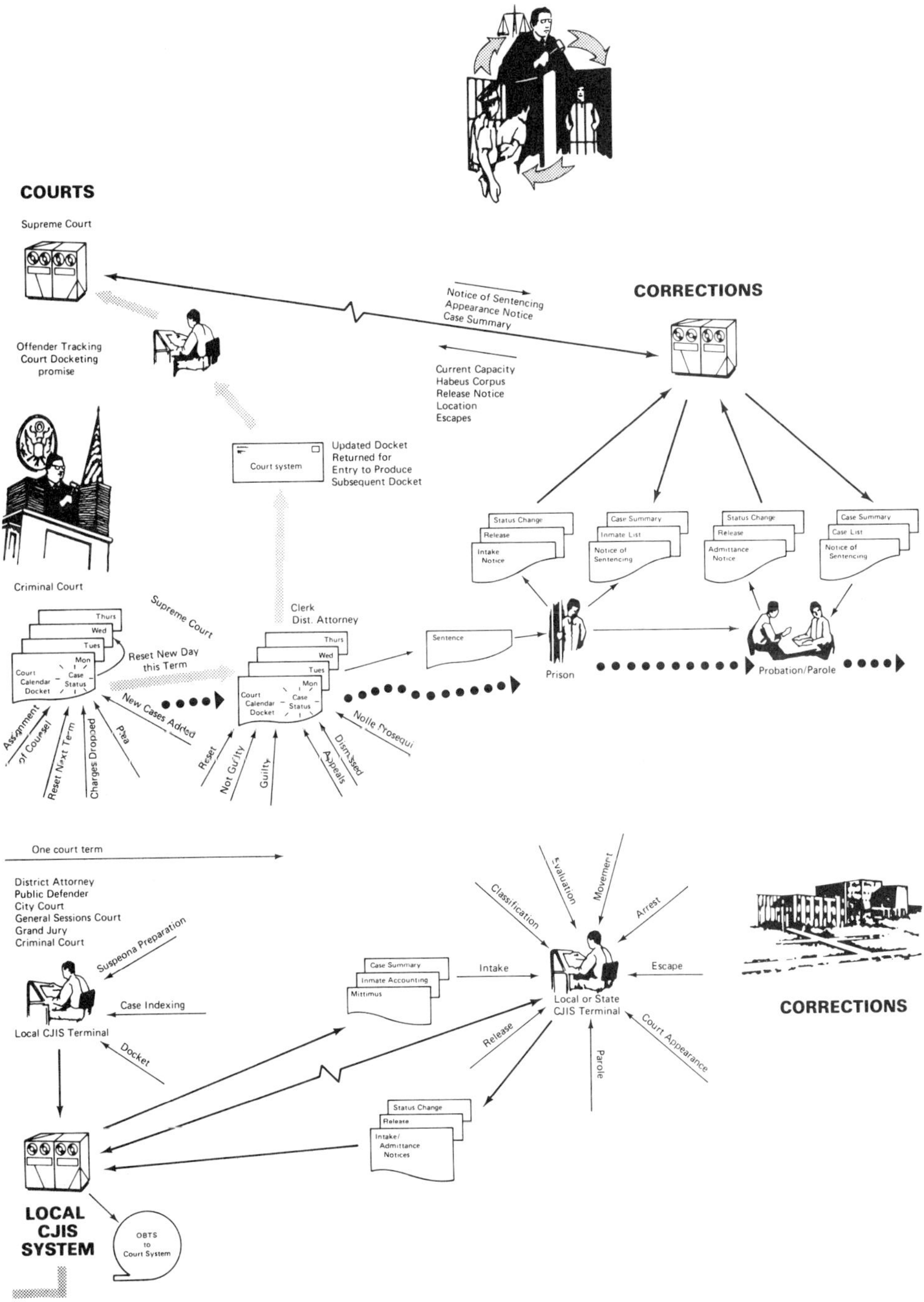

now maintains a CJIS in some form or another, in various stages of computer sophistication. Funding provided by the government carries the proviso of uniform reporting and uniform procedure, thus facilitating interstate exchange of information.

Most CJISs contain the following subsystems, listed with their functions:

1. *UCRs:* The reporting and recording of all available crime data.
2. *Radio Log:* The assignment of resources under a CADS, a Computer Aided Dispatch System. This very vital system gives an immediate statistical analysis for disposal and allocation of vehicles and manpower. Radio Log is a computer assist in the apprehension of the criminal.
3. *Warrants:* Records the warrants requested and all data.
4. *Criminal Court System:* Performs jury selection prior to court, pays the jury and keeps records, sets the trial and court calendars, keeps track of motions.
5. *Juvenile Court:* Records data on juveniles, keeps track of nonsupport cases.
6. *Motor Vehicles:* Used for inquiry only.
7. *Summons:* Records data on all summonses.
8. *Interface:* Exchanges information with state Information Search and Enforcement Systems, NICC, NLETS.
9. *Organized Crime:* Records organized-crime data and checks files.
10. *Offender Tracking System:* Keeps track of the movement of offenders through the criminal justice system.

Offender tracking is the largest and most-used subsystem. At each point of entry for it, the appropriate agency files the pertinent case history on the offender, and the data are fed into the central terminal and made available to each participant. The flow of data is as follows:

1. Field reports: crime scene, complaint, police report, investigation
2. Station report: warrant, arrest, I.D., booking
3. Pretrial status: D.A., preliminary, higher court, grand jury, bond
4. Court reports: D.A. and defense review, trial, sentencing
5. Corrections reports: prison, probation or parole, release

Access to data is relatively easy because of uniform procedures. The OTS thus becomes a Criminal History System (CHS).

The data flow in the offender tracking system is shown in Figure 15-2. From the diagram it may be seen that a routine check at the time the offender comes into contact with the criminal justice agency sets the entire tracking system into operation. This is especially true of fingerprinting. Offender Tracking, or Offender Based Transaction (OBT), is also interfaced with programs such as BOND STATUS, PROMIS, and ICAP.

Some Special Programs

All data are fed into the State Information Enforcement Systems (SIES). Once fingerprints are identified, either at the scene of the crime or at booking of the

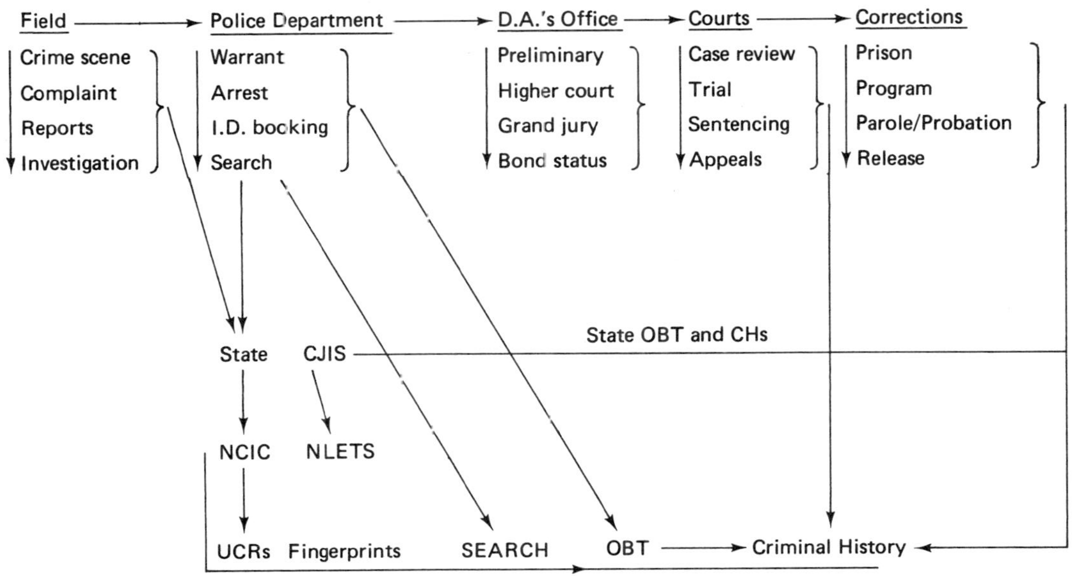

Fig. 15-2 Offender tracking and criminal history

offender, a computer search is made for positive I.D. of the suspect. The computer search is aided by automatic high-speed search, optical scanning, and holographic comparison. Thus, fingerprints from a crime, a booking, an application for a gun permit or liquor license, or any other special application may be processed through a single high-speed terminal. Similarly, vehicles, pawned or stolen property, or any other coded or numbered property may be entered and searched on the terminal.

As indicated in Figure 15-2, the offender is tracked from apprehension to trial, sentencing, and correction. At any point, a trained officer may enter or access data on the offender. The computer is highly efficient in making positive I.D., even when the suspect is mobile or changes names. The errors occur when the arresting officers are too busy to access the computer, and thus miss a wanted person.

The County Offender Tracking System is linked to the State Offender Tracking System and the NCIC criminal histories. Four agencies feed data into the system: law enforcement, the D.A.'s office, the courts (through the court clerk), and corrections. The computer systems are still being developed, and new programs are added regularly. Two recent programs have dealt with bond status and forfeiture (bond-jumping), and nonsupport cases and welfare fraud. In both instances, the computer saved about 90 percent of working time.

One of the most useful aspects of the computer is that it can work and search on its own once a program is entered. The operator is then free to perform some other task while the terminal is printing. The computer comes into its own when performing routine tasks, such as (in addition to payroll and budget):

1. Traffic: Produces statistical reports of all accidents; processes all citations issued by police; lists stolen vehicles, stolen tags, stolen parts; lists suspect vehicles, recovered vehicles, driver and vehicle registrations, violation histories.
2. Courts: Generates jury list, jury payroll, court docket, case load, record of dispositions, grand-jury docket, motions and appearances, judges' blotters, clerks' blotters, no-bill files, calendar files, bond files, completed case files, warrants index, appeals file, habeas corpus file, commitment files.
3. Corrections: Tracks offender from I.D. at reception; keeps records of work assignments, cell assignments, discipline, transfers, progress, mail and visits, time served, release, detainers, parole record; completes prison files; informs local agencies.
4. Police: Personnel control and planning, vehicle control and disposition, UCRs, stolen property, jail population, fingerprinting, crime-pattern graphic analysis, graphic I.D. and composite I.D. (I.D. module), citations, arrests, allocation, appearances.

(It should be noted that not all agencies have implemented the programs above; some do not have the funding or training to implement them.)

Other unique programs are available, such as:

1. JURIS: Provides statutory retrieval, computerized bill drafting, photo com-composition of new laws from passage to publication. Used by the U.S. Department of Justice.

2. PROMIS: Prepares a dossier for the prosecutor's office giving warrant, grand-jury report, jail list, rap sheet, lab report, detainer request, outstanding warrants, court calendar, proceedings, dispositions, petitions. Lists cases not docketed but pending, with jail lists showing order and length of detention, assessment of case, probability of success, age of case, schedule conflicts, and case order based on date of arrest.
3. ICAP (Integrated Crime Apprehension Program): Provides crime analysis data based on computer search, method of operation, stolen property, and type of suspect vehicle. Provides a daily and weekly statistical printout of type and frequency of crime in geographic locations. Furnishes a daily breakdown of UCRs by statistics and histograms, with mean and standard deviation provided for each precinct on a daily or weekly basis. Lists descriptions of stolen property (unlike NCIC, which lists only a serial number). Special programs may be requested, such as lists of robberies by location, patterns of criminal operation, suspect vehicle locations, related crimes, etc. ICAP is an administrative aid in the disposition and use of police resources and the computerized delivery of police services.

Although these special programs and all other government and state programs are written in COBOL, scientists in the behavioral sciences are writing new programs in FORTRAN, which lends itself to use of the SPSS packages and similar processes. There are currently programs in development of profiles, homicide studies,[5] rape prevention,[6] stress,[7] and jury selection. Newer programs are also being written in BASIC II for security systems.[8]

To illustrate progress in the use of computers, entry on the ICAP terminal is made by answering questions flashed one at a time on the terminal screen. Typed responses are then relayed to the main computer. The format is standardized and is also printed. Thus, an entire police report is entered in seconds, as is a document report or a report on a suspect vehicle. Statistics are entered on a crime analysis short form.

METHODOLOGY IN INFORMATION SYSTEMS

Statistics and methods in contemporary use are mainly in the area of applied science. Criminal justice operations require the entry and use of hard data. Although most of this type of data is quantified for inventory and retrieval from high-speed computers, it is accessible for other types of methodological analysis. Operational use in the detection of crime and offenders utilizes the computer's speed in listing and sorting. However, once the input is made, the computer will perform other programs that are available.

[5] Matthew Parsons, "Study of Homicide in Western New York," unpublished ms., 1978.

[6] Dr. Fred Klyman and Brit Goodroe, ERITCA for Southern Illinois University, Carbondale, Ill., 1979.

[7] Dr. Thomas S. Hickey, stress study for Memphis, Tennessee, police department, 1979.

[8] Specialist E. McDonald, USAF, Arkansas, writing security programs. University of Ark, 1979.

A great deal of research effort has been made in designing computer programs to fit the needs of operational requirements and then linking these programs to agency needs throughout the criminal justice system. In this way, local or regional computers may interface with other large computer systems. For police operations, where the need is for rapid communications, on-line systems have been designed to asssist in the booking and apprehension of offenders.[9] The advantage of these systems is their simplicity and rapidity of response.

Consistent with accumulation of data on crime, criminal histories, methods of operation, and listings of stolen property, statistical analysis centers are being set up in various regions. These SACs go far beyond the routine of normal operations and begin to look into the deeper problems of the epidemiology and the ecology of crime and criminal behavior.

The Uses of Hard Data

Fingerprinting is a form of positive identification. Now that it has been computerized, the training required by manual experts has been reduced from 18 months to eight hours of classroom time for computer operation. Only three steps are required for computer entry:

1. Pattern identification:
   (a) Two types of LOOPS, ulnar and radial
   (b) Two types of ARCH, plain and tented
   (c) Types of WHORL
2. Ridge counts for the LOOPS, between the delta and the core, must be within plus or minus 4.
3. Tracings of WHORLS must be determined by following a ridge leaving a delta center to see if it meets (M), or falls inside (I) or outside (O) another delta.

The old Henry classification is virtually eliminated. The computer even permits mistakes in the entry of data. Once the computer has made an identification, it can be accessed by or circulated to over 40,000 other law-enforcement agencies across the country. Because fingerprints are virtually infallible, a superior program of identification has been built. Even if an offender changes the color of his hair, eyes, or skin, or changes name, age, race, or even sex and build to avoid I.D., the fingerprints afford immutable identification.

Similarly, serialized and nonserialized property that has been reported stolen may be entered. Again, the advantage of a serial number provides positive I.D.

Figure 15-3 shows how the data are entered on-line, stored, retrieved, and communicated to other computers.

[9] Sam Alexy, "On-Line Booking Systems," *Target*, January 1975. This is an LEAA publication available from the U.S. Government Printing Office, Washington, D.C. Mr. Alexy has also designed a Juvenile Court System (JCS) and a Bond Status System (BSS).

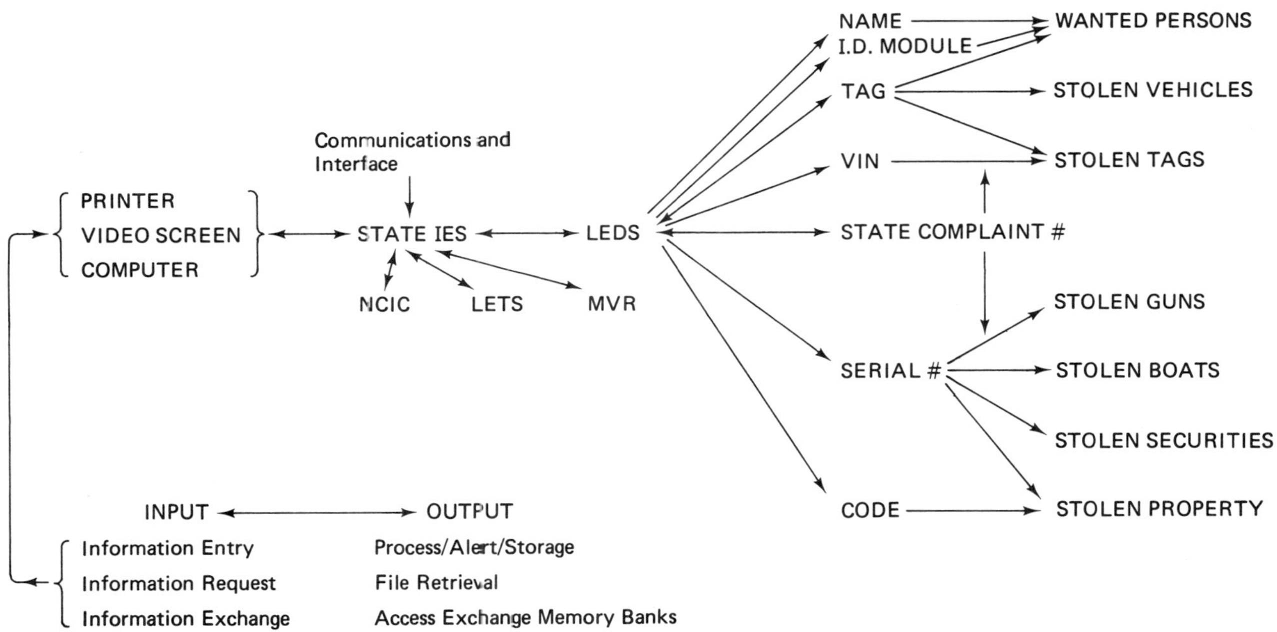

Fig. 15-3 Computer communication and on-line use of hard data by criminal justice information systems

The type of input of data finally determines the quality of crime statistics. For example, because of the capacity of the memory bank of the computer and its ability to store information, entries may be made that were not previously considered. Even though a great deal of this type of data will not be used in routine operations, it will be available for statistical analysis. Within crime analysis units, there is now increasing emphasis on the quality of information control. Format and entry procedures are improving, as are security measures on the operation and access of computers. Not only are certain information requests highly classified (sensitive), but new procedures can now selectively alert agencies to information without other agencies knowing.

In terms of statistical analysis, daily and weekly breakdowns can be made of crime information. This information can be plotted (graphed) and located (pinpointed). For example, homicide statistics are well reported in most agencies. Crime analysis units can also generate the following data:

1. Precinct or tract distribution of incidents
2. Residential location of crime, offender, and victim
3. Critical events in processing, trial, and disposition
4. Comparison tables with other and/or related offenses
5. Characteristics of offender, victim, and profile
6. Table of causes of homicide
7. Table of type of weapon used
8. Status of offender to victim
9. Comparisons of disposition and status
10. Comparisons of courts and disposition
11. Tables of motives, times, and locations of crimes
12. Probability tables for case outcome, trial by jury, rehabilitation outcome, and social risk

The tables include the use of frequency data, correlation, regression/prediction, chi-square, analysis of variance, and probability outcomes.

It would appear that the crime analysis units can provide a great deal of material for research analysis. In many cases, a great deal of information is stored that requires merely access and recode. Much of it is coded in COBOL, but it may be accessed and recoded for FORTRAN.

Computers aid not only in the efficiency of operation but in providing theory (through technological means) for improving that efficiency. The problems of allocation of resources and manpower (management operations) are made easier by computer use. The computer is a tool in providing information for decision making. It gives quantitative facts upon which we may make a qualitative decision.

But despite their incredible speed, computers are limited by input, they do only what they are programmed to do, and they lack the vital ingredient, the research imagination. The researcher, with this valuable tool to aid him, is limited only by innovation and imagination. Whatever the output, it must still be used and analyzed by human beings; so, impressive as computer operation may be, it is even more impressive when you know what you are doing and how you use and apply the computerized output.

SUMMARY

If we use the computer properly, it can assist us in a logical analysis of data without the tedium of calculation. We need to know how to summarize and how to interpret the variables we are using.

New computers and on-line terminals have changed the face of police activity and operations. The computer aids in the disposition and allocation of resources as well as in the apprehension of the criminal.

Terminals are fast and efficient, but programmable calculators are even faster for statistical work. They will carry more data than terminals—almost as much as computers—are more compact, are faster, and save a great deal of time and inconvenience. Terminals carry many libraries, but now calculators are also carrying interchangeable libraries. Terminals come into their own when tying into other systems. Calculators, with the new solid-state modules, printers, and easy programming, have a tremendous potential for survey research.

You should have a calculator as part of your regular daily equipment, much like a watch, as you will use it often. It saves having to use tables, it gives you instant solution to difficult math, and it readily solves complex statistics. The only mistakes it makes are yours. Take care of your calculator, it is fragile; it hates direct strong light, physical abuse, and old batteries.

With your calculator, your knowledge of computers and terminals, and your training in research methodology, you are now ready to enter the field of survey research. My final advice to you is be careful, be precise, be accurate, be logical, be substantive, be truthful.

EXERCISES

1. Comment on the impact of computers on the social sciences.
2. Name some ways in which the police now use computers.
3. There are six important computer languages; what are they, and what are they used for? What are the four most-used programs in the social sciences?
4. Computers have five main parts; name them. What are the two kinds of computers? What is meant by BCD? What is switching algebra? Who invented it? When?

5. The "brain" of a computer is often no bigger than a thumbnail. What is this electronic gadget?
6. Define *fourth-generation computers, 4K bytes, analog, digital, module, binary logic, interface, acoustical coupler, integrated circuit, terminal.*
7. When was the first digital computer invented?
8. Most computers can do only one thing. Explain.
9. How do you get on-line with a terminal?
10. What is the APL command for Pearson correlation? What kind of printout do you get?
11. Use the data on juvenile arrests and convictions in Table 11.13 for APL entry. Correlate, use chi-square, use STAT and FDIST. Be sure to use them in the right order.
12. Use a preprogrammed calculator with correlation to check your terminal data.
13. Run the data on "Crimes by Accidents," (Chapter 11, p. 284).
14. Use these data: Cell A = 42; low number of accidents, 106; high number of accidents, 44; high crime = 94; low crime = 56. Calculate χ^2, also internal percentages. What are your conclusions? (Check APL on your calculator.)
15. How would you develop a criminal history for the computer?
16. Describe a logical way of handling masses of data and variables. Be sequential.
17. Explain how fingerprinting may be quantified. What would you need to enter?
18. What tables could you develop from homicide data? rape? robbery?
19. Comment on CJIS, NLETS, OBTS, PROMIS, ICAP, NCIC, SIES, SEARCH.
20. Comment upon what the computer *cannot* do.

FOR FURTHER READING

Albrecht, Robert L., Leroy Finkel, and Jerry Brown, *BASIC*. New York: John Wiley, 1973.

APL Language Systems, GC26-3847-2, 3rd ed. San Jose, Calif.: IBM Corporation, 1976. With Library Info. 1–654.

Barr, Anthony J., et al., *A User's Guide to SAS*. Raleigh, N.C.: SAS Institute, Inc., 1976.

Bates, F., and M. L. Douglas, *Programming Language/One* (2nd ed.). Englewood Cliffs, N.J.: Prentice-Hall, 1970.

Borko, H., ed., *Computer Applications in the Behavioral Sciences*. Englewood Cliffs, N.J.: Prentice-Hall, 1962.

Bowles, E. A., ed., *Computers in Humanistic Research*. Englewood Cliffs, N.J.: Prentice-Hall, 1967.

Brier, Alan, and Ian Robinson, *Computers and the Social Sciences*. New York: Columbia University Press, 1974.

Cooley, W. W., and P. R. Lohnes, *Multivariate Data Analysis*. New York: John Wiley, 1971.

Day, A. C., *FORTRAN Techniques, with Special Reference to Non-Numerical Applications*. Cambridge, England: Cambridge University Press, 1972.

Dixon, W. J., ed., *BMD Biomedical Computer Programs* (3rd ed.). Berkeley: University of California Press, 1973.

Goldstine, H. H., *The Computer from Pascal to Von Neumann*. Princeton, N.J.: Princeton University Press, 1972.

Hollingdale, S. H., and E. C. Toothill, *Electronic Computers*. New York: Penguin, 1965.

Infosystems. Wheaton, Ill.: Hitchcock Publishing Co., 1978.

McCracken, D. D., *A Guide to FORTRAN Programming*. New York: John Wiley, 1961.

——, and U. Garbassi, *A Guide to COBOL Programming* (2nd ed.). New York: John Wiley, 1970.

Mano, M. Morris, *Computer Logic Design*. Englewood Cliffs, N.J.: Prentice-Hall, 1972.

Martin, J., and A. R. D. Norman, *The Computerized Society*. Englewood Cliffs, N.J.: Prentice-Hall, 1970.

Mims, Forrest M. III, *Understanding Digital Computers*. Fort Worth, Tx.: Radio Shack, Tandy Corporation, 1978.

Moore, Richard W., *Introduction to the Use of Computer Packages for Statistical Analysis*. Englewood Cliffs, N.J.: Prentice-Hall, 1978.

Nie, Norman H., et al., *Statistical Package for the Social Sciences (SPSS)* (2nd ed.). New York: McGraw-Hill, 1975.

Randell, Brian, ed., *The Origins of Digital Computers*. New York: Springer-Verlag, N.Y., 1973.

Reeves, C. M., and M. Wells, *A Course on Programming in ALGOL 60*. London: Chapman and Hall, 1964.

Scientific American, September 1977, Special Edition on Microelectronics. See also May 1975, pp. 32–40, and March 1976, pp. 88–98.

Sharpe, W. F., *BASIC: An Introduction to Computer Programming Using the BASIC Language*. New York: Free Press, 1967.

Stark, Peter A., *Computer Programming Handbook*. Blue Ridge Summit, Pa.: Tab Books, 1975.

Sterling, T. D., and S. V. Pollack, *Introduction to Statistical Data Processing*. Englewood Cliffs, N.J.: Prentice-Hall, 1968.

Stone, P. J., et al., *The Users Manual for the General Inquirer*. Cambridge Mass.: M.I.T. Press, 1968.

Taviss, I., ed., *The Computer Impact*. Englewood Cliffs, N.J.: Prentice-Hall, 1970.

Turn, Rein, *Computers in the 1980s*. New York: Columbia University Press, 1974.

Veldman, D. J., *FORTRAN Programming for the Behavioral Sciences*. New York: Holt, Rinehart & Winston, 1967.

Waite, Mitchell, and Michael Pardee, *Microcomputer Primer*. Indianapolis: Howard W. Sams, 1976.

See also federal (LEAA) and state Law Enforcement Planning Commission manuals (you may need clearance); also instruction manuals and program manuals for calculators and microcomputers from APF, Cannon, Casio, Commodore, Hewlett-Packard, National Semiconductor, Sharp, Sinclair, Radio Shack, Texas Instruments, and Unisonic.

Appendix 1
Student's Quick Reference Table for r, t, χ^2, and F Values

df	= 0.05	= 0.01	
1	r = 0.99 t = 6.4 χ^2 = 3.84	r = 0.99 t = 31.8 χ^2 = 6.64	r, t, χ^2 values are given for 0.05 and 0.01 for 1-10 df.
	F = 161 200 216 225 230		
2	r = 0.9 t = 2.9 χ^2 = 5.99	r = 0.98 t = 6.9 χ^2 = 9.2	F values are given for 0.05 only, with $n - k$ = 1 to 10 df down the side and $k - 1$ = 1 to 5 df across.
	F = 18.5 19 19.2 19.2 19.3		
3	r = 0.8 t = 2.35 χ^2 = 7.8	r = 0.93 t = 4.54 χ^2 = 11.34	Tables on squares, square roots, and random numbers are calculated much faster on most calculators.
	F = 10.1 9.6 9.3 9.1 9		
4	r = 0.72 t = 2.13 χ^2 = 9.5	r = 0.88 t = 3.75 χ^2 = 13.3	Programmable calculators will also give distribution programs for most statistics.
	F = 7.7 6.9 6.6 6.4 6.3		
5	r = 0.67 t = 2.02 χ^2 = 11.1	r = 0.83 t = 3.37 χ^2 = 15.1	Most computer programs will print out the required statistic and significance level.
	F = 6.6 5.8 5.4 5.2 5		
6	r = 0.62 t = 1.94 χ^2 = 12.6	r = 0.79 t = 3.14 χ^2 = 16.8	(Values are adapted from *Biometrika Tables for Statisticians*, Vol. 1, 3rd ed., by Pearson and Hartley.)
	F = 5.9 5.1 4.7 4.5 4.4		

7	r = 0.58	t = 1.89	χ^2 = 14.1	r = 0.75	t = 2.99	χ^2 = 18.5	F = 5.6 4.7 4.4 4.1 3.9
8	r = 0.55	t = 1.86	χ^2 = 15.5	r = 0.72	t = 2.89	χ^2 = 20.1	F = 5.3 4.5 4 3.8 3.7
9	r = 0.52	t = 1.83	χ^2 = 16.9	r = 0.68	t = 2.82	χ^2 = 21.6	F = 5.1 4.2 3.9 3.6 3.5
10	r = 0.49	t = 1.81	χ^2 = 18.3	r = 0.66	t = 2.76	χ^2 = 23.2	F = 4.9 4.1 3.7 3.5 3.3

Appendix 2
Review, Rules, and Research-Methods Tables

A REVIEW OF TERMS AND DEFINITIONS

Survey research is a study of a section, segment, or sample drawn from a parent population for the purposes of making inferences about that population.

A *population* or universe is a specific aggregation of a variety of individuals (or items, or events) that have measurable differences in such attributes as age, race, sex, religion, occupation, and marital status; these attributes are called *survey elements* or *variables*. Although a population may be statistically defined as a group of anything, a universe, or an entirety, for survey purposes we prefer that it is thought of as a collection of survey elements. From those elements we select a *sample*. A good sample is representative of the parent population. *Sample error*, which occurs because of sample differences from the parent population, can be reduced by increasing the size and homogeneity of the sample.

We take a sample in order to gather data. *Data* are the record of facts, of phenomena, of observable events. All *statistics* start out with data. We have two kinds of statistics: *descriptive statistics*, which help us describe large masses of data, and *inferential statistics*, which enable us to make inferences from the sample concerning the parent population. Because the sample is a group selected from the population and is in fact a small part representing the whole, theoretically it should contain data that are distributed throughout the parent population.

The whole object of survey research is to describe the effect of one variable upon another. A *variable* is a set of mutually exclusive *characteristics*. If an individual, item, or event does not fall into one *category* or characteristic, it must fall into the other. We are concerned with differences in characteristics. The data that we gather on those characteristics for the sample are called *sample statistics*. If an event, item, or individual characteristic occurs more than once, it is collected and called a *frequency*. By collecting sample data together on a particular characteristic, we can divide the sum of the frequency by the sample size and get a *sample mean*. The *mean* is an average or central measure, rather like a balancing point or fulcrum. From the mean, we can measure the differences of scores. These differences are called *variations* from the mean. Because their sum equals zero, we square them and use the square root of the calculation, which is called *deviation*. Deviation helps us to tell how scores are dispersed about the mean. When we collect data from the parent population, we assume that equal variances of the characteristic exist in the population; this quality is called *homoscedasticity*. We also assume that that characteristic is *normally distributed* and approximates the *normal curve*.

The way we test differences in variables is to state a *hypothesis*, a statement of a testable proposition. We begin by making a statement of no difference, or a *null hypothesis.* Based upon statistical calculation derived from the normal curve, we are able to construct a *confidence interval* and a *confidence level.* From the sample size, we decide upon *degrees of freedom.*

All variable data are dependent upon the quality of the instrument that is used in the survey. We assume that we have representation by using *stratification* in the sample, which is the selection of subcategories in a particular variable; we also use *random sampling* to ensure that each item, event, or characteristic has an equal chance of selection. There are various methods of sampling that we call *probability* (selection by chance) and *nonprobability* (selection by quota or convenience). We prefer probability methods.

Having controlled for sample error, we now control for *data error.* Data error occurs when either the instrument or the interview techniques are faulty. *Instrument error*, or error in the questionnaire, happens when wrong variables are selected, or when questions are badly designed. *Interview error* is the result of poor conversational techniques, or fabrication or manipulation of the sample data.

The probability of simple dichotomous variables in terms of the frequency of outcomes is called the *binomial probability distribution.* The plotting of a probability graph follows certain rules, and a curve may be used to approximate the distribution. This is called the *normal curve.* Not only do characteristics, items, and events have a normal distribution in the *parent population*, but *sample statistics* may also have a *normal distribution.* Scores may also be transformed into *standardized scores.* Sample means may be used in a *sampling distribution of the means* to construct *confidence intervals*, based upon *standard error*, to give a *confidence level* indicating where the *population mean (population parameter)* may fall.

Test statistics are used to show *correlation* between *variables: levels of significance*, and *degrees of freedom* upon which to base the *retention or rejection of the null hypothesis.* The level of significance gives an *area of rejection* for the null hypothesis; this is known as *statistical significance.* The interval chosen invariably indicates the *statistical test* chosen, such as *r, t, or* χ^2 *(Pearson r, T-test, chi-square).* The *assumptions* for such test depend upon whether the data are *continuous*, as in Pearson *r* or *t*, or *discrete*, as in χ^2. Continuous data are called *parametric*, discrete data *nonparametric.*

No matter what type of data is used, certain *errors may occur in the decision process* of rejecting the null hypothesis. *Type 1* occurs when the true null is rejected (we reject the truth); *Type 2* occurs when we retain a false null (we retain a lie). We can avoid error by choosing a *level of significance about 0.05, and keeping the sample size large.* A large sample will ensure that in the distribution of the sample means (when $n = 100$), our distribution will follow the *central limit theorem*, and we may apply the normal curve regardless of the form of the parent population. Statistics may be used for *sampling, comparison, central tendency, dispersion, association, prediction*, and *elaboration.* However, *the real force of the normal distribution and the normal curve lies in the final application of test statistics.*

Calculated values from data are compared to tabled or previously computed values. Usually when *calculated values equal or exceed tabled values*, the null hypothesis is rejected. Nevertheless, *statistical significance is always compared to substantive significance.*

There are numerous *fallacies* to be avoided in the research design and its application. *Halo effect* occurs during the interview, when the client gives the interviewer the responses that he thinks the interviewer wants. *Ecological fallacy* happens when sample inferences are applied to populations other than that from which the sample was drawn. The *reduction fallacy* assumes that only one cause is responsible for the effect—a single-factor explanation for a complex problem.

Another factor in gathering data is the matter of ethics. *Ethics* are the standards of behavior or code of conduct by which the researcher lives. We must protect our sources of information and guarantee anonymity, confidentiality, and freedom from harm.

Proper sampling is the door to good research, and the questionnaire is the key that opens that door for the gathering of accurate data. We select our *element*, or unit of analysis, as representative of the parent population. The *sampling unit* is an element or set of elements considered for selection, particularly if we use *multi-stage cluster sampling*, sometimes called *proportional probability sampling* (*PPS*, probability proportionate to size). Each stage is decided by probability and ratio. The *statistics* from our sample are descriptions of the variables in quantitative terms. *Sampling error* tends to be larger when we use cluster designs.

We use those statistics to describe *parameters*, limits or range of a given variable in the population. If we are careless in the selection of our sample, bias occurs. *Bias* is the nonrandom selection of any group that will influence the outcome of the study.

Prejudice is the effect of using people with the same beliefs and interests. We seek to avoid this. Our aim in research is impartiality and precision of measurement.

Research is based upon the concepts of description, exploration, and explanation. We seek to quantify, to solve problems, to be faithful to the highest standards in our pursuit of knowledge. Another aim of research is *prediction*. Prediction is the mathematical anticipation of outcomes owing to the understanding of trends that develop in the population. Prediction is developed from a statistical technique called *regression* that occurs in *correlation*. Correlation is the relationship of one variable to another. It gives *direction* of relationship. After significance and direction, one other measure is used, strength of *association*. Association may be measured using *Pearson r* for *continuous data*, or *chi-square* for *discrete data*. However, whereas correlation does not indicate *causal relationships*, chi-square does. Chi-square also aids in the *elaboration* of the variables to determine *causal order*. Causal order is based upon *asymmetrical relationships*, and they are the central core of research, particularly that of *characteristic* causing *disposition*, or background variable causing a particular course of action.

Misunderstandings in the Use of Terms

There are certain semantic effects to beware of:

1. In *zero-order relationships*, only two variables are used. *A zero relationship* (note that the word *order* is omitted) occurs when the relationship is reduced to zero, or when in fact no relationship exists between the two variables.

2. *Positive direction* means that when variable A increases, so does variable B—they both increase (or decrease) together. *Positive findings* means that the final results are acceptable for positively accepting or rejecting the null hypothesis.

3. *Negative direction* occurs when variable A increases as variable B decreases, or vice versa. *Negative findings* mean that there is no real basis for acceptance or rejection of the null hypothesis.

4. *Independence* between variables means that their distributions are alike and there is no relationship or association between them. An *independent variable*, however, is one that is assumed to have causal effect upon a dependent variable; it is determined by the criteria of time order, dominance, and influence. It stands as the main or dominant variable in the causal chain or model. It may be preceded or caused by an antecedent variable, or it may cause an intervening variable, which in turn causes a dependent variable.

5. *Statistical significance* occurs when the nature of the calculations is such that the null hypothesis is rejected at a set level of alpha (usually 0.05), and with the appropriate number of degrees of freedom. *Statistical inference* is the use of the statistics from the sample to make population estimates; or the generalizing of the sample statistics to the parent population. The inference must consist of the sample statistic based upon calculations derived from the data, and a confidence level for that statistic—that is, the degree of confidence upon which the null was rejected or accepted.

6. *Validity* refers to the truth, substance, and effectiveness of our research. *Construct validity* is the way in which we have applied our instrument to our sample—its "fit," its appropriateness, the correct selection of questions, to the characteristic we seek to examine in the candidate. *Internal validity* refers to the controls used in the research design itself to establish the truth of the conclusions. Validity refers to authenticity and soundness as well as factual resonance. It also implies verification, which literally means "to make true."

7. *Expected values* are not the same as *predicted values*. Expected values occur in chi-square analysis, wherein the observed scores are compared to expected scores or expected values. The expected values are hypothetical, but if they coincide with the *observed values*, the variables are independent of each other. Predicted values occur in regression when the value of the dependent variable is predicted from the effect of the independent variable. Expected values and predicted values are both hypothetical but may actually occur—expected values with nonparametric data (qualitative), predicted values with parametric (quantitative) data.

8. *Control variables* are those variables used to control or test a hypothesis in a first-order or multivariate analysis. Control variables are used to establish or disprove the hypothesis, reorder the variables in the model according to time or logical order, or indicate further research. *Controlled sampling* occurs when random samples are taken from two or more carefully defined groups. *Controlled experiments*, like controlled samples, contain at least two groups. One group receives a treatment, the other does not. In controlled experiments, the researcher may manipulate the variables. In both groups, the sample that is *not* treated is called the *control group*; the one exposed to the experimental variable is called the *experimental group*.

9. *Partial relationships* are found inside the chi-square bivariate tables. They are also known as contingent relationships, and the tables are sometimes called contingency tables. In effect, one part of a variable is compared to one part of another variable; this is usually done by comparing percentages of the dependent variable across each category of the independent variable. *Partial correlation* happens when more than two variables are used in correlation. One is held constant—as we say, is controlled—and the effect of the other two is measured. In this way, we can measure the effect of the relationship by Pearson r and determine if the relationship increases, decreases, or remains constant. *Partial regression*, or partial regression slopes, or beta weights (small b) are unstandardized regression coefficients that occur in multiple regression. They measure the impact of each independent variable after holding all the other independent variables constant. Remember, *slopes measure change; correlation coefficients measure variation.*

10. *Multiple correlation* does exactly what its name implies. It gives a coefficient, a statistic, R, which tells us how well we may predict the dependent variable from the several independent variables used in the equation. Whereas r^2 explains the variation in the dependent variable caused by an independent variable, R^2 explains the variation caused in the dependent variable by *several* independent variables, or *multiple* variables. *Multiple regression* is simply the use of multiple variables in the regression equation. Instead of finding the best-fitting regression line for only two variables, for correlation and prediction, we now use several (independent) variables to find the best-fitting line showing the effect on the dependent variable. Notice that as in using a control variable in nonparametric analysis, the final result is made up of a study of partial relationships. Multivariate analysis, whether it be elaboration in chi-square or elaboration in multiple regression, is made up of several two-variable relationships; these partial relationships contribute to the final result. In multiple regression, we have an accumulation of partial correlations, partial slopes, and partial predictive patterns. All these may be standardized, which they usually are, into Beta (large B) weights. In this way, just like using percentages in chi-square, we may compare the effects of the independent variables upon the dependent variables.

Be careful in your use of words when explaining relationships, and when reading for explanation, be precise. An understanding of terms will help you in setting up your own research design. The language is new, and when you get into programming, you will encounter a lot more. Terms used in one way alone have different meanings when used with other terms; "zero order" is a good example. In other parts of the text, confusion related to "sample" and "standard" has been explained. Keep the definitions clear in your own mind.

RULES FOR HYPOTHESIS TESTING

1. State the hypothesis in its proper form as a logical research hypothesis and the derived alternates. This should be in both descriptive and statistical form (H_a and H_o).
2. Set the level of analysis. Describe the statistical methods to be used and their sequence. Make the analysis proceed through various levels of sophistication. Move from frequencies to correlation to chi-square, or whatever the problem demands.
3. *Specify the level of significance and the region of rejection.* Make sure that your statistical statement shows whether you are using a one-tail or a two-tail test. If you are using a two-tail test, state both areas of rejection. State the degrees of freedom in your calculation. Your statistical symbols should indicate your level of statistical analysis—i.e., χ^2, r, etc.
4. Compare your calculations and computer printouts with the tables, as well as taking heed of the computer information and the level of significance printed for you.
5. Estimate the possibility of Type 1 and Type 2 error. Check your calculations against sample size; enlarge your sample and see what happens to your calculations—it could change your mind on retention or rejection of the hypothesis.
6. Although you may make statistical conclusions based upon numbers, do not be overwhelmed by statistics; consider the substance of your conclusions. *Always compare statistical significance with substantive significance.*

These simple rules may make a world of difference in your final decisions. Consider that most statistical studies have contributed very little to solving problems. Therefore, it is vital that rather than adding to the mass of problems that exist around us, your findings attempt to solve problems. The use of the normal curve and probability theory have enabled us to make decisions quantitatively. We now have the technology to speed this process up. It would appear logical to put theory and technology together to improve our research ability.

RULES FOR PRELIMINARY STUDENT SURVEY RESEARCH

1. The hypothesis should be stated in the form of a research and a null hypothesis (no relationship).
2. Variables should be described, defined, and explained. A model should be proposed. A population should be selected.

3. The model should be related to the research instrument. The questionnaire should be on one page.
4. Sampling method should be cross-sectional, systematic, random sampling, aiming at as representative a sample as possible. Sample stratification should agree with the parent population.
5. Time and cost should be considered carefully for completing the survey project. (*If pretest is possible, do it.*)
6. Team survey work is preferred to individual projects. Tasks should be divided evenly. Techniques should be uniform.
7. Each member is personally responsible for completing his or her part of the sampling honestly and accurately.
8. The data must be coded and a research statistical analysis selected. Be alert for unexpected results.
9. The program must then be run through the computer and the data analyzed, first by FREQUENCIES, then CORRELATION, and finally CHI-SQUARE.
10. Presentation of the report follows a definite format. Use the format, report all your findings, bring out what is significant; make your report clear, concise, and relevant. Remember, the object of your research is to discover the effect of the independent variable upon the dependent variable.

Do not:

1. Keep putting off getting started.
2. Use impossible variables, scales, or questions.
3. Curbside, fabricate, or manipulate your results.
4. Use a complex design with many variables—the data will overwhelm you.
5. Lose your temper with the computer. It only does what you tell it to do.

Populations and Samples

Parent population	More than one sample	Single sample
The population mean is unknown and is estimated from the sample.	Each sample has its own mean. The means may be put in one category and then the mean of means may be calculated.	*The mean* is calculated from sample data and is an average. Data are grouped about the mean.
The population standard deviation is estimated from the sample standard deviation.	*Sampling error* is the degree of error for a given design. It is a measure of *standard error* and is related to sample size and dispersion of sample means about the parent-population mean.	*Sample error* or *standard deviation* is the square root of the variation. It is the average square root of the distance of the raw score from the sample mean.
The *normal curve* that approximates the parent population is a distribution model made up of infinite samples from an infinite population.	*Sampling distribution* is the distribution of sample means for infinite samples that can be drawn from the parent population. The normal curve is a model of the *sampling distribution of the means* of each sample.	*Sample distribution* is the frequency distribution of sample statistics–mainly raw scores about the mean.
The normal-curve theory is the base upon which sampling theory is constructed. It is also the base for rejection or retention of the null hypothesis using confidence intervals and confidence levels.	Whenever a particular statistic is taken from each sample, its plotted frequency is a *sampling distribution*. The sampling distribution is used to find error in samples of varying sizes. Sampling distribution is also known as probability distribution. It is a theoretical distribution.	It is assumed that *sample elements* are drawn randomly. Elements are drawn from the *sampling frame*, which is an exact listing of all available elements in the population.
The central limit theorem is useful for populations of any form of distribution.	Each sample is assumed to be randomly sampled independently of the others. No element is sampled twice.	*Random sampling* of the population assumes that every element has an equal chance of selection.
A *parameter* is a description of a variable in a population.	Multiple samples should increase randomness, homogeneity, and representation. *Triangulation* is preferred.	The sample has all the elements present in the parent population. The sample should be equal to or greater than 30. $N = 100$ is preferable. A *statistic* is a description of a variable in a sample.

Process, Methods, and Theory in Statistical Research

Process	Symbol	Method	Theory used
Normal population	μ σ N	Estimated Not known Mean is fixed	*Probability theory*, based upon chance outcomes and proportional distribution
Sample	$\bar{x}$ s z n	Observed Measured Transformed Standardized scores	*Sampling theory*, randomization and representation (homogeneity), linear transformation
Sampling (means) distribution	$s_{\bar{x}}$ s_e	Calculated $= \frac{\sigma}{\sqrt{n}}$ Means vary	*Central limit theorem*, dependent upon sample size and distribution of means and *normal curve*
Statistical significance	H_0 α, df	Calculated comparison of means Use of tails	*Normal-curve theory*, based upon C.I., C.L., sample size and selection, of region of rejection
Test statistic	r, τ χ^2 t F	Computed Compared to tabled values to be $<$ or $>$	*Power of the test*, selection of the proper level of analysis for the statistical design
Conclusions	R:	Rejection or retention of H_0 Further research indicated	*Theory of logic*, inductive vs. deductive reasoning; statistical significance vs. substantive significance. Use of *decision theory*
Evaluation	EV	Review of project Possible replication Verification	*Accountability*: cost–benefit ratio; contribution to the discipline; practical problem-solving application; steps to improving project design

Methods of Research Analysis

Analysis	Sample	Parametric	Formula	Non-parametric	Formula
Frequencies	1 random/ representative	Interval ratio	Numbers and percentages	Nominal Ordinal	Numbers and percentages
Correlation	1 R/R 2 variables	Pearson r	$r = \dfrac{n\Sigma xy - \Sigma x \Sigma y}{\sqrt{[n\Sigma x^2 - (\Sigma x)^2]\,[n\Sigma y^2 - (\Sigma y)^2]}}$	Spearman's rho	$r_s = 1 - \dfrac{6\Sigma d^2}{n(n^2 - 1)}$
Difference of means	2 R/R (x and y)	T-test	$t = \dfrac{x - y}{\sqrt{\dfrac{s^2}{n_x} + \dfrac{s^2}{n_y}}}$	Mann-Whitney U-test	$U = n_x n_y + \dfrac{n_x(n_x + 1)}{2} - R_x$ where x is smallest sample and R_x is sum of ranks
	2 matched pairs	T-test	$t = \dfrac{\Sigma D}{\sqrt{\dfrac{n\Sigma D^2 - (\Sigma D)^2}{n - 1}}}$	Wilcoxon matched pairs	Also use Sign Test
	2 samples random or matched	. . . . .	Analysis of variance		
Data analysis (Frequencies) (Subfiles) (Recode)	1 or more samples	Regression (zero-order)	$\hat{Y} = a + bx$ (a = intercept; b = slope)	Chi-square (Yule's Q)	$\chi^2 = \Sigma \dfrac{(O - E)^2}{E}$
	Several independent variables–2 or more	Multiple regression (first-order) Multivariate analysis	$\hat{Y} = a + b_1x_1 + b_2x_2 + b_3x_3$	Elaboration	Using control variables Checking percentages (partials/ marginals)

Appendix 3
Casino Gambling Survey

by David LiBassi

TOPIC

The study of city residents' attitudes on legalized gambling and the comparison of two types of surveys, telephone and interview, on this issue.

PURPOSE

The research hypothesis is that there is a relationship between attitude toward legalized gambling and background variables of age, race, sex, religion, ethnic origin, education, income, marital status, and political preference. The testable null hypothesis is that there is no relationship between the attitude toward legalized gambling and the stated variables. Also measured was the stress of the respondent at the time of interview. Two surveys of equal sample size, one by telephone and one by interview, would be compared for similarities and differences.

VARIABLES DESCRIBED

The variables used were: *age* in the categories 18-25, 26-35, 36-45, 46-55, 56 and over; *race*—black, white, and other; *sex; religion*—Protestant, Catholic, Jewish, Other; *marital status; political preference; education level; income* in the categories \$0-5,000, \$5,001-10,000, \$10,001-15,000, \$15,001-20,000, \$20,001-25,000, and over \$25,000; *ethnic background*—Irish, Italian, German, British, Polish, Afro-American, Oriental, Spanish, Other.

The variable *stress* was measured on a scale. Several questions on gambling attitude, questions 11-17, were totaled to give a scale of 7-28, 7 being a low attitude toward gambling and 28 being approval of legalized gambling and in favor of it. No opinions were scored as zeros. Scoring on Q13, 15, 16 was reversed to avoid set. Other variables were participation, estimation, and ownership, as seen on the instrument. The model may be seen:

Note: Many of the tables originally included in this report have been omitted here. However, the substance has been retained.

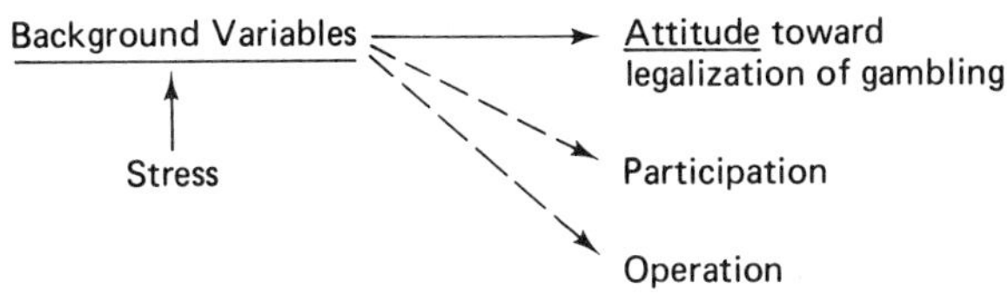

POPULATION, PLACE, AND DATE

The surveys were conducted in the city of ____________________, from April 20, 1977, to April 27, 1977. The interview sample was taken throughout the city to achieve an accurate ethnic cross-section of the varied ethnic groupings in this city. The telephone sample was selected randomly from the city telephone directory. From a city population of approximately 300,000, the sample size was 400, 200 in each category.

SAMPLING

For the *Interview Survey*, the city was divided into six demographic zones, one for each team member. The zones approximated the ethnic concentrations, which fell into a grid-like division:

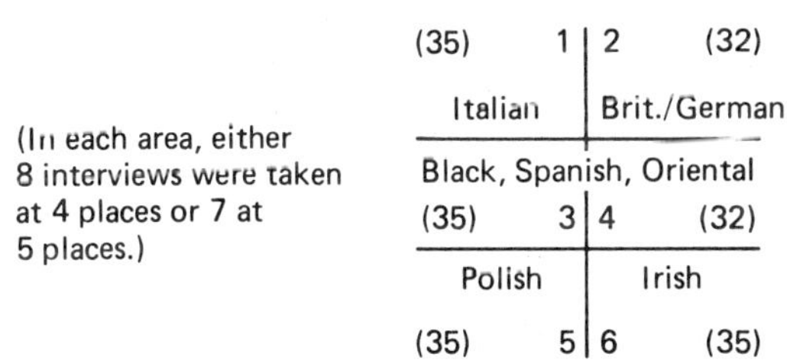

Each team member selected busy locations within the prescribed area—shopping malls, public buildings, or work centers—and successively interviewed every fiftieth (50th) person until 35 interviews were completed—200 were selected. From the total city population, the sampling frame was 10,000, the sample 200. Knowing census estimates for stratification, the sample was also kept within those parameters as much as circumstances would permit, in terms of age, race, and sex.

For the *Telephone Survey*, the directory was divided into six equal sections, each member having 132 pages. Every 1,003rd resident was selected. If refused or no answer, the next person was taken. 200 interviews were completed by phone. (Note that the unlisted phones and those without phones increase this figure to the population size.)

On average, one in four, or 25%, refused to participate or were not available. This heavy "nonresponse" did not appear to affect the outcomes, due to sample size and reduction of sample error.

THE INSTRUMENT

A copy of the questionnaire is attached. (See p. 403.) The first nine questions determine the respondent's background. He or she is then asked for a self-rating on the stress line in terms of present anxiety. Questions 11-17 are totaled to determine the variable, *Attitude toward Legalized Gambling*, with scores on questions 13, 15, and 16 being reversed. A total score of 28 would represent a person completely in favor of legalized gambling. Questions 18 and 21 concern participation. Question 19 concerns the decline of present gambling if made legal, and 20 is one's view of who should own the casinos.

CODING

Coding appears numeric, in that each category is sequentially numbered—e.g., *Age*: 1, 2, 3, 4, 5, with a number for each category, 1 = 18–25, etc. For questions 11-17 (with the exception of 13, 15, and 16), *Agree* = 4, *Somewhat agree* = 3, *Disagree* = 2, *Somewhat Disagree* = 1, *No Opinion* = 0. No coding is shown on the instrument, as all coding is scored on FORTRAN sheets and then keypunched on IBM cards. 27 columns were used.

DATA COLLECTION

Actual interviewing took a few minutes in most cases. Respondents were cooperative, and the survey was completed over the period of one week. Several locations in each area were chosen, to achieve the widest possible selection and stratification.

STATISTICS USED

The following programs were used with SPSS: FREQUENCIES, PEARSON CORR, RECODE, CROSSTABS. Sample size for each batch was 200. Some data may be inaccurate due to misleading responses. For example, information on income is sometimes cautiously given, because respondents are afraid of being robbed or simply do not want you to know what they were earning: or, to be impressive, they

STATE COLLEGE RESEARCH COMMITTEE

Sample Questionnaire

GAMBLING ATTITUDE SURVEY

CHECK THE APPROPRIATE AREAS BELOW:

1) AGE: (18-25) (26-35) (46-55) (55-OVER)
2) RACE: Black X White____ Other____
3) SEX: Male____ Female X
4) RELIGION: Protestant____ Catholic X Jewish____ Other
5) MARITAL STATUS: Single X Married____ Widowed____ Divorced/Separated ____
6) POLITICAL PREFERENCE: Democrat X Republican____ Other____
7) EDUCATION: Grade School____ H.S.____ A.S.____ B.S. X M.S.____ PHD.____ Professional School____
8) INCOME: $ (0-5,000) (5-10,000) (10-15,000) (15-20,000) (20-25,000) (Over 25,000)
9) ETHNIC BACKGROUND: Irish____ Italian____ German____ British____ Polish____
Afro-American X Oriental____ Spanish____ Other____
10) BASED ON THE ANXIETY YOU FEEL PRESENTLY, RATE YOURSELF ON THE STRESS LINE BELOW: 0____ 1____ 2____ 3____ 4____ 5____ 6____ 7____ 8____ 9 X
LOW MEDIUM HIGH

	AGREE	SOMEWHAT	DISAGREE	SOMEWHAT	NO OPINION
11) Casino gambling should be legalized within the city of ?	X				
12) Sports gambling should be legalized within the city of ?	X				
13) Organized Crime would influence legalized gambling.			X		
14) Legalized gambling would help the economic situations in		X			
15) Legalized gambling would cause an increase in other forms of crime.			X		
16) Present opposition to legalized gambling is organized crime related.		X			
17) Tourism into the area would increase.	X				

18) If legalized, how much would you participate? NEVER X SOMETIMES____ OFTEN____ MORE____
19) By what % would gambling decrease. (0-25%) (25-50%) (50-75%) (75-100%)
20) If legalized, gambling casinos should be operated: A) Privately owned____ B) City owned____
C) State owned X D) Combination private and public owned____
21) Do you presently participate in any form of gambling? YES____ NO X

THANK YOU FOR YOUR PARTICIPATION

	Interview		Telephone	
Age	#	%	#	%
18-25 yrs.	42	21%	68	34%
26-35	45	23%	53	26%
36-45	36	18%	29	15%
46-55	34	17%	22	11%
56+	43	21%	28	14%
Race				
Black	42	21%	41	20%
White	155	78%	153	77%
Other	3	1%	6	3%
Sex				
Male	93	47%	99	49%
Female	107	53%	101	51%
Religion				
Protestant	61	30%	49	25%
Catholic	85	42%	104	52%
Jewish	16	8%	13	6%
Other	38	20%	34	17%
Marital status				
Single	54	27%	90	45%
Married	94	47%	78	39%
Widowed	27	13%	18	9%
Divorced/ Separated	25	13%	14	7%
Political preference				
Democrat	97	48%	97	48%
Republican	56	28%	53	26%
Other	48	24%	50	26%
Education				
Elementary	27	13%	22	11%
High School	91	46%	91	46%
A.S.	35	17%	32	16%
Bachelor's	37	19%	37	19%
Master's	6	3%	6	3%
Ph.D.	1	½%	8	4%
Professional	3	1½%	4	2%
Ethnic background				
Irish	33	16%	35	17%
Italian	27	14%	28	14%
German	36	18%	28	14%

	Interview		Telephone	
Income	#	%	#	%
$0-5,000	57	29%	56	28%
5,001-10,000	50	25%	51	26%
10-15,000	45	22%	54	27%
15-20,000	28	14%	23	11%
20-25,000	18	9%	8	4%
25,000+	2	1%	7	4%
Casino gambling				
Agree	128	64%	118	59%
Disagree	61	31%	68	34%
No opinion	11	5%	14	7%
Sports gambling				
Agree	131	66%	124	62%
Disagree	55	27%	59	30%
No opinion	14	7%	17	8%
Organized crime				
Agree	128	64%	126	63%
Disagree	54	27%	56	28%
No opinion	18	9%	18	9%
Economic stimulus				
Agree	133	67%	133	67%
Disagree	47	23%	53	26%
No opinion	20	10%	14	7%
Increase in crime				
Agree	95	47%	96	48%
Disagree	84	42%	82	41%
No opinion	21	11%	22	11%
Tourism				
Agree	150	75%	148	74%
Disagree	30	15%	32	16%
No opinion	20	10%	20	10%
Participation				
Never	79	40%	93	47%
Sometimes	102	51%	91	45%
Often	19	9%	16	8%
Casinos owned by				
Private	30	15%	29	14%
City	27	13%	33	17%

Age	Interview #	Interview %	Telephone #	Telephone %	*Income*	Interview #	Interview %	Telephone #	Telephone %
British	10	5%	8	4%	City/State	76	38%	73	36%
Polish	26	13%	43	22%	State	67	34%	65	33%
Afro-American	35	17%	34	17%					
Oriental	12	6%	10	5%	*Currently gambling*				
Spanish	20	10%	14	7%	Yes	105	53%	103	52%
Other	1	1%	–	–	No	95	47%	97	48%

give an inflated income. Again, on ethnic origin, even though a person may be more Italian than Irish, the choice of origin would be Irish. Afro-Americans do not have the variety of choices that whites have. Overall, however, the income distribution and ethnic origin do appear to be fairly representative for the city.

From the various correlations, hierarchies could be established for further testing by chi-square. Finally, the two surveys on the same subject could be compared to each other.

Data analysis will compare the two sets of frequency data, correlations, and finally chi-square associations. Although profiles are not given, they may be constructed from the tables.

[For the sake of brevity, nonsignificant data have been omitted from this appendix. Full tables may take up many pages of computer printout.]

Ranking of Pearson Correlations with Attitudes toward Legalization of Gambling

Rank	Interviews	*r*	*Signif.*	Telephone	*r*	*Signif.*
1.	With sex	0.19	0.003	With income	0.17	0.009
2.	With participation	−0.17	0.008	With participation	−0.13	0.036
3.	With age	0.12	0.040	With marital status	0.12	0.048

Ranking of Chi-Square Statistic with Attitudes toward Legalization of Gambling

1.	With sex	$\chi^2 = 6.04$, 1 df, sig @ 0.02–Interview
2.	With participation	$\chi^2 = 4.06$, 1 df, sig. @ 0.05–Interview
3.	With income	$\chi^2 = 11.8$, 5 df, sig. @ 0.05–Telephone

No other correlations were significant at 0.05; no other chi-square values were significant at 0.05 level. However, we do know that sex is related to income and that age is related to marital status. Nevertheless, on all cross-tabulations, no other significant values were found. The dichotomization along the mean for "Attitude toward Legalization of Gambling" resulted in 145 high and 55 low for telephone surveys and 153 high and 47 low for interview surveys. There is every indication that had the mean been set higher, the results would have been similar. As indicated by the frequency tables, comparison of the two surveys revealed no significant differences with the exceptions of those above.

CONCLUSIONS

There is only one major exception to the similarity of findings of the two surveys. In the interview process, sex does appear to be a causative factor in attitude toward gambling. It appears that men favor legalization of gambling more than women do. It would also appear that those who participate favor legalization to avoid the penalty of being apprehended. Also younger, single people in lower income groups favor legalization. These facts may be observed in the internal percentages of the contingency tables. Nevertheless, there is little difference between the results from the interview surveys and from the telephone surveys: rather, there is agreement.

Statistical research books point out that there are many errors in a phone survey, and therefore it is not as accurate as an interview survey. However, it is our conclusion that the particular issue determines the outcome of the survey. For example, on the issue of voting, the Dewey–Truman election has made researchers apprehensive about the results of telephone surveys. Voting would appear to be an *individual* choice and thus leave room for considerable error if the sample was not stratified. Gambling is a *group* issue and it appears that, on this issue, stratification does not assume priority over randomness. The survey indicated the residents favorable to legalization of gambling (casinos), and frequency data showed a mean of 61.5% in favor, with 56.5% willing to participate. 74.5% feel that casino gambling would aid the city in terms of tourism, while 67% felt it would help economically. On the darker side, 62.5% feel that organized crime would move in with gambling, with 47% opting that crime would increase in the city.

From the survey we could assume that a vote on casino gambling, or legalization of gambling, would be favorable, although this question was never asked directly. Neither religion nor ethnic background made any difference. The Polish people did show a slight lead in a preference for gambling over Orientals and blacks. It is safe to assume that this sports-minded city also favors casino gambling. 64% of those asked favored sports gambling.

From the frequency data, one can see early in the analysis that there is very little of significant difference in the two surveys. (Frequency data occur as the marginals in contingency tables.)

SUMMARY

Although only a slight majority gamble and only about 20% are hard-core, the city favors legalization of gambling, accepting the good with the bad in terms of economic improvement. Whether this is a vote of desperation or emancipation remains to be seen. Certainly, the choice is not due to either stress or political preference.

Index

D

E

T

Y

Z